STRANGERS AND KIN

Barbara Melosh

STRANGERS AND KIN
The American Way of Adoption

HARVARD
UNIVERSITY
PRESS
Cambridge,
Massachusetts
London, England
2002

Library of Congress Cataloging-in-Publication Data
Melosh, Barbara.
Strangers and kin : the American way of adoption / Barbara Melosh.
   p. cm.
Includes bibliographical references and index.
ISBN 0–674–00912–6 (alk. paper)
  1. Adoption—United States.   2. Adoption—United States—History.   I. Title.
HV875.55 .M444 2002
362.73'4'0973—dc21   2002017159

03

Contents

For Mike

Preface

This book would not have been possible without the generosity and trust of those who maintain the records of the Children's Bureau of Delaware (CBD). My heartfelt thanks to Iris Synder and Lisa Reticker, who first alerted me to these records and encouraged me to think I might be able to gain access to them. The CBD no longer exists as an organization, but the several social agencies that succeeded it have been faithful stewards of its records and of the adoptive families whose stories are told in them. Al Synder believed in the importance of the history of adoption and trusted me to use the records to tell that story. Lydia Durbin supplied me with useful background information and assisted my work at the agency in many ways large and small. Typical of both her thoughtfulness and sense of humor, she supplied me with a table and chair in the corridor outside the record room, and dignified my labors with a printed sign over it: "Center for the Study of the History of Adoption."

I also wish to acknowledge the prodigious memory and faithful stewardship of Susan Burns. When I first began to use the records, I was pleased, and also puzzled, to encounter newspaper clippings in many of them that supplied information about adoptive families years after their contact with the CBD ended. The mystery was solved one day when I met Susan in the record room, filing clippings in the records of clients she still remembered. Later, I benefited from her detailed comments and criticisms as she read a full draft of the manuscript.

I have used those records under the terms of a confidentiality agree-

ment that binds me to maintain that trust. Neither my research notes
nor this book contain any proper names from those records. I use simple letter designations—Mr. and Mrs. G.—when I have needed to use
names for adult individuals. I have frequently changed the prospective
adopters' initials when repetition would lead to confusion within a
chapter. I identify children by assigned pseudonyms ("George," Mary,"
etc.). In cases where unusual circumstances might identify the persons
involved, I have changed other details to protect that confidentiality. My
notes and draft manuscripts identify cases by a numerical code whose
key is stored at the agency. Because these records are not available for
public access, I do not include identification numbers in the documentation for this book; instead, I indicate the year of the record so that
readers can follow the chronology I trace.

The language of adoption is a revealing index of its anomalous
status, and any choice of terms itself represents an implicit position or
evaluation. I use "prospective adopters" to describe adults seeking
children to adopt, and "adoptive mothers," "adoptive fathers," and
"adoptive parents" to identify those in families formed by law. At the
time of this writing, there is no consensus on the best term for those
who give birth to children and then decide to plan adoption for them.
Adoptive parents object to the phrase "natural parents" as a term that
denigrates adoptive kinship. "Biological parents" strikes many as cold
and clinical, even dehumanizing. "Birth parent" acknowledges the tie of
reproduction, and the term emerged as a protest against the erasure
embodied in the term "illicit pregnancy." "Birth parent" does not work
well, though, in the earlier decades of adoption, when few mothers
placed children at birth. Still, I take up this terminology as the best
among available alternatives.

In describing termination of parental rights, I use the term "relinquishment." No longer current in social science literature, the term
seems to me worth rescuing; I find it a compelling expression of both
the intentionality and the pain that attend this act. Another alternative,
also currently in disuse, is "surrender"; this poignantly expresses the
loss of relinquishment, but I am uneasy with its connotations of war
and defeat. Adoption professionals currently favor the phrase "to make
an adoption plan." More respectful of relinquishing parents, the term

nonetheless seems to me too bloodless and instrumental and therefore not a faithful rendering of the complicated emotions and constrained choices that attend adoption.

Many colleagues and friends assisted this work over the years by reading drafts, listening to conference papers, sending me newspaper articles and references, sharing their own work, and talking with me about adoption. I am pleased to acknowledge their good company and their help: Margo Anderson, Susan Porter Benson, E. Wayne Carp, John Gillis, Cynthia Harrison, Ellen Herman, Brian Horrigan, Richard John, Deborah Kaplan, Lee Klesius, Rebecca Knight, Michael Lacey, Amy Levine, Elaine Tyler May, Judith S. Modell, Marianne Novy, Leslie Reagan, Roy Rosenzweig, Ellen Ross, Margaret Rossiter, Sarah Sherman, Christina Simmons, Judith E. Smith, Rickie Solinger.

I am pleased to acknowledge also the support of George Mason University, especially for the 1994–1995 Faculty Study Leave that enabled me to get this project underway. The National Endowment for the Humanities and the Woodrow Wilson International Center for Scholars assisted at the crucial writing stage. The generosity of Cornelia and Lawrence W. Levine was a source of much-appreciated support during my residency in Washington, DC, as a Wilson Center Fellow.

I benefited from the fine readings of the penultimate draft by Ellen Herman and Daniel Walkowitz, who provided detailed comments. At Harvard University Press, Joyce Seltzer offered superb editorial guidance and encouraged me to broaden my argument and address. Susan Wallace Boehmer brought a discerning ear and careful editorial eye to the copyediting.

Zofia Burr read many versions of this book. Her comments guided my rethinking and rewriting, and the gift of her friendship sustained me in the intellectual and emotional labor of writing.

Finally, I want to thank the strangers and kin in my own family. My mother and father (he is now deceased) were compassionate supporters as my husband, Gary, and I faced infertility and turned to adoption. Gary has spent many hours thinking with me about adoption. With his encouragement, I was able to accept the Wilson Center grant; he handled things at home to give me the luxury of focused time to think and write. His readings of the manuscript in its later stages were crucial in guiding my revisions and sustaining me through them. Mike was a baby when I began to think of writing this book. Now sixteen, he has supplied frequent reminders of my deadlines and assisted my work in other ways as our household computer specialist. For these many years he has enlivened our household with his energy, quick wit, and spontaneity and blessed us with the gift of parenthood. This book is for him.

Introduction

Some years ago, a curious document came into my hands. A birth certificate from the state of Connecticut, it bears the name of a child born in July 1985. Listed underneath are the names of his mother and father, the attending physician, the name and location of the hospital where the birth occurred.

This document is my son's birth certificate, and my name and my husband's appear under his. But we have never met the attending physician who signed this document, or entered the building where my son was born, or visited the city named here.

Strictly speaking, this document is not a falsification. My son was born on this day, in this place, and we are his parents. Nonetheless, it is not what it seems. Unlike most birth certificates, my son's does not name the woman and man whose genes he shares. It obscures the woman whose body nourished his, who labored to give birth to him, and who made the consequential decision to relinquish him. Her name is written on another document, the original certificate of my son's birth, sealed in the court record of our adoption. The document I hold is his amended birth certificate, issued as the final legal confirmation of our adoptive kinship.

The three of us are strangers and kin. The amended birth certificate tells just half of our story. Its representation of kinship reveals much about the contradictory cultural meaning of adoption in the United States. Codified in law, the bonds of adoptive kinship are acknowledged and affirmed in a welter of formal and informal practices. The amended birth certificate attests to that acceptance. It creates a public record that declares the adoptive family the full legal and social equivalent of the biological family. Adoption has been accepted more readily and practiced more widely in the United States than in any other comparable industrialized nation—an acceptance that observers have attributed to the relative openness of American society, its fluid class and social structure, its racial and ethnic diversity. This embrace of adoption attests to the vibrant optimism of many Americans, to our belief in the malleability of human nature and the beneficence of social institutions.

And yet the lingering sense of anomaly that surrounds adoption reveals the limits of that optimism, the underlying conviction that no social relationship can match the natural kinship of blood. In the nuances of language and informal social exchange, adoption is marked as difference. We speak of adoptive families and adopted children, modifying the unmarked category of families linked by biological kinship. Sometimes we frankly name adoption as second-best, in terms like "natural" parents, "their own" children, "real" parents. In print and conversation, a common phrase refers to children "put up" for adoption, a usage that equates adoption with cold-hearted buying and selling. Our language signals that adoption is "other" and, often, inferior—but in either case, a difference that makes a difference.

The contradiction embodied in my son's birth certificate, I found, is emblematic of adoption throughout its history in the United States. This book tells the story of how adoption became familiar, and how it remains strange. Legal adoption is a relatively recent institution, at least in its American form, where the use of adoption as "substitute family," a relationship established by law as the equivalent of biological family, became common only in the twentieth century. This book deals with "stranger" adoption, that is, adoption in which there is no genetic kinship between parents and child. On average, half of all adoptions involve relatives by blood or marriage, as in stepfamilies. However, these adoptions by family members have always been treated quite differently, perceived as natural extensions of blood kinship rather than as social kinship crafted by law.

Adoption in America took shape at the edges of a reform agenda driven by an informal network of women that emerged at the turn of the century.[1] A generation of women educated in elite women's colleges in the 1880s and 1890s turned from nineteenth-century charity work to new social and political commitments—public health reform, settlement house work, legislative efforts including mother's pensions, protective legislation for women workers, and prohibition of child labor. They got the attention of Theodore Roosevelt and claimed a prominent role at the 1909 White House Conference on the Care of Dependent Children. There, they generated momentum for the establishment of a federal Children's Bureau, which Congress authorized in 1912. The U.S. Children's Bureau (USCB) became the nerve center of child welfare reformers, a community that came to include increasing numbers of social workers, as that field emerged in the first two decades of the twentieth century.[2]

Adoption was not, at the outset, high on the agenda of these child welfare reformers, even though they were energetically revising nineteenth-century approaches to the care of dependent children. By 1910 they were dismantling the orphanages. Critical of institutional care, they turned instead to "placing out"—caring for dependent children in paid foster homes. Even as childless adults importuned them, child welfare workers resisted placing children for adoption. Skeptical of the kindness of strangers, they doubted that adults could accept as their own children not born to them.

Adoption gradually became established in the 1920s and 1930s. Pressured by eager prospective adopters and their supporters—for adoption quickly won the favor of middle-class constituencies—child welfare workers began to consider adoption as an acceptable form of substitute care. Social workers belatedly claimed adoptive placement as part of their domain and sought to manage it through professional protocols and expert supervision. Social work manuals articulated prevailing professional wisdom on adoption. The USCB actively shaped the expert consensus, monitoring adoption practices and seeking to develop and promote common standards. The Child Welfare League of America, established in 1921, was the USCB's counterpart in the private sector. This association of private child welfare agencies was influential in gathering information about adoption practice and advocating better regulation. By the 1930s and 1940s adoption had become less strange, accepted by both lay and professional constituencies.

Adoption reached its apex in the 1950s and 1960s. Scarcely a generation earlier, social workers had accepted relinquishments of children only with reluctance. Now, imbued with the fervor of new converts, they promoted adoption as the "best solution" for the growing numbers of children born out of wedlock. Once regarded as a useful and humane alternative for some dependent children, adoption assumed a prominent role as social policy. With the support of a broad white middle-class consensus, social workers supervised an exponential expansion of adoption. Their advocacy echoed larger social themes of post-war optimism and mobility. Adoption was a "second chance" for all involved: in one bold stroke, it rescued children from illegitimacy, offered a "fresh start" to "girls in trouble," and conferred parenthood on infertile couples longing to join the post-war domestic idyll. By the late 1960s adoption had expanded past its old boundaries: a few white adopters crossed racial lines to claim black children as their own; and some Americans found children to adopt in other countries.

After 1970 the numbers of adoptions declined precipitately. From a historic high in 1970, when there were 89,000 stranger adoptions, the number dropped to 48,000 in 1975. The federal government stopped collecting statistics then, but subsequent estimates suggest that this number has remained relatively constant.[3] Births out of wedlock continued to climb through the 1980s, and the population has grown. But adoption is now a highly exceptional practice; one might say that it has again become strange. This claim will itself seem strange to many readers, since prospective adopters continue to find children against the odds. Still, adoptive families of the early twentieth-first century are scarce, and they live in a climate of renewed skepticism about the kinship of strangers. In the 1970s and 1980s, critics across the political spectrum—from those who identified with black nationalism, anti-imperialism, and feminism to those who espoused sociobiology—challenged the wisdom of stranger adoption.

What do we have to learn from the odd history of this anomalous family form? Its very difference, I propose, makes adoption a clarifying lens, a way to discern the arbitrariness of what passes for common sense—our received truths about family, identity, and kinship. Adoption is "other" because it disorders and disrupts our expectations of choice and chance in family life. Its difference, then, reveals what we usually take for granted. From early debates about which children were "fit" for adoption to contemporary dramas of search and reunion, adoption illuminates questions of identity: Who am I, and where do I belong? Adoption is a case history of the shifting boundaries of American pluralism. The questions of the adoption "home study" are also the questions of American civic life and national identity: What makes a family? Who belongs together? How wide is the circle of "we"?

At the center of this history are the stories of hundreds of adoptive parents, children, and relinquishing parents, recorded in the rich case narratives of the Children's Bureau of Delaware (CBD). Established in 1918, the bureau was a non-sectarian child welfare agency supported by private contributions. Its name suggested its affinity with the child welfare reformers in the USCB, and social workers in the Delaware agency communicated regularly with the federal agency. However, the CBD had no formal affiliation with the USCB, which in any case was not a member agency but rather part of the policy-making and educational apparatus of the federal government. At first, adoptions constituted a very small part of the CBD's practice, which included supervision of children in foster homes, investigation of child neglect and child abuse complaints, and assistance to needy families in their homes. But after World War II, adoption dominated that practice, and in 1951 the CBD became a full-time adoption agency. By the 1990s, when I did my research there, the CBD and its successors had supervised the formation of over 2,000 adoptive families, many of which returned to the bureau to adopt additional children.

The CBD records are stored in a locked basement room, protected from dust, light, and prying eyes. Dimly lit with overhead fixtures, the cinder block vault is filled with row upon row of gray steel filing cabinets. On the right, the cabinets contain records of adoptive families. For the earlier years, ledger books covered in marbled paper provide a key to the records; hand-written entries in black ink list names, record

numbers, and dates of placement. On the other side of the room, records of relinquishing mothers are filed among an array of client files
that document other aspects of the CBD's work, including child neglect
investigations, foster children's records, and families receiving other social services. A discreet number on the adoptive family's record links the
two sets of files, allowing the researcher to reconstruct the full adoption
triad of adoptive parents, adopted persons, and birth mother. The records themselves vary in size and contents, reflecting seventy years of
changing staff and practice. Yet the basic form of the case record is dis-
cernible throughout, testament to the consistencies in case work
method.

The records of adoptive families include several kinds of documents
that mark the stages of the adoption process. On top of the file, one
finds the application for adoption, a form provided by the agency and
filled out by prospective adopters. Next follows the case narrative; it is
titled "Adoptive Home Investigation" in the earliest records, but that
phrase is soon replaced by "home study." Beneath the home study, the
next sheaf of stapled pages is the child's record. This section includes
medical records, information about birth relatives, a copy of the legal
document executing the relinquishment, and notes documenting the
agency's supervision of the child in foster care. Next, one finds the
CBD's report to the court: a summary of the child's history and the reasons for relinquishment; evaluation of the prospective adopters; and the
agency's recommendation about the suitability of the adoption. Some
files also include scraps of information about the adoptive family after
the agency's formal involvement had ended. A few adoptive families
sent notes or cards, sometimes including photographs of their children.
Quite a few files include newspaper clippings that announce marriages,
births, deaths; on occasion, special honors or arrests—valuable
glimpses of how CBD clients fared later in life. Some returned to seek
social workers' advice on parenting. Some records from the 1950s and
1960s contained inquiries from adopted persons or birth relatives who
were seeking reunions; in the 1990s, the bureau offered its services as
mediator in searches.

Case narratives are the key documents in the records; they include
the home study, the child's record, and records of relinquishing moth-

ers. Crucial to the professionalization of social work, the case record is both the technology and the testament of case workers' accuracy, accountability, and objectivity. Observing common standards of professional record-keeping, CBD workers painstakingly reconstructed interviews and home visits, attempting to write verbatim accounts of what was said and to amplify them with the social worker's observation of non-verbal aspects of the encounter. The home study, for example, began with a description of prospective adopters as they appeared in their initial interview at the CBD's offices—their physical features, grooming, clothing, and demeanor. Interviews at clients' homes captured not only what they said but the information disclosed through their domestic spaces. Social workers astutely observed and described clients' neighborhoods, houses, and yards; their furnishings and décor; their standards of housekeeping and maintenance; their pets; their books and magazines; sometimes even their mail, as in several cases where social workers noticed piles of bills. After a child was placed, social workers visited the home every three months, documenting the child's health and emotional adjustment and advising adopters on child-rearing. (Before 1935, children had to be in a prospective adoptive home for a two-year probationary period before the adoption could be legalized. From 1935 to 1951 the mandated interval, renamed the "supervisory period," was one year; after 1952 it was reduced to six months.) Social workers also turned their assessing gazes on themselves. As part of their professional self-evaluation, they noted their own responses to clients during the interview and reflected on case work goals, accomplishments, missed opportunities, or outright missteps as they recorded each encounter.

The changing shape and volume of the records reflect the historical evolution of the bureau's adoption practice. In the 1930s and 1940s some of these narratives ran to 100 single-spaced pages, evidence of the measured pace of adoption at that time. Children's records were usually at least 10 pages, and often many more, for most children were under the bureau's care for at least a year before they were deemed ready for adoption. The CBD did not place newborns for adoption until the mid-1950s. Their records, then, documented the agency's supervision and testing, the child's medical care, and foster placements. In the 1950s and

1960s most individual files were slimmer, even as their numbers prolif-
erated. More children were placed as infants, and so their records might
occupy only a page or two. As social workers raced to keep up with their
busy adoption practice, record-keeping became more perfunctory.
Some home studies are only a few paragraphs long; in the narratives
themselves, social workers noted the hectic pace of their work and indicated that they were hastily recording summaries of successful placements. In the 1980s and 1990s the agency might complete only a half
dozen adoptions a year, a fraction of the annual caseload during the
1950s and 1960s, but a single case record often fills an entire drawer, testimony to the complicated lives of children served by the CBD in these
years. Many had multiple disabilities, which were documented in voluminous medical records. Virtually all had long histories of dependency,
and many had lived in a string of different foster homes and institutions
before they were adopted. These later records lack the richness of those
compiled before 1970. Social workers discarded traditional case narratives, suspicious of their claims to objectivity. Instead, files are stuffed
with forms that document social work administration and medical bu-
reaucracy.

Strangers and Kin relies on a sample of about 400 of the 2,000 CBD
records of adoptive families, complemented by an examination of the
records of the women who bore these children. (Since many adoptive
families adopted more than one child, I looked at well over 400 children's and mothers' records.) I read all the records of adoptions done in
the 1920s and 1930s. As the bureau's adoption cases increased, I began
to sample. I tried to find all adoptions by Jewish or African American
adopters, since these groups are less well documented in other studies. I
also looked for records of adoptions that ended in disruption. These exceptional cases tested social workers' protocols and captured them in especially acute moments of self-examination. In addition to looking for
exceptional cases, I selected every sixth record for close reading.

My understanding of adoption practice was enhanced by reviewing
records of clients who came to the bureau but who, for one reason or
another, did not end up adopting or relinquishing children, as they had
initially planned. Midway through my research, I discovered another
locked room across the hall. It proved to be a kind of discard pile of re-

cords culled from those carefully maintained in the main vault. About 500 file folders were grouped in boxes labeled "rejected/withdrawn." These were records of contacts—often very brief—with prospective adopters who had come to the agency but had not proceeded to the home study. Most of these are dated after 1950, so they do not provide a full view of clients who did not proceed to adoption or who were rejected outright; nonetheless, they offer a valuable glimpse of the agency's procedures and selection policies. Another set of records, marked "withdrawn," documents the agency's contact with women who came to the bureau to plan adoptions but who did not, in the end, relinquish their children to the agency. Some are dated as early as 1943, and they continue into the 1990s. These records, numbering close to 400, are brief and fragmentary. More than half of the women broke off contact with the agency, and so we do not know the outcome of the pregnancies that brought them to the bureau to begin with. From the records at hand, though, we can get a sense of the alternatives to CBD adoption that some women pursued, including single motherhood, private adoption, long-term foster care, or informal placements with relatives. Finally, I have gleaned useful information about the CBD itself in organizational records: annual reports, budgets, and minutes of committee and board meetings.

Although CBD case records stand at the center of this book, *Strangers and Kin* is not a case history of this agency or of adoption in Delaware. I read these case narratives alongside other sources that allowed me to locate this agency's practice within the larger national context. The records of the USCB at the National Archives and Records Administration provide a wide-angle lens that complements the close focus supplied by one agency's records. The USCB coordinated efforts of social workers and child welfare reformers across the country, assisting them to articulate common standards and to lobby for more public regulation of adoption. The bureau also collected data from professional colleagues across the country and conducted periodic studies and surveys that provide valuable snapshots of adoption practice. In addition, its files contain hundreds of letters from prospective adopters, affording a glimpse of the expectations and experiences of those in search of children. The professional literature on adoption—published manuals and journals—supplements the picture of an emerging expert consensus that is evident in USCB records.

Other primary sources provide further evidence on specific topics and serve to document the broader cultural history of adoption. Archival records from the National Urban League supplied evidence about the adoption work of this civil rights organization in the 1950s. Over the last fifteen years, I have followed public portrayals of adoption through journalistic accounts, novels, and film. These interests surface directly in Chapter 4 as I interpret the contemporary debate over transracial adoption. First-hand accounts of adoptive parents, adopted persons, and relinquishing parents—mostly mothers—comprise another important primary source for this study. These take center stage in Chapter 6, where I examine the proliferation of adoption memoirs in the 1980s; they inform my understanding of adoption throughout.

Of course, this book is also grounded in my own story. I am an adoptive mother and a historian. Like other histories, this one is a dialogue between past and present. Like other historians of the recent past, I was a historical participant in some of the changes that I observe as a scholar. And more directly than many historians, I am a character in this story. *Strangers and Kin* is not a memoir, but it is inflected by my personal experience of adoption and deeply informed by who I am as a mother, a feminist, and a cultural historian. In turn, I make sense of motherhood and family by seeing myself and others historically.

Finally, though, this book is not my story or a story only for those touched by adoption. Rather, it is a cultural history of family as it is refracted through the kinship of strangers. The law and practice of adoption reveal the larger historical changes that shape all families: the intersecting histories of child welfare, sexuality and motherhood, upward mobility and assimilation. Adoption is a quintessentially American institution, embodying the recklessly optimistic faith in self-construction and social engineering that characterizes much of our history. The confident experts and their middle-class constituencies have sometimes been too ready to separate mother and child; adoption follows the contours of a long history of American social reform that often was prone to arrogant intervention into the lives of those who are weak and marginalized. And yet as it forges kinship among strangers, adoption also suggests the possibility of a more expansive community, of mutuality across the boundaries of blood. For if we trust that strangers can become kin, then maybe we can also forge families, communities, and nations that welcome the stranger.

1

Wanted—A Child to Raise as Our Own: Claiming Strangers as Kin

In 1918, the mayor of Bogalusa, Louisiana, wrote the Children's Aid Society of New York to request "some white babies . . . a carload . . . by a carload, mean about thirty to fifty. We do not care to know anything about their antecedents or parentage. All we want to know is that they are healthy. We would be interested in about one half Protestant and one half Catholic children, both boys and girls."[1]

In the early 1920s, the following notice appeared in *Outlook*, a nationally circulated magazine directed to social workers and reformers: "Desirable home is available for boy of seven or eight with superior mentality and healthy heredity. Family consists of university graduates, and child would receive skillful attention in respect to health and education, including music if desirable, also college and professional training later. Neighborhood and general environment the best."[2]

The two documents illustrate the competing models of family and child placement characteristic of the 1910s and 1920s, a transitional moment in the history of adoption. "Instrumental adoption" had dominated nineteenth-century child exchange, influenced by apprenticeship and its calculus concerning the worth of a child's labor. In this kind of adoption, older children were far more desirable than infants, who were, consequently, rarely the subjects of adoption. By the early twentieth century, some began to turn to adoption in search of children to cherish, eschewing considerations of their economic value. Indeed, "sentimental adoption" was predicated on the economic uselessness of the child and on a heightened sense of the child's emotional value.[3]

The mayor's letter suggests the persistence of older forms of child exchange. His letter addressed the Children's Aid Society of New York. Under the leadership of Charles Loring Brace, that organization collected children from the city's streets to transport them to the supposedly more salubrious environs of midwestern farms. Begun in the mid-1850s, these orphan trains had fallen into disrepute by 1918.[4] Progressive-era reformers instead turned to "home relief," that is, keeping children with their original families and caring for them in their homes. The mayor's request for a "carload" of "thirty to fifty" children was strikingly at odds with emerging new middle-class models of childhood: his casual quantification seemed to posit children as readily exchangeable surplus commodities, an affront to the sentimentality and emotion associated with childhood. Moreover, the unsavory whiff of apprenticeship clings to his letter. Though he does not say why his constituents seek to import children in such numbers, the mayor's concern with their health might imply the expectation that they will be put to work—a characteristic of the "instrumental family" that was under assault by reformers who agitated for child labor laws and compulsory schooling. Requesting a mix of Protestants and Catholics, the mayor was apparently planning to place children with families of their own faith, thus implying some kind of religious nurture or supervision—a traditional obligation of apprenticeship, and one that survived into modern child adoption. In two telling details, however, the mayor signals a clear shift from the child exchange of nineteenth-century apprenticeship. His letter requests "babies"—children too young to work. And the mayor offers a puzzling disclaimer: "We do not care to know anything of their antecedents or parentage." The citizens of Bogulosa, he seems to be saying, are commendable for their openness to children of unknown background.

The *Outlook* announcement, written just a few years later, implies a very different world of child nurture and family. In sharp contrast to the mayor's order of a job lot of healthy children, these petitioners seek one particular child, meticulously specified by sex, age, intelligence, and inheritance. If these petitioners are far choosier about the child they seek, they are also far more concerned to present their own credentials as parents. Saying nothing about religion, they offer as inducements the material and cultural advantages of middle-class life. The two documents reveal radically different assessments of the economy of adoption. The mayor assumes that the Children's Aid Society has large numbers of children on hand, ready to be distributed for the asking. The *Outlook* notice, in contrast, implies an economy of scarcity. The prospective adopters, or whoever is writing on their behalf, have resorted to national advertising to find a single child.

As different as they are, these documents have one thing in common: they both drew the reproach of child welfare professionals. Both documents ended up in the records of the U.S. Children's Bureau (USCB), sent by correspondents who offered them as exhibits of the lamentable state of contemporary child placement. The mayor's letter was forwarded to the USCB by a worker at the Children's Aid Society itself, then beating a rapid retreat from policies it had pioneered in the nineteenth century. By 1918 the CAS was largely out of the business of exporting children. In the reply attached to the mayor's letter, the society refused his request, advising him to turn to local child placement agencies rather than interstate transport of children. The letter gently rebuked the mayor for his undiscriminating offer: "Your attitude is based on a generous motive but is extremely fallacious and dangerous," the worker cautioned, explaining the importance of knowing as much as possible about children who might come into one's care.

The *Outlook* notice, then, might seem a laudable counter-example; certainly it demonstrated careful attention to the characteristics of individual children. But the disapproving reader who sent it to the federal Children's Bureau considered it, too, an exemplar of undesirable placement practices. It violated an emerging social work article of faith, which called for local case study of child placements and held that trained social workers were the appropriate experts to direct child welfare. At issue was this fundamental question: who would define and defend the best interest of the child?

During the 1910s and 1920s, adoption emerged as an ambitious new social transaction, a legal and cultural institution that conferred kinship on parents and children unrelated by blood. Adoption, and arrangements resembling adoption, existed long before the twentieth century. Apprenticeship and indenture were established forms of labor regulation and child exchange, with reciprocal obligations between master and apprenticeship or servant stipulated by contract and longstanding social practice. Twelve states still had indenture laws in 1927, attesting to the durability of this arrangement.[5]

Outside the boundaries of formal legal institutions, children circulated among extended families and neighbors when economic pressure or a parent's death left children without adequate means of support. In the United States, the first adoption law was passed in 1851 in Massachusetts. However, many earlier laws were directed primarily to the regulation of inheritance, and even as they made provision for bequests to those outside the circle of blood kinship, they also explicitly defended the rights of biological heirs.[6] By contrast, the evolving institution of adoption in the twentieth century made adoptive families in the United States the full legal equivalent of families formed by biology. In some times and places, adoption had established a new relationship between adults. In the United States, adoption meant *child* adoption, and by decree of adoption, biological strangers became legal and social kin.

Adoption was crafted in the context of Progressive reform and modernizing culture, as the religious and moral commitments of Victorianism yielded to the new understandings of social and behavioral science. The emergence of modern adoption required a radically different understanding of family, one that overturned deeply held beliefs about blood and nurture, obligation and love, choice and chance. It was no accident that the United States was the crucible of this kind of adoption: in its repudiation of the past and its confidence in social engineering, adoption is quintessentially American.

Environmentalism both reflected and fueled this optimism about remaking social life. In the two decades before and after 1920, sociologists and anthropologists turned away from the belief that inherited traits determine the life of an individual. The Chicago School of Sociology pioneered studies in urban ecology that replaced hereditarian views with the notion that environment shapes character. In anthropology, Franz Boas, Ruth Benedict, and Margaret Mead popularized the idea of culture as the shaper of a malleable human nature. Such views helped undermine longstanding fears of the "bad seed" and made adults less anxious about adopting children of unknown heredity. Boasian views also challenged the intricate hierarchies of ethnic and racial groups that had been an article of faith for educated white Americans. He and his students argued that differences among human groups were not biological but cultural in origin.[7]

The new adoptive family reflected another change within American culture: the ongoing transformation of middle-class family life. For nearly a century, Americans had made marriage a more individual affair, as young people insisted on choosing their own partners. They added romantic love to duty in the marriage contract. In the twentieth century, companionate marriage elaborated this consensual and individual view of matrimony: its ethic of marriage affirmed mutuality and sexual fulfillment.[8] The growing use of contraception contributed to this sense of family as chosen and intentional, and this view in turn made adoption more acceptable: if couples could claim control over the timing of parenthood, those denied parenthood by nature might in turn defy the sentence of infertility through adoption. Adoption reflects, too, the loosening bonds of family and its increased privatism in the twentieth century, especially for middle-class whites. As inheritance became less important in assuring one's prospects and as kinship obligations became more attenuated, married couples were more at liberty to add unrelated persons to the family circle.

These changing conditions created an extraordinary groundswell of popular support for adoption, one that coincided with shifting approaches to child welfare. Beginning in the 1890s, a spate of exposés and reform tracts decried the deplorable conditions of children trapped in poverty, neglected, abandoned, or orphaned. Nineteenth-century reformers had responded to a range of social problems from disabilities to child dependency by building institutions, confident that they could remake society through the salutary effect of a controlled environment.[9] But that optimism waned by the end of the century, and increasingly the orphanage came under attack. The 1909 White House Conference on the Care of Dependent Children gathered a new breed of child welfare workers. The benevolent reform of charity workers and evangelical missions yielded to a new professionalization of reform, one that appealed to the expertise of social science. Child welfare workers renewed their commitment to "home relief," seeking to keep children with their families and provide services to them at home. If children could not be cared for at home, providing a substitute family through "placing out" was the recommended alternative. Institutional care was the last resort, and Progressive reformers sought to supplant orphanages with smaller and more intimate places, such as "cottage-homes" that housed small groups of children with one or two adults.[10]

Still, these "experts" were slow to consider adoption as a likely alternative for such children. Certainly, they knew, it was not a broad solution to the problem of child dependency, since then—as now—most children in the care of people other than their parents were not available for adoption. Rather, parents used "placing out" and institutional care to supplement their own care of the children; they did not intend to relinquish them permanently. "Orphanage" was itself something of a misnomer, for most residents had at least one living parent and most children committed to orphanages did not spend their entire childhoods in these institutions. Even for children who had no kin to claim them, child welfare reformers were doubtful that adoption was the solution: they were skeptical that permanent homes for children could be found among strangers.[11]

A growing faith in nurture over nature, and child welfare experts looking for new solutions for dependent children, were two crucial factors in the emergence of modern adoption. The third was a new attitude toward women pregnant out of wedlock and their "illegitimate" offspring. Nineteenth-century evangelical reformers had reached out to the "fallen woman," first with rescue homes for prostitutes and then, at the end of the century, with maternity homes that offered care for pregnant women along with the rehabilitative agenda of domesticity. In a home-like environment, women could recover the virtues of true womanhood, a rehabilitation that would be completed by motherhood itself. In the Florence Crittenton homes established by Kate Waller Barrett in 1896, the goal was to keep mother and child together, both for the good of the child and for its mother's redemption. The Salvation Army's mission to unwed mothers also sought to reform the sinner through motherhood. The prescription of maternity had a punitive edge, as revealed in one matron's prescription for a young resident: "The girl had committed a terrible sin and . . . she should do her duty by her child."[12] Single motherhood, then, was both penalty and restitution for having illicit sex. By assuming the duties of woman's highest calling, the sinner was redeemed.[13]

An illicit alternative to this rehabilitative agenda soon emerged, as revealed in a classic Progressive era exposé. Published in 1914, George Walker's *The Traffic in Babies* reported the results of an investigation of two Baltimore "baby farms." For a fee, they took babies off the hands of mothers looking to save themselves from the disgrace of single motherhood. Some also boarded pregnant women until their babies' births, further helping to conceal an illicit pregnancy.[14] The profit in such services depended on a grisly calculus: at a time when bottle feeding was not yet a reliable substitute for breast milk, most babies did not survive separation from their mothers and so did not become a financial burden for the proprietors. Only the hardiest newborns could survive a regimen that often combined bottle feeding with poor sanitation and negligent care. Walker's investigation reported a death rate of over 80 percent of all babies admitted and gave a grim account of the mass graves to which their small bodies were consigned.[15] When investigators interviewed persons who referred women to the baby farms, they found that at least some were well aware of these mortality rates. "It was better that it should die," opined a woman as she explained to an investigator why she referred mothers of "illegitimate" babies to one such institution. When an investigator posed as a concerned relative of a woman pregnant out of wedlock, one doctor advised, "I will place the baby in Institution No. 1; it will not live more than five weeks, but I think that is the best thing that can happen to it."[16]

Reformers and middle-class observers like Walker were appalled by the terrible conditions of these institutions and outraged by those who knowingly sent infants to their probable deaths. But tellingly, they often voiced the very moralism that created the market for the baby farms. Walker opened his exposé by pronouncing, "All this is done in the effort to preserve a family's good name; to prevent a girl's reputation from being smirched; to save a man from facing the consequences of his act. Altogether it is a well-organized hushing up, by a system of subterfuges and repressions, in order that certain individuals shall not have to face openly what they have done."[17] But others expressed more sympathy. One member of the Board of Lady Managers for one baby farm defended herself by explaining, "She thinks it is her duty to save the good name of unmarried mothers who have children."[18] Clearly, some women chose to avoid the strenuous rehabilitation afforded by single motherhood, and they were abetted by the doctors, nurses, midwives, clergymen, and hospital administers who referred them to the baby farms.

Along with Progressive reform, the developing profession of social work helped to displace the moralism of nineteenth-century evangelical reformers. The pioneering work of sex theorists and the sexual revolution of the World War I era charted this change in attitude, at least among urban Americans. Though very few people publicly advocated sex outside of marriage, psychological accounts of sexual behavior provided an alternative to the stern moralism of Victorian culture. Evangelical reformers had reached out to the "fallen woman," but for them, the retribution for sin was the sentence of single motherhood. A new generation of secular reformers was both less concerned with punishing the sinner and more concerned about the effects of such redemption on the child. Between 1910 and 1930, one manifestation of that commitment was the campaign to defend children from the stigma and legal disabilities of illegitimacy.[19] Later, social workers would endorse adoption as another solution for a child born out of wedlock—a way to give the sexual transgressor a second chance while saving the child from the consequences of its mother's mistakes. By the 1940s, the "fallen women" of the nineteenth-century moral tale became "problem girls" in the narrative of social work, susceptible to the interventions of experts.

Through the second and third decades of this century, social workers strongly advocated keeping mother and child together, though not from any conviction about redemptive motherhood. Aware of the uncertain prospects that awaited children without families, they were motivated by their concerns for children's health and welfare. Certainly, the existence of such institutions as baby farms would have deepened their doubts about adoption as a practical solution for dependent children. If baby farms were able to charge unmarried mothers for the service of taking their babies, it hardly seemed likely that large numbers of adults were clamoring to take these children into their homes. And yet by 1910, there were other indications of a growing demand for children. Some baby farms exacted fees from mothers wanting to relinquish children born out of wedlock, and then turned around and collected fees from adults eager to claim the children as their own. Newspapers reported that some prospective parents had paid baby-selling rings high prices for infants.[20] An extensive investigation by the Illinois legislature in 1913 reported a brisk trade in child-placing at private maternity hospitals, and its summary concluded, "The demand for children has been greater than the supply."[21] Despite newspaper and magazine reports that adoption had become widespread, with adults eagerly seeking scarce children, the federal Children's Bureau was skeptical. In reply to an inquiry about this claim in 1920, the bureau said, "So far as we know, there is no such movement afoot in this country; certainly there is no Governmental movement of this character."[22] The bureau was only half right. The government was not involved, but some unmarried mothers and infertile couples were seeking new solutions to their plights. Single mothers were refusing disgrace and penury; and infertile couples were searching for children to raise as their own.

In the 1920s and 1930s, child welfare workers were cautious and reluctant advocates of adoption, viewing it as a limited and exceptional response to the problems of dependent children. This position set them increasingly at odds with adults seeking to adopt, who soon attracted the sympathetic attention of a broad collection of middle-class allies. Judges and legislators often resisted efforts to regulate adoption more carefully, instead defending the laissez-faire status quo—a measure of their confidence in adoption, but also of their skepticism about the professional expertise of social workers. In one example, the president of the board of the Knoxville, Tennessee, Children's Bureau wrote the

USCB in 1939 to complain about a local judge who had approved the petition of a divorced man to adopt two children in his care. The agency had placed the children with him and his wife, but since the placement he had begun drinking heavily and the marriage had dissolved. The Tennessee Children's Bureau now advised against the adoption, but the court allowed it. "Our Juvenile Court has sometimes placed children for adoption almost as pets are placed," the board member complained, "with no records, no supervision, and freedom to pass the children from one person to another without reporting to anyone."[23] Self-appointed adoption facilitators such as lawyers, doctors, nurses, and members of the clergy matched children and adopters according to their own criteria, thwarting social workers' efforts to implement professional standards of child placement. Radio shows featured children for adoption, evidence of the popular appeal of adoption—and of the limited influence of child welfare advocates, who deplored such casual approaches to child placement. Commercial maternity homes became another venue of adoption practice—a kind of parallel institution to the professional agency adoption encouraged by the U.S. Children's Bureau and exemplified by agencies like the Children's Bureau of Delaware (CBD).[24]

On their own part, social workers and other child welfare experts viewed this groundswell for adoption as well-meaning but wrong-headed. Their own professional charge was not to assist adults seeking children but to defend children's best interest. The advocates of adoption, they believed, were too ready to separate mothers and children. Moreover, they were alarmed at the cavalier attitude about child placement exhibited by those pressing them to approve more adoptions. Many allies of adoption, in their view, grossly underestimated the work of child placement. Indeed, some seemed to think that it required no more than finding a child for a couple who expressed a desire for one, and helping out a desperate mother in the process—a gratifying exercise all around, and one hardly requiring the application of professional expertise. Social workers, by contrast, regarded child placement as a grave responsibility, one properly undertaken by a trained professional guided by tested protocols.

The example of the CBD illustrates the very limited place of adoption in child welfare prior to the 1930s. Established in 1916, the CBD first operated as an umbrella organization to coordinate the activities of eighteen member agencies. Its second constitution, passed in December 1918, exemplifies the ongoing professionalization of child welfare reform: the Progressive era commitments of efficiency and "scientific charity," assistance offered through the methods of social science, with coordination of private and public efforts. As the CBD's constitution stated, its objectives were "to develop higher standards and to maintain closer cooperation among these organizations"; and "to serve as an agency through which to secure united effort for a definite and comprehensive program of child care throughout the state."[25] In March 1920 the affiliated organizations agreed that all child placement would be done under the supervision of the CBD, with one full-time director and a part-time staff person to carry out its activities. Initially supported entirely by private contributions, most from one benefactor, Mrs. Irenée du Pont, the bureau began to receive some funding from member organizations that paid fees for the agency's placement services and supervision. The next step was to evaluate and reform existing services. In April the CBD hired another worker and part-time assistant to conduct a survey on child placement. In 250 cases investigated, none met the standards prescribed by social work experts, the worker concluded. Placements were often highly informal, the children were placed without case work documenting their family histories, and many children were placed from out of state because of Delaware's lax apprenticeship law, which did not require "bound" children to attend school. The bureau then recommended a cessation of all child placement until the Delaware legislature repealed its child indenture laws, which occurred in 1921.

Through the 1920s, adoption was only a small part of the CBD's rapidly growing case load. From April 1921 to April 1922, the agency served 472 children. Most of the children got help in their own homes from agency workers who investigated complaints of child neglect and abuse or who responded to parents' requests for assistance. Even for children not in the care of their parents, adoption was seldom the outcome. Instead, 74 were placed in institutions (orphanages or state institutions for older children). Some were cared for in foster homes; the bureau recorded 137 supervisory visits to children in foster care.

Twenty-five went to "free" homes, an arrangement intermediate between foster care and adoption. In such homes, the caretaking parents received no payment for board, but neither did they assume parental rights through legal adoption; the Children's Bureau retained legal custody. Free boarding was an arrangement that emphasized the emotional ties between family members and wards, since foster parents received no payment. At the same time, the CBD's legal custody offered a safety net for families that lived close to the edge: if a family faced economic reversals or unanticipated medical expenses, care of the child would revert to the bureau. Another 22 children were placed with relatives. As of March 31, 1922, 117 children were "placed out" under the supervision of the bureau. Adoption, by comparison, was an uncommon outcome for children in the bureau's care. During this period, only seven adoptions were completed.

The Annual Service Report for April 1925 to January 31, 1926, told a similar story. Many children received services in their own homes. The Department for Dependent Children had handled 166 cases involving 272 children. Of 133 children in foster care on April 1, 1925, 32 were released by the end of the year. Seven returned to their parents; eleven came of age; others were placed in institutions. Only two were placed for adoption. As of January 31, 1926, 137 children were in foster care; those few who had circulated out of the system were replaced by others coming in.

Annual reports from 1921 and 1922 reveal a slightly broader scope of adoption practice than revealed in the accounts of children under CBD supervision in foster care. One role of the agency was to advise the court on pending adoptions by filing reports for adoption petitions. These petitions included information on the child, the relinquishing mother, and the prospective parents, along with the agency's recommendation about whether the adoption should be approved. The CBD completed reports for 16 petitions in 1921 and 14 in 1922; it is not clear how many of these ended in legal adoptions.

For the entire decade of the 1920s, though, there are only three CBD case records documenting adoptions that took place under the agency's supervision. These were stranger adoptions, that is, adoptions of children unrelated to the prospective parents. From the start, adoptions by relatives were treated differently, subject to less investigation and thus generating less documentation. Moreover, the agency separated these files from the case records of stranger adoptions.

From the outset, the CBD sought to apply systematic principles of child placement in its adoption practice. Its protocol was deliberate and extended. The process opened with an interview of prospective adopters, who received an application form if they passed this initial assessment. The "Adoptive Home Investigation" included several home visits, during which CBD workers conducted further interviews with each petitioner individually and with the couple together. The agency assessed all the information gathered to determine whether the couple met its requirements. These included financial qualifications, primarily an income adequate to ensure a modicum of economic security for an adopted child. CBD workers also investigated the physical environment of applicants' homes, with an eye for the standard of housekeeping and domestic comfort on offer. They also wanted assurance that the child would have adequate sleeping quarters separate from the parents (its own bed and some private space, though not necessarily a room of its own). They sought to assure that children would have a place to play outdoors (whether a private yard or nearby park). They wanted children to have educational opportunity—"all that they could use," in a common parlance in the records—which meant not only placing them in households with a measure of financial security but also with parents who would recognize children's abilities and support their aspirations. The Adoption Home Investigation included the assessment of many other qualifications for adoptive parenthood, including good character and marital stability. As social work took on more psychological methods in the 1930s and 1940s, that list expanded to include emotional maturity, flexibility, and "adequacy" in meeting life's challenges.

The questions on the CBD's first application form—and the standard protocol that such forms implied—indicated the agency's concern for its charges and its expectations of adoptive families. Used from 1919 until the mid-1930s, the form reflected the CBD's wariness about the motives of adopters. Child-placing had often been combined with informal apprenticeship or, until 1921, legal indenture, a history that the CBD tacitly repudiated in its question, "Do you expect to treat the child in every way as a member of your family?" They further inquired of adopters, "Will you send the child to school until sixteen years of age?" Although the bureau was not a religious agency, adopters were expected to provide religious education for their children. The application queried, "What church do you attend?" "Will you send the child to Sunday School with reasonable regularity?" (That last phrase suggests a rather perfunctory attitude toward religious education; bureau workers seemed to regard church attendance more as a form of good citizenship than as an essential spiritual discipline.) Adopters had to provide the names of four persons who knew them well, including one member of the clergy. The bureau asked recommenders to comment on a battery of questions that probed the character, reputation, health, finances, and religious practice of prospective adopters. "Is Mr. ___ of temperate habits? Is he kind and just? Is Mrs. ___ a good, sensible woman? Is the moral standard of the family high? Is the family in good health? What is their financial condition? Have they a comfortable home? Would you consider it *a desirable home for a child?* What church do they attend? How long have you known the family? Are you related to them by marriage or otherwise? Please state any further particulars regarding their character and standing." Bureau social workers supplemented the written testimony of letters of recommendation by conducting personal interviews with each reference.

These procedures became more elaborate as the CBD claimed an expanded public role in child welfare. In its revised constitution of 1923, the agency added to its mandate the charge "to initiate and execute plans for the general welfare of children . . . To take an active part in the perfecting of laws relating to children." This agenda reflected the CBD's participation in the reform agenda of a national network of child welfare advocates. The U.S. Children's Bureau acknowledged CBD's important legislative activity in a letter written in September 1923, and CBD staff maintained close contact with the federal bureau as it conducted its review of Delaware law. The Russell Sage foundation supported the study. The result was a 1925 law that required a petition to the court to adopt and established a procedure for relinquishment of parental rights. The judge could request an investigation of the adoptive parents, but this was not mandatory. Still, weak as this law appears, it was one of the more stringent in the country. In 1929, only seven states required a court investigation of adoption petitions. In five others, including Delaware, adoption laws stated that such investigations could be required, and in six states the board of welfare investigated the case when the court notified the board that an adoption petition had been filed. Thirty of the 48 states had no provisions for supervision of adoption.[26]

Further revisions to the law in 1933 gave the CBD a more expansive role in Delaware adoptions. Petitions had to include the report of a "social investigation" that included medical and mental tests of the birth parents, some family medical and social history, and signed release of custody from the birth parents, or the mother alone if parents were unmarried. The law also provided for a two-year "probationary period" before a placement could become a legal adoption; the prospective parents could submit an adoption petition to the court after one year but could not get full parental rights until two years had passed. (The interval between placement and legalization was reduced to one year in 1935, and renamed the "supervisory" period.) These changes greatly increased the role of the state in child placement, and the court frequently called upon the bureau to assist with investigations and supervision. This law conformed more closely to social work prescriptions for adoption practice, offering a limited mandate for more expert involvement and oversight in matters of child placement. However, agencies remained advisory to the court. In Delaware and other states that passed similar legislation, judges could and did make decisions that contravened the recommendations submitted by social workers, and petitioners could submit social investigations done by someone other than a social worker or agency.

In the 1920s and 1930s, the agency often found itself in the awkward position of assessing and supervising placements that it would not have made in the first place. Such adoptions were essentially ratifications of already existing arrangements. As they considered the cases of petitioners eager to adopt children already with them, social workers were under considerable pressure to proffer a positive recommendation. These records illustrate the agency's struggles to apply emerging professional protocols to complicated situations that defied easy management. The first placement supervised by the bureau, made in 1919, apparently never ended in a formal adoption. Mr. and Mrs. S, the prospective parents, were an African American laborer and "housewife" living in modest circumstances. They had three children already, ranging in age from six to twelve years old, and lived with a sister and brother-in-law who had three children of their own. The petitioners sought to add a three-week-old boy to their family, a foundling recently received at Colored Babies' Hospital. Bureau visitors found the home satisfactory, even as case notes signaled their cultural distance from these clients: one reported, "The house was neat and clean. It consists of six rooms all furnished in distinctly colored people's tastes." But as the months passed, no adoption petition was submitted to the court. Mr. S seemed to think the legal work was done, since he had "signed papers"; these papers, though, were the placement agreement between the family and the bureau, a preliminary step to adoption. Later, when Mr. and Mrs. S separated, the bureau continued to supervise the little boy, now living with Mrs. S in a house that the visitor described as "rather dilapidated, but . . . about as comfortable as the average negro home." Neighbors reported that the child was receiving good care, and CBD visitors concurred. But the bureau seems to have tacitly reclassified the case as free boarding rather than a pre-adoptive placement, no doubt because of the marital separation. Mrs. S eventually married a second time, but neither she nor her new husband had gotten divorces from their legal spouses. This common-law partnership did not meet the agency's marriage test: adopters had to verify that they were legally married to one another. Still, the bureau never moved to disrupt the placement. Its supervision apparently ended in 1925, the date of the last note in the record: "Family moved, whereabouts unknown."

In another of these early cases, six years elapsed between placement and legal adoption. Again, the prospective adopters already had three sons by birth, three, four, and six years old. Their fourth child, a daughter, had recently died in infancy. These parents sought to adopt a foundling girl. The bureau initially refused to place the child: "It was decided, as Mrs. L has three little children and is having children just as fast as she can, that it would not be wise to place the foundling in this home." But the agency reconsidered when Mrs. L's mother came to petition the bureau on her daughter's behalf. She invoked a more expansive view of informal adoption, one that social workers would later resist as they sought to codify adoption practice. She explained, "Their people for generations had been in the habit of caring for large numbers of children, usually have large families of their own and then take in some waif in addition, who was given absolutely the same care as the others." The bureau did place the child, but again avoided bringing the case to court for legalization. Visitors found that the girl was healthy and growing well but were concerned about the chaotic household, now comprised of the girl and four boys, "one ungovernable," and the sometimes unkempt condition of the children. By 1924 no adoption had taken place. Mr. and Mrs. L chafed at the bureau's inaction, to no effect. Notably, though, both parties were apparently willing to let the matter slide. Some time later, the family moved to Pennsylvania and again sought to adopt the little girl in their care. In response to their lawyer, the bureau finally recommended approval for the adoption.

Another application, made in 1930, found the bureau doubtful from the beginning. This time the worker had misgivings about the prospective father, Mr. M, who among other shortcomings "was such a constant talker that it was very annoying." Before the CBD had a chance to reject this application, Mrs. M withdrew it, concerned that her husband was not really ready for adoption. Some months later, though, the couple went to the Wilmington Florence Crittenton home and arranged to board a baby recently born there. Because of "hard times," the couple had decided to take a foster child rather than to pursue adoption. Mrs. M assured the worker that "she expects to love it as her own child and bring it up so." Still concerned about Mr. M, the bureau's director nonetheless approved this placement, reasoning, "As child is a boarding one it can be removed if it seems best." But the placement went well, and when their finances stabilized, the couple went on to adopt the child. In the case of Mr. and Mrs. M and others like them, both the bureau and the prospective adopters showed a willingness to tolerate considerable ambiguity about the boundaries between foster care and adoption.

With the agency's approval, Mr. and Mrs. M also accepted a fluid boundary between the adoptive family and their child's blood kin. At this time, the bureau did not seek legal surrender of parental rights until an adoptive family had been identified for the child in question. This little girl's mother was "in a terrible state of indecision," her worker reported. She had visited the baby at the foster family's home, giving foster parents the opportunity to make their case for adoption directly to her. The CBD worker recorded the agency's misgivings about this pressure: "While Dir. [director] feels that foster parents have done a good deal of urging she also feels that the foster parents can give [the little girl] a much better chance than mother." When the agency asked the mother to sign a formal document relinquishing her daughter, she agreed on the condition that she could visit the child annually. The CBD not only agreed but indicated its approval in the record, noting "Foster mother took a very nice attitude toward mother, is going to allow her to see [the girl] once a year." The court, too, gave its imprimatur to the arrangement, for the final adoption petition included an affidavit stipulating that the mother could have an annual visit.

In the 1930s, the agency worked to establish its own adoption practice, and as a result, more and more of its cases reflected the CBD's placement protocols; the agency was less often in the position of supervising placements it had not made. In an effort to avoid the drift and ambiguity of some of its early cases, the bureau developed policies and working methods to move placements to a definite conclusion. The CBD also took the initiative to develop its own clientele of caretakers: the agency actively recruited foster and adoptive parents through newspaper notices, professional networks, church organizations, and word of mouth (perhaps the most effective of all in this small and closely knit state).

Faithful to the commitments of child welfare experts elsewhere, the CBD's practice was characterized by caution and the conviction that adoption was no job for amateurs. The CBD became gradually convinced that adoption could be a good solution for dependent children, as a last resort. Most babies, social workers believed, were better off with their mothers. The USCB counseled keeping mother and baby together at least three months, so that the mother could breast feed. "From the point of view of the child there is an additional advantage of keeping the mother and baby together; this is that the mother has a period to decide what she really wants to do and is much more apt to be able to make arrangements to keep the child."[27] Moreover, the CBD did not accept relinquishments until the babies had been determined "fit" for adoption. The bureau regarded adoption as appropriate only for selected children, whose "eligibility" it determined through careful study and observation. Therefore, the agency never placed children under six months of age; usually, children who came into the bureau's care as newborns were not placed in adoptive homes until they were nine months to a year old.

In counseling pregnant women who came to the agency, social workers took an approach that might be described as cautiously meliorative. Pragmatic about the constraints that pressed upon single mothers, they sought to offer advice and services that might improve the limited prospects of such women and their children. They helped clients take inventory of available resources, such as help from relatives or assistance from the New Deal's Aid to Dependent Children. They advised women about the legal recourse of paternity suits to wrest child support from men reluctant to meet their responsibilities. But social workers rarely counseled clients to relinquish their children for adoption. Acutely aware of the narrow confines of single mothers' lives and the bleak futures that their children often faced, social workers were even less sanguine about the prospects of children dependent on the kindness of strangers.

For mothers unable to care for their children, the CBD provided a two-tier system of foster care. "Temporary" foster care was intended as an interim measure, with a time limit of six to nine months, after which mothers were expected to make a definite long-term plan for their children. During this time, the bureau assumed legal custody of the children, including responsibility for providing medical care. Mothers were expected to assume some financial responsibility for children in temporary foster care, with fees negotiated according to what they could pay. Meanwhile, social workers advised mothers as they worked out permanent plans of care—raising their children themselves; planning long-term foster care; or, as a last resort, relinquishing children for adoption. In long-term foster care, children essentially became wards of the CBD, which assumed all financial responsibility and held legal custody. Mothers still retained parental rights and were encouraged to visit their children, but they could reclaim custody only with the bureau's approval or a court order.

Temporary foster care supported new mothers by relieving them of the daily cares of children and affording an extended period of reflection and planning for their futures. However, it also brought them under the scrutiny and jurisdiction of the agency, which exerted a maternalistic social control on behalf of children and their mothers. Some mothers were dismayed with the agency's control over visitation, which was limited to once a week or once every two weeks, scheduled at the convenience of foster mother and social workers. Mothers met their children at the CBD office, where social workers observed and assessed the interaction of mother and child.

The agency's fee structure helped to defer the costs of foster care, but its symbolic uses were equally important. Mothers were not required to pay the full cost, and indeed social workers counseled them to consider carefully what they could realistically afford as they drew up agreements for foster care. Fees then served as a litmus test of maternal realism and responsibility: case records carefully noted whether mothers rendered their payments fully and on time. Financial support of children was both a parental responsibility and a mark of parental rights; in recognition of the latter, the agency refused to take payments of accounts that were in arrears after mothers had signed relinquishments.

Social workers considered temporary foster care as a necessary safeguard against hasty and ill-considered relinquishments. Sometimes this policy brought them into conflict with clients who wanted to make the decision ahead of the bureau's schedule. For example, Mrs. J, whose husband had deserted the family in 1938, placed her two youngest children in care with the firm intention of relinquishing them for adoption. When the social worker tried to persuade her to care for the twins for a time, she demurred: "She was afraid she would get fond of them and then she couldn't give them up . . . I asked her if she thought it would be giving her a little better chance to know how she really did feel about these babies if she had them with her for a time and she said no, she didn't want that at all; she didn't see how she could look after three children." She visited infrequently, which social workers interpreted as a sign that she had little interest in her sons. In six weeks, she signed her consent to terminate parental rights. The worker noted that she hesitated as she filled out the form, unable to recall the children's names,

and "apparently showed no conflict whatsoever" about the relinquishment.

The case record contains a whiff of disapproval for Mrs. J's cool deci-
siveness. But perhaps Mrs. J simply recognized outright her own limited
resources and wished to save herself from the pain of extended deliberation. Subsequent events, in any case, were to confirm her estimation of
her straitened circumstances. In 1943, this mother's seventh child was
removed for neglect. "It seemed evident that he had not been given
sufficient food," the medical report noted in understated prose. "This
may have been due to the fact that Mrs. J had insufficient money to buy
food for all her children."

Miss R was another mother who made a firm decision ahead of the
schedule established by the Children's Bureau. Accompanied by her sister, she came to the bureau in 1940 to request adoption for her newborn
daughter. A doctor had offered to help place the child, and this mother
was weighing the relative advantages of private and agency adoption.
The social worker made the case for agency adoption with its thorough
investigation of adoptive homes, and Miss R placed her daughter in
temporary care. However, the negotiation underscored the appeal of
private adoptions, for the worker also warned Miss R that she would be
responsible for the child until she was deemed "eligible" for adoption.
The dismayed mother told the social worker that "she didn't know what
she would do if the baby wasn't accepted for adoption, as she wouldn't
be able to take her herself." In subsequent meetings, this mother discussed plans for her child with the CBD social worker, who acknowledged the difficulties of earning a living, securing child care, and dealing with the stigma of illegitimacy. Still, the worker argued that
maternal devotion could outweigh the disadvantages of illegitimacy,
advising Miss R, "if she felt she really wanted B, the child would derive a
great deal from being with her own mother in spite of the fact that she
would not have a father she could call her own." By contrast, social
workers in the 1950s would see illegitimacy as a pressing reason for relinquishment.

After two months, Miss R declared herself ready to sign a surrender
of parental rights. But the worker dissuaded her, convincing her to visit
her daughter once more before making the decision to relinquish. A

week later, Miss R came to see the baby at the agency and then signed her consent to relinquishment. They parted, with the social worker issuing a final warning that the agency would be in touch again if the child was not suitable for adoptive placement. The agency believed that such meetings were important for mothers, to ensure that their decisions were firm; social workers also used them as an occasion to observe and report the interaction between mother and child. In this case, the worker noted that the baby screamed vigorously throughout the visit and would not smile at her mother, who observed her daughter fondly but expressed little emotion. She concluded, "There was no deep feeling of attachment between the two of them and I felt that she was looking at Betsy as if she were a curiosity just to see what she looked like." Case records such as this suggest that the structure of temporary placement served social workers as well as clients, allowing them to reassure themselves that the consequential decision to relinquish was right for mother and child.

In a 1936 case, the CBD's lone male social worker himself believed that adoption was the best plan, but he hesitated to accept a decision that he thought the mother herself did not embrace. His client was an inmate at the Girls Industrial School, "dismissed by her family" when she was found to be pregnant at eighteen. He and the matron at the Industrial School talked with the girl, both counseling her about the difficulties of raising a child as a single mother. The social worker even made an argument that was then uncommon, suggesting, "It would seem to him to take a good deal more love on the mother's part to give [the child] up than to keep him." In his notes, the case worker speculated that she would decide on adoption, but he had doubts about "how much the decision will impart what she really wanted to do." Though he himself thought adoption was best, he wanted her to come to that conclusion herself. He ended his note wondering "if she can ever be happy giving up the child without having made some effort to look after him and take responsibility for him." Temporary foster care served this purpose, CBD workers believed.

CBD practice regarding relinquishment conformed to social work standards as articulated by the U.S. Children's Bureau and in professional literature—standards repeatedly reaffirmed in the 1930s. These

sources show, at the same time, that such professionals were facing increased pressure from adults eager to adopt children and from others
who thought social workers were needlessly cautious. In 1930 Henry W.
Thurston's *The Dependent Child* restated the consensus of leading experts in a manual that exhorted child welfare workers to keep families
together.[28] For Thurston, a model agency was one that he himself had
supervised between 1909 and 1912, now under the direction of Wilfred
S. Reynolds. Writing in 1921, Reynolds recounted with pride a dimin-
ishing number of adoptions. Eight years previously, the Illinois agency
had accepted 300 for adoptive placement. The year before, in 1920, they
had accepted only 140. Reynolds attributed the decline to superior case
work: the agency's personnel had doubled in ten years, and more intense intervention had helped troubled families stay together.[29]

Thurston also approvingly quoted the 1921 Annual Report of the
Boston Children's Aid Society, which declared: "It is not the practice of
the Society to agree to very many adoptions of its children. It cannot
guarantee physical and mental soundness for some of them, and for
others it is anxious to exercise supervision until majority is reached and
in some cases long afterwards."[30] Telling in its assumptions, the statement implies that only "sound" children are fit subjects of adoption;
that prospective parents will require, or should require, "guarantees";
and that the CAS is better suited than parents to exercise the necessary
supervision over dependent children. Even as Thurston applauded this
cautious approach, he documented a surge of adoptions as he be-
moaned counterexamples of disturbing and ill-considered practices.
Surveying thirty-two member societies of the National Children's
Home and Welfare Association during 1917 and 1918, he found that
children waiting for adoption comprised the great majority of the total
caseload: of 14,792 children receiving services, 12,379 were in "free foster family homes," a prelude to adoption. Thurston feared that these
numbers derived from a lack of good temporary foster homes, perhaps
resulting in unnecessary permanent separations of children from their
natal families.[31] Like-minded social workers turned up reports of adoption burgeoning elsewhere. A Pennsylvania observer, studying thirteen
counties, was critical of the rapid and unsystematic adoptions made

possible by that state's laws. A 1926 study by the Child Welfare League of America found many agencies doing large numbers of adoptions. The authors thought the agencies were too ready to accept relinquishments of children for adoption. One Pacific area agency, they noted, accepted eight applications for every one that was rejected. "This would mean that the Society separated eight times as many children from their natural families as it enabled to stay with them," the report concluded, and it found some child welfare workers too ready to encourage clients in "the drastic action of permanent surrender of their own children which violates one of the deepest human instincts."[32]

But as a growing number of exigent adults found themselves frustrated in their search for children to adopt, some charged that it was social workers who were unnatural, standing between needy children and adults eager to become their parents. In 1936, a frustrated adopter from Chicago wrote Franklin D. Roosevelt to appeal for presidential support of an "Adopt a Child" campaign. "Through questioning both Catholic and Protestant 'welfare' agencies, I gather they are not very anxious to part with their wards. They remind me of the average county sheriff who is happy when his jail is full of prisoners for the winter!" These social workers inflicted suffering on prospective parents as well as homeless children, the author complained, "for everyone of normal intelligence *loves* [underscored three times] children, but—try and get one!"[33]

Adoption gained national visibility as journalists took up the cause of prospective adopters. Dorothy Thompson, a widely known and influential journalist, lambasted social workers in her column in the *Ladies Home Journal* for May 1939. In "Fit for Adoption," she expressed outrage at agency practices that she believed excluded many promising would-be parents while needy children waited in institutions. (Thompson failed to recognize that most such children were not available for adoption.) She found social workers too reluctant to accept relinquishments, and proposed a more forceful approach: "The healthy unwed mother ought to be persuaded—if possible in advance of the birth of the child—that the best possible thing she can do for the child is to give him to eager, loving parents who will do for him what she, by her very circumstances, cannot do." Thompson denounced the testing and observation of children in agency care, charging that social workers were applying standards that were all too reminiscent of eugenic practices in Nazi Germany.

U.S. Children's Bureau files on adoption swelled during the 1930s and 1940s, and these records attest both to the dramatically increasing public interest in adoption and social workers' cautious responses. Hundreds of people wrote letters soliciting the assistance of the federal agency in their quest for children to adopt, dramatic evidence of the "shortage" of children that in fact has been typical of formal adoption for most of its history. By the mid-1930s, almost every letter from prospective adoptive parents recounted long and discouraging searches for children to adopt. "I have found out that becoming Adopted Parents is no small task," a disheartened Georgia woman wrote.[34] Another requested a list of addresses of agencies, plaintively explaining, "I have applied to a few and their waiting list is so long I have quite given up hope."[35] In response, as early as 1932 the Children's Bureau began to use a standard reply that warned, "Most institutions and agencies . . . find that they have more applicants for children than children who are available for adoption."[36] Some of these letters were referred to the USCB by Eleanor Roosevelt; prospective adopters appealed to the celebrated compassion of the First Lady for help in their quests. One such woman, from Iowa, explained that they had been applying for a child for eight years. "In each case though our credentials were satisfactory, we were told that for every child available, there are about a hundred or two hundred applicants and that it might be years before our turn came."[37] Stung by the perceived rejection of agencies, correspondents rehearsed their qualifications for parenthood, appealed for the bureau's sympathy, or criticized adoption practices.

Alternatives to agency placement were readily available, and many prospective adopters turned to them. In the 1920s, most adoptions took place without agency supervision. In a 1922–1925 study done in Massachusetts and another in New Jersey in 1928, investigators found that two-thirds of adoptions took place without agency involvement. Until 1951, when Delaware became the first state to require agency supervision of adoption, no state compelled prospective parents to adopt through agencies, and in Delaware as elsewhere, many formed adoptive families without the involvement of CBD or any other agency. As late as 1955, an estimated three-quarters of all adoptions in the United States were done independent of agencies.[38] Some of these adoptions were arranged directly by the mothers themselves, with adopters they knew or whom they located through intermediaries.

Commercial maternity homes were other sources of adoptive placement. One such institution was the Vail, a Pennsylvania maternity home whose practices are documented in a 1935 CBD record when the court asked the agency to report on the placement. Reading the file through the critical lens of the CBD worker, we can discern the reasons that such institutions enjoyed a robust clientele. Confidentiality was one. The CBD worker lamented, "They advertise their services widely as an institution which will provide secret maternity care for unmarried mothers and dispose of the infant." She went on to note with disapproval that the Vail did only sketchy case work with expectant mothers, violating social work standards; likely, though, some unmarried mothers sought out places like the Vail to avoid what some perceived as probing and intrusive case work. Commercial maternity homes placed infants at a very young age—this child was less than two weeks old when placed with his adoptive parents. By contrast, social work practice mandated a long period of observation and testing.

Clearly, though, some adopters were prepared to forego such caution in order to adopt children "as young as possible," a common preference of prospective adopters expressed in CBD records and USCB correspondence. Moreover, commercial maternity homes did not conduct home studies of prospective adopters, and no doubt many were happy to escape the professional scrutiny of social workers. Child welfare advocates condemned such places as "adoption mills," engaged in baby-selling. Indeed, they were profit-making institutions; such concern was not unwarranted. It seems possible, at the same time, that these homes and their clientele may be taken as evidence of a different understanding of adoption—one closer to the casual exchange implied in the letter that opens this chapter. Such arrangements suggest a sweeping confidence—social workers considered it recklessness—about the ease with which strangers might become kin.

By contrast, social workers viewed adoption as a consequential transaction that required care and discernment. Along with caution about relinquishment, social workers like those at the CBD advocated very careful design of the adoptive family. This process began with meticulous selection of children. Until after World War II, child welfare professionals counseled that adoptive placements should not take place until the children were at least six months old, allowing time for close observation and scientific testing. Social workers made that determination through an elaborate protocol that included periodic medical examinations; psychological testing, especially intelligence testing; assessment of emotional development; and direct observation of children during home and office visits. In counseling prospective adoptive parents, social workers often referred to the "risks" of adoption. Their own practice was dominated by the assumption that such risks were considerable, manageable only through the careful application of medical, psychological, and social work expertise.

In the social work practice of the 1930s and 1940s, "eligibility" for adoption was an achieved status, and one accorded only after measured deliberation by experts. No other practice so starkly reveals the extent of expert caution about adoption. Social workers assumed that only some children were appropriate "candidates" for adoption, to be identified through elaborate screening and observation. The language of risk loomed large, revealing the persistent influence of hereditarian social science and eugenics. For social workers, infants were not blank slates upon which adopters would write their own scripts but rather were disturbing ciphers to be painstakingly decoded. As one worker explained in the early 1930s to prospective adopters hoping for a newborn, "the risk involved in too early placements was so great that we could not be responsible for doing it that way." Social workers were confident about placement only when they were dealing with a child known to them through assessment of its "background," medical examinations, intelligence and psychological tests, and extended observation. In this approach to placement, CBD workers reflected the consensus of other professional experts in social work: the Child Welfare League and the U.S. Children's Bureau both recommended careful study of the child before placement.

The first popular adoption manual, Eleanor Garrigue Gallagher's

The Adopted Child (1936), endorsed social workers' cautious approach to placement in revealing language: "It is unwise, if not dangerous, for parents to ask a physician to find and give them a newborn infant, or to take a baby directly from the hospital in which he was born, without having him under the scientific observation of pediatricians, graduate nurses and, if need be psychologists, for a long enough period to determine, so far as possible, whether the baby is physically sound and mentally normal."[39] This pervasive sense of adoption as risky, even "dangerous," stigmatized the adoptive child as different, potentially damaged in ways that required heightened vigilance and expert intervention. The whole structure of testing bespoke suspicion among experts about the unknown child: presumed defective, he had to be proved normal.

Hereditarian views strongly inflected social work practice. Though social workers would have scoffed at the outdated notion of inherited criminality, they did share more recent versions of such ideas in the form of eugenicist views of "mental defectiveness" as a major source of crime and social pathology. Unwed mothers were stigmatized in a circular logic prominent in the 1910s and 1920s: "feeblemindedness" put a woman at high risk of pregnancy out of wedlock, and, in turn, such pregnancies themselves were grounds for a diagnosis of feeblemindedness.[40] By the 1930s and 1940s, unwed mothers were more likely to be figured as "sex delinquents," and yet their babies were still seen as especially at risk, suggesting the continuing influence of eugenic views of these women as carriers of heritable defects.

At the same time, the language of risk suggested suspicion of adoptive parents and a sense of adoptive kinship as tenuous and fragile. Later critics of such screening practices would argue that social workers were inappropriately trying to shield parents from the "normal risks of parenthood," kow-towing to the unrealistic demands of adopters rather than considering the best interests of children. But adopters themselves sometimes protested against screening or reluctantly acquiesced to it. (And many, of course, avoided it altogether by adopting without agencies.) Social workers believed that careful screening was necessary for children, betraying an unspoken concern that adoptive parents could not be relied on to provide the unconditional love and acceptance that is the hallmark of biological kinship. To compensate for this difference,

it was not enough to construct adoptive families in the image of the biological family; social workers sought to improve on nature by offering a
hedge against risk.

The perceived risks of adoption opened up a space for the exercise of
professional expertise. Until Delaware's legislation in 1951, no state required agency involvement in adoption. Many prospective adopters
avoided agencies, disliking social workers' investigations of family
finances, marital stability, medical records, religious commitments,
work records, and the like. Social workers' caution about severing parental rights was also a source of some contention; prospective adopters
and many judges, lawyers, and doctors criticized social workers for
standing between needy children and capable adults eager to adopt. To
establish themselves as the reigning professionals in adoption, social
workers had to lay claim to a body of specialized knowledge and to gain
the legitimacy conferred by a clientele that valued and sought out their
services. Moreover, to compete in the unregulated market of adoption,
they had to convince potential clients that agency adoption was prefera-
ble to other ways of finding children. Social workers' rhetoric of risk was
not calculated as a marketing device; clearly, they were acting on their
own convictions as social scientists and advocates of children. Nonetheless, prospective adopters who believed that adoption was risky were
more likely to turn to expert intervention.

Agency evaluation of the child began even before its birth as social
workers investigated its "background"—the social history and heredity
of parents and relatives. For example, one record from the late 1930s described a birth mother with "very poor background . . . she stated she
has one sister who is 'no good,' and her own history is one of drinking
and probably prostituting." Though notions of inherited criminality
had been discredited, eugenicists still believed that much social pathology could be attributed to defective heredity, and such ideas seemed to
influence CBD social workers. "Poor background" might also refer to
insanity or "feeblemindedness"; workers were aware that many people
believed these conditions to be hereditary. Social workers themselves
thought that some mental illness might be inherited, and that intelligence was largely hereditary. Workers also assessed educational attainments and work histories of birth families: high school diplomas, col-

lege degrees, stable employment, and professional status all were taken as markers of intelligence. Social workers did recognize that class and race might pose barriers to such attainments, and they were careful not to assume that a client was dull simply because he had only a grade school education and worked in an unskilled job. Many records noted signs of "native intelligence" in clients who had limited schooling and modest achievements. Nonetheless, they believed in the importance of heredity and shared the eugenics thinking prominent among psychologists of the day. Delaware passed a eugenics sterilization law in 1923, part of a resurgence of such legislation during the decade.[41] CBD social workers themselves sometimes recommended clients for involuntary sterilization, legal for men and women deemed "unfit" because of low scores on intelligence tests.

Bureau workers monitored babies' development by recording their own observations, interviewing foster mothers, and consulting other experts. Children received regular medical care, including "clearance" for adoption near the time of placement. At three-month intervals, social workers took their charges to consulting psychologists at the Mental Hygiene Clinic who examined and tested the children. They recorded developmental milestones, assessed temperament, and administered standardized tests. First widely used in World War I military recruiting, IQ tests became an article of faith for many socials science experts in the 1920s. The CBD used them regularly until the 1950s, when the agency began placing infants too young for such assessments to be done.[42]

Agency social workers' case notes and summaries during the 1920s and 1930s, when they supervised children in foster care for at least six months, offer remarkably vivid portraits of children, rendered with texture and dimension. These verbal descriptions served as useful signposts of children's transformation from unknown and potentially threatening entities to familiar subjects of agency care.

Letters to the USCB from prospective adopters make clear that some of them valued this technology of expertise; they asked for advice about reliable agencies that tested children and knew something of their backgrounds. In CBD records, likewise, some applicants indicated that they came to the agency because they felt more secure adopting with the guidance of professional expertise, including testing. Undoubtedly, prospective adopters were aware of alternatives to agency services; case records are full of testimony about other routes to adoptive parenthood. Some of the CBD's own clients had adopted children through private arrangements before approaching the CBD for subsequent adoptions. Others received offers of children from birth parents, relatives, doctors, or lawyers during the course of CBD home studies. Those who chose agencies—in some ways more cumbersome and intrusive than other methods of adopting—often did so because they deemed social workers a reliable source of information about children available for placement. Cautious adopters indicated that they shared social workers' views of "fitness" for adoption. As one such prospective father indicated in the 1930s, "It was important . . . that the child they take comes from good stock and they would be anxious to know as much as possible about the parents and the possibility of the child's development."

In large part, adopters' and social workers' perceptions of risk turned on their assumptions about the influence of heredity. Overall, the record shows that adopters were less concerned than social workers about the risks of adoption. The majority, who adopted without agencies, were apparently willing to forego *any* testing. Not surprisingly, many prospective adopters professed themselves to be committed environmentalists, rendering them both less fearful of adopting untested infants and particularly eager to shape them from the earliest possible age. Social workers themselves, though, invariably issued demurrals when their clients discounted the influence of heredity. In a 1938 home study, for example, the case worker pressed Mr. and Mrs. T about their expectations of a child's potential, skeptical of their claim that they were not very concerned about a child's intellectual potential. The prospective parents discounted intelligence tests (the worker agreed they were often unreliable) and opined that a stimulating environment was likely to produce intelligent children. The social worker replied, "Little children seemed to be truly plastic, except that you must have something to begin with and we don't place a child who doesn't have this something." This caveat sums up the perspective of the CBD.

In some case records, prospective parents chafed at social workers' caution, urging the agency to allow them to adopt children whom CBD social workers viewed as poor risks. Such cases often arose in the 1930s, when the CBD made probationary placements of children before it had concluded intelligence and psychological evaluations. In 1933, for example, a childless couple pressed the bureau to support legalization of their adoption of Peggy, a two-year-old child provisionally placed with them. The psychological evaluation portrayed the little girl in dire language: she was "temperamentally deficient . . . emotionally unstable," and with "seriously psychopathic heredity." The CBD report concluded, "Her hereditary and temperamental manifestations suggest that she is a risk." Nonetheless, "The [prospective adopters] are devoted to the child and leave the impression that they want to adopt her regardless of any affliction that may be revealed." Under these circumstances, the bureau reluctantly endorsed the adoption, with the caveat that the prospective parents should be warned "that the child comes of inferior stock."

In another case, the bureau mediated among conflicting assessments of one little boy. Mr. and Mrs. P came to the CBD in the early 1930s to ask about a little boy they had seen at St. Michael's Home for Children. When tests showed a low IQ, the official conclusion was that the boy was "poor adoption material." Nonetheless, the matron at St. Michael's urged the bureau to consider the little boy for placement, and the agency acquiesced, offering him to the prospective parents. At first they declined, intimidated by the guarded official prognosis. But Mrs. P kept writing to the CBD to inquire about Eddie, and the couple finally decided to adopt him regardless of his possible intellectual limitations. In its final summary, the case record noted that the CBD's consulting psychologist at the Mental Hygiene Clinic did not recommend adoption, but registered the agency's demurral: the bureau regarded this child as a good fit for the home, which was "mediocre culturally and intellectually speaking."

As social workers struggled with ambiguous cases, prospective adopters sometimes settled the question by their decisive claims to children. The bureau hesitated over placement of another little girl in the early 1930s, concerned about her mother's positive Wassermann test (diagnostic of syphilis) and the possibility of congenital infection, though repeated tests of the child were negative. As was often the case, intelligence tests were inconclusive, showing wide fluctuation. Reporting the latest test results to the prospective adoptive parents, the social worker noted, "Although they knew that she rated poorly in her last test they were nevertheless so much interested in her that they wished to take her for adoption at once."

In a 1934 case, social workers again struggled with inconclusive results of intelligence testing. Trying to make decisions about Catherine's care, agency workers pondered the maddeningly ambiguous counsel of the Mental Hygiene Clinic: "It can be stated that she is not definitely mentally defective." Meanwhile, Catherine's prospective parents were eager to legalize their relationship to the little girl. A follow-up test yielded more promising results, and Mr. N used the occasion to press social workers to endorse their adoption petition. He declared, "Even if she is a moron we want to keep her." Such cases clearly refuted social workers' concerns that adoptive parents could not form enduring bonds with less-than-perfect children. Instead, for these adopters, the ties forged by family intimacy and nurturance prevailed over workers' counsel about the children's defects.

Both foster parents and prospective adopters of one-year-old Doris brushed off the bureau's warnings about her possible intellectual limits. Mr. and Mrs. C had cared for Doris almost since her birth, and when they learned in 1936 that her mother had relinquished her for adoption, they quickly appealed to the bureau to become her legal parents. The social worker reminded them that she had not yet been tested for intelligence and that they were concerned. Mrs. C responded that this didn't matter to the family, "so long as she wasn't feeble minded, they would love her as she was, and not as they wanted her to be." The bureau was ambivalent about this family—worried that the couple's straitened finances could not stretch beyond their two birth children to accommodate another child. Mr. and Mrs. C themselves reluctantly concluded that they could not afford to adopt Doris, saving the bureau from rejecting their application.

The bureau then discussed the little girl's case with another pair of prospective adopters. The social worker warned them that Doris was the child of a factory worker "and a good one but did not have a great deal of general intelligence." Mr. and Mrs. H nonetheless decided to meet the child and afterward spent some time discussing their concerns about her background. They themselves didn't think it "absolutely essential" that a child have the potential for college education, but they were concerned that Doris might feel inferior by comparison to their other child, whom they deemed very bright. However, Mr. H ended the discussion by spontaneously declaring that he wanted the one-year-old for his daughter, and Mrs. H "joyously" agreed.

Some adopters dismissed the CBD's concerns about inheritable defects. In 1937, for example, Mr. and Mrs. A sought to adopt a girl to add to their current family of two children. The bureau presented a two-year-old girl for their consideration, but warned that her mother was "psychotic" and "feebleminded" and that another relative also had mental problems. The agency felt the little girl was fine, but warned that *her* children might bear the taint of undesirable inheritance. "Mr. A tried to reassure me . . . it made no difference to him. It was the child herself in whom they were interested. He felt that she might or might not have children who were limited intellectually but that seemed a risk they were willing to take and, in fact, it did not seem like a very great risk." Cases like this one underscore what social workers were later to affirm themselves: that "risk" was a relative and subjective matter.

The CBD recognized that its placements shaped the agency's reputation, and records indicate a self-conscious effort to educate others in the community about adoption. When they interviewed the references of prospective adopters, for example, their contacts often initiated discussions about adoption that CBD workers seized upon as a pedagogical opportunity. Many clients came to the CBD by word of mouth, or because they knew of neighbors, friends, or relatives who had adopted from the agency. In 1944, when the CBD acquiesced to one couple's entreaties against the agency's own judgment of the child, a social work took pains to explain to their lawyer that "Dinah "was not the type of child we could show to many types of adoptive parents, but . . . she seemed the right little girl for [these adopters], and they for her. I indicated that she was not up to the usual standard of the child that we usually place on an adoption basis."

Observation and testing supplied essential data for the professional design of adoptive families—for making good matches between prospective parents and children. "Fitness" yielded to "fit" in the art and science of these placements.. Without the ties of biological kinship, the

chances that strangers would become family was far from assured, social workers believed, and they sought to improve the odds through expertise.

The home study and other placement procedures carefully managed
the crafting of an adoptive family and marked significant transitions
into adoptive parenthood. Social workers believed that adoption was a
matter of the head and the heart, and they designed their procedures to
cultivate and assess both responses. In a sense, they offered substitu-
tions for the biological stages and cultural rituals of pregnancy and
childbirth. At the same time, this process was sharply distinguished
from biological reproduction by its intentionality and the screening and
deliberation that attended each stage. After adoptive homes had been
investigated and approved, social workers would select a child for potential placement in that home. The worker then met with prospective
adopters to "present" the child—a term invoking at once the idea of
"gift" and of "presence,"—the presence of a particular, singular child
who would fill the empty space of longing. The children themselves did
not appear at presentations, however. Presentations were narrative bi-
ographies that described the child's appearance, temperament, health,
and psychological development. They included selected information
about the child's birth parents, social history, and the circumstances of
relinquishment. Prospective adopters received a photograph of the
child, which brought them closer to the imaginative reality of parenthood—through a cultural artifact redolent of family ritual and sentimental parenthood. At this crossroads, adopters were asked to decide
whether they wanted to meet the child in person (as almost all did) or
to wait for another.

Next, meetings brought prospective parents and children face to face.
These carefully staged and orchestrated encounters occurred in the
playroom of the agency's office. The social worker in attendance was
there to reassure the child and observe the initial interaction. After a few
minutes, the social worker would withdraw, to allow the clients and the
child to spend an hour alone. Immediately following the visit, the
worker would meet with the adopters again to discuss (and observe)
their response to the child. With young children (up to about eighteen

months), placement followed within a few days. For older children, the transition was more gradual; adopters would take the child for an outing during the second meeting, and on a third occasion they would bring the child to their home for a visit.

With its enactment of deliberation and choice, the ritual of meeting accentuated the "difference" of adoption. In a few cases, prospective adopters protested the idea of meeting the child before making a commitment, revealing their desire to be more like birth parents, who accept a child sight unseen. In a 1930s case, Mr. and Mrs. Y declared themselves fully committed to the child offered in presentation, and they tried to decline the meeting. This was their second adoption through the CBD. The baby's "looks" weren't important to them, they explained. But social workers believed that far more than appearance was disclosed at a meeting. This worker refused their suggestion, declaring that placement without a meeting was "a little risky."

However, such demurrals were rare, and it seems likely that meetings helped to mitigate adopters' fears of the stranger. Social workers themselves believed that meetings were indispensable, a crucial test of adopters' commitment and even of a kind of chemistry of mutuality. In a successful meeting, they believed, adopters and child reached out to one another. Their social worker fondly described the first encounter of Timothy and his future parents. Mrs. F could barely contain her excitement on seeing the little boy; her worker described her hands trembling as she fumbled to unbutton his sweater. Later, "I came back . . . and found the three of them awfully close together and [Mr. and Mrs. F] looking as though they found this wonderful baby delicious enough to eat." As the approving tone of the description makes clear, meetings were supposed to invoke this kind of emotional response, which social workers read as a promising sign of appropriate parental sentiment. Social workers spoke in almost mystical terms about the chemistry of meeting and were extremely reluctant to proceed with placements if they did not sense some palpable connection. After one 1930s meeting, for example, prospective adopters pronounced themselves ready to take three-year-old Christine for their daughter, but the social worker demurred: "Maybe I was wrong, but I thought that really nothing had

happened [during the visit] between [the child] and them." She arranged another meeting, coaching the adopters to be more emotionally
expressive toward the little girl during their interactions.

CBD workers deliberately emphasized the meeting as a ritual of
choice, a choice that they believed might deflect the stigma of adoption
as "second best." They disapproved the kinds of adoption that presented
children as objects of consumerism, selected from a line-up, or, as occurred in some orphanages, by browsing among the inmates for a child
that appealed. But they used the idea of choice themselves to promote
parental attachment—to draw adopters into a process of actively claiming a child as their own. In one ritual of meeting that did not survive
past World War II, workers even encouraged adopters to ask older children if they would like to join their family. Choice—and even mutuality—might compensate for adopters' infertility and for the child's loss
of birth family.

Though social workers did not assign the same agency to children, to
a striking extent they did portray their small charges as intentional participants in the process. Case workers discussed impending meetings
with children as young as eighteen months, explaining that they might
be moving from foster homes to "new mommies and daddies." Older
children were supposed to understand already that their foster homes
were temporary, as social workers had explained during supervisory
visits. On the way to one meeting in 1938, a social worker told three-
year-old Charley that he might soon have "real" parents. "Real Mommy,
real Daddy," he repeated wonderingly. At the meeting, the entranced
prospective adopters followed the worker's prompting to ask Charley if
he wanted to be their little boy. He accepted with alacrity. Of course,
young children did not always follow this script. One quick-witted five-
year-old responded to another couple's invitation by proposing a bargain: he would be their little boy if they would buy him a cowboy suit
and a new tricycle. Others children clung to their foster parents, like
four-year-old Marie, who declined the offer of her eager prospective
adopters with an emphatic no. Of course, social workers did not allow
children so young to be the arbiters of their own placements. Rather,
they watched adopters to gauge their resilience, confidence, and resourcefulness in reaching out to children.

Still, social workers did see children as active participants in the outcome of presentation. In her account of a 1940 meeting, the social
worker described two-and-a-half-year-old George as willfully resisting
prospective adopters. As she drove him to the meeting, the little boy had
refused her opening ploys: "George looked cute in his new suit . . . but
made absolutely no response when I [told] him about playing with our
toys or seeing a man and lady who wanted him to come with them and
be their little boy." Confronted with the "man and lady," George was adamantly unforthcoming: "He was shy, turned his head away, stuck out
his tongue, and put both hands in his mouth slobbering over them . . .
he seemed to be trying to make himself as unattractive as possible." Social workers imputed such intentional behavior even to infants. Of a
six-month-old boy, one opined in 1937, "Actually I don't think Harry is
a baby with immediate appeal, as he is cautious and does not bother to
put himself across." Such records are telling: social workers seemed to
believe that they could apply their professional expertise to placement,
but families were forged, finally, by members' own emotional assent and
mutuality.

In the 1920s and 1930s, social workers like those at the CBD had developed an adoption practice that rejected both the casual approach of the
mayor of Bogalusa and the disturbing particularity of the prospective
adopters who placed the *Outlook* ad. In Delaware and elsewhere, a network of child welfare advocates had developed and articulated standards for assessing the "fitness" and "fit" of both children and prospective adopters, even as they reaffirmed their commitments to casework
with unmarried mothers or families in need of their assistance. As the
CBD and other agencies accumulated a history of successful adoptions,
social workers became more confident. By 1940, adoptive parents themselves had convinced the professionals that strangers could become kin.

But which strangers? How much difference could an adoptive family
embrace? Who belongs together? What was a good "fit"? The history of
adoption is largely a history of changing answers to those questions.
Over the twentieth century, changes in adoptive families serve as one
telling measure of the shifting boundaries of race, ethnicity, and religion in American society. Social workers were never the sole or even

primary determinants of the boundaries of adoptive families; law and custom always powerfully shaped ideas and practice. Prospective adopters brought their own expectations to agencies, which in turn were influenced by relatives, neighbors, and community members. "Matching" was the revealing term that social workers used to describe the process of designing adoptive families. Its curious history is revealed through CBD practices, social work literature, and letters written to the federal Children's Bureau, as we will see in Chapter 2.

2

Families by Design:
"Fitness" and "Fit" in the Creation of Kin

In 1936 Eleanor Garrigue Gallagher's manual for adoptive parents exuded confidence in families formed by law: "The child enters the hearts and affections, the kinship and the home of his new parents as their own." A few pages later, though, she counseled, "There should be very careful matching of homes and babies."[1] Her admonition reveals the paradox at the heart of adoption: the apparent naturalness of its kinship was an achievement of social engineering. The history of matching demonstrates the cultural ambivalence that has surrounded this difference.

In common usage, matching most often refers to the construction of adoptive families whose members resemble one another enough to appear biologically related. In professional parlance, matching covered a much broader terrain, comprising a long list of characteristics that social workers considered as they assessed birth parents, prospective adopters, and children. "Fit" was professional shorthand for the goal of matching—through the skilled application of expert knowledge, social workers would design an adoptive family whose members would flourish together. By this more capacious definition, matching exists wherever where is any non-random principle of placement in operation—that is, in just about any adoption. Social workers no longer use the term; it became anachronistic as adoptive families became more visibly diverse in the late 1960s and 1970s, and it took on volatile overtones as the adoption rights movement of the 1980s repudiated adoption secrecy (which had been abetted by physical matching). Nonetheless, whether mediated by social workers or done independently, adoptions have always involved some kind of matching.

Matching has long evoked unease, for it represents an exercise of intentionality that disorders and disrupts our usual expectations about family life. As prospective parents of already existing children, adopters could defy the maxim, "You can pick your friends, but you can't pick your relatives." Adoption violated this tacit category rule about kinship, rendering parent-child relationships too much like the contractual and consensual relationship of marriage. The term "matching" itself suggests arranged marriage by way of an intermediary.

Even as matching underscores the difference between biological and adoptive families, it has been used most often to minimize or obscure those differences. "Fit" has usually meant creating an adoptive family in the image of the biological family—matching adults with a child like the one adopters might have had by birth. The "as if begotten" family attests to a supreme confidence in the reach of social engineering: what nature has denied, adoption can achieve. And yet ultimately, argues the anthropologist Judith S. Modell, this model of adoption signals and reproduces the inferior status of adoptive families, because it tacitly accepts blood as the only authentic medium of affinity. "The symbolism of blood sustains the fiction of adoption, but it also lends the transaction a fatal flaw—an inevitable comparison with 'real' blood ties."[2]

Families are generally taken to represent a primary domain of intimacy and private life; at the same time, they are also public institutions, regulated by law, interwoven into economic life, the subject of political agendas, and the source of rich cultural meanings. Adoptive families share this dual citizenship in both public and private realms, but their public face is more visible because adoptive kinship is established by law alone. Traditionally constrained from interference in family life, the state is permitted—even mandated—to intervene actively in adoption, on the grounds of defending children's best interest. Moreover, adoption is a matter of compelling public interest because it challenges social boundaries of class, religion, and race. Adoption can bring together families whose members are more diverse than any imaginable biological family. In large part, matching has served to limit these transgressions of religious and racial boundaries and to calm the fears, usually unarticulated, that such potential violations often raise.

Through matching, social workers expressed and consolidated their gradual endorsement of adoption. Influenced by growing evidence of successful adoptions, inundated by prospective adopters, and pressured by public opinion favoring adoption, social workers moderated their view of adoption as a risky and exceptional solution. Instead, they became strong advocates of adoption if carried out under the supervision of trained professionals. Matching was one key element in the design of a practice that sought to improve the odds of successful adoption.

Impatient with social workers' cautious, even wary, approach to adoption, some advocates of adoption were so confident about its general benefits that they dismissed the need for extensive deliberation over placement. This stance generally went hand in hand with a confident assumption that children are highly malleable and a belief that parental love and altruism are expressed as naturally in adoptive families as among blood kin. Social workers were markedly more skeptical of the kindness of strangers. They feared that adopters would reject children if they seemed too different, and that even if adopters themselves were genuinely open to children unlike themselves, the surrounding community might stigmatize them. Social workers rejected the environmentalist tendency to see children as interchangeable. Case workers viewed children as psychologically complex individuals with specific needs that not all prospective adopters could meet equally well. Their own approach to matching took into consideration both communal concerns, such as religion and ethnicity, and individual characteristics, especially intelligence and temperament. Until at least 1950, social workers dedicated much effort to measuring children's intellectual potential and then to placing them with adopters of similar apparent intelligence. Even when adopters themselves insisted that intelligence did not matter to them, social workers doubted the wisdom of placing children with parents who might expect too much of them—or, who might provide too little intellectual stimulation and educational opportunity for "bright" children.

Matching was an arena of intense negotiation. Social workers believed that they ought to be the arbiters of adoption, and they claimed that their professional expertise enabled them to make better matches—and therefore to improve the odds that children would land in happy adoptive families. However, they were never the sole architects of matching even in agency adoption. Prospective adopters also expressed preferences about the children they sought for their families— preferences that sometimes overlapped and sometimes conflicted with social workers' ideas of what made a good match. In letters to the federal Children's Bureau and case records from Delaware, adopters described the kinds of children that they could imagine as kin—and sometimes specified others that they would not welcome into their family. Most often, they mentioned age and sex preferences. Social workers generally counseled prospective adopters to be flexible on the matter of sex preference, to facilitate placement. Nonetheless, throughout the history of adoption in the United States, prospective adoptive parents have exhibited an enduring preference for girls. Ethnicity, race, and color were consequential categories openly discussed in some home studies. A few adopters also mentioned intelligence and temperament; and, occasionally, physical appearance (including but not limited to race and ethnicity) appeared among their concerns.

Matching was most openly and extensively practiced from about 1930 to 1960. It was claimed as part of social workers' professional domain as they began to articulate standards for adoption practice. By 1960 the scope of matching had been dramatically reduced. In part, this was a measure of the soaring confidence in adoption after World War II. Social workers and clients alike came to believe that adoption was the "best solution" for children born out of wedlock and that those children were likely to flourish as long as their adoptive parents had been adequately screened. In part, it was a register of broader social change. Ethnicity, once a prominent concern of adopters, nearly disappeared from case records by the 1950s, as post-war assimilation and Americanization blurred older distinctions. Intellectual matching, once dear to social workers' hearts, was also emphasized less by 1960 because experts had become convinced of the importance of early placement, which precluded the developmental testing and extended observation that social workers had used to predict children's intellectual potential. "Direct placement"—moving children from the hospital nursery directly to adoptive homes—had become the favored practice by the 1960s. During that period, most adopters had also become flexible on the question of their child's sex, and by 1970 children available for adoption had become so scarce that sex preference was essentially a moot point.

Matching did not so much disappear, though, as take new forms. It could hardly be otherwise. Child placement is always a powerful statement about identity. As we decide where children belong, we are also making claims about who they are as individuals, and who they might become. Adoption also identifies children as members of social groups, and its history limns the expanding boundaries—and limits—of American pluralism.

Sex preference occupies a singular position in the history of adoption, a startling marker of its difference. Adoption enables parents to choose the sex of their child, an exercise of choice sharply at odds with the ordinary experience of expectant parents. Speculating about the undisclosed sex of the fetus remains part of the culture of pregnancy, even in the era of prenatal screening; the only difference now is that, for women who choose to know, the suspense is resolved earlier. After prenatal screening, a woman might choose to abort a fetus of the undesired sex, but those who do so are subject to strong moral disapproval, and many physicians refuse to perform abortions that are elected solely because of the fetus's sex. Even conventional expressions of sex preference are tacitly disapproved in contemporary American culture. It is customary for relatives, friends, and acquaintances to ask a pregnant woman which sex she and her husband are hoping for—and customary for her to deny a preference by responding, "We just hope the baby is healthy." This ritualized exchange seems to enact a cultural performance of "good" motherhood. The question acknowledges the temptation of preferring one sex over the other, even as it allows the expectant mother to demonstrate the approved stance of neutrality. Being willing to submit to chance on the question of sex, then, is in a sense a token of biological parents' willingness to accept other unknowns about parenting;

it is a demonstration of their proper attitude toward chance. In adoption, by contrast, while sex selection has been subtly discouraged, it has never been countermanded absolutely. Indeed, though such adopters are unusual, a few have sought adoption in order to add a child of the desired sex to their family.

Thus, adopters are "strange" for choosing at all, and then stranger still for *how* they choose: in contrast to biological parents, who—when they express any sex preference—consistently prefer boys, adopters seek girls.[3]

The tilt toward girls was widely noted in social work literature and U.S. Children's Bureau correspondence. One prospective adopter recounted that at the midwestern agency where they had applied, he and his wife were advised that they would wait a year for a boy, and two for a girl.[4] A 1947 article in a national news magazine noted, "A couple requesting a girl must wait longer than those who want a boy."[5] Another discouraged correspondent wrote Eleanor Roosevelt plaintively about their three-year effort to adopt a daughter. They had applied at many agencies, but "we always receive the same answer: 'Little girls are hard to get.'"[6] As social workers discussed the disproportion between eager adults and children available for adoption, some blamed adopters' choosiness: "It does seem strange that we have so many applications for babies that we cannot possibly supply the demand. Probably the reason is that they all want a girl baby with 'blue eyes and light brown hair.'"[7] This writer was exaggerating; among correspondents to the USCB, over half expressed no preference. But she was right about adopters' yearning for girls: of those who did indicate a preference, nearly three times as many sought daughters as sons.[8]

Clients at the Children's Bureau of Delaware exhibited the same preference for girls. "Baby girls seem to be on the preferred list," advised a social worker in 1938, suggesting to prospective adopters that they might want to reconsider their own request for a daughter. "Therefore, we are usually out of balance in terms of little girls." That same year, a worker at the agency let her clients know that they would have to wait for a child, but noted encouragingly "that it does help them . . . that they are as interested in a boy as a girl, because somehow or other a good many people want little girls." This situation was chronic at the agency. In 1953 another CBD social worker tried to discourage adopters hoping for a daughter: "I did let them know quite definitely that boys far out-numbered girls." Adopters in CBD home studies preferred girls by a considerable margin: 41 percent hoped for daughters, compared to 23 percent seeking sons. They were more likely than USCB correspondents to state a sex preference: less than 40 percent said "either" at the outset of the home study.[9] In sharp contrast to biological parents, adopters preferred to start their families with a girl. Among childless white Christian adopters at the CBD, 57 couples preferred girls (or indicated "girl only"); 37 indicated a preference for boys. By comparison, two-thirds to three-quarters of biological parents prefer boys when they have a preference, and less than 10 percent prefer girls as first-born children.[10]

In one important way, adopters resembled biological parents: they imagined one boy and one girl as the ideal family. This preference comes into view in narrative records of the many first-time adopters (39 percent of white Christians) who declared themselves ready to welcome either sex.[11] Some of these apparently neutral adopters were actually making a strategic compromise; husbands and wives who wanted children of different sexes split the difference by responding "either." For eleven couples, "either" was a compromise between wives who wanted girls and husbands who preferred boys. (In one more case, adopters divulged that they hoped eventually to adopt a boy and a girl but did not care which was first.) At least some adopters who said they preferred "either" were hoping for a family that included a child of each sex. They reasoned that they would start their families with whatever child came along first, and then try to adopt a child of the opposite sex later. Perhaps many others who wrote "either" on the application form had the same calculus in mind. This pattern conforms to the expressed sex preferences of biological parents, who are more likely to say "either" about an anticipated first child, and more likely to desire the opposite sex of living children with each subsequent pregnancy.[12] In a few cases, adopters tried to negotiate with the bureau in order to get "one of each" as soon as possible. One such couple, adopting in 1945, told their worker that they wanted a girl first, and then a boy, but offered to take a boy for starters if the bureau would promise them a girl for their second adoption.

Adopters' preference for a family that included both sons and daughters is clearly evident among couples who were already parents. These adopters were more likely than childless adopters to prefer one sex over another, and much more likely to restrict their application to just one sex. For example, white Christian adopters who were already the parents of boys were more likely than others to restrict themselves to "girls only" (16 of 34 couples), and another 8 couples with sons indicated they would prefer a girl. On rare occasions, fertile couples turned to adoption because of the chance to choose their child's sex. Six such couples appear in the sample, and five of them sought to adopt a child of the opposite sex of those already in the family. In 1966, Mr. and Mrs. M told their social worker that they had decided to adopt a boy if their third child turned out to be another girl, a decision that was confirmed when the doctor advised Mrs. M not to have more children after their third daughter was born. Mr. M had a vasectomy, and they turned readily to adoption. Their preference was decisive: "must be male." Another couple, parents of two daughters born to them, were still fertile but had determined they could not raise more than three children. They turned to the bureau in the late 1960s: "Both would like a son and they could be assured of this through adoption."

Social workers themselves shaped adoptive families in the image of this ideal: when adopters already had a child, the CBD tried hard to place a child of the opposite sex. This commitment followed contemporary professional wisdom that emphasized children's individuality and strove for placements that would allow each child to find a special niche in the family. To some extent, this logic ran counter to the idea of "fit," which favored similarity of temperament, appearance, and intelligence among family members: when it came to sex, social workers believed it was better to have un-matching children. Measured by different gender expectations, a brother and sister were less likely to be compared directly by parents and others and therefore might escape the more intense versions of sibling rivalry. Opposite-sex placement also allowed the new child to claim a unique role in the family. In this matter, social work policy conformed to adopters' common preference for a child of each sex.

But even when adopters disavowed such a preference, the agency sometimes considered such clients only for a child of the opposite sex from the one they had. In 1959, Mr. and Mrs. F returned to the CBD hoping to adopt a second child; they had adopted a girl earlier. The social worker assumed that the adoptive parents would prefer a son, even though the couple declared that they wanted to be considered for either. Nonetheless, she believed she discerned signs of an undisclosed preference for a boy: Mrs. F, she noted, would on occasion "slip out with something about a baby boy. Since this only coincided with my own feeling that I would prefer to see the second child male sex, I did not comment on this other than to say 'baby boy.'" But when she did try to encourage an overt statement of this preference, the adopters demurred: "Both . . . laughed with Mrs. F saying . . . that they had thought so long that their second child would be a boy and then had surprised themselves after talking it over that they really did not want to put in this limitation." The bureau placed a boy.

In another 1950s case, the parents of an adopted daughter waited two years for a second child because the bureau wanted to place an older child with them and would consider them only for a son—even though, as the record made clear, "the family was ready for a child of either sex." Social workers were particularly concerned to make opposite sex placements when the child in the home had been born to the prospective adopters. When parents of a son by birth sought to adopt a boy in 1960, the bureau explained that this was not advisable: "I pointed out that actually it was really very rare that we would place other than a child of the opposite sex where there is a natural born child, feeling that in this way the child being adopted has a greater chance of finding a special place in the family." Even when social workers began to discourage sex preference in order to facilitate placement of very young infants, they made an exception for adopters who were already parents. Prospective adopters who already had a daughter by birth declared themselves ready for either sex, with preference for a boy. The bureau decided to place only a boy, even though, as the record noted, this would make a direct placement difficult.

Placement policy thus encouraged adopters to exercise sex preference in a way that would allow the composition of families to include a boy and a girl, an assortment that emerges as the ideal in many studies of sex preference. Notably, though, adopters exercised this preference differentially, in ways that again demonstrate their strong bias toward girls. Two-thirds of adopters who already had sons requested daughters. Adoptive parents of daughters were also likely to try "balance" their families by seeking a son, but not as likely to prefer the opposite sex as adopters who had sons. White Christians who already had daughters account for more than half of the couples who request "boys only" (10 of 19 couples), and two more indicated they would prefer a son. But 5 couples who were parents of daughters had no sex preference for this adoption, one preferred another girl, and one wanted a daughter only. Slightly over half of the parents of daughters preferred sons, a less decisive preference for the opposite sex than that found among parents who had sons.

Oddly, parents with daughters are markedly underrepresented in the sample: 34 adopters already had sons, but only 19 had daughters. This imbalance prompts the speculation that people who already had daughters in the family were less likely to seek another child to adopt. If so, it is a striking mirror image of boy preference among biological parents, who are more likely to stop having children when the family already includes a son.[13] Given the widespread American preference for families including boys and girls, one might think that adoption would afford parents with one child the ideal opportunity to "balance out" their families. And indeed, parents of sons did seize this opportunity. Why were parents of daughters less likely to do so?

One possibility is that adopting a boy did not fulfill the same needs as having a son by birth. Perhaps biological parents prefer boys for reasons that are specific to biological kinship: that is, they want to reproduce male progenitors to perpetrate the family name and its genetic heritage. Rearing a son, then, does not quite substitute for bearing a son. Of course, girls born to their parents also carry the family genetic heritage into the next generation, but since married women usually assume the name of another family, the genetic heritage of the family of origin is not culturally "marked" as it is for the children of sons. (This marking has survived feminist revisions of naming; even when women keep their own birth names, their children usually bear the paternal family name.) Or, it could be that adopters considered adopted boys a potential liability as family members—strangers not readily assimilable as kin.

Social workers and adopters themselves assumed that men and women were often divided on sex preference, with men hoping for sons and women preferring daughters. "Most men like boys," one prospective female adopter asserted in 1938, even as she explained that her own husband wished for a girl. This view in itself requires some explanation, since studies indicate that among biological parents, both men and women prefer boys, and among adopters, both prefer girls. However, it is also the case that among biological parents, women's preference for boys is weaker, and among adopters, men prefer girls but less strongly than do their wives. The bureau's own marital compromisers—couples who said "either" when the wife wanted a girl and the husband wanted a boy—suggest that sex preference statistics might reflect this kind of accommodation on a larger scale.

It appears that some men themselves tended to prefer girls rather than boys as adoptive kin, and that others readily deferred to their wives' preference for girls. Why? It may be that men were more invested in bearing sons than in rearing them. In a 1966 home study, the adopters told their social worker they preferred a girl. When the worker probed about the reasons for this, a prospective father himself acknowledged, "had he been expecting a natural born child he would have preferred a boy but he found it didn't matter at all in anticipating adoption." Once men recognized that they would not sire a son, perhaps the perceived advantages of rearing girls became more salient. Or, men, like women, may have found the prospect of a male stranger in the family more threatening than the addition of a little girl.

Most adopters believed that they would be closer to a same-sex child, and this view was offered as a veritable truism to explain men's preference for sons and women's hopes for daughters. This parental division by sex would seem to present an insuperable obstacle to marital consensus on the sex of an adopted child, and one response was the strategic "either." Another possibility, of course, was deferring to one's spouse. The records suggest that adopters and social workers alike believed that women's preferences ought to weigh more heavily than men's in this consequential matter. Indeed, men often deferred to their wives, indicating that this was only fair because of mothers' disproportionate investment in child-rearing. "His wife would be having the care of the child so it was up to her," one prospective adopter told his case worker in 1948, explaining his willingness to go along with her preference for a daughter. Social workers routinely accepted men's deference to their wives in this matter.

The converse was not true: social workers questioned women whom they thought were deferring too readily to men's requests for sons. In a few cases they expressed disapproval of men who insisted on sons. In a 1955 home study, Mrs. W readily deferred to her husband's strong desire for a boy, averring that she herself had no preference. The couple got their boy, and then returned for a second adoption. Again, the husband wanted a boy. His worker commented critically in the case narrative, "I had a pretty definite impression that his interest in another little boy was a pretty self-centered one and at no point did he give any indication that it might be nice for his wife to have a little girl who might be more companionable for her." This sentiment, though, was apparently based on the worker's expectation that women would want daughters, for Mrs. W herself expressed no partiality. The CBD case worker questioned another couple applying in 1955 when it became clear that their stated preference for a boy was really the prospective father's idea: "He put it in terms of a little boy being more companionable and being able to go about different places with him, and really put this preference in quite a strong term. I wondered then, where this would leave Mrs. G, to which she responded in a rather light vein that she guessed she would have to get herself a little girl to keep her company."

African-American adopters and Jewish adopters complicate the picture, for both groups showed distinctive patterns of sex preference that diverge from the Children Bureau's white Christian majority. African Americans showed a remarkably strong desire for daughters: 60 percent preferred girls, and half of these adopters wanted to consider girls only. Thirty-two percent indicated they preferred boys, and half of those adopters restricted their consideration to boys alone. Prospective African American adopters stand out as the clients who were most "choosy" when it came to the sex of their prospective children: only 8 percent declared themselves to have no preference. Jewish adopters occupied the other end of the spectrum. More than three-quarters (16 out of 21 in the sample) disclaimed any preference. Of the five who did state a preference, three wanted a girl and one a boy; only one couple (already parents of a son) limited themselves to one sex (female).

These sharp disparities bespeak the very different prospects that African Americans and Jews faced as adopters, prospects shaped by each group's demographics and by the politics of racial and religious matching. African American adopters were in short supply throughout the entire history of the bureau: that is, children available to adopt always outnumbered prospective adopters. By the mid-1940s, the CBD was actively recruiting African American adopters, soliciting help from local ministers and other community leaders to find prospective parents. African American adopters often told social workers that they had come to the bureau in response to community meetings or newspaper, radio, or television publicity about the need for black adopters. These prospective parents may not have realized that the bureau's eagerness to recruit them meant that they could exercise more choice over matters such as sex preference. Nonetheless, social workers did in fact treat black adopters differently than others, applying more flexible standards on matters such as family income, housing, mothers' wage-earning work, and duration of marriage. Likewise, they seldom pressed these prospective adopters on the issue of sex preference.

Jewish men and women, by contrast, faced severe constraints as adopters, for prospective parents in this group vastly outnumbered children available for adoption. Very few Jewish children were born out of wedlock, and, by law and custom, religious matching constrained placement of children born to Christians with Jewish adopters. By the 1930s the special plight of Jewish adopters was widely recognized. Acutely aware of the formidable odds against them, Jewish adopters were not likely to limit their chances voluntarily by stating a preference for one sex over the other.

The distinctive patterns of African American and Jewish adopters suggest the ways in which contingency and choice shaped the expression of sex preferences for all adopters. African Americans demonstrate sex preference at its least constrained: their strong preference for girls, then, might be interpreted as the predisposition of adopters writ large. On the other end of the spectrum, Jewish adopters' nearly unanimous "either" reflects the relatively low priority of sex preference in a hierarchy of concerns that adults brought to the process of adoption. Their child's sex mattered to adopters—two-thirds registered some preference. But many exercised this choice weakly, by stating a preference but not limiting themselves to "boys only" or "girls only." When they recognized that "flexibility" improved their chances, most adopters readily revised their preference to "either." The sex of their adopted children mattered, but it was not important enough to most adopters that they would accept a longer wait or risk not getting a child at all.

Why did so many prospective adopters favor girls? When social workers asked clients their reasons for seeking a particular sex, most offered one of two contradictory explanations. Some said they were seeking gender balance, either in their immediate family or their extended kin network. This rationale was shared by respondents in sex preference studies—the expressed ideal of a family of "one of each," though adopters sometimes also invoked a larger group of kin. For example, a couple applying in 1952 wanted a boy because "both of them grew up in families that were predominately feminine." Another couple sought a boy to fill an empty niche in the extended family: they had a dozen nieces and hoped to adopt a child who would be the first male in that generation of the family. A prospective father who wanted a girl was one of nine sons himself; his family had more than enough males, he thought. For such prospective parents, adoption could supply an opportunity that biology had denied to other family members, a "gift" to the extended family that perhaps might offset other perceived risks of incorporating a stranger.

Curiously, some adopters explained their preference with just the opposite logic: they hoped for a child of the sex that had been more common in their experience. Ten couples justified their stated preferences on this basis. In a 1950s home study, one prospective mother wanted a girl because she had grown up with sisters and therefore was more accustomed to girls. A prospective 1950s father wanted a son because "it is mostly little boys he has known and been around." In a 1930s home study, the prospective mother wanted a boy since "she practically raised her brother." Another woman told her social worker, "She has had more experience with little girls and felt she would therefore be a little more at ease in taking on a girl baby." For these adopters, choosing the sex that seemed more familiar might have been a way to temper the perceived risks of adoption. Only one adopter, a prospective father applying in the 1950s, cited experience with one sex as the reason for preferring the *opposite* sex. While growing up he had felt burdened by his responsibility for managing his unruly younger brothers, and dealing with boys was not an experience he cared to repeat.

These adopters assumed that the child's sex made a difference for parenting; sons and daughters each offered distinctive rewards and challenges. Some adopters relied on assumptions about gendered characteristics that they considered too obvious to require explanation, as for one couple who indicated in 1958 they hoped for "a little girl, who would like all the things that little girls like," and a 1930s adopter who specified only a "feminine type female." Other adopters told their case worker in 1966 that they wanted a girl because "their home is just [needing] a little more femininity." Others offered explanations that provide some tantalizing hints about why adopters preferred girls. A 1930s adopter hoped for a child who was "tractable and loving" and gave this as the reason for seeking a girl. Mr. E endorsed girls by way of a revealing contrast with boys: he told his case worker in 1965, "He enjoys the feminine qualities rather than the boys' more aggressive independent nature." Social workers themselves sometimes inferred such connections between sex and temperament. In a 1969 record, the case worker noted that "it seemed to me that Mrs. E's wish for a clean and obedient child might be related to her preference of a baby girl."

Boys had their partisans, and those who preferred male children cited their alleged qualities of spirit, "spunk," and independence—qualities attributed to boys in records from the early 1930s to the late 1960s. Others hoped for boys to share interests seen as masculine. One couple, applying in 1967, wanted a boy because "both love the outdoors and the things that are associated more with boys." One exceptional couple told the social worker in 1969 that they hoped to adopt five children eventually, all boys, because they themselves were enthusiastic athletes and sports lovers. The bureau worker cautioned that not all boys liked sports. The prospective mother countered that she "believed in the influence of environment and she therefore, was presuming that the child would be interested in athletics." Perhaps she was saying what she thought the social worker wanted to hear. In any case, her confidence in environment was not so robust as to allow her to imagine that a girl might be readily recruited to share these interests. Even though in both of these cases the prospective mothers were themselves eager participants in outdoor pursuits and sports, the couples nonetheless believed that boys were more likely than girls to enjoy their active lives.

A few adopters, all hoping for boys, invoked issues of inheritance and lineage. Three couples wanted a boy to carry on the family name. Nearly a truism for boy preference among biological parents, this idea rarely appears in adoption case records. Indeed, some observers have suggested that many adopters may prefer girls because girls do not pass the family name to their children. Two couples seeking boys wanted a son so they could leave valued property to a male heir. Of course, parents could and did leave inheritances to adopted daughters as well as sons, but none mentioned this as a motive for adopting a girl. Another prospective father, adopting in 1951, hoped for a boy who could take up the family business eventually, a role he apparently did not envision as a possibility for a daughter. Another couple, who were African American, had been able to purchase a house that represented hard-won upward mobility; they hoped to leave this symbol of their achievement to a son.

Two couples candidly disclosed that they preferred to adopt girls because they were cheaper to raise. In 1942, one prospective father explained that he saw no reason to send a girl to college, since "if she were the least attractive and had nice ways she probably would be getting married, anyway." Social workers took a dim view of such attitudes. As children's advocates, they sought to make placements that would enable both boys and girls to have all the opportunities they could use. And, as educated professional women themselves, they would have been unlikely to assent to the proposition that college was unnecessary for girls. A 1947 adopter who wanted a daughter surely imperiled his chances when he explained that "he would want to send a boy through high school and if he had that kind of interest, he would want to send him to college. However he feels that college is a waste of money for a girl." Belatedly recognizing that his case worker might have reason to demur, he tried to backtrack: "Of course there were exceptional women like me who probably needed to be educated, but . . . he thought most girls would be wasting money in a college education because they would get married." Social workers disapproved of such attitudes about girls' prospects, and they also were suspicious of prospective adopters who were considering the economies of child-rearing with such a calculating eye.

Adopters frequently opined that girls were "easier to raise." Several believed that girls were "easier to manage," "possibly less aggressive," and "a little less trouble in their basic nature." These attitudes, too, appeared throughout the records. One prospective mother commented "that she had seen too many sons spoiled" and felt that she and her husband would find it easier to discipline a girl. Such comments imply that boys posed unarticulated threats of disorder.

A surprising number of prospective adopters, mostly women, explained that they wanted girls because "you can dress them so cute." Social workers were not inclined to view this explanation as a compelling reason to place a girl, and some adopters themselves recognized that it sounded inadequate. One woman reflected in 1942, "She supposed that she just wanted a girl because she thought you could dress them up to look so cute but that was silly, too, because she thought you could get cute things for little boys nowadays." Apparently superficial, this response may hold a significant clue about adopters' preference for girls. The imagined act of dressing a child conjures up an idealized vision of parenting as physical intimacy and emotional nurture—and also as order and control. A dressed-up little girl implies feminine passivity and compliance, in contrast to the image of active little boys heedless of their clothes and demeanor.

Many adopters portrayed girls as more committed family members who "stayed closer to home," in the recurring phrase, and would "offer more companionship" than sons. Social workers tirelessly challenged this assumption, concerned that such parents might cling to girls and impose undue restrictions on them. "Girls as well as boys did grow away from home," one case worker counseled 1930s clients who were looking forward to gaining the companionship of a loyal daughter. Another social worker paraphrased a prospective father's hope of adopting a home-loving daughter this way: "Girls naturally have more interest [in being] around the home and stay in closer touch with home than boys whom he finds to be more naturally gregarious and independent and soon having their activities out with other boys." The social worker interjected that girls, too, needed to get out of the house, to which the prospective mother responded that they wouldn't keep a girl from her friends and outside interests. Nonetheless, she affirmed that she too believed "a girl was more likely to be staying closer to home." Adopters who preferred boys seemed to agree that girls were more placid and domestic, even though they themselves wanted children who were active, athletic, and "spunky"—qualities they attributed to boys.

A few comments provocatively suggest that adopters found girls less "strange." Boys, by comparison, more readily evoked fears of the unknown. One couple seemed to feel that adopting a girl would offset some of the perceived risks of adoption. The prospective mother explained, "When they had first talked of wanting to adopt a child they had a lot of fears and thought that perhaps a girl would be easier to manage." Seen as more passive and malleable, girls also seemed easier to assimilate—strangers that might more readily be embraced as kin. This consideration appeared to be the motive for the mother of a prospective adopter, who strongly encouraged her daughter and son-in-law to seek a girl. "She [the mother] was sure if [her daughter] adopted a little girl that she would be able to love it as much as she would a child she might have had but she was not quite as sure about a boy."

Social workers had many reasons of their own to try to moderate clients' exercise of sex preference. If adopters insisted on a girl or boy only, social workers were constrained in their ability to match children and adopters by criteria they considered more important, such as age, religion, intelligence. And given the strong preference for girls, social workers faced the prospect of needy boys being passed over by adopters who were waiting for daughters. As the bureau began to handle many adoptions and to place children at younger ages, social workers discouraged adopters from limiting their consideration to one sex only. As they became more confident about adoption themselves, they began to demand more flexibility of prospective adopters; by the mid-1950s, social workers expected adopters to be "willing to accept the normal risks of parenthood." In most cases, that included the willingness to adopt either boys or girls.

Social workers emphasized intellectual matching over any other criteria of "fit," striving to place children with parents of similar intelligence. As one CBD worker explained to prospective adopters in 1942, "Our selection was not based on physical appearance but rather on the potential capacity of the children . . . if a family wanted a child who would go on to college, we tried to take that into consideration." Their assessments of both children and parents were blunt: of one little girl, for example, a 1930s report noted, "dull-normal intelligence . . . would benefit from placement in a home of average opportunities." In another 1930s case, CBD workers weighed two placement decisions and made them on the basis of a calculus about intellectual matching: "Because the Rs were interested in a good background, and were on a higher intellectual level than the Hs, it was felt that they should have Sarah, whose background was better than Rebecca's and whose psychological test report was more promising." A social worker's evaluation of one home concluded that it would be good for a child of average intelligence: "While there are not so many cultural interests as might be desired for a child of above average intelligence, the feeling of happiness which one gets from the home would in a great many cases offset the lack of cultural interests." Another home study ended with the assessment, "Excellent adoption home for an average child . . . A high type child could not fit into this home as the Js would not be able to manage. They make a few small mistakes in grammar, but are the kind of people who would have ambitions and would want to send the child to a small college." A conventional lower-middle-class couple, the CBD director decided, might offer "a good home for a child of average mental ability, one not too sensitive to its surroundings."[14]

In principle, the logic of intellectual matching attached no special value to superior intellect, instead simply endorsing a good "fit"—that is, intellectual parity among adoptive family members. In practice, though, social workers' assessments of intelligence often functioned as a kind of coded language of class. In 1938, for example, as a CBD social worker recorded her first meeting with Mr. and Mrs. C, she described them in details that registered her own class distance from the prospective adopters; the father, she noted, was "chewing his gum hard," and his "fat, uncorseted wife" was wearing a "cheap" dress. She assessed them bluntly as "barely average in every way." Nonetheless, the social worker's disparaging description of this couple's demeanor and grooming did not prevent her from recognizing other qualities that the bureau valued in potential adopters. She concluded, "I don't think I've ever talked with adopting parents that I felt more confidence in. Their feeling about a baby was so rich and so warm and so right." At other times, social workers betrayed a bias toward more advantaged parents and "superior" children. When Mr. and Mrs. B petitioned to adopt one child in their care, the bureau acquiesced with a lukewarm endorsement recorded in 1938, "The placement has been satisfactory on a mediocre level, for both Edward and the parents are very mediocre people." The same record betrayed a patronizing attitude toward adopters with such low standards: "They are mediocre people and Edward's sweetness and need for them is apparently more satisfying to them than the qualities of a more superior child might be." In another 1930s adoptive home investigation, the social worker was clearly entranced with the prospective adopters, both graduates of Ivy League colleges and members of "cultured and scholarly families." When the bureau placed a lively little girl with them, the record concluded, "In short, we consider [them] prize parents and Monica a prize child."

Though defended on the grounds of the best interest of the child, matching was sometimes subject to an invidious calculus of parental entitlement. "Superior" parents deserved "superior" children, with the corollary that inferior parents merited children no more prepossessing than themselves. Two records from the 1930s illustrate this axiom in use. One CBD social worker reported of a prospective adoptive mother, "She is anxious to have a child who would be as good as one they would have themselves and who would come up to what they could give it. She would hope to send a child through college." In an unusual example, a CBD social worker appeared to endorse such logic when she commiserated with an adoptive mother struggling with a difficult adolescent daughter. "I said I thought it was unfortunate she had been permitted to adopt a child like Margaret when she had so much to give a child."

This calculus of entitlement also appeared in letters and interviews of those who served as references for prospective adopters in the 1930s. One recommender concluded his letter with this appeal to the bureau on behalf of the adopters: "I do hope you will give them a child whose heritage is such that their love and care for it will be rewarded." In another example, when a case worker interviewed a doctor who was serving as a reference, she let him know that the bureau was considering these adopters for an "average child." "Just right," the doctor declared. "What they would want would be an average child. That is what they are, average people." In a poignant example, foster parents nearly gave up their struggle to adopt little Michael in 1935 when they discovered (by means they refused to reveal to the social worker) that he "came from such a good background . . . they felt that perhaps they could not give him as much as he deserves. Fos[ter] mo[ther] said that since some of his uncles are doctors and lawyers they feel he should be placed in a home where he can be given a college education."

Social workers were convinced that intellectual matching was crucial for successful adoptions. Parity, they believed, would protect children from undue pressure from parents who expected more than children could reasonably accomplish—and shield them from the hurt that parental disappointment might inflict. In 1936, one social worker hesitated about adoptive placement of a little boy in the care of a local orphanage. The matron considered him "poor adoption material," citing test results that indicated "limited mental ability." Nonetheless, Mr. and Mrs. S persisted in their appeals to adopt the child. The CBD worker reported her concern "that anyone adopting him should understand the situation sufficiently well that their ambitions for the child would not soar beyond his abilities, as this might develop real personality difficulties." In another home study, the social worker sought to temper the unrealistic demands of college-educated adopters who wanted a child with "a college background," that is, born to parents with educational accomplishment in their families. Few birth parents could claim such pedigrees, the worker reminded these prospective parents, and she suggested that an "average baby" might well develop into a college-bound child if raised in a stimulating environment. In the end, these parental aspirations for educational achievement kept them from getting a very young infant, which they also requested. Their social worker feared that these adopters were likely to demand more academic success than most children could achieve, and therefore she would not consider them for placement of a baby who had not undergone intelligence testing. "It would take a child of ability to keep up with [the prospective adoptive father] . . . We felt it wasn't fair to a baby to place him in circumstances where he would always be out of step."

Social workers also wanted to make sure that intellectually promising children were placed with parents who would recognize and nurture their abilities. When the court asked the CBD to investigate a private placement in 1935 as part of legalization proceedings, the agency's report noted, "The natural parents of the child for adoption have had more education and are probably endowed with more native intelligence than the adopting parents. Should this child prove to be substantially superior intellectually to the adopting parents in later life, unhappiness for them and for her may result." In recommending the legal adoption of a two-year-old child who was the prospective mother's niece, another 1935 report concluded "that this home is a good one for Joanna, as she is with her own family and hence probably with people of her own intellectual level."

Some adopters themselves ranked intelligence high on the list of desired attributes, as shown in these examples from 1930s records. "Intelligent child with a loving disposition," one couple requested. Other prospective adopters, both college graduates, wanted a child with "blue eyes, bright mentally, musical aptitude if possible." A prospective mother, herself a high school graduate, wanted a bright child to adopt because she thought she and her husband would have given birth to such a child: "She is anxious to have a child who would be as good as the one they would have themselves and who would come up to what they could give it. She would hope to send a child through college." Another applicant forthrightly requested "a child that was perfect physically and mentally." This prospective mother proudly wore her Phi Beta Kappa key to her first interview at the CBD and emphasized her wish for a child who was "college material." (Her husband, himself a high school graduate, dissented, opining that a normal "well rounded" child was more desirable.) Others wanted bright children to match children already in the family. One couple, seeking to adopt a second child, noted that their little girl was very smart and wanted a boy who would be similar, with "college potential." The social worker warned that a child might not want to go to college, but opined in the record, "I do feel that Georgia [their daughter] is superior and that in considering another child for this home we should consider that."

It is likely that parents with such views are over-represented in the records of agency adoption, since intelligence testing was one of the reasons that prospective adopters would choose to work with an agency rather than pursue independent adoptions. It is all the more striking, then, to find that quite a few adopters in the CBD case records challenged the bureau's insistence on intelligence testing and matching. Prospective parents did not uniformly view intelligence as a necessary or even desirable characteristic. One prospective father, himself a college graduate, "felt he should not have a very bright child as he thought that people who were quite bright were a little harder to manage. He would like a good average child." In a 1947 home study, another couple let the social worker know that "they did not want a child of unusual promise or one in the genius group," preferring an average child. Some adopters accepted children that social workers deemed poor prospects because of low scores on IQ tests and developmental measures, such as the devoted father who avowed, "Even if she is a moron we want to keep her."

Others candidly assessed themselves and their other children as average. Such responses endorsed the idea of matching, yet at the same time implicitly resisted the hierarchy of value implied in such CBD designations as "superior," "mediocre," "barely adequate," or "inferior." For these adopters (all from the 1930s), a child who fit the family was not "mediocre" but just right. One prospective adoptive mother told the social worker, "She would want a child of normal intelligence, but it didn't have to be overly bright." Her husband agreed: "Their own girl is just average, although the boy is somewhat higher . . . Mrs. M said that if the child was too smart she might make their children feel badly." Another couple, judged "purely average in every way" by the CBD worker, wanted a child of average intelligence, capable of finishing high school, "but they didn't care for any more intellectual capacity than this." The social worker reported, "I said, then they aren't demanding a brilliant child? They both laughed and Mrs. A said, "'We wouldn't have one ourselves.'"

Discussions of IQ were often stalking horses for class, and as such they disclose the promise and unease about upward mobility that inflected adoption.[15] In intellectual matching, parity was seen as the appropriate goal for adopters: that is, parents should get a child "as good as the one that would have been born to them." But no better than that—adoption was not supposed to be an opportunity for families to rise above their own genetic station. By contrast, Americans could and did freely use marriage as a vehicle for upward mobility, a practice that might incur some social disapproval but that operated under no formal constraints. For children, though, parity was the minimum goal of placement: that is, the adoptive family should be at least as "good" as the birth family. The overt expectation of "expert" adoption was that placement would significantly improve children's life chances—otherwise, how could social workers countenance the separation of blood kin?

The preoccupation with intelligence, so prominent in the 1930s and 1940s, diminishes notably in the case records of the 1950s and 1960s. The predictive value of intelligence testing was challenged by social scientists who emphasized the influence of environment. These studies were widely publicized; in 1940, a CBD client lent her social worker a recent issue of the *Ladies Home Journal* reporting on the findings. More immediately, CBD social workers may well have been influenced by their own experience with testing. In more than a few children, test results fluctuated wildly. One baby boy, first thought to be severely retarded, ended up (at one year) with an IQ in the "superior" range. Initially classified as "dull," another little girl later tested as well above average. Family background, also used as a guide, sometimes proved just as confounding. One baby girl had three maternal aunts who were deemed retarded, a finding that put social workers on guard. She herself, though, was ranked "very superior" in intelligence testing at one year. Surely such results must have given pause to CBD social workers. Even if testing was deemed reliable, most of the time it simply confirmed what common sense would predict: most children were normal, and scores a little below or above the average could not be taken as precise measures of children's intellectual potential.

Ultimately, though, intellectual matching was not so much rejected as it was attenuated by competing pressures—especially, the desire of adopters to get children "as young as possible." Letters to the U.S. Children's Bureau confirm, by the hundreds, the widespread preference for infants. At the CBD, many applicants expressed disappointment when they learned the agency did not place newborns. Social workers eventually revised their practice, both because of pressure from adopters and because they were persuaded by new evidence about early emotional life and the importance of infant attachment to a consistent caregiver. In the 1930s, studies of hospitalized infants documented the devastating effects of impersonal care, changing caretakers, and limited physical contact. Adding to this work, John Bowlby pursued the question of attachment and in 1951, published *Maternal Care and Mental Health*, which quickly gained a large audience. By 1955, half of all agencies were placing children less than a month old. A study at the prestigious Yale Clinic of Child Development bolstered the shift to early placement by showing that testing, so important to professional practice in the 1930s and 1940s, in fact had no value in predicting children's intellectual development. The report concluded, "Our data imply that the general emphasis on evaluating adoptive infants has been excessive."[16]

Still, intellectual matching was not repudiated in principle so much as subordinated and rendered less visible. As social workers began to place younger children, they partly replaced testing and observation of infants with closer observation of their parents. At the CBD, direct placements from hospital to adoptive home were done only when workers could meet and assess both birth parents, enabling them to make estimates of intellectual potential on the basis of observation and family history. In the early twenty-first century, intellectual matching persists in more coded forms—as in the case of prospective adopters who advertise in college newspapers to find pregnant women who are considering adoption. (In a corollary, sperm banks have long made IQ a marketing factor by recruiting medical students as donors.) But as early placement became a priority for both social workers and most adopters, the overt assessment of intelligence receded, and the discourse of intellectual parity became muted.

By the close of the twentieth century, religious affiliation was an almost forgotten dimension of matching, yet it was more likely than any other to be codified in adoption law. Delaware's 1935 code mandated that adoptive parents and child "are suited to one another by religious affiliation."[17] Before World War II, many adoptions were of older children, and the law aimed to ensure that children would not be moved arbitrarily from one faith community to another; even as it sought to preserve a child's affiliation with a familiar faith, it indirectly acknowledged the claims of religious communities on their members. Increasingly, children were relinquished as infants and placed for adoption before they became members of any faith community. In such cases, CBD social workers interpreted "suitable religious affiliation" to mean that prospective adopters should have the same faith as the child's birth mother.

The records at the CBD and elsewhere declared infants "Protestant," "Catholic," or "Jewish"—a usage that bespoke the politics of boundary maintenance. Theologically, such assignments were all but meaningless. Persons become Christian not through birth but through baptism. Indeed, the New Testament uses the metaphor of "adoption"—not birth—to describe the Christian's relationship to God.[18] Judaism is a matter of both covenant and inheritance. One is Jewish if born to a Jewish woman, but Israel's covenant with God is marked and sealed by faithful observance of Jewish law. Religious assignment in the early part of this century was instead a legacy of nineteenth-century social reform, as Catholics and Jews sought to defend themselves against the evangelizing efforts of the Protestant majority. Nineteenth-century charitable organizations, including orphanages, were mostly religiously affiliated, organized to serve members of their own faiths and to preserve their religious traditions.[19] Religious boundaries in New York were maintained so vigilantly that even *abandoned* babies were designated as either Catholic or Protestant, in alternation. Jews protested their exclusion from this rotation in the 1930s, when they constituted one-third of the population of the city; nonetheless, the division between Protestant and Catholic continued until the rotation's demise in the 1950s.[20] In many states adoption laws retained religious matching clauses well into the 1970s.

Delaware law represented a moderate and permissive use of religious matching. The wording of the 1935 Delaware law was ambiguous, and it appears that judges tolerated some flexibility in interpreting "suitable" religious affiliation. Case records included a "religious waiver" that served as a relinquishing mother's statement of intent, including the option of indicating no religious preference in placement. Waivers were a testament of the weakening of communal claims in favor of a more individualistic understanding of religious affiliation. CBD workers used such flexibility only rarely, for they themselves believed in the importance of shared religious affiliation. In their deference to religious matching, they recognized children as members of communities, with identities that should be maintained even as children were moved into new families. The amended law of 1951 spelled out "suitable" religious affiliation more specifically, even as it also explicitly allowed for some flexibility.[21] It declared, "At least one of the prospective adopting parents shall be of the same religion as the natural mother." The law codified the use of religious waivers, with two important results: birth mothers' preferences became a legal mandate, as the law directed that agencies "shall make placement in accordance with such statement"; and social workers were explicitly empowered to cross religious lines if no preference was stipulated: "then the authorized agency may make placement without regard to religion." In 1967, Delaware law was amended further to allow the court to waive religious requirements if they created a hardship for children by delaying placement.[22] By the end of the twentieth century, that law was further liberalized by the change of a single word: if birth mothers stated no preference, then the authorized agency "*shall* make placement without regard to religion."[23] Delaware's treatment of religious matching was unusually liberal in requiring only one adopter to have the same affiliation as the child. In other ways it was typical: most states followed a similar trajectory of increasingly permissive law combined with protection of maternal preference.[24]

Much religious matching happened silently because it was done, in effect, even before adopters reached the CBD. Both relinquishing mothers and adopters selected agencies to correspond to their own religious

affiliations. Although the Children's Bureau of Delaware was a non-sectarian private agency open to clients of all faiths (or none), in practice it
served primarily Protestants. The Catholic Welfare Guild (CWG) considered all Catholic families as within its purview, and CBD social
workers were sensitive to this claim. When Catholic clients appeared at
the agency, they were invariably referred to the CWG. Most Catholics
who came to the CBD, though, had their own reasons for avoiding the
CWG—or had been rejected there already—and the agency did accept
Catholics as clients. Delaware's Jewish communities could turn to the
Jewish Welfare Society, but since so few Jewish women relinquished
children for adoption, that agency usually referred prospective adopters
to other agencies, including the CBD.

The CBD appears to have anticipated the post-World War II secular-
izing turn of American culture by endorsing, early on, a kind of "civic
religion."[25] That is, the agency approved of clients who practiced some
kind of religion, but without making any distinctions among creeds. Instead, social workers appeared to regard religious observance as a sign
of good citizenship and social adjustment. In this position they shared
an underlying assumption embodied in custody and adoption law in
the United States: "a policy favoring religion as against irreligion," including the conviction "that some form of religious surrounding" is vital to children's welfare.[26] This practice was seldom questioned until the
1970s, when a spate of cases posed constitutional challenges to what
amounted to a de facto requirement of religious affiliation.[27]

The bureau's earliest application form queried adopters, "Will you
see that the child attends Sunday school with reasonable regularity?"
Both the question and its phrasing were telling. Social workers believed
that it was important for children to get some religious instruction, and
the assumption that they would do so in "Sunday school" betrayed the
bureau's Protestant bias. But they did not uphold a very high standard
of parental vigilance in the matter, as suggested in the qualifier, "with
reasonable regularity." In fact, CBD workers held that religious devotion
could be excessive. Home studies revealed social workers' ideal of mod-
eration in religious observance. One 1939 record described the prospective adopters (Methodists) as "deeply religious themselves but not intol-
erant." In evaluating applicants who were members of Delaware's

Holiness (Pentecostal) churches, case workers were wary; they feared that religious enthusiasm might go hand in hand with narrowness and "fanaticism." Religious observance was never a formal requirement for approval, and, indeed, intense identification with a faith community might even count against applicants.

Nonetheless, social workers considered religious affiliation a significant marker of parental fitness. Through the 1950s, such participation was important enough to the bureau that social workers discussed religious observance in the home study and confirmed what prospective adopters said by asking for recommendations from their clergy. The rare unchurched applicant was viewed with concern, and social workers urged prospective adopters who were lax in their attendance to become more regular church-goers. They also insisted that applicants come to some resolution of their own religious differences, if any, in order that they could present a united front on the matter of children's religious education.

The bureau's civic religion was less demanding than the standards of some local faith communities, creating the potential for conflict between the secular agency and its religious counterparts. The CBD's work with Catholic adopters illustrates the agency's careful negotiation of these differences. The CBD considered adopters to be Catholic if they identified themselves as such and declared an intention to take their children to church. But the Catholic Welfare Guild adhered to the church's own more rigorous definition of what it meant to be Catholic, requiring both adopters to be actively practicing Catholics in full communion with the church. The difference lent a certain tension to relationships between the agencies. The CBD, in response, sought to avoid any appearance of competing with the CWG. Bureau workers advised all Catholic clients that the CWG was the agency for Catholic placements, and the CBD served only those Catholics who were refused at CWG or who themselves asserted a preference for the secular agency.

Catholic birth mothers probably came to the Children's Bureau for reasons similar to those motivating Catholic adopters: that is, aware that they had violated the Church's standards, they chose to avoid its scrutiny. Miss E was no stranger to the CWG; she had been a foster child under the care of the agency since she was nine years old. But when she got pregnant out of wedlock in 1953, she turned to the CBD instead, not wanting the Catholic agency to learn of her illicit relationship with the baby's father. Likewise, in another 1950s case, when Mrs. A decided to seek adoption for her second child, fathered by a man married to someone else, she avoided the Catholic agency rather than face its judgment. Remarried after her first marriage had ended in divorce, Mrs. A was an adulteress twice over, according to the canons of the Church: she had been unfaithful to her husband, and that marriage itself was invalid in the eyes of the church.

A CBD adoption done in the late 1940s illustrates the agency's careful negotiation of religious matching. Clients from "mixed marriages"— one Catholic and one Protestant partner—were unacceptable to the CWG and thus often found their way to the bureau. Mrs. D, herself a practicing Catholic, harbored "some bitterness" against the Church after the CWG rejected their adoption application because her husband was Protestant. Although he had agreed that the children could be raised as Catholics, this promise did not meet the Church's standard for Catholic adoptive families. But it was good enough for the CBD, and the agency accepted Mr. and Mrs. D as clients after issuing the standard warning that most Catholic babies were placed through CWG (so they might have a long wait). Still, even though the CBD allowed adopters in mixed marriages to find their way around the strictures of the Catholic church, the agency supported the principle of religious matching. When Miss K, raised a Catholic, relinquished her son to the Children's Bureau, she signed a religious waiver that allowed either Protestant or Catholic placement for him. Nonetheless, social workers actively sought a Catholic placement for the little boy, Thomas, and he became Mr. and Mrs. D's son.

In what sense was Thomas a Catholic? His mother was not a practicing Catholic. She did not seek out the services of the Catholic Welfare Guild, which would have sought to ensure that Thomas was raised as a faithful Catholic. Indeed, she did not even exercise her legal right to have him placed with Catholic adopters. Such cases suggest the communal claims embodied in religious matching. CBD social workers were sensitive to the turf issues between their agency and the CWG: they did not want to be seen as poaching on the constituency that rightfully belonged to the Church.

Even when religious waivers gave mothers the right to make individual decisions about religious matching, the agency continued to act in ways that suggest deference to communal claims about religious identities. In some cases, the CBD acknowledged Catholic identity even when clients themselves had turned away from that religious practice. The CBD tried to observe religious matching even when a Catholic mother had waived it, as Delaware law allowed. When a twenty-year-old Italian-American Catholic came to the bureau in the 1930s to plan an adoption for her expected baby, the worker who interviewed her suggested the CWG. The woman explained that she did not want Catholic placement for the baby, but the CBD social worker countered, "This was something the agency felt was important, even if she did not." The CBD was not alone in this broad interpretation of religious affiliation, which persisted until well after World War II. In an influential 1954 decision in Massachusetts, the state Supreme Court upheld the denial of a Jewish couple's petition to adopt twin boys born to a Catholic mother, even though the mother herself had consented to the placement.[28] Surveys of judicial practice done in 1965 (in Nebraska) and 1971 (in New York) found that judges were considerably more conservative on religious matching than statutes required.[29]

Jews are treated as both a "race" and a religious group in agency records, and thus the records on Jewish children and adopters illuminate the intersection of ethnic and religious matching. Protestant and Catholic adopters rarely specified that they would not want Jewish children, but policies of religious matching and the dearth of Jewish children available for adoption made such assertions unnecessary. In a few exceptional cases, adopters indicated they wanted children who were "Gentile," a phrase that excluded Jews; however, we cannot assume that adopters who did not specify religion were open to placements of a child from another religious background. Indeed, the few adopters who did indicate such openness learned what others probably knew already: both law and practice in Delaware strongly encouraged religious matching, though birth mothers' waivers allowed for some flexibility. Quite a few birth mothers checked both "Protestant" and "Catholic"; it was much less common, though, for women identified as Christian to sign a waiver allowing Jewish placement for their children.

At the CBD, adopters and social workers alike grappled with a question that has long generated debate within and outside the Jewish community: What is a Jew? Is Jewish identity a religious affiliation, a racial category, or both? Orthodox congregations interpreted Jewish identity according to maternal blood lines and thus did not accept adopted children as Jews unless their birth mothers were Jewish. Conservative Judaism and Reform Judaism were more flexible on the issue, accepting "Jewish heritage" anywhere in the natal family as a sign of Jewishness. Still, adopted children usually had to undergo rituals of conversion. The most liberal rabbis interpreted Jewish identity entirely as a matter of nurture: that is, children raised by Jewish parents were Jewish, regardless of their maternal blood line.[30]

Wilmington's Jewish Welfare Society was licensed to place children for adoption, but it had so few requests for placement that by 1957 it had asked the bureau to accept referrals of all their clients. In Delaware and across the country, prospective Jewish adopters might first turn to Jewish social services, but their quest for children rarely ended there. As members of a minority community in the United States with a very low rate of birth out of wedlock, Jews faced formidable obstacles to adoptive parenthood. Jews were the first group to experience the extreme imbalance that would come to characterize adoption more generally: far more clients hoping to adopt than children available for adoption.

During 1941 and 1942, the U.S. Children's Bureau initiated inquiries about Jewish adoption as it recognized the special difficulties encountered by members of this group. Surprisingly, their query even included the Cradle, a private maternity home in Evanston, Illinois, considered a notorious adoption mill by child welfare reformers (including those at the USCB). The Cradle's matron reported that the home had placed only eight Jewish babies in 1940, and with a backlog of 109 applications from Jews on file, "we have to be especially discouraging to Jewish applicants."[31] A social worker from the Free Synagogue Child Adoption Committee in New York City acknowledged the very dim prospects of Jews hoping to adopt, especially those living away from the east coast, only to conclude, "I frankly do not know what the answer is for them." Even in New York, with its large Jewish population, prospective adopters faced long and uncertain waits. In 1941, she reported, they had interviewed 800 families and placed just 57 children for adoption.[32] In a letter to the Child Welfare League, USCB chief Mary Ruth Colby indicated that the bureau received many inquiries from Jewish adopters and knew of only five agencies in the country that specialized in Jewish adoption. The bureau, she wrote, had turned to the National Conference of Jewish Social Welfare in hopes of coming up with some way of assisting Jewish adopters.[33]

The first Jewish adopters in the CBD records appear in 1935, self-identified as "Hebrew." The home study's discussion of matching turned on finding a child who "looked Jewish." Although the wife was blond and thus presumably *not* Jewish-looking as that is usually understood, the adopters and their social worker both felt that it would be best to place a child who would resemble the adoptive father. Without further elaboration, the record described him as having "typically Jewish features" and noted, "both he and his wife stated that any child whom they would adopt would preferably have a sufficiently Jewish appearance that there would be no startling contrast between Mr. W and the child." Perhaps aware of their "otherness" in the eyes of the bureau—or perhaps claiming their own place within the widening circle of American pluralism—Mr. and Mrs. W wrote on their initial application that the boy they hoped to adopt "will be given every opportunity to be raised as a typical American boy."

When Dr. and Mrs. G approached the bureau in 1940, even the application form declared them strange. To indicate their religion, clients were asked to check either "Protestant" or "Catholic." Not to be deterred, these applicants drew another line and wrote "Jewish." The home study demonstrates the social worker's preoccupation with her clients' difference. "Neither is distinctly Jewish in appearance," she reported. "He looks definitely like a young professional man. Mrs. G . . . is dark with lovely brown eyes and softly waved dark brown hair. Her features are typically Jewish." Later in the record, the worker described the baby offered to these clients according to her own notions of "typical" Jewish appearance. Hannah "was very small and quite unattractive looking. She had a decided Jewish nose and a very broad forehead." The worker examined even their furniture with an eye peeled for signs of ethnic distinctiveness. "The dining room is the only room which seemed really Jewish," she reported. "They have heavy carved oak furniture."

True to the strictures of melting-pot pluralism, the CBD approved Jews who acknowledged their difference without emphasizing it: "They talked with me about themselves as Jews with no defensiveness and, on the other hand, with no objectionable pride." In her discussions with Dr. and Mrs. G, the worker drew them out about presumed racial characteristics, in particular her "impression that the Jewish race as a whole had a greater ability to feel and express feeling than perhaps an average person." Observing that this did not seem to be true of this particular couple, she asked them how they would deal with a Jewish child who might manifest this characteristic. Dr. G conceded that temperament might indeed be "inborn," but he opined that it was also shaped by environment. He and Mrs. G agreed that they would be firm about squelching any excessive displays of sensibility in their children. The prospective father implicitly defended his own group with a counter-charge against Italians: "He had a number of Jewish and Italian patients both and he felt that perhaps, if anything, the Italian race were more temperamental than the Jewish."

As she supervised this home during the probationary period, the case worker continued to evaluate Dr. and Mrs. G through the lens of her own preconceptions about Jews. The CBD endorsed a style of child-rearing that valued discipline, order, and limits, standards that many clients failed to meet to the agency's satisfaction. In their assessments of adoptive families during the probationary period, social workers often expressed disapproval of over-indulgent parents. But when she observed such tendencies in Dr. and Mrs. G, the social worker attributed their "spoiling" of little Hannah to racial tendencies. "Their attitude toward her is in many ways characteristic of Jewish families."

As in their placements involving Catholics, the bureau sometimes asserted the importance of religious matching even when adopters and relinquishing parents did not. Hopeful of a second adoption, Dr. and Mrs. G indicated that they "saw no problem in our placing a non-Jewish child with them." The social worker demurred: "I told her that aside from our feeling, it would be a legal requirement." In fact, though, the 1935 statute allowed broad judicial interpretation about what constituted "suitable" religious affiliation, and waivers were already in use during the 1930s and 1940s.

In this case, Hannah's birth mother (who was Jewish) had initially planned to sign a waiver that would send her daughter to Protestant or Catholic adopters. Though her social worker explained that the CBD favored religious matching, Miss P saw adoption as an opportunity for her daughter to escape the pressures of anti-Semitism: "She expressed a lot of feeling about how she felt the baby would have real advantages if she were brought up in a non-Jewish home since there is such great prejudice against Jews." Miss P was on the verge of using the waiver to subvert religious matching altogether—not only to broaden social workers' discretion in placement but to actively constrain them from placing her daughter with Jews. Glimpsing this scenario, the social worker moved deftly to deflect this outcome, counseling Miss P that it was best to make no exclusions. In the end, she did not exclude Jewish adopters on her release, allowing the CBD to honor her preferences and to place a scarce Jewish baby with the Dr. and Mrs. G.

By the mid-1950s, the bureau was routinely placing children of non-Jewish backgrounds with Jewish adopters, as enabled by religious waivers from relinquishing parents and by judges willing to approve such placements. However, home study records indicate evidence of silent matching: that is, even when Jewish adopters indicated they did not want to wait for a religious match and were open to children from any religious background, the bureau sometimes decided that they were not appropriate parents for non-Jewish children. Though one Wilmington rabbi noted that "he was not convinced there was an essentially 'Jewish look,'" social workers apparently were: they continued to record impressions of adopters as "distinctly Jewish"—or not.

Applying in 1958, Mr. and Mrs. O were adamant that they did not care about the religious background of an adoptive child, and further indicated that they would freely share with that child information about the religious background of its birth family. The CBD social worker, though, was clearly concerned that a non-Jewish child would stand out too much in this family: "I have found them to have Jewish characteristics in their appearance, speech and with Mr. O in his manner somewhat too." By contrast, the bureau did not hesitate to place a child from non-Jewish background with an adoptive mother, formerly Protestant, who had converted to Judaism and an adoptive father with "no strikingly Jewish characteristics . . . people who do not know him are not aware that he is Jewish." In the case of Mr. and Mrs. O, their CBD worker may have been confusing regional differences with religious and ethnic differences, for she noted that these adopters had recently moved from Brooklyn—decidedly "other" for Delawareans. The bureau placed a baby with them who, very exceptionally, had been born out of wedlock to two Orthodox Jews. The case record itself acknowledged that religious matching was a concern of the agency, not of the adopters: Mr. and Mrs. O expressed no feeling one way or another upon learning that their child had been born to Jewish parents, and their social worker noted that she felt sure they would have accepted a non-Jewish child as warmly as they welcomed this baby. Still, the CBD believed that children would fare better if others did not recognize them as visibly different from their parents.

"Looking Jewish" was a designation that CBD social workers applied liberally, with an imprecision that reflected the blurring of ethnic difference after World War II. By contrast to the 1930s record, in which "Jewishness" included everything from religious practice to temperament and taste, later records focus almost exclusively on appearance—difference had become only skin deep. The placement of little James, born in 1967, was delayed for several days while social workers and others struggled with his racial assignment. His mother was a Moor, an ethnically distinct group clustered in two enclaves of southern Delaware. The origins of the group are obscure, but Moors had long been identified as a distinctive community. Their tri-racial heritage reflected the intermingling of whites, African Americans, and American Indians (Lenni Lenape and Nanticoke). Some Moors were visually indistinguishable from whites and, according to comments in CBD records, were known to direct considerable animosity toward African Americans; other Delawareans, though, often saw Moors as "Negro." Some of the many legends of the group's ancestry held that Delaware's Moors were descended from a Moorish colony, from Spanish pirates, or an exiled Spanish beauty, and a 1940s observer opined, "Some would indeed be inconspicuous among Spaniards, Cubans, or Italians." Moors themselves sometimes identified with their tribal heritage, calling themselves Indians; others refused to subsume their identity as "Moors" under any more widely recognized ethnic or racial category.[34]

Clearly, the social worker had a formidable task before her as she contemplated this child's racial assignment. In the case record, she mulled over her own and others' impressions of mother and baby. "Anyone familiar with the Moors might recognize her as Moorish," she opined, "but otherwise I suspect that she would pass readily as Caucasian." When the baby was born, the social worker solicited the opinions of others, including a nurse at the hospital. "Both nurse and I feel we would think he was completely Caucasian if we did not know his mother is a Moor. Knowing this, however, there may be something just a little 'different' about his nose and he has an abundance of thick straight black hair which stands out in all directions." This child was placed with a Jewish couple; if they were privy to the bureau's initial uncertainty about his racial assignment, the record does not show it. Rather, the placement suggests provocatively that the social worker decided that James himself looked Jewish—or close enough to make a good "fit" with these adopters.

Mr. and Mrs. I also indicated their openness to a child from any religious background, but the social worker hesitated. They had a child by birth, and moreover, "I did have a pretty definite impression that this couple's social contacts are primarily within a Jewish circle." Apparently, though, the social worker resolved these issues to her satisfaction with the flimsiest of matches. The child's birth mother was Protestant. She knew little about the father's background (and he had since departed for places unknown), but, the record noted, she recalled that "He had a large, hooked nose and [the birth mother] thought he was unmistakably Jewish in appearance." The record also strongly suggests that the bureau actively encouraged the birth mother to sign a religious waiver that allowed Jewish placement. She "agreed to either Protestant or Jewish placement—preferring Protestant herself but feeling that a Jewish family might be better for [her daughter] and knowing that in all probability we would place her in the Jewish faith." The baby herself did not "look Jewish," in the eyes of the case worker, who instead described her as a kind of blank slate: "Her appearance does not suggest any particular nationality."

Social workers seized this opportunity to create a kind of symbolic Jewish identity, in order to improve the "fit" between family and child. Mr. and Mrs. I themselves insisted they did not care about the child's religious background. The bureau may have felt, nonetheless, that the child would have a more secure place in their predominantly Jewish community life if adopters and others thought she had a Jewish parent. It almost certainly mattered that the little girl was joining a family that already included a biological child. In such cases, social workers were especially concerned than an adoptive child could become an outsider in the family, and perhaps this influenced them to emphasize ethnic commonality—even to the point of manufacturing it.

The CBD's capacious definition of Jewishness after World War II was emblematic of the larger cultural shift—a measure of the embrace of American pluralism and its redefinition of ethnic and racial identities. By contrast, pre-World War II records reveal intense preoccupation with ethnicity as a defining mark of difference. After World War II, ethnic identities were elided into a generalized affirmation of "American" identity, though in the eyes of most white Americans, black people remained outside the expanded boundaries of who counted as American. Commonly perceived as the most intimate domain of social life, the family was a charged arena for the expression of American pluralism. Many who endorsed full equality in public life—citizenship, employment, public accommodations—shrank from full integration of private life, eschewing intermarriage. Constructed by choice and chance in ways that violated ordinary expectations for kinship, adoptive families raised fears of boundary-crossing among both prospective adopters and larger public constituencies. The family of adoption had no inherent constraints on difference: adoptive families could be much more heterogeneous than any given biological family, however different the man and woman. This unrestricted potential, combined with the intentionality of adoption, made adoption a potent site for the expression of American visions of identity and otherness.

Ethnicity and race matter in American culture, and they mattered to adopters. Yet case records contain relatively little discussion of these subjects—far less, for example, than consideration of sex preference. Ethnic and racial preferences were often unarticulated, not because they were unimportant but because they were so entrenched that this kind of matching "went without saying." Much ethnic matching took place within religious matching. Direct discussion of ethnicity emerged most often in response to the open-ended question posed on the CBD application: "In what type of child are you interested?" Interviews probed deeper: social workers asked prospective adopters to explain their preferences and to declare forthrightly what kinds of children they did *not* want. Some prospective adopters responded to the question by describing the appearance of the child they hoped to find, a category that sometimes overlapped with or encoded race or ethnicity. In a 1940s home study with the CBD, Mr. and Mrs. Z indicated a preference for "a child who is blonde or light in coloring," because such a child "would be the right color scheme for their whole family group." A prospective adoptive mother wrote the U.S. Children's Bureau about her hope to find a little girl, preferably one with "light curly hair and fair."[35] These respondents did not directly exclude or request children of any particular ethnic background, but children with the coloring they described would likely have northern European heritage. Other adopters specifically linked appearance and ethnicity. Applying in the early 1940s, one couple indicated they preferred children of "Nordic, English, German or Swedish" descent, "since both she and her husband are fairly blond." In a 1935 record, the prospective adoptive father was a naturalized citizen born in Greece. He recognized that the bureau was unlikely to have any children with Greek heritage in its care, but he and his wife hoped for a "brunette" who would not look too different from themselves.

Adopters often simply stipulated that they wanted an "American" child, a designation that revealed the ideal—and the limits—of assimilation. In a letter to the U.S. Children's Bureau, for example, one prospective adopter declared she was hoping simply for an "American" child—a category she explained, and qualified, by placing in parentheses, "Protestant."[36] Of course, most African Americans would fit this description, but no doubt this white adopter did not imagine herself as the parent of American Protestants of color. A prospective adopter in the late 1930s told CBD workers that she hoped for a child "of American parentage," but in her mind that category did not include Italian Americans. In a 1943 CBD record, another couple indicated that they sought a boy, six to twelve months old, "one of American nationality." The home study revealed, though, that the boundaries of their ethnic preference were narrower than indicated by the expansive designation of "American." "They feel very strongly that they could not accept a child of Polish-Italian or other foreign ancestry." Just such persons often counted themselves as Americans. When the CBD worker interviewed a Catholic couple of Polish background in 1936, they resisted her suggestion that they would prefer a child with Polish heritage. The prospective father declared that they were "American" and did not care about national background.

Some adopters expressed concern about purported racial characteristics that they identified with ethnic others. Applying in the 1930s, a woman who had taught Italian American children "thought they were adorable as babies, but when they get older they did seem so different temperamentally from herself. She didn't think an Italian child could ever seem exactly like hers." A 1937 case summary noted of a prospective father, "When speaking of nationalities he said that that really would not be an obstacle except that from his experience he distrusts Italian and Polish people rather generally." In a 1942 record, prospective adopters "thought they would feel all right about a child with dark coloring if she did not seem to have this foreign look about her. They have decided that they would probably not feel right about an Italian child or a Polish child, because such a child might seem different not only in looks but in temperament from themselves." Yet the prospective mother then concluded this discussion with an endorsement of pluralism: "As far as other nationalities went, Mrs. K laughingly said, 'We're all mixtures, anyway.'" Apparently contradictory, this adopter's views offer telling evidence of the influence of a pluralist ideal, even as her response also suggests the tenacity of ethnic particularism. Or perhaps Mrs. K was only saying what she thought her social worker wanted to hear. In the end, the couple's reservations about Poles proved so strong that they declined to meet a little boy with Polish grandparents on one side of his birth family. Another prospective father came to the defense of the much-maligned Poles when his and his wife were presented with a child who had Polish background, but he took the opportunity to disparage Germans: "He felt Polish blood was good and said he was glad that there was no German parentage, because Germans are 'tow-headed and stubborn.'"

For many, though, reservations about ethnic "others" often appear surprisingly superficial. Most often, prospective adopters expressed reservations about such children on the basis of appearance alone—that they would be too different from the rest of the adoptive family, or too "foreign-looking." One couple, applying in the 1940s, avowed that they did not care about a child's ethnic heritage, "providing that the child did not look too foreign in appearance." In 1939, a prospective adoptive mother told the CBD "that she wouldn't want an Italian or Jewish child and then added Polish, saying that she thought that when these children grew up they looked like foreigners." A social worker reporting on the preferences of a couple applying in 1946 summarized, "They have no nationality prejudices, and if the child were not too different in appearance, could accept Italian or Polish." In the mid-1930s, prospective adopters—one of whom was considered "mixed race" (American Indian and white)—considered whether they should accept a little girl with one Puerto Rican parent. They wanted a "dark" child, to match the mixed-race adopter, but they, too, queried the social worker about whether the child was "foreign-looking." Another couple said they did not want to consider children with Italian or Polish heritage because such children might feel uncomfortably different when they learned they did not share their adoptive parents' ethnic background.

Of course, stated concerns about appearance could be coded prejudices against other features associated with ethnic others. Yet many CBD cases confirm that adopters in fact accepted children of different ethnic backgrounds when they were not visibly identifiable as "other." Irish American adopters in a 1958 case told their social worker that they did not want a child who would be "too dark-complected." When the CBD presented a child of "Italian descent" as a possible addition to their family, they agreed to go ahead, "Just so long as there is nothing about this baby that makes the Italian come out in him." Whatever this meant, the prospective parents were apparently reassured after one meeting with the little boy. "They really could see nothing that let them feel he looked Italian," and so they adopted him.

Social workers and other experts sometimes revealed their own ethnic biases in the records. Such views often appeared in the physical descriptions and characterizations of clients that opened each case record. One 1940 home study described the prospective adoptive mother as "quite Italian in appearance, with big brown eyes and very dark brown hair." In a 1933 record, a Bureau social worker described another prospective mother as "gifted with a particularly good sense of humor such as is characteristic of the Irish." In a medical report, a physician opined of the prospective mother, "She is fairly high strung and nervous but he supposed that she was not too different in this from many Italian people . . . he knew with Italian people they felt a very strong urge to have children and when she had a child perhaps she would be less nervous."

After World War II, such ethnic attributions all but disappeared, and discussion of ethnicity became perfunctory. Social workers continued to raise the issue, but adopters rarely stipulated ethnic exclusions or proffered derogatory comments about ethnic others. In one record after another, the issue of ethnic matching is dismissed in a recurring phrase: most adopters were "flexible—willing to consider any nationality." The common pre-war prejudice against Italians and Poles was likely a covert anti-Catholicism, and the waning of this concern after World War II attests to the broad assimilation of American Catholics. Though the war did not banish anti-Semitism, Jews, too, became "American" in the 1950s, a shift reflected in the growing willingness of the CBD to accept Jews as adoptive parents of children born to Christians.

Flexibility had its limits. By "any nationality," CBD workers of the 1950s and 1960s were referring to the heritage of American-born children, rather than to adoption of children from other countries. By the mid-1950s, social workers did ask adopters if they wanted to consider "Oriental" children; though the CBD itself did not do international adoptions, it referred interested clients to Welcome House, Pearl Buck's organization of networked agencies that placed Korean-born children with American adopters. And "flexibility," for almost all white adopters, did not include openness to American Indian or African American children. Both the revisions and continuities in adoption practice reflected broader social changes. World War II marked a watershed, as Americans self-consciously embraced an ideal of pluralism—but one based on a shared American identity rather than a celebration of ethnic distinctiveness. This melting pot sensibility subordinated ethnic and religious difference to proclaim Americans' common participation in a culture of postwar abundance. Only racial boundaries remained rigid.

Racial matching was, and is, the most pervasive and persistent form of matching. Well after intellectual matching had been rendered largely impractical, ethnic boundaries had blurred, and religious matching had been rendered voluntary, adopters, social workers, and others remained deeply invested in maintaining racial boundaries between black and white Americans. The consensus on racial matching went so deep that it is quite sparsely documented. Such matching "went without saying"; unlike religious matching, it was seldom codified in law; in contrast to sex or ethnic preference, race is usually not explicitly discussed in home studies. The history of race in adoption becomes available, then, primarily through exceptional cases. Two kinds of occasions elicited talk about race: category violations, in the form of children or parents who did not easily fit into customary cultural boundaries of race; and matching in African American adoption. In both cases, color was often destiny.

Biracial children born to white mothers posed "an impossible situation" in the eyes of most Delawareans, as one case record acknowledged. Born in 1945, Alice was the child of a white nineteen-year-old factory worker. The mother had applied to the CBD for adoptive placement of the little girl, but her aunt and mother opposed the plan: they offered to care for the child themselves and took her home. After a few weeks, though, Alice "began to look more and more like a colored baby," at which point the female relatives changed their minds about raising her. As the case worker noted, "They rejected her pretty completely when they learned of her colored blood." Race, then, was the reason that Alice was relinquished for adoption.

Alice's birth mother apparently told no one of her African American lover. When she discovered her pregnancy, she told her white lover that the baby was his, and he acknowledged paternity. "When [the birth mother] discovered the baby was colored, she could not bring herself to explain this to him, so she simply ended her relationship with him abruptly, so he still considers himself the baby's father." The CBD interviewed a man that she then identified as the probable father, a black tenant farmer living nearby, though the man did not admit paternity. The case record suggests that he had ample reason for this reticence: "There is a good deal of feeling in [the area] around a colored man having relations with a white girl, and there would be a good deal of reality in his being fearful of making any such admission."

Color determined Alice's fate at two critical junctures. She was relinquished when her color disclosed the secret of her African American father. Then, she was placed with black adopters who chose her, in part, because of her color. In 1947 Mr. and Mrs. B came to the agency seeking a child with "light complexion." They themselves represented a study in contrast, as the social worker described them: Mrs. B had "light coloring, a round face, and some of the features which are not distinctly negroid," while Mr. B "is extremely dark . . . definitely negroid features." At first, the social worker presented a little boy, Robert, twenty months old, whom she described as "much lighter than Mr. B and much darker than Mrs. B." Color was destiny for Robert: after an awkward meeting, Mrs. B explained "that Robert was certainly a cute little boy but . . . his skin was far too dark." Soon after, the couple accepted Alice as their daughter.

When children's racial identity was ambiguous, social workers and others scrutinized the children in an intense effort to place them in a recognized cultural category. They examined hair color and texture, complexion, and facial features for clues. The skin tone of genitals, especially scrotums, was considered predictive of the skin color babies would develop as they grew older. Social workers looked at babies' buttocks to discern "Mongolian spots," areas of darker pigmentation found more often on African American and Asian babies. A little girl born in 1938 posed a conundrum to CBD workers trying to figure out how to assign her for adoptive placement. She had one Puerto Rican parent, and her case worker opined that at first encounter the child looked "very foreign" with "tightly curled and sometimes matted hair, and dusky skin." In such cases social workers often enlisted doctors in their efforts to "read" the race of the child. Asked if they thought the child had "colored blood," the physicians who examined the infant declared in the negative. When the agency worker presented the girl to prospective white adopters, they asked if the child was "foreign-looking." "I told him both professionally and personally she was not a foreign-looking child now. However, I stressed the fact that in the beginning she had been an odd-looking child . . . She seemed to me . . . now not to be so different-looking." Her ungrammatical construction spoke volumes about race: the phrase "both professionally and personally" revealed social workers' awareness of the subjectivity of racial assignment. By "professionally," the worker presumably meant her trained eye and experience in observing coloring, features, hair and the like. By "personally," she seemed to invoke a more subjective and holistic perception of the child. Social workers themselves appeared unconcerned with essential racial characteristics; rather, they sought to discern how children would fit into available cultural categories of race—not who they were by dint of race, but how they appeared to others. The idea of race as a cultural heritage and a collective identity did not appear until the 1970s.

Rare cases of abandonment posed the sharpest challenge to social workers' powers of discernment. In a 1975 case, the bureau had no information about either parent, and scrutinized the baby in search of clues. The social worker opined that the child "has Caucasian features yet overall appearance strikes me as somewhat different, perhaps Oriental." An interracial couple became the parents of another child of unknown parents, born in 1968. At the hospital, some thought it likely that the baby was "white . . . with the possibility of Puerto Rican ancestry." The bureau worker recorded, "in coloring seemed to be essentially white though he did have a dark scrotum perhaps indicating some mixed blood." She concluded, though, that this child's race could not be read from the only evidence available: his own body. "One would be hard put to try to decipher [his] racial background from his appearance."

But if social workers saw race as only skin deep, they recognized that it was nonetheless consequential. In ambiguous cases, social workers delayed placement until they could make a clear racial assignment.

These situations appeared more frequently in records of the late 1960s and 1970s, as the sexual revolution and the civil rights movement changed private life: women could have multiple sexual partners without courting certain disgrace, and more people crossed racial lines as they chose sexual partners. The increase in casual sex, though, posed complications for the CBD, rendering paternity uncertain in some cases and fathers out of reach in others. In 1968, when one client (herself white) described the father of her coming baby as "dark complected," her worker suspected that the father might be African American. The young woman herself opined that the father "might be of Spanish or Mediterranean descent," but she felt sure he was not African American. The worker was not so sure: she decided that this baby could not be a direct placement. After the baby was born, the social worker satisfied herself that the baby was white by prevailing standards. Born in 1970, a child with "very mixed racial background" defied ready classification; the social worker and her foster parents thought they discerned "an orientale caste [sic] to her eyes but other than this there seems to be little identifiable difference . . . she is a child who merits a second glance because of her difference but a kind of difference that one finds hard to describe." The language of "passing" was explicitly applied in some cases when social workers commented on the appearances of children with one white and one African American parent. Of a child born in 1967, the social worker noted, "Baby passes as white but I think skin is on the dark side, hair is black but straight. Nose slightly flared, cute looking, some pink coloring in face." This little girl was placed with African American adopters. "Skin looks as though it could darken later but right now baby could easily pass as Italian," the social worker recorded, describing another such child born in 1967, placed with white adopters who indicated their readiness for an "interracial" child.

When social workers sought to match African American children and adopters, they recorded their own impressions of racial appearance and carefully explored the preferences and perceptions of adopters. Such home studies demanded a more open discussion of color than would have ordinarily occurred between white and black interlocutors; indeed, it violated racial etiquette. Color mattered to many African Americans, but the topic was a source of tension within African American communities and certainly one rarely aired with racial outsiders. Social workers (most of whom were white) sometimes found themselves embroiled in miscommunications with African American clients, and they were aware that such adopters might be reticent about discussing color with a white social worker.

One such record suggests the complications of these exchanges. An African American couple applied in 1950, requesting "normal average baby, one who would not be too dissimilar from them in general coloring." The social worker then set about to discern what that might mean. She recorded her own impression that both applicants were "medium brown," but noted that he described himself as "brown" and she considered herself "dark brown." In a later meeting, she pressed the couple for a more specific description of the kind of coloring that they would find suitable in a child. The prospective parents remained rather reticent, indicating only that they hoped for a child "to fall somewhere between their two skin colorings."

Experience had taught CBD social workers the hazards of such parameters. She warned them that it could be difficult to predict the coloring that a baby would eventually have, and told them forthrightly that she was not sure what they considered acceptable. Her concern was vindicated when the couple rejected a little boy who they found "too light for them . . . They were quite certain that this was the only reason and said they were awfully sorry because in every other way he seemed to be such a nice little boy, but they felt it would be impossible for them to take a child who would be so light in skin coloring." At this point, the prospective mother provided a more specific color name: they hoped for a "nut brown child." At a later meeting, the clients and the case worker returned yet again to the question of color. The social worker expressed concern again about understanding how to "get the color right" and acknowledged, "it was a difficult thing for someone else to know what skin coloring was going to look right to them."

A 1953 home study found another CBD worker puzzling over the vexed issue of color matching. "They want a child whose complexion would fit in with theirs," she noted. "I let them know that it was very difficult for us sometimes to decide what was a complexion that was suitable for another person." Mr. and Mrs. S averred that they were not that particular but did not want a child who was "very black." At the same time, though, they mentioned that a neighborhood child, who had been placed by the bureau, was "much too light" for them. The worker struggled to describe the couple's own coloring, which seemed to her "that kind of color that is rather indeterminate, sometimes they look lighter and in different lights they look lighter than other times and it is very hard for me to tell exactly how dark either one of them are, although I note that they consider themselves light brown."

In a 1958 home study, adopters expressed relief that their worker was African American like themselves, feeling that "they could have more confidence in her ability to evaluate a child's appearance and some of the things that it would be important to take into account." They described themselves as "light complexioned" and sought a child who would be the same. The case worker herself did not assume that she could rely on any shared racial sensibility about color; like other bureau social workers, she used home study interviews to try to understand how these clients saw themselves and what they wanted in a child. These particular clients, she knew, cared deeply about the matter: they had recently returned a foster child because of their disappointment with her appearance. Mr. M "told me he didn't fault the worker because white people think all Negroes look alike but they had just offered them a 'horrible looking' child. He said her nose was runny, her blankets and clothes filthy dirty and she was plain ugly and very dark." The worker pressed Mr. M to be more specific about the little girl's color; in response, he "estimated she must have been the color of Jackie Robinson (very dark)." To measure the priority of their concern about color, she posed this test: "I asked what would be his choice . . . of two boys available, one very dark with the potential of becoming a surgeon or lawyer and the other very light who would finish high school but not without a struggle. Mr. M quickly said, the light one . . . Like her husband, Mrs. M felt she would place skin coloring foremost in their choice of a child . . . She let me know she wasn't prejudiced against other people's dark children, 'but just could not take one into her heart to be her own.' As for hair, the they didn't care if they got a boy (since his hair could be cut short), but definitely did not want a girl whose hair was 'kinky.'"

On their initial application in 1959, Mr. and Mrs. P both described themselves as "light brown," but in person, the social worker judged Mrs. P as considerably lighter than her husband, "who is really brown skinned." In this home study, photographs served as a visual aid to clarify the notoriously subjective language of color. Reviewing family photographs, Mrs. P pointed out the children that most closely conformed to the kind of child she hoped for—"always stressing the children who were the lighter ones and some of these were extremely light." Because color seemed to loom large for Mrs. P, her case worker took the unusual step of showing her photographs of two children available for adoption. (Later, photographs would become an important medium of home studies; at this point, though, adopters were not shown visual images of children until presentation, when the case worker used a snapshot to introduce a particular child.)

Social workers sometimes inferred preferences that adopters did not state directly. For instance, when the agency's first black social worker assessed the case of Mr. and Mrs. Y, they told her they wanted a child "with ways and looks as much as possible like ours." Hair texture and features did not matter, they maintained. But the worker nonetheless noted, "I judged a child with straight hair, like Mr. Y, would be found satisfactory to them. Mr. Y commented that parents whose children had straight hair probably kept them themselves."

These preferences for light skin and "good" hair might seem painful testimony to African American internalization of white standards of beauty. In talking about color with one African American couple, the CBD social worker prompted them to be frank on the issue by observing that some African American adopters preferred light-complexioned children even if they themselves were dark. But read together, case records of African American adoption do not confirm a pattern of preference for lightness. Indeed, one African American foster mother opined that, on the contrary, "light" children were harder to place, because they would not readily fit into either white or African American families. If some adopters refused placements of children they deemed too dark, just as many others refused children who looked too light to them.

Like many other adopters, African Americans seemed concerned that children would blend into their immediate and extended families. One couple, for example, applying in 1942, requested a child with "light brown skin, fair hair, and fair looking"; both of them, the record noted, were light-skinned. In a 1955 home study, another couple evocatively requested a child "not too odd from us." Of adopters who requested a child with "brown skin" in another 1950s case, the social worker noted, "They would definitely not want a light skinned child, and were think-ing of one who would have some physical resemblance to them in col-oring." This couple later told the social worker that a child darker than they were would also be acceptable.

Others, though, proved more expansive in their preferences than so-cial workers had expected. One couple requested a child that was "fair looking brown skin fair hair." The social worker described the prospec-tive father: "He seemed to me quite dark in coloring, although not of the very black colored group." In 1942, when she presented a little boy, she described his color in careful detail and told them that the foster mother considered him "definitely a dark child." But Mr. N dismissed her concerns with a hearty laugh, twitting her gently, "Well, you know I did expect him to be colored." Other prospective adopters also stead-fastly denied concern about color in a 1960s case even as the social worker probed for a concealed preference by hinting, "some people had very strong feelings about having a light-skinned child even if they were darker skinned." "Good hair" was not a requirement either, they averred. The worker doubted that these clients were really as flexible as they claimed: "It was my feeling that [the clients] were so eager for a child that they might not be able to express their feelings about these matters which are usually emotionally very important to the negro group." The couple confounded her expectations, joyfully accepting a little girl rejected as "too dark" by other African American adopters.

As the CBD began to place children at younger ages, racial matching was further complicated by developmental changes in children's ap-pearances. Home study records contain some evidence of the folklore of predicting future skin color and hair texture. Considering a baby who was a few months' old, a prospective adoptive mother opined in a 1950s record that "having very little hair at this age meant she would have a soft fine texture when she grew up," but the social worker demurred: "I didn't hold out any hope in this direction." Others held that a baby's hair did not reveal its long-term disposition until the third or fourth month, at which time prediction was a less hazardous endeavor.[37]

By the 1950s, child welfare workers were well aware of the many black children waiting for homes, and efforts to recruit more African American adopters included probing discussions of matching. Between 1953 and 1961, the interracial National Urban League sponsored an Adoption Program to address the problem. Its initial "cultural study" criticized African American adopters for an undue color consciousness: "There is too much emphasis on color and a negative approach on the part of prospective parents on the way a child will turn out in terms of coloration and hair texture," noted a summary memo.[38] Other comments in the NUL records provided a more sympathetic interpretation of matching in African American adoption, as one that noted, "Some emphasis on physical matching is not unusual regardless of the racial group."[39] Some African Americans did complain that agencies were insensitive to color matching, like the couple who replied on a survey, "The agency . . . wanted us to take a light-skinned child, but we didn't accept it. We are brown-skinned."[40] Others resented white social workers' bluntness about color. One recounted bitterly that a social worker had asked them, "'Do you consider yourself colored? You don't look like an American Negro.' What does she expect a Negro to look like? That's the trouble with whites, they are always trying to divide us."[41] In a revealing artifact of the vexed matter of racial matching, one agency attempted to overcome the ambiguous language of color by developing standardized categories of hair texture and color. The Department of Public Welfare in Nashville, Tennessee, classified children according to six categories of hair texture: "fine or coarse; tight curls close to skin; unmanageable (thick and bushy); fine with little curl; coarse with little curl; straight without curl." The same department experimented with a hand-colored chart designed to correspond to a range of skin color, enlisting the African American artist Aaron Douglas in the project.[42] The classification scheme was cited approvingly by social workers from other states, and apparently some agencies attempted to use it for their own case work.

The vocabulary of color was more expansive in African American case records not because such adopters were "choosier" but because they were more "flexible"—willing to consider a wider range of children than did most white adopters. African American adopters accepted biracial children (with one white and one black parent) as their own throughout the history of the bureau. These were, in practice, the first transracial adopters, though that boundary-crossing was not named until white adopters began to venture across the border themselves in the late 1950s. When they did, talk of ethnicity and race became more detailed in their records, too.

Even as many African American adopters proved ready to welcome children of a broad range of skin tones, some of whom had parents of different races, white adopters remained fearful of racial mixing. Appealing to Eleanor Roosevelt in 1941, a prospective mother indicated the racial boundaries of her imagined adoptive family: in search of a little girl, she noted, "I will love it, as my own, of course I don't want a brown baby."[43] A lawyer, serving as reference to a couple applying at the Delaware agency, frustrated the social worker interviewing him in 1953. He would not keep to the subject of the prospective adopters' character and fitness to adopt, instead asking repeatedly "how we could be sure that any child we placed did not have any colored blood." Racial matching underscores the dual role of matching more generally. Social workers emphasized matching as a tool used to craft a good "fit" between child and family. Matching also served the larger social purpose of boundary maintenance, and thus was a stay against fears of transgression associated with adoption.

Rumors about adoption persistently raised the specter of white children placed with African American adopters. In all likelihood, such children were light-skinned offspring of at least one African American parent. Yet even the U.S. Children's Bureau fell prey to white panics about such unseemly placements, or was willing to credit such rumors when crusading for more regulation of adoption. In 1938 a paper presented by a staff member of the bureau noted that regulation of adoption had been spurred by a 1917 investigation that "uncovered" problems such as "white children adopted by colored petitioners."[44] If so, the results of the investigation were not known (or not found credible) by bureau staffers in 1931. In that year, a law school student wrote to ask if the bureau knew of any reports of white children in custody of Negro families; the staffer replied in the negative.[45]

At the end of the 1940s, one couple faced the harassment of a Pennsylvania judge determined to uphold racial separation, at least in his domain. These African American adopters were described with warm approval in the CBD case record; their social worker considered them good parents who nurtured their child wisely and lovingly. They moved to Pennsylvania during the probationary period and therefore undertook the legalization of their adoption in that state's courts. The judge demanded to see "what proof they could offer that they really loved Billy," and subjected them to a public review of their "entire personal life" in search of discrediting information. All he could come up with was the fact that they had been on relief for three months during the Great Depression; nonetheless, they were embarrassed to have this history brought up in court. At the heart of this harassment was the judge's intense concern about racial boundaries. He demanded that they bring Billy to court and, having seen the child, demanded proof that he was "really a Negro." He refused to approve the adoption, imposing a year's residency requirement on the adopters. When they came back in 1950, he again demanded "documentary evidence" of his racial background.

Such responses reveal the depth of white fears of racial mixing. By contrast, the bureau itself tended to view racial identity as its clients did ethnic identity—that is, as a matter of appearance and social assignment rather than one of essential difference. In a 1938 case record, the prospective adopters repeatedly raised concerns about "colored blood." They told their social worker that they knew of a white adoptive mother whose baby had turned out to have "definite Negroid characteristics"; the birth family, adopters later discovered, included some "colored blood." The case worker refused to supply the unqualified guarantee that these adopters sought. She did reassure them that the bureau took "every precaution" to ensure accuracy in its study of children, but that in the absence of complete family histories, it was not possible to be absolutely certain of a child's background. At another point, she reminded the couple that "anyone might have some [colored blood]," averring that white children placed by the bureau were no more (or less) likely than other whites to have a mixed racial heritage. Since in fact the bu-

reau went to considerable lengths to verify the race of children in its
care, it seems that this social worker was using the applicants' concern
with "colored blood" to school them in the "risks" of adoption—that is,
as adoptive parents they had to be prepared to accept some unknowns
in their children's backgrounds. At the same time, her response was unusual for its forthright acknowledgment—and acceptance—of the in-
tertwined histories and genealogies of white Americans and African
Americans.

Matching—the hallmark of the "as if begotten" family—would falter as
adoption expanded across national and racial borders in the 1950s and
1960s. The principle of matching would be repudiated soundly after
1970, as a broad critique of adoption rejected the post-war ideal of
adoptive families who were indistinguishable from blood kin. As practiced before 1970, the overt effort to match IQ, religion, ethnicity, and
race reveals the complicated negotiation undergirding the expansion of
adoption. Americans accepted the transfer of "strange" children with an
alacrity unmatched in the world, and for the most part adopters were
more ready than social workers, co-religionists, legislators, and judges
to transgress the boundaries of the "as if begotten" family. Matching is
now decried as masquerade—a species of passing, despised for its evasion of the difference at the heart of the adoptive family. It might be
seen, instead, as a signally American kind of self-construction: even kinship, the last redoubt of biology and destiny, might be imitated and improved by social engineering.

3

The "Best Solution":
Adoption Embraced

A sea change swept adoption in the years following World War II. Once practiced as a limited and marginal response to the needs of dependent children, adoption became social policy; it was proclaimed the "best solution" to the "problem" of out-of-wedlock pregnancy. No longer seen as an exceptional and anomalous arrangement, adoption became widely accepted as an alternative family form. In the twenty-five years following World War II, adoption had the broad support of an unprecedented white middle-class consensus. Adoption practice expanded proportionately. A U.S. Children's Bureau study estimated 16,000–17,000 adoptions for 1937; by 1945, the number had increased to 50,000. In 1957 improved statistics cited 91,000 adoptions, a number that increased each year until the historic peak of 1970, with 175,000 adoptions.[1]

These shifts corresponded to changes in sexual behavior among white women, as rates of pregnancy out of wedlock grew rapidly in this group. The rising numbers of adoptions signaled a newly interventionist attitude surrounding "illegitimacy." Reversing their former reluctance to separate single mothers and their children, social workers came to consider adoption the best solution for unwed mothers and their children. The popular and professional embrace of adoption reflected the larger American scene, too, during the 1950s and 1960s. In this era of unprecedented economic expansion and global dominance, adoption gained new credibility as a kind of social engineering that appealed to American dreams of upward mobility and self-invention.

Experts and a lay public alike endorsed adoption as a "legitimate" response to "illegitimacy": that is, as a legal institution that designed social kinship as the full equivalent of biological kinship. Adoption was touted in popular and professional sources as the best solution for all its participants. The unwed mother might recover from the stigma of pregnancy out of wedlock, gaining a second chance for marriage and respectable motherhood. The child placed for adoption would benefit from the emotional stability and improved life chances afforded by growing up in a two-parent family. Adoptive parents could recoup the losses of infertility by forming the families denied to them by biology. A bold intervention, postwar adoption took on the expansionist character of contemporary political culture and social life. And it served as a vehicle to enable wider access to the good life as figured in postwar culture. The "second chance" of adoption allowed unwed mothers and their children a new opportunity to participate in the social mobility of a booming postwar economy and gave infertile people a way to enter into its celebration of domesticity and family.

This postwar consensus rested on a set of interrelated understandings about family, sexuality, and child welfare, many of which were already in place by 1945. Eager prospective adopters had long insisted that nurture mattered more than nature; by the 1950s, expert opinion had shifted in the same direction. Frustrated prospective adopters had long complained about child welfare workers' reluctance to separate mothers and children, and experts had indeed seen relinquishment as a desperate last resort. But after World War II, experts advocated it for nearly all children born out of wedlock.

Largely unregulated at the opening of the twentieth century, adoption had come under state supervision by World War II. A variegated patchwork of laws emerged, the result of jurisdiction at the state level and also an indication of the lack of consensus about how to regulate adoption. But variable as they were, adoption laws nonetheless codified a consensus that accepted families created through adoption as kin—as the full equivalent of biological kinship. Adoptive families were permanent: what law had ordained was not subject to disruption or renegotiation, except under the same extraordinary circumstances that might call for the disruption of families joined by blood. Adoptive families were singular and exclusive: adoption permanently severed the bonds of blood kinship and replaced them with the legal ties of adoption. Child welfare advocates were often frustrated by the permissive character of adoption law. They themselves consistently pressed for legislation that would require expert supervision of adoption and investigation of children and prospective adoptive parents. The persistent disposition in most states, though, was for laws that regulated adoption lightly—a permissiveness that attested to public confidence in kinship forged by law.

The new attitude of Americans toward adoption in the postwar period was, in part, a response to expanding prospects for upward mobility. In 1935 a working-class woman who found herself unhappily pregnant faced a limited set of options and was unlikely to imagine that, whatever she did, she might expect a life dramatically better than her mother's. Or perhaps some did have such dreams, but social workers themselves seemed to expect little on behalf of such clients. By 1950 a woman of the same class situation had reason to hope that she might claim a share of the material abundance of postwar America. In this context, an unwanted pregnancy loomed as a formidable obstacle to the middle-class status that would otherwise have been within her grasp. By mid-century, social workers supported such aspirations by advocating adoption as a second chance for women who had made a "mistake." These attitudes were also influenced by the narrowing class distance between social workers and their clients, as more middle-class young women became pregnant out of wedlock.

By the 1950s and 1960s, women pregnant out of wedlock had become "girls in trouble"—neither sinners, like the fallen women of the nineteenth century, nor sexual delinquents, like the problem girls of the 1930s and 1940s.[2] Looking back on this era, some have seen the "best solution" as a prime example of Cold War hypocrisy and repression, and indeed its narratives bear some resemblance to the paranoid poli-

tics of the period, with young women whisked away to bear their children in secrecy and relinquish them in silence.[3] The "second chance" of
adoption was undeniably and unabashedly a form of sexual containment—of policing traditional boundaries of respectability by
reaffirming the ideal (as well as the "deal") of conjugal relations. Despite these drawbacks, the "best solution" nonetheless bespoke a new,
more tolerant attitude toward sexual transgression. Social workers believed that wayward girls could be rehabilitated, not just forgiven or dis-
ciplined, and that they *deserved* a second chance.

Race set the limits of the postwar era's broadening definition of
"American" and "middle class," and adoption in these years predominantly served a white clientele. By the mid-1950s, an estimated 150,000
children were born out of wedlock each year, of whom the great majority—96,000—were "non-white." But in 1951, for example, of 80,000
adoption petitions filed, only 4 percent involved African American children.[4] To some extent, the disparity reflected different communal standards: black communities, like white working-class and rural communities, often disapproved of relinquishment. African American children
whose mothers could not care for them were frequently absorbed into
substitute families that did not get recorded in adoption statistics; informal adoption was a traditional resource of black communities. But
the low number of African American adoptions was also a glaring example of racial exclusion and inequality. In Delaware and across the
country, black women who sought adoption services were usually
turned away.

During this period, adoption practice among whites became more
uniform than ever before—or since. By 1970 most adoptions were mediated by public or private agencies under the control of social workers.
Courts accepted their expertise in counseling relinquishing parents, assessing adoptive homes, and defending the best interests of the child.
Though most states allowed adoptions that were arranged outside agencies, relinquishing mothers and adopters turned to agencies in record
numbers. In 1945 only about a quarter of nonrelative adoptions were
done under the supervision of licensed agencies. That rate had almost
doubled by 1951, and by 1971 nearly 80 percent of nonrelative adoptions occurred under agency supervision.[5] The figure was almost cer-

tainly much higher in Delaware, where private adoption had been outlawed in 1951.[6]

Confidential adoption became standard practice during this period. Birth parents had no contact with their children after they relinquished them. Birth and adoptive parents did not meet or encounter one another, and agencies kept birth and adoptive families from learning one another's identities. Most states sealed birth records and substituted the names of adoptive parents on the birth certificate of adopted persons.[7] This practice powerfully symbolized the cultural status of adoption as substitute family. The amended birth certificate erased blood kinship from the public record, silently substituting legal for biological kinship. This kind of adoption required the diligent intervention of an intermediary, and social workers were well situated to serve in that role.

Their unprecedented support for adoption brought these professionals into closer accord with lay publics who had long criticized social workers' cautious and skeptical approach to relinquishment and placement. However, even at this high point of public confidence, social workers enjoyed only a limited mandate. The U.S. Children's Bureau had long encouraged state agencies and child welfare organizations to lobby for adoption codes that mandated social workers' supervision of adoption. In state after state, such efforts failed. Americans were more willing to turn to social work agencies for adoptions, and many state codes required some form of public investigation of prospective adopters and supervision of adoptive homes. But the gold standard of child welfare reformers—the provision that adoption should take place *only* under the supervision of licensed and trained social workers—was seldom met. Even by the end of the twentieth century, only six states had such legislation; adoption has operated mostly within a durable tradition of wide juridical discretion. In most states, the courts are authorized—and in many, they are required—to undertake some investigation of adoptive homes. But the investigator may be a social worker or other officer of the court (probation officers were often delegated to this task), and the findings and recommendations of such investigations are not binding. The courts, not social workers, continue to be the arbiters of adoption, and the role of social workers in that process remains one of negotiated power—of influence, not clear professional authority.

The story of the CBD in these years demonstrates the extent—and the limits—of social workers' control at the zenith of their authority in adoption practice. In 1951 the bureau's social workers and other child welfare professionals in Delaware successfully won support for the first model adoption legislation in the country. Formulated along the lines approved by the federal Children's Bureau, the Delaware law was the first to require that all non-relative adoptions be conducted through a licensed social work agency. In anticipation of the enactment of this law, the bureau revised its historical role as a child welfare agency in 1951. For years, the bureau had offered a broad range of services to the community, with adoption comprising a relatively small part of the work. Social workers investigated complaints of neglect and abuse; helped clients find food and housing; advised on access to mothers' pensions and Aid to Dependent Children (ADC); offered family counseling services; placed and supervised children in foster care. In 1951 the CBD became an agency solely dedicated to adoption. The change was made in response to dramatically rising numbers of relinquishments and in anticipation of the increased demands for service when the new law went into effect in July 1952.

Before World War II, out of wedlock birth, in itself, was rarely considered a reason to relinquish a child for adoption. Instead, social workers assisted pregnant single women as they faced the daunting prospects of raising a child without the usual advantages of marriage: access to a male wage; the economic and social resources of an extended kin network; the father's help in child-rearing, or at least the presence of a partner whose masculine authority might bolster a mother's directives. Social workers certainly recognized the social burdens that illegitimacy unfairly placed on children. For decades they had challenged the legal disadvantages incurred by children born out of wedlock, such as restrictions on their ability to inherit.[8] Yet before World War II they did not argue that single mothers should place children for adoption so they might avoid the stigma still attached to illegitimacy.

The zeal for relinquishment was driven partly by the conviction that women pregnant out of wedlock were by definition unfit mothers. In the postwar version of Freudianism, these women were deemed neurotic—as manifesting a disordered femininity. Leontine Young's widely circulated 1954 manual for social workers reveals how the tenets of the best solution derived from and served 1950s gender regulation. In a convoluted logic, Young branded unwed mothers as covert man-haters. "Few . . . are interested in men," she asserted. "They show much less concern and initiative in attracting men than the average girl and have often lacked normal social and romantic contracts. For many, their only sexual experience seems to be the relationship which results in pregnancy, and this has usually been brief and unhappy."[9] One feature of such personalities, Young theorized, was a kind of hyper-fertility caused by their neurotic desire for a baby. "The majority of unmarried mothers seem to become pregnant more quickly than is usual with married women," she observed, apparently not considering the possibility that the unmarried mothers of her acquaintance might have underreported their sexual activity. "Once they have become pregnant, seemingly they almost never lose the baby." Young believed she observed "an unusual degree of contentment" among these women.[10] The desire for a child, fecundity, and a contented pregnancy—hallmarks of feminine "adjustment" among married women—were signs of pathology in the unwed mother. "The serious problem of the unmarried mother is that her urge for a baby has been separated from its normal matrix, love for a mate. In fact, this is precisely the one thing that the unmarried mother avoids consistently."[11] Wanting a baby but unwilling to take on a man, the unwed mother violated the terms of postwar domesticity.

On the other side of the equation, adoptive mothers were potentially suspect themselves, for childbearing was the ultimate test of femininity. Most adopters were motivated by infertility, turning to adoption only after sexual reproduction had failed them.[12] By 1950 many agencies had codified this tendency in policies that excluded most fertile persons from adopting.[13] Like age limitations, such requirements were often responses to the chronic pressure of adopters, who greatly outnumbered available children; it was a widely accepted way to winnow down the numbers of prospective adopters. Social workers supplied another logic to buttress the policy that favored or required infertility, for they believed adoptive children were better off without siblings who had been born to the adopters. Biological children, they feared, might have—or seem to have—an insuperable advantage in the inevitable competition for parents' attention and favor. The Child Welfare League of America endorsed the policy of restricting adoption to infertile couples in 1952: "If they can have children and do not, their reason for wanting to adopt is highly questionable."[14] Such attitudes reflected postwar pronatalism, directed with special intensity toward women. In a discussion of agency requirements of infertility, a 1957 adoption manual explained, "This is not merely because there are not enough children to go around. It is also because the motive for adopting, if not based on an organic sterility that precludes having one's own children, might be a neurotic one. No matter how desperately anxious for motherhood a woman claims to be, social workers know that a potentially good mother makes every effort to have her own child before she tries to adopt one." The authors also suggested psychological counseling to rule out a "rebellious unconscious," speculating that infertility might be a telltale symptom of hidden reservations about maternity.[15] Male infertility was not subject to the same kind of psychoanalytic speculation, and, indeed, it was long under-estimated in medical literature and neglected in medical research.[16]

Social workers had long advocated careful scrutiny of prospective adopters, but in the postwar years that examination began to include a heightened attention to their gender performances. From their first appearance at the bureau, women were evaluated for signs of appropriate "femininity." The case record typically opened with a physical description of adopters that included a detailed account of the prospective mother's clothing, grooming, and hairstyle. One 1955 record approvingly noted, for example, that the client was "dressed today in a frilly white blouse and skirt and made a quite soft and feminine appearance." Men, too, were expected to meet appropriate standards for their sex; in conformity with postwar expectations for masculinity, the most important was to establish themselves as responsible breadwinners.[17] This meant a good work record and a job that yielded a "family wage"—an income adequate to support the entire household. Through interviews with references and through police records, social workers sought to establish that prospective fathers eschewed the masculine vices of excessive drinking, gambling, "running around," and fighting. Social workers endorsed standards of companionate marriage, well established by World War II. In conformity with postwar domestic ideals, they wrote approvingly of men who shared leisure time activities with their wives and "helped out" with housework. They were uneasy with husbands who seemed too domineering or bullying, but also leery when they encountered couples in which a passive man followed the lead of a forceful woman. Of one promising couple, a social worker summarized approvingly in 1959, "Mr. K is very much the masculine head of the family and Mrs. K is very domestic and feminine in her role."

A 1955 record illustrates the preoccupation with gender—and particularly with femininity—evident in many postwar home studies. The record opened with the worker's observation of Mrs. C, "dressed today, which was hot, in a thin cotton dress . . . wearing high heeled shoes, but no other accessories. Mrs. C appeared to be a feminine person with a soft gentle manner." Social workers regarded prospective adopters' response to infertility as a valuable indicator of their personal qualities and marital relationship, and the couple passed with flying colors. Mr. C. had taken the news of his own infertility like a man: "I have no indication that he sees this as any reflection at all on his masculinity or pride," and had unselfishly suggested that Mrs. C could have a baby by artificial insemination. Mrs. C, for her own part, "knew for herself that it was something she could never accept, feeling that her joy in being pregnant could only come from knowing she was carrying her husband's child." In her summary of the home study, this social worker was gratified to recommend Mrs. C as the epitome of womanhood: "Mrs. C . . . seems to accept completely and with great satisfaction her role as a feminine person, as a wife, homemaker and potential mother. She shows great admiration and pride for her husband and certainly seems ready to put his career ahead of other personal considerations."

Even tiny babies were scrutinized for signs of conformity to prescribed gender roles. Mr. and Mrs. C soon received a five-month-old girl, described as "a small, petite, dainty, very feminine little girl, quite sensitive in nature and inclined to hold her feelings in a bit." The same worker adjudged a two-month-old male, placed two years later with this family, to be "a large and long, masculine looking infant . . . a large, lusty, dynamic kind of baby, very active and strong and definitely all boy." She concluded with satisfaction, "The C's seemed very pleased that their little girl was so feminine and their little boy so masculine."

The very picture of ideal domesticity was presented by an Air Force man and his wife, according to a 1957 case narrative. The prospective mother had already given up her clerical job in anticipation of mother-hood. "Mrs. F does seem like quite a feminine individual and one who is really far happier being at home even though they might not have chil-dren." On another visit, the social worker again noted Mrs. F's satisfac-tion with home-making: "I would say she is really quite a domestic indi-vidual, one who really enjoys cooking, keeping house and all the essentially feminine occupations." Mr. F was not above housework him-self, and the case narrative included a detailed inventory of his domestic skills: "When she was working her husband did help a great deal with the household chores; he himself likes to cook . . . There are only two chores he has absolutely refused to help in: making beds and ironing. She knows he surely could though he says he doesn't know how to iron. He is really a 'model husband' in everything else." The bureau approved this kind of limited male participation as the sign of a healthy companionate marriage, and in this case the social worker was pleased to note that Mr. F himself shared this view. "He feels it is not sissy to pitch in and help your wife when she is working. He knows of some marriages that failed because the husband has taken the attitude that it is her job to do all the household chores as well as to take on some of the financial responsibility for bringing home a paycheck."

The bureau enforced postwar gender expectations by prohibiting women's paid work. Prospective adoptive mothers were required to quit their jobs before the bureau would undertake a home study. For many, this policy never arose as an issue, for they were unemployed at the time of their initial application. Though the proportion of wage-earning married women had grown steadily over the twentieth century, working wives were still in the minority as late as 1970. Mothers of young chil-dren seldom worked for wages: under 11 percent in 1948, and fewer than one in three in 1970.[18] Full-time motherhood was a middle-class ideal, and almost a practical necessity for families of all classes, given the very limited child care available for babies and toddlers. In anticipation of motherhood, some prospective adopters had left their jobs when they first began to try to get pregnant. Informed of the bureau's policy, most employed wives agreed and quit their jobs, duly reporting their resignations to their social worker.

A few wage-earning wives greeted this news with considerable dismay. As they recognized, there was no guarantee that they would be approved for adoption, and even if they were, a considerable time might elapse between the home study and placement. As social workers countered such objections, the bureau's designs come into view. Mrs. W, a telephone operator, saw no reason to quit until their home study had been approved. Her case worker explained in this 1955 record that women had to leave their jobs so they could be readily available for appointments and home visits during the home study. Though it was undoubtedly more convenient for social workers to schedule visits with clients who had few fixed demands on their time, this was hardly the whole reason for the policy. They did not expect men to quit work. When they needed to talk with prospective fathers, they offered to meet them at their workplaces or to schedule appointments outside normal business hours.

In truth, the policy served primarily to allow the bureau to assess and enforce women's commitment to the approved version of motherhood—a full-time job undertaken in a household supported by a male breadwinner. This ideal, of course, was widespread in popular culture and prescriptive literature of the period. Female domesticity was initially heralded as the fruit of military victory, and women who had aided the war effort through paid work were urged "back to the home." But soon female domesticity, enabled by postwar prosperity, was being celebrated as the epitome of women's social and sexual fulfillment. While most Americans encountered this ideal as a cultural prescription, women who wished to adopt confronted it as a requirement. Like many professional experts, CBD social workers believed unswervingly that this arrangement was in the best interest of children; as mediators of adoption, they were in a position to forego persuasion and simply mandate full-time motherhood. Men's responsible performance at a steady job was seen as an important qualification for adoptive fatherhood. Women, on their part, demonstrated their qualifications for motherhood by willingly abjuring paid work. Therefore, Mrs. W's proposal—that she would quit work once approved for motherhood—raised a red flag for her social worker.

Such a policy also served straightforward practical aims, as revealed in the social worker's admonition to her reluctant client: "I let Mrs. W know that we felt it important that there be a period when she was dependent on her husband's income and at home for a while before she had a child." The bureau based its assessment of a family's financial position on the husband's income alone, but recognized that strictly quantitative evaluations of income did not tell the whole story. Some families managed well on small incomes, while others in apparently similar circumstances were perpetually indebted and overextended. The best test of financial ability to adopt, then, was the demonstration of adopters' adjustment to the income they would have as parents. In addition, they wanted adopters themselves to become accustomed to managing on one income before placement, adjusting to the constrictions of a leaner budget before a child placed new demands on the family income. Then, the arrival of a new child would not be associated with the privation of a suddenly reduced income.

In effect, the policy served as a dress rehearsal for the prescribed gender roles of postwar domesticity. Though social workers seemed straightforwardly committed to this ideal, the policy nonetheless suggests a tacit acknowledgment of the demands it imposed on marriages and especially on wives. Social workers recognized that wives' dependency on husbands' wages might involve emotional adjustments as well as financial ones. And their vigilance for any signs of untoward commitment to paid work suggests, implicitly, that social workers understood that jobs held attractions for women that might compete with the touted fulfillment of home-making.

Social workers were convinced that women who invested themselves in their jobs were lacking in femininity and maternal feeling. In 1957 Mrs. G, a secretary at a large corporation, must have been a seasoned and valued worker, for she earned almost as much as her husband, who worked as a hospital administrator. Their social worker's first impression was that Mrs. G seemed "pretty used to her career," and largely for this reason the couple were not promising prospects. Another prospective adopter vacillated for months, torn between her job and her desire to become a mother. When the couple applied to the bureau in 1953, Mrs. S, a nurse, indicated "she does not want to give up all her work because she enjoys it and also wants to keep her hand in." She hastened to explain, "It is not a financial necessity," a risky admission. She was probably aware that the bureau would not ordinarily place a child in a family that relied on two incomes, and so it was prudent to indicate that her husband's income was sufficient. But Mrs. S placed herself under suspicion by admitting that she was working for reasons other than need. A few months later, she confessed that she had been dragging her feet a bit, "finding some difficulty in thinking of giving up her work, although she said that having the child is much more important." Nonetheless, a year later, Mrs. S was still working as a nurse, and the couple decided to defer their application. When they returned for a home study several months after that, Mrs. S received special scrutiny because of her attachment to her job. Interviewing their references, the case worker asked them point-blank about the issue and got the answer she was looking for: "They both let me know quite strongly that they knew Mrs. S was working more to fill in her time than from being the type of person who prefers working to enjoying her home."

Social workers reluctantly accepted black working women as adopters, for the bureau's urgent need for black prospective parents forced the agency to recognize and accommodate to the exigencies of African American life. National studies confirmed that prospective black adopters were often deterred by agency prohibitions against women's work. In surveys and interviews conducted as part of a study by the National Urban League, some prospective adopters revealed that they had withdrawn from home studies when confronted with such requirements. One woman remembered, "We were moving along nicely and then they told me I would have to give up my job. I did not continue [the home study] because I couldn't afford to give it up."

Examining a questionnaire returned by an African American woman, the investigator concluded "that the only thing blocking her from adopting was the fact that she was working. Cannot afford to stop working. The family needs the income of both." A union official who had referred prospective black adopters to the league was indignant at the way they had been treated when they applied to adopt: "What are these agencies doing? She was told she would have to quit her job. Who can afford to do that?"[19]

Bureau workers encouraged African American prospective mothers to quit their jobs once a child was placed, but they did not require them to resign before beginning the home study. In practice, CBD social workers accepted the policy implied in a recruiting pamphlet published by a Wisconsin public agency. Addressed to prospective black adopters, the pamphlet supplied information about adoption in a question-and-answer format. "Is it all right for the adopting mother to work?" The answer was a qualified yes: "An adoptive mother may work but she is expected to be at home enough to really know her child and to have her child know her as a mother."[20] This more flexible standard allowed social workers to affirm a maternal and domestic ideal but without enforcing full-time motherhood, as they did with white clients.

When Mrs. D and her husband applied at the bureau in 1952, she volunteered that she planned to leave domestic service when they got a child. The bureau placed a little girl with them in 1954. But about half way through the probationary period, Mrs. D told her social worker with some anxiety that she had taken a seasonal job, working at night in a cannery. Her husband cared for their daughter when she was at work. The bureau accepted the situation with a note of resignation: "Since this is a temporary arrangement of only a few weeks and since they seem to have worked out well [sic] in their arrangements together, this did not seem too unsatisfactory for the time being." The agency was not about to risk a placement that was clearly going well—especially when it involved promising black parents. When this child's adoption was finalized, the bureau appealed to them several times to see if they might be willing to consider another child.

In a case record that spanned eight years, wage work was a source of extended negotiation between the bureau and another African American couple, Mr. and Mrs. B. When the couple first came to the agency in 1953, Mrs. B was a leather worker who earned a weekly wage only a few dollars less than what her husband brought home as a truck driver. As she anticipated motherhood, Mrs. B told her social worker (the bureau's first black case worker) that she would quit work, at least for a time, after a child was placed with them. The worker confided in the case narrative, though, that she was not sure if the couple were really committed to this plan, or only saying what they knew she wanted to hear. At the moment, the discussion was moot, since Mrs. B had recently been laid off. Later in the same conversation Mrs. B admitted that she would go back to work as soon as called. Mr. and Mrs. B calculated that their current income was adequate, but they worried that they had little reserve against unexpected reversals. The bureau approved these adopters with some misgivings, concerned both about their financial insecurity and her intention to work.

Mrs. B's episodic employment was, indeed, crucial to maintaining the household. In 1954 a three-year-old boy was placed with them. A few years later, the bureau called to see if they might be able to consider another child. The couple declined, for they did not think they could support a larger family. Not long after, the bureau asked Mr. and Mrs. B if they could serve as foster parents of four-year-old Ella. The social worker felt that they hesitated only because family finances remained precarious; she noticed several bills and collection agency notices on the table when she visited. (Foster parents received a stipend, and the bureau covered medical expenses; nonetheless, many foster parents probably spent more than they received for children in their homes.) Mr. and Mrs. B did take on the little girl, who became their daughter in all but law. They considered Ella their own, but repeatedly told the bureau they were too hard pressed to make the commitment to adoption.

Social workers continued to view Mrs. B's employment with suppressed disapproval, whereas she continued to regard it as a necessary contribution to the family income. Leather workers were subject to frequent layoffs, and so Mrs. B's wage-earning was interspersed with periods of full-time home-making. In 1958, the case record noted, "Mrs. B has been laid off her job indefinitely and is glad to be home with the children." A year later, the social worker found Mrs. B "very anxious to return to work," this time hoping for employment as a practical nurse. "Mrs. B seemed on the defensive about going to work and explained that after fourteen or fifteen years of two salaries it is hard to get along on one." Called back again to the leather-processing plant, she returned to that job. On a supervisory visit, she told her social worker, "Both children had been happy that Mrs. B was going to work because then she could buy some more toys, etc., which they had been wanting." She hastened to add, "she would like not to have to work but it is just about mandatory . . . Working not only meant luxuries for the children but helping with some of the bills." Mrs. B's social worker was not convinced: "The Bs say they are financially in debt but still seem to spend a considerable amount of money on extras for the children. Mrs. B always supplements Ella's agency wardrobe, and both children have an abundance of spending money." The bureau preferred mothers who stayed at home and managed the family finances carefully. Reading between the lines of the case record, we might speculate that Mr. and Mrs. B, for their part, sought at least a limited participation in the burgeoning consumer economy of the 1950s.

Prospective adoptive mothers confronted a subtle but pervasive stigma attached to their infertility, and as mothers by adoption, they had to prove their femininity by meeting social work protocols for appropriate gender performance. Single mothers, or mothers-to-be, faced a much more visible and overt stigma: they were bad women, their sexual transgressions exposed by pregnancy. Postwar social work affirmed contemporary mores about sexual morality, upholding prescriptions that limited sexual intercourse to marriage. Yet at the same time, the rise of the best solution was predicated on a newly optimistic view of the possibilities of rehabilitating women who had transgressed. As it was redefined and practiced in the postwar period, relinquishment was a distinctive expression of that era's culture of self-improvement and upward mobility.

Social workers had never shared evangelical reformers' confidence in the redemptive possibilities of motherhood. As secular professionals, they placed their faith in personal transformation as wrought by psychological insight rather than religious devotion. Advocates of children, they doubted that children's own happiness and prospects would be served by making them the instruments of their mothers' salvation. Social workers believed that "illegitimacy" imposed an enormous burden on children, both because of the stigma attached to it and because of the limited life chances available to single mothers and their children. But they rejected the older idea that an out-of-wedlock pregnancy meant a woman's certain ruin. Through adoption, single mothers could redeem the past by erasing their own "mistake" and securing a better future for themselves and their children. The "second chance" of adoption extended the boundaries of the American dream to include women who had violated postwar sexual mores.

The widening constituency of "problem girls" reshaped professional and popular views of out-of-wedlock pregnancy. By 1945, CBD workers (like social workers elsewhere) were confronting a far more varied clientele than they had before. Earlier, most women who sought their services were from what case workers described as the "client class"—poor or working-class Delawareans whose familial and communal resources had proved inadequate to address the life problems they confronted and who thus turned to social service agencies for assistance. CBD workers, for the most part, treated such clients with respect and considerable empathy; nonetheless, they addressed them over the distances of class (and sometimes ethnic and racial) difference.

With the upheavals of the home front in wartime—Delaware was the site of a large air force base and defense industries—CBD social workers began to encounter women pregnant out of wedlock who otherwise were more like themselves—women of middle-class standing or prospects. Across the country, rising rates of "illegitimacy" strained social work services—even as they also challenged prevailing assumptions about such pregnancies. Some worried that wartime would strain existing services past capacity. Others, though, noted a newly defiant clientele of unwed mothers who wanted assistance but refused to be shamed by their sexuality or their out-of-wedlock children. Through the 1950s, steadily increasing rates of pregnancy out of wedlock indicated that this was more than a problem of wartime upheaval. By the 1960s, the rhetoric of sexual revolution challenged older languages of morality and psychology.

The changes gradually inflected social work as well. Clark Vincent's 1961 *Unmarried Mothers* overturned earlier views with its matter-of-fact conclusion that such women resembled their age peers in every other way except for the accident of their pregnancies.[21] Many social workers, including those at the CBD, continued to see out-of-wedlock pregnancy as social pathology, and proffered treatment to their clients.

Still, the characteristic label of the postwar years was telling. Earlier, "fallen women" implied moral failure and "problem girls" suggested an unhealthy psyche. By contrast, "girls in trouble" suggested a more transient social condition, even a place—a specific social space—that an individual could enter and then exit.

Adoption both maintained and moderated the contradictions of postwar sexual ideologies. Since the 1920s, prohibitions on sex outside marriage had been losing force. During the war, traditional strictures yielded as young people seized the day in the face of war's uncertainties and as communities were destabilized by wartime migration to defense industries and military service. Yet raising a child as a single mother remained a formidable undertaking in a society that had made only a limited commitment to a welfare state, and one rigorously concerned to sort out the deserving from the unworthy.[22] After World War II, new forms of sexual regulation raised the price of sexual transgression. Practiced with some openness before the war, abortion now became the target of 1950s moral panics, driving providers underground and narrowing women's access to this traditional response to an unwelcome pregnancy.[23] The "feminine mystique" promoted heterosexual domesticity with new insistence. Glossy depictions of suburban bliss purveyed the allure of consumption, even as popular Freudian narratives warned that women could find sexual fulfillment only as wives and mothers. In this combination of contradictory pressures—liberalizing sexual mores, the promise of upward mobility (though a mobility dependent on male wages), the widening constituency of unwed mothers—adoption served to meliorate the harshest consequences of sexual transgression even as it supported a version of social order that contained women's social, economic, and sexual possibilities.

The presumption of relinquishment dominated CBD case work. Defined as an *adoption* agency after 1951, the bureau extended its services to pregnant women or mothers who were considering adoption plans—not, as previously, to any woman who sought their help as she confronted an unexpected pregnancy or struggled to care for her children. In a new community-wide division of labor, the CBD no longer supervised any children in long-term foster care. Instead, the Department of Public Welfare assumed custody of all dependent children. The bureau handled temporary placements only, supervising the care of children while their mothers made decisions or while the children waited for adoptive families. The new arrangement provocatively suggests the underlying class character of the best solution: adoption served as a vehicle for recovering or attaining middle-class status for both mother and child, while mothers who did not relinquish faced the prospect of having their children raised by the state.

Social workers still saw themselves as supportive listeners rather than as outright advocates of one course or other, and professional ethics still staunchly maintained that the worker's role was to support the expectant mother as she made her own decision. But they now believed strongly that adoption was the best decision for most, and this commitment inevitably colored their relationships with women considering relinquishment. With the uncritical enthusiasm of a novice, a social work student at the bureau articulated the qualified neutrality of social workers' approach to relinquishment. In a term paper written in 1963, she delivered the received wisdom of social work: "Unwed mothers cannot be treated as a group, for each one has a unique personality and problem. These girls must realize that the worker is as interested in them personally as she is in placing their babies. Their feelings and wishes must be respected, but at the same time the worker has to help them see what is the best thing to do." That "best thing" was usually adoption, she went on to explain, in prose that aptly captures the tenets of the best solution: "Our society just does not accept illegitimacy. So both the mother's and the child's chances for a happy life would be hindered if they tried to live together in the community. Through adoption, they are both given a fresh start."[24] A bureau social worker explained this logic to a pregnant teenager considering adoption in 1957: "The primary reason that a girl gave up her baby was not because she was unable to take care of it or did not have feeling for it but rather because she wanted the baby protected from its illegitimate status."

Social workers themselves were convinced that illegitimacy was the primary justification for adoption, and they worried that clients who did not agree were not good candidates for rehabilitation. The CBD case worker seemed dissatisfied with one mother in a 1959 case, who "felt adoption was the best plan for her baby in view of her age and lack of financial security although she also gave lip service to her feeling that [her child] should have both a mother and a father." A 1963 record captured the social worker leading her witness with determination, but not getting the answer she wanted to hear: "I wondered if the baby's illegitimacy had anything to do with it [her request for adoption] and although she said she guessed so in a way, I really wonder. I had the feeling that she was wanting adoption for this new baby because of practical lacks, such as money and baby sitter and responsibility." These "practical lacks," in the minds of bureau social workers, were not in themselves adequate reasons for relinquishing a child. Instead, they promoted adoption for the young woman who sought a "fresh start".

In its turn toward adoption, the bureau conformed closely to wider shifts in social work practice. The Florence Crittenton Homes, which had once strongly discouraged relinquishment, now became influential advocates of adoption as the best solution. In Wilmington as elsewhere, the FCH rendered its services *only* to women who said they were planning to relinquish their children, and it concentrated on pregnant single women with no children, presumably the most likely candidates for rehabilitation. As pressures mounted on the home, with rising numbers of women clamoring for admission, FCH staff scrutinized applicants with an eye to selecting the "girls" who would use the institution as they felt it should be: to keep their pregnancies secret and to relinquish their babies.

This protocol often translated into a tacit racial and class screening. In 1963 the matron became suspicious of a fourteen-year-old African American resident, fretting to the CBD social worker that "maybe M is in the Home only because of their school program [the FCH was the only maternity home in the region that enabled residents to keep up with high school classes] . . . if this is true, it would mean that the Home is being used inappropriately." Adoption workers viewed such young girls as prime candidates for adoption services; in all likelihood, the FCH matron questioned this girl's motivation only because of her race, knowing that most African American women did not relinquish children born out of wedlock. In the same year, a CBD worker was skeptical when a sixteen-year-old white woman from rural Delaware came to the bureau to inquire about maternity home care. Aware of this community's disapproval of adoption, the worker warned, "Right now, the home is still filled to overflowing with a waiting list so it is extremely important that the home accept only those girls who are going to follow through with adoption, because otherwise they would be using a valuable vacancy for somebody who really needs it." As defined by both the FCH and CBD, services to pregnant women were no longer aimed at supporting or sequestering women during a difficult life passage but at facilitating adoption to rehabilitate both mother and child.

CBD social workers did not tell relinquishing mothers that their decision would be easy or that they would forget their children. In 1953, during her initial interview with a pregnant eighteen-year-old, her social worker acknowledged the young woman's apprehensions: "It seemed good to me that she should realize this was going to be hard. It always is and is an experience that she will not forget." They viewed relinquishment as a weighty and consequential decision that was properly attended by studied deliberation. Case records show their efforts to engage clients in a searching life review that included psychological exploration and planning for the future. They also sought to set a particular pace and staging for the decision. They were troubled by both women who moved too quickly toward adoption and those who "wavered."

Older scripts of penitence and redemption were replaced with a therapeutic narrative, though one that bore more than a trace of the outlines of moral reform. The best outcomes, according to social work standards, were those that rehabilitated the errant mother as well as securing her child's future. Of one young resident at FCH in 1957, her case worker noted with satisfaction, "Although [the client] was not without her problems, she was a joy to work with because she really wanted casework help and tried to think clearly." The "good" unwed mother felt remorse, achieved insight, and learned from her experience, like the exemplary Miss P, who "has literally writhed in self-condemnation at becoming illegitimately pregnant yet she has had enough balance to be able to look at it as a valuable though costly experience." Sadder but wiser, another bureau client understood the error of her ways after her married lover let her down: "It is difficult to speak of one's having an illegitimate baby as being a profitable experience and yet, in one sense, Mrs. O's experience in this area could be called profitable. As she said, she finally stopped to look at her behavior and the meaning of it." These three cases, all from the 1950s, rang the themes pervasive in 1950s and 1960s records.

Faced with an unplanned pregnancy, women were apt to see it as bad luck or accident; social workers, by contrast, viewed such pregnancies as symptoms of social or psychological pathology. Counseling began, then, with social workers asking why the pregnancy had occurred. Understandably, this query left some clients confused, wondering if perhaps the social workers of the CBD were in need of a refresher course in sex education. One such exchange, recorded in 1960, was a comedy of misapprehension: "Miss H seemed genuinely distressed about her four illegitimate pregnancies, however, when I asked her if she had any ideas as to why she had had so many pregnancies, and what she might do to prevent any further, she came through with: 'I just don't understand it. I use jellies and a douche every time and I try to be careful.'" Contraceptive failure was not the sort of reason social workers had in mind, and the social worker tried valiantly to steer Miss H toward the bureau's view of the problem (illicit sex) and its solution (abstinence): "I wondered if she saw sexual relations as a very essential part of life." But Miss H did not take the hint, replying that "she guessed it was a habit by now." Probably perceiving her worker's disapproval, she went on to explain, "She recognized that she was the kind of girl who is easily aroused and swept off her feet . . . [she] knew it was wrong but she just did not seem to be able to stop." The bureau took a dim view of such explanations.

Asked to account for their pregnancies, others responded by narrating the circumstances of their illicit sex—a high school romance, an affair with a married man, a casual date or boisterous party where too many drinks had rendered the woman incautious—better, but still not what the bureau had in mind. Rather, social workers assumed there were psychological reasons for out-of-wedlock pregnancy, and sought to elicit a therapeutic narrative about it. The successful encounter, then, ended with women understanding their pregnancies as meaningful, not simply unhappy mischance. The social worker reported this satisfactory outcome of a 1957 case in which she convinced her client that she had actually *wanted* to become pregnant: "She, with help, had come through to some clarification of the meaning of this experience. She recognized that it was very likely she had become pregnant intentionally hoping that Mr. R would then feel duty bound to marry her." As another worker explained to a skeptical teenager in 1962, "Oftentimes . . . girls who have illegitimate babies do so because they want the baby subconsciously." Her client, she recognized, "did not go for this too much." A more cooperative teenager, also pregnant in 1962, volunteered that perhaps she had gotten pregnant to get attention.

Social workers often interpreted pregnancies as a sign of emotional deprivation or family conflict. In 1957, Miss S's case worker felt that her client's sexual behavior was a symptom of pitifully low self-esteem: "Her own needs are so tremendous that any male attention is a boost to her ego and she is not very discriminating. She sees herself as an ugly duckling and she impresses me as being emotionally drained." Adolescent rebellion was another key theme, with social workers critical of overcontrolling parents who goaded their restive daughters into bad behavior. Counseling a sixteen-year-old mother who had just given birth to her second child in 1953, her case worker speculated that she "has a real need to get back at her mother for some reason and so far has succeeded in doing this with two illegitimate babies."

The combination of a manipulative mother and a passive father, social workers believed, was a particularly potent recipe for premarital pregnancy. In a 1970 case, the worker suggested to her client that her pregnancy was the result of anxious perfectionism: pressured by her parents' unrelenting expectations, perhaps she got pregnant as "one way to say that she was not perfect but unfortunately instead of easing off the pedestal [she] took a nose-dive." Her client "eagerly accepted this hypothesis," believing, to her worker's gratification, that "since there seemed to be some reason for her involvement with [the birth father], she felt better able to prevent a similar situation from reoccurring."

Less often, social workers acknowledged the devastating influence of deprivation in lives constricted by poverty and isolation. Reviewing the life story of her young client, a CBD social worker mused in 1955, "One could almost have predicted that Miss R would become illegitimately pregnant. I have visited in one of these little mining towns and the drabness of life and the intense poverty is almost unbelievable." This kind of explanation, though, appeared infrequently in 1950s and 1960s accounts, reflecting the dominance of psychological interpretation.

Bureau social workers believed that adoption was best for children born out of wedlock, but they wanted women to reach this consequential decision only after studied deliberation and careful review of their options. Summarizing her work with a client who gave birth in 1954, the social worker wrote, "I tried to help her look closely at plans other than adoption for [her infant] but one by one she ruled them out . . . She felt ADC at best provided only a hand to mouth existence. She . . . wanted more for [her] than foster care. She seemed to see adoption as a guarantee that her baby would have a life far different from her own."

When women declared themselves set on adoption without such deliberation, CBD workers were skeptical and probed for signs of ambivalence. One high school senior, a maternity home resident in 1953, declared that she wanted adoption so she could finish school and go on to nursing school. "I remarked that it sounded as though she was very definite about wanting adoption for her baby and I wondered if it was this clear cut. Were there times when she felt uncertain or perhaps dreaded the idea of giving her baby up?" At times, social workers' insistence on extensive deliberation met resistance from clients, who declared they already knew their own minds. One apprentice social worker (a student earning her Master of Social Work degree) described what amounted to a struggle of wills as she pressed her CBD client to follow the social work script for a "good" relinquishment. Miss B, she felt, was in denial, refusing to express the ambivalence she must surely feel about her decision to place her baby for adoption. Specifically, she refused to admit she loved her expected baby. The student ended up in strategic retreat and responded by redefining the situation: Miss B's resistance, she came to believe, showed the strength that a client might derive from denial. When the apprentice social worker backed off, victory was hers at last: Miss B was then "able to acknowledge her feelings" for her baby.[25]

The "good mother" was one who showed "real feeling" for her child, even as she demonstrated the maturity to temper maternal emotion with the deeper mother love of selfless rationality. Of a 1956 relinquishment, the social worker summarized approvingly, "I felt [the client] evidenced feeling and concern for [her child] and she felt keenly the responsibility of making a plan that would be right for her baby." A "good" relinquishment was not rendered easily. "When she was not on the verge of tears, she was convulsed with sobs which were sometimes loud," her social worker recorded of one emotional scene that took place in the early 1960s. "She obviously dreaded the signing." Nonetheless, the new mother, a young teenager, executed the relinquishment, even though she was crying so hard that a nurse intervened with smelling salts. Her social worker did not take this as a sign of "wavering" or indecision but rather as the appropriate response to a painful decision. "I sat by her and tried to console her as much as I could and thought it was good that she was able to express her feeling so clearly and for a while I began to wonder if [she] was ever going to pull herself together." Moved by the girl's love and resolve, the worker concluded, "This was really one of the most meaningful and difficult signings I have witnessed."

Social workers accepted relinquishments not executed in this spirit, but they were clearly less satisfied with this kind of client. Case records included an assessment of the mother's state of mind as a way of demonstrating the validity of the relinquishment, which was not legal unless executed by a competent person acting freely. At the same time, these summaries also served as social workers' own assessments of the success of case work. Of a woman who had relinquished one child and was now placing another for adoption, her social worker noted, "Fundamentally I think she has little maternal instinct so that signing her Consent did not seem very difficult for her." A single mother who had tried to care for her child and then returned to the bureau to relinquish him signed "with a complete lack of feeling," her social worker thought. Social workers certainly believed that children with uncaring or unattached mothers were better off in adoptive placements. Nonetheless, such women also represented troubling failures of case work, since they had refused to involve themselves emotionally in the process of relinquishment.

Recidivists posed a particular challenge to the narrative of rehabilitation that dominated social work of the time. Doggedly, CBD workers intoned the same message about the values of celibacy and the hazards of illegitimacy even to women who were already single mothers, sometimes of several children. Miss A, expecting her sixth child in 1957, volunteered that she had gone to Planned Parenthood in hopes of preventing further pregnancies. Her social worker "raised some question about this being a real solution to her problem." Dutifully, Miss A then supplied the answer her worker wanted to hear: "Miss A is quite aware that there is only one real solution and she is going to try to 'control' herself." Some CBD social workers tempered the counsel of celibacy with a measure of pragmatism. As she interviewed one woman who had given birth to three children (all relinquished for adoption), the social worker learned that her client was currently earning her living as a prostitute. Dismayed to find she had never practiced any method of birth control, the worker suggested that she might discuss the matter with a doctor. But she also pressed her client to consider the bureau's counsel of abstinence, the "one real way to stop having babies." Discussing her four pregnancies with her social worker in 1960, a single mother explained that she used birth control sometimes but then got "caught" during her occasional lapses. Her worker was quick to supply the bureau's irrefutable logic on the subject: "There was no sure way of avoiding pregnancy unless she just avoided sex relations." By the early 1960s, bureau workers routinely suggested contraception for women who had more than one child out of wedlock, even as they continued to argue for sexual abstinence as the superior course of action.

Social workers set themselves against the rising tide of sexual revolution as they continued to intone the virtues of abstinence for unmarried women. Their views of sexuality adamantly emphasized women's vulnerability to men. In a sense, the CBD case records are cautionary tales, outlining the cost of violating postwar conformity and its middle-class code of sexual containment. Social workers advanced no critical perspective on that morality—indeed, they were active agents of shame, relentlessly inculcating the harsh lessons of the cost of sexual transgression. To read these records is to be reminded of the profound sexual alienation of 1950s white middle-class culture.[26] As bureau workers grimly counseled their clients, sex was women's capital. The woman who squandered it had only herself to blame. When one client confided miserably in 1957 that her boyfriend had started drinking, driving too

fast, and "running around," her social worker replied that his bad behavior was her fault. A girl who "gave in" to her boyfriend's entreaties
for sex could expect to lose control of him, just as she would lose his respect and, soon enough, his interest in her. Complaining of men's
perfidy in a 1963 case, a woman in her mid-twenties appealed to her
worker's sense of gender solidarity, only to be firmly deflected: "She
spoke as though she guessed I knew how men are and how they don't do
right by women. I thought I knew what she meant but in another sense,
I supposed you could say that women don't do right by men, that is,
when a woman allows a man to have the privileges of marriage without
any of the responsibility and then gets . . . irritated at his lack of responsibility." In the battle of the sexes, it was every woman for herself; and
men were the enemy, not to be relied upon without the contract of
marriage.

This grimly pragmatic view of heterosexual relations was conveyed
in chilling popular metaphors of sexual exchange. In the language of the
market, young girls were admonished that their marital futures depended on wise, cool-headed conservation of sexual capital. Men won't
buy the cow if they can get the milk free. Men won't buy a used car
[marry a sexually experienced woman] when they can get a new one.
The logic of this argument, of course, led ultimately to the literal exchange of sex for cash, as a few bureau clients recognized. In a 1962 case,
the CBD social worker suspected that Mrs. T might be making her living from selling sex since she claimed to have no idea about the paternity of either of her children. She asked her client outright if she was
"prostituting." "Mrs. T denied this though admitted she had had some
propositions and sometimes she wondered why she didn't just go ahead
and get some money for it." A client who was incarcerated for prostitution explained to her social worker in 1963, "It's a way to make a living.
There is no point in just giving it away because when you get money,
then you can afford treatment if you catch anything."

Nowhere in the records did bureau workers acknowledge that
women themselves might find pleasure as well as danger in sexual expression. A few years later, at the height of the women's liberation
movement, some women would claim sex as a domain of "freedom and
power"—a possibility supported by the material conditions of more re-

liable contraception and legal abortion.[27] Bureau workers, instead, saw women's raw vulnerability in a risky sexual marketplace. Both medical practices and social attitudes limited women's access to reliable birth control. Many physicians would not supply contraceptive devices to single women under twenty-one years of age. Sterilization—the one form of contraception as reliable as abstinence—was rarely available to young women, as nineteen-year-old Miss Y, mother of two children, learned. Waiting for the birth of a third child she knew she could not support, she asked her worker to help her arrange a tubal ligation. The bureau worker informed her she was "ineligible." And so she was—by the "rule of 120," the widely observed medical standard that withheld voluntary sterilization from women until their age multiplied by the number of their living children equaled 120.[28] (Meanwhile, through the 1950s bureau records coolly referred to other women who were "eligible" for involuntary sterilization. Along with many other states, Delaware's eugenics law enabled this drastic intervention for women adjudged feeble-minded.)[29] In the 1950s and 1960s, as now, limited sex education and guilt about sexual activity inhibited other young people from practicing contraception. And then there was the woman who explained, in 1960, that she had always used contraception but had stopped doing so at the behest of a boyfriend who complained that it interfered with his pleasure. "She spoke in rather philosophical terms about how girls in this day and age try to do what their boyfriend wants them to and she wanted to please him." When she became pregnant, her boyfriend reciprocated by making it clear that this was "her problem" and then claimed that the baby was not his. Sex was not "freedom and power" for such women. In the face of such conditions, bureau workers recommended abstinence as the best guarantor of women's security and their future prospects.

If social workers accepted the overall logic of the sexual marketplace, they nonetheless resisted its all-or-nothing tenets of respectability. In a peculiar way, the market logic itself opened up a space for a narrative of redemption. In the old narrative of the fallen woman, a repentant sinner might hope for forgiveness and redemption, but the sin itself was irrevocable. By contrast, the market metaphor of sex as capital suggested more fluid and flexible forms of exchange. Once bankrupt, a person was not consigned to permanent impoverishment but might hope to re-cover assets or generate new capital. In this cultural context, the bureau's single-minded counsel of abstinence emerges as a striking instance of postwar optimism—the belief that the past could be not only redeemed but erased. Virginity is ordinarily understood as absolute and unrenewable: once surrendered, it is gone forever. But in the logic of bureau workers, the body could be managed not as misspent capital that was forever irrecoverable but as a depreciated asset that, carefully reinvested and managed, might grow in value.

Another recurring analogy, however, was less optimistic. Sex was figured as an addictive drug or irresistible compulsion. This attitude—and its covert misogyny—is captured in the experience of a maternity home resident who returned from a medical check-up with an unsolicited prescription for birth control pills. Her doctor told her "that now that she had started having sex, she'd never be able to stop."[30] Bureau workers refused such a logic. Women could and should stop, they believed. They encouraged women to reclaim their sexual capital, withdrawing their investments from the risky marketplace of sex outside marriage. In a postwar ethos dominated by consumption, influenced by popular psychology and its insistence on heterosexual expression, and then reshaped by the cultural revolution of the 1960s, the counsel of abstinence would strike many as too constricted and self-denying. Nonetheless, in a limited way, CBD social workers anticipated the 1970s feminist critique of the sexual revolution: that is, they understood that there can be no authentic sexual freedom unless women can claim their bodies for themselves.

The price of the "second chance" extended to sexual transgressors was high: denial and repression of women's sexuality and maternity. If the redemptive narrative were to succeed according to the broad ambitions of the best solution, the incriminating evidence had to be hidden. "Confidentiality" became the hallmark of postwar adoption. Maternity homes redefined themselves to serve this function: to get transgressive pregnancies out of sight and to rescue the spoiled identity of the "illegitimate" baby through adoption.

Birth mothers' memoirs vividly recall the shame of pregnancy out of wedlock in the 1950s and 1960s. In her memoir of relinquishment and reunion, Rebecca Harsin recalled the intense social shame of appearing in public as a single pregnant woman: other shoppers, she felt, viewed her and her friend (also pregnant) "as if we both had horrible disfigurements. I had never before been looked at as though I were something distasteful."[31] Many narratives offer examples of efforts to hide a transgressive pregnancy—lonely efforts to conceal the nausea and vomiting of morning sickness, rigorous control of weight gain, hiding pregnant bodies under loose clothing and confining girdles.[32] Some women attempted abortions. Memoirs and case records offer a grim catalog of folk remedies, including vigorous jumping; scalding hot baths; taking quinine, gin, hot ginger, and castor oil; douching with turpentine; lifting heavy objects. Pregnant at sixteen, one teenager had heard of coat hanger abortions. She straightened out a wire hanger but was not sure how to proceed and could not bring herself to insert the instrument she had fashioned.[33] A few recounted fleeing back-alley abortionists as their resolve faltered at the last minute.[34] When abortion failed and the changes of pregnancy defeated strategies of disguise, some took the next step—going into hiding for the duration.

During this period, many maternity homes redefined themselves. Once temporary refuges for women disgraced by an out-of-wedlock pregnancy, they now became liminal spaces between respectability and disgrace—spaces into which an "illegitimately" pregnant woman could disappear, arrange adoption for her baby, and re-emerge with her respectability restored. Maternity homes were "total institutions" whose control of every aspect of residents' lives served the rehabilitative agenda of the best solution.[35] Women left behind their old identities on admission to the maternity home. In some homes, women took assumed names; in most, residents used first names only and were strongly discouraged from communicating with one another after their discharges. Maternity home staff monitored all contact with the "outside." Visitors, phone calls, and mail all had to pass the scrutiny of staff.

One reason was to maintain the confidentiality of the maternity home stay; the other, to keep pregnant women away from the men who had brought them to their present condition. As one woman recalled wryly, "We were made to understand soon after our arrival that the Salvation Army considered our boyfriends stumbling blocks to our future restoration to the ranks of the virtuous."[36] Bodily discipline and control were expressed in a strict dietary regimen monitored by weekly weighing in some institutions. As reported in a memoir of a 1960 stay in a maternity home, residents were counseled to aim for a total weight gain of fifteen pounds. While consistent with contemporary medical prescriptions for small weight gains during pregnancy, the restriction was enforced through disciplinary measures that exceeded anything a pregnant woman might experience in private life. If one of the "girls" gained more than the allowable limit for that week, she lost her "privileges"— the daily and weekly passes that regulated inmates' excursions out of the maternity home. This regimen modeled the message and discipline of the maternity home more generally: controlling one's appetites led to freedom, while yielding to them meant punishment and confinement.

Dietary restriction was also a part of the systematic denial of the maternal body, the most challenging feat in attaining the restored identity promised by the best solution. One former resident uncritically endorsed the goal of erasing the signs of maternity: "Most of us want to look as if we'd never had any babies when we leave here, of course. Some of the girls manage to keep their total weight-gain down to five pounds or less and look fashionably slim when they leave. If we thought we could starve ourselves into *feeling* as if we'd never had a baby, I bet we'd quit eating all that junk between meals."[37]

Another relinquishing mother noted the irony of this alienated relationship to the body. Her maternity home provided intensive counseling on post-partum dieting and exercise—but no preparation for labor and no information about contraception. Instead, as she recalled indignantly, the program sponsored the visit of a woman from a modeling agency who advised on "how to get our figures back and be attractive again. Really! Even at the time I was sitting thinking, they're just telling us how to get pregnant again! . . . The whole point of that was to get us to feel glamorous and marriageable."[38] If sex was women's capital, then their bodies were a crucial asset that had to be returned to mint condition.

Maternity homes used space to reinforce the sense of passage through stigma to restored identity. Pregnant women were separated from women who had given birth, often in wings on opposite sides of the building. Labor was the rite of passage from one side to the other. Final steps in rehabilitation were relinquishing the baby and then leaving the whole experience behind. Residents were not even supposed to say goodbye to other inmates. Instead, a silent departure dramatized the break with the past. Maternity home histories were supposed to disappear into silence and secrecy. If the adoptive family was ideally "as if begotten," the out-of-wedlock pregnancy was to be "as if forgotten."

This strenuous rehabilitation worked for some women, by their own accounts. Jean Thompson's narrative portrays the maternity home as discipline—a ritual banishment from society—but also as a source of solace and redemption. The home offers a place where Thompson can sequester herself from the shame of unwed motherhood, find ease in the camaraderie of other women in the same situation, and regain respectability through the second chance of adoption. In conformity with the postwar narrative, she depicts relinquishment as a painful necessity, and portrays her motherhood as a temporary stewardship: "He is someone else's son . . . I'm not giving him away. He was never mine. I've just been responsible for him for a little while."[39] Thompson's epilogue affirms adoption as the best solution. Married, with "two children of my own," Thompson joyfully watches them and considers the hard-won wisdom of her experience of pregnancy out of wedlock: "I am reminded of the lesson I learned several years ago; your children are not your children—they dwell in the house of tomorrow."[40] Relinquishing her first child, she implied, allowed her to secure the future for all her children.

Other accounts endorse the best solution even as they depict the grief and anguish of relinquishing a child. One woman remembered sobbing so hard as she signed her relinquishment that she could hardly hold the pen. But she remained convinced that she had made a good decision. "I never felt guilty or that I'd done the wrong thing with the adoption," she recalled. "I was made to feel guilty for having had sex and having gotten pregnant. That was absolutely the sin, and I've carried that guilt all along. But I never felt guilty about relinquishing. And all along I told him [her baby, while in utero and after his birth] that this was absolutely the best thing for him."[41] Another woman shared her resolve, even as she grieved for her child for nearly a decade. As she relinquished her son, "I wished him well, and all that . . . Just horrendous sadness and the

crying . . . Still, I could not let myself change my mind." She kept a photograph of her relinquished child and observed his birthday in sorrow
for ten years. "It finally hit me," she wrote, that this unresolved grief was
robbing her second son of his childhood. "I finally threw the picture
away and tried to let go of it so that I could enjoy my own child that I
did keep."[42] Accounts like these vividly render the maternal sacrifice advocated by the best solution, portraying relinquishment as a costly decision made for the child's good.

By the 1980s and 1990s, other women who had relinquished in the
1950s and 1960s described their unresolved grief as evidence of the false
promises of the best solution. Many regretted their decisions. Birth
mothers defined themselves as a social group and repudiated the postwar consensus. For these women, there could be no "choice" to relinquish a child. Interviewed in the 1990s, a woman who had relinquished
her child years earlier denounced the terms of the best solution. She declared flatly, "No mother in the world, human or animal, would *decide*
to give up her baby. It isn't normal or natural. It wouldn't happen if
mothers had the power to decide. It only happens when they don't."[43]

Yet we know that women did relinquish their babies, by the thousands. Supported by a broad white middle-class consensus, the presumption that adoption was best resulted in an unprecedented rate of
relinquishment. For the first time, most white single mothers placed
their children for adoption. In 1963, 70 percent of children born out of
wedlock were relinquished. That rate reached 80 percent in 1970, the
year that recorded the highest numbers of adoption in United States
history.[44]

Why did they do it? "We were coerced," some birth mothers responded later. Women pregnant out of wedlock did face formidable
pressures, both the shame imposed by postwar gender ideologies and
the limited prospects that awaited single mothers and their children.
But does that mean that relinquishment was inevitably coercive? What
of the corollary—when women kept children they had considered relinquishing, are we to conclude they were freely exercising their "power to
decide"? This formulation has become commonplace, but it is simply
not adequate as an account of women's decisions. Postwar adoption offers an excruciating demonstration of the costs and limits of women's

choices; at the same time, it also reveals women's exercise of agency within those constraints.

Maternity homes and social workers loom large as repressive agents in critiques of postwar adoption. Sources from that era confirm that some women were pressured by others who argued single-mindedly that adoption was the only acceptable alternative. CBD social workers themselves felt that the staff at the Wilmington FCH were too directive. When a young woman expressed misgivings about adoption and wondered aloud if her mother might help her raise her baby, "Mrs. G's [the matron] response was to remind F that she had caused her mother a lot of worry and heartache already and she advised her 'not to start that kind of thing.'" Young's 1954 manual, addressed to social workers, firmly advocated such directive counseling. Addressing colleagues who might feel qualms about "imposing an arbitrary decision upon the girl," Young pronounced such fears "a delusion," and reminded her readers that the clients were deviants in need of a firm hand: "When a worker can see that, had the unmarried mother wanted a baby for normal reasons, she would have fallen in love, married, and had a child under normal circumstances, the worker's problem begins to resolve itself."[45]

CBD workers eschewed this forthright pressure in favor of deliberative counseling, but one might argue that their therapeutic approach was itself a form of repression, a covert discipline that was the more effective for its seductive display of empathy.[46] Undeniably, their support of women's choice was framed by their own belief that adoption was the best solution, and this conviction inevitably colored their counseling. On rare occasions, CBD social workers discarded even the appearance of neutrality to become direct advocates of relinquishment. In case records, they themselves recorded their qualms over the ethics of such advocacy.

The extreme youth and troubled family situation of one pregnant fourteen-year-old convinced her bureau worker that relinquishment was an urgent necessity. Cathy avowed that the birth father could be one of two boys she was dating, but it soon emerged that a male relative was the most likely father. Her mother knew this, it seemed, but had threatened to kill her daughter if she told. Under the circumstances, social workers had little chance of rescuing the daughter who remained dependent on this troubled family. Still, it seemed all too likely that adding an infant to the mix would make things worse, so adoption could be seen as a form of melioration for the girl at the same time as it offered the hope of a more stable family for her baby.

The bureau worker set herself to the task of convincing this family that adoption would be best, though Cathy and her mother both remained doubtful. When the baby was born, Cathy declared that she had definitely decided to keep her and to raise her with the help of her mother. The bureau worker went to her hospital bedside to try to dissuade her. The case narrative evokes a scene that uncomfortably recalls an interrogation: "[Cathy] would sit with her head and eyes downcast ... [she] did, at one time, acknowledge that adoption was probably best for the baby and I thought that a small victory had been won with this admission." In the same interview, the worker asked again, "Did she want us to find a good adoptive home for her baby and [Cathy] finally and slowly nodded her head in the affirmative. With this she burst into hard long sobs and buried her head in the pillow." The CBD worker left, planning to bring relinquishment papers for her signature the next day.

When Cathy changed her mind again and indicated that she would not sign, the worker turned to Cathy's mother, who remained unconvinced. She did agree, though, that if Cathy wanted adoption she would not oppose it—a crucial concession, because Cathy was a minor and her mother would have to co-sign the relinquishment papers. When Cathy continued to demur, the bureau broke its own rules and accepted her baby for temporary foster care, hoping against hope that she would come around to recognizing the wisdom of an adoption plan. By this point, the worker had abandoned even the appearance of neutrality on the question: "I was quite open in saying that I couldn't see this plan [to raise the child herself] as working out either to [Cathy's] or the baby's interests."

This social worker intervened forcefully, and she recognized herself that she had crossed ordinary lines of professional objectivity by urging relinquishment. In this case, her commitment to "best interest" trumped therapeutic neutrality. Were her efforts an abuse of professional authority? She used her position to exert considerable pressure on a client who was rendered vulnerable by her youth, her troubled family situation, and her pregnancy. At the same time, she saw herself as an advocate for both Cathy and her baby, and in her judgment that meant encouraging adoption.

This story also reveals the limits of professional authority. Despite her social worker's energetic intervention, Cathy did not relinquish her daughter. In the end, the worker voluntarily restrained her own exercise of authority. Likely, given the girl's age and the suspicion of incest, the CBD could have sought and won a court-ordered termination of parental rights. Though convinced that relinquishment was the best course, the case worker ultimately accepted her client's decision.

The CBD social worker interpreted this outcome as a defeat; others might read it as a triumph of resistance. Cathy set her own course, defying both professional expertise and postwar conformity. In an emphatic claiming—or was it a disturbing over-identification?—she gave the little girl both her own first name and the pseudonym she had assumed during her maternity home stay. We do not know what became of her daughter, but Cathy herself continued on a troubled course. Her home life remained tumultuous. Less than a year after she had taken her baby home to her mother and stepfather, word reached the bureau that Cathy's mother was trying to commit her daughter (probably to Woods Haven, the local facility for delinquent girls), declaring her "unmanageable." By the time another year had passed, this troubled young woman had been admitted to the state mental hospital. Cathy's record ends with a newspaper clipping that announces her marriage. Whether or not this union supplied a happy ending for her, we do not know, but it does refute the common prediction that a disreputable past would render a woman unmarriageable.

Later accounts by birth mothers who regretted their decisions often portray the overwhelming pressures of parents and experts who insisted on adoption. But the historical record shows that even at the height of the best-solution rhetoric, alternative narratives persisted. Many women approached the bureau to plan relinquishment and then changed their minds; their experiences are captured in four hundred files marked "withdrawn." Some decided to raise their children themselves. Others placed their children with relatives or negotiated private adoptions (even after 1952). Some turned to foster care, hoping it would be a temporary expedient. Moreover, even when women did make adoption plans, some did so for their own reasons, and made it clear to social workers that they did not accept the reigning therapeutic narrative.

Some of the bureau's clients resisted social workers' views of sexuality and "illegitimacy." CBD social workers were aware that African American communities, among others, were tolerant of pregnancy out of wedlock. Even when African American women sought adoption for their children, they often refused to display the shame and penitence that social workers thought necessary for rehabilitation of problem girls. Instead, some clients undertook to educate their workers in the mores of their own communities. An African American woman, pregnant with her second child in 1957, had been born out of wedlock herself and instructed her social worker "that illegitimacy did not pose the problem for the Negro child that it did for the white child." A seventeen-year-old African American sought adoption for her expected child in 1956 because she wanted to finish high school, but she dismissed the CBD worker's efforts to get her to renounce non-marital sex. Instead, she counted herself unflinchingly as a member of the growing ranks of sexually active young women. "She claimed no problem about the illegitimacy angle and tended to excuse this on the basis that other girls do it and she is no better than other people." A twenty-one-year-old black woman informed her worker in 1957, "Nowadays everybody had illegitimate babies." Pregnant with her second out-of-wedlock child, another African American woman told her worker in 1953, "It's no disgrace."

This view was widely shared by white women from "downstate," as rural southern Delaware is known. A CBD worker recognized that her discussion of the stigma of illegitimacy was probably not finding a receptive audience when she talked with one such client in 1963. "I am not sure this means too much to her because she spent some time telling me all about all the girls on her street in [a town in rural Delaware] who have illegitimate babies and have kept them." In 1963, when the Wilmington FCH was filled to capacity, the bureau worker was inclined to discourage the application of a sixteen-year-old from downstate. She advised the girl that "the home's experience has been that girls from the very rural sections of Sussex County where illegitimacy seems to be less of a stigma, are more apt to change their minds."

In still other cases, white women endorsed views of sexuality that foreshadowed the more widespread rejection of middle-class morality in the 1960s. Awaiting the birth of her child at a maternity home in 1955, one fifteen-year-old girl proved a hard case for the bureau worker, who found her "uncommunicative" and thus not readily susceptible to the talking cure offered by social work intervention. Shamelessly leading the witness, the social worker elicited only defiance. "When I wondered how she felt about getting pregnant under these circumstances, if perhaps she felt guilty, she let me know that she did not feel guilty and added that after all it is no sin." The worker soldiered on sternly—"I said some people thought it was a sin"—but to no avail. (This young woman was considering adoption not to save her reputation but because she did not want to take her baby back to a conflict-ridden home with her stepmother and father.) In a 1954 case, an eighteen-year-old client who had just given birth to a son shrugged off her social worker's warnings about the disgrace of single motherhood: "The way she talked it sounded as though almost every girl in this high school had either had an illegitimate baby or an abortion and yet had come back to school and resumed their place in the community [a predominantly working-class town in Pennsylvania]." Young women like these resisted social workers' diagnoses even as they sought their help.

If workers were preoccupied with the stigma of illegitimacy, some of their clients were more concerned about the stigma of relinquishment. Disapproval of adoption was pervasive among African Americans. One twenty-year-old single mother, pregnant with her third child in 1963, struggled to maintain her plan for adoption even though "anyone she talks with thinks it is terrible that she is giving this child away." A fourteen-year-old black girl entered the FCH home in 1963 hoping to salvage her dreams of becoming a lawyer. There, she faced the concerted opposition of her mother and her minister, backed by other family members who "think anybody who will give a baby up is hard as iron." A fifteen-year-old who wanted adoption in 1957 encountered resistance from the baby's father and his mother, who told her, "It is awful to give up a baby." Indeed, the stigma surrounding adoption was so great among Delaware's black communities that some women sought the confidentiality of maternity homes not because they were shamed by their pregnancies but because they wanted to conceal their adoption plans.

Like African American communities, white rural and working-class communities often censured relinquishing mothers. An eighteen-year-old white woman faced her girlfriends' disapproval when she considered adoption for her newborn son in 1954. When her married lover reneged on his promise to get a divorce in 1959, a twenty-one-year-old factory worker came to the bureau to discuss adoption for her expected child. But she decided to keep her child, influenced by her father's strong opposition to adoption. It was "not right," he believed, claiming the child for their family. According to the social worker, "They keep and take care of what they have." A working-class woman considered adoption in 1957, with the support of her parents. But her sister weighed in, telling her that "the neighbors would think a great deal more of her if she kept her baby than if she gave it up," and in the end, she took her baby home.

Evangelical communities—both white and African American congregations—represented yet another strand of cultural resistance to the best solution. Women in Delaware's Pentecostal churches were shamed by out-of-wedlock pregnancies and sometimes made their way to the bureau in hopes of concealing their transgressions from their religious communities. However, when Pentecostal ministers and congregations learned of such plans, they intervened to prevent adoption. Though these communities disapproved emphatically of sex outside marriage, they believed relinquishment compounded the sin.

Women who felt they had been pressured to relinquish might well have wished for the support of relatives or communities such as these. And yet CBD records provocatively suggest that familial or communal opposition to adoption might also operate as an instrument of coercion. These women's stories forcibly remind us of the ambiguity and moral complexity of choice under constrained circumstances. We have women's testimony that some felt coerced to relinquish, pressured by middle-class morality, parents' expectations, and their own vulnerability and limited resources. We also have historical evidence of women who kept children that they themselves felt unable to raise. Some changed their decision about adoption in response to pressure from friends and family members. Married women were a special case: some of them were unable to relinquish because their spouses wielded their legal power to refuse consent. And, most troubling of all, we have startling evidence of women who decided to relinquish, only to be refused by the bureau.

One lengthy record illustrates the ambiguity of "choice" in a situation of intense family conflict. When bureau workers found themselves in the middle of mother-daughter struggles, they tried to make sure that their pregnant clients were making a decision that was really their own—a professional ethic complicated, though, by the legal requirement of parental consent when the relinquishing mother was a minor. When Joanne got pregnant at sixteen, her "domineering" mother marched her to the agency to make an adoption plan. But when Joanne agreed that adoption would be best, her mother abruptly changed tactics, "indicating that if she keeps the baby maybe it will 'learn' her a lesson." Soon after, this mother left a message informing the bureau that its services were no longer needed: the baby would remain with them. Suspicious of this sudden change of heart, the social worker recorded her concern that Joanne had been browbeaten by her mother. So she ignored the dismissal, noting in the record, "I decided I might try to find a way back into the situation." After the baby was born, a hospital social worker asked her to affirm her decision to raise the child herself; in response, "Joanne indicated that she would prefer to give the baby up." The bureau worker then visited Joanne in the hospital and concluded, "I do believe that given a free choice, she would want adoption for her baby." In the end, Joanne took the baby home.

Was Joanne coerced, and by whom? What did this young woman really want? The social worker acknowledged the ambiguity of the situation in her case summary, for "a part of Joanne's wish for adoption seemed to me to be based also on the fact that she would be in opposition to anything her mother wanted." She predicted, "Unless there is some shift within the family relationships I can see Joanne continuing on with many more illegitimate pregnancies." Joanne did soon return to the bureau, pregnant again, and wanting to keep the child. Her mother, though, was insisting on adoption—and then, again, when Joanne agreed, her mother changed *her* mind and insisted that Joanne would keep her expected child. The record remains intractably ambiguous on Joanne's real wishes in this battle of wills. And how are we to regard the outcome? One might say that her mother's support enabled her to raise her two children as a single mother. Bureau workers, by contrast, saw it as the unfortunate perpetuation of a history of family pathology—one that left two children hostage to the struggle between this daughter and her overbearing mother.

A pregnant woman's choices were often complicated by her own am-bivalence and the pressure of family members. In 1971 a twenty-nine-year old woman gave birth to her fifth child, and called the bureau to re-quest adoption. A waitress, she was already hard pressed to support the four children in her care. None of the children's fathers paid child sup-port, and she had no expectation of getting any help from this child's fa-ther. As soon as they learned of this plan, though, her mother and sister (with whom she lived) protested vehemently. Her CBD worker inter-vened to try to bolster her decision to relinquish: "I helped her to think that even though the two closest people of her family might disagree with her thinking, that she had a primary responsibility to herself and her children and that this should take precedence over what her rela-tives choose. This would be her life, her child and the decision she will need to live with. I for one could see how adoption could offer a lot more than she could under the circumstances." The bureau's view of choice relied on assumptions about individual autonomy that had little relevance in this client's life. She did have to live with her decision, as her social worker said. But she also had to live with her mother and sis-ter, who were undoubtedly crucial resources for this single mother and her children. She ended up keeping her last-born child, resolving, "She will manage somehow."

Social workers were keenly aware of the influence of relatives, espe-cially mothers, on women's decisions; as part of assessing the likelihood that a woman would follow through with her plan to relinquish, they routinely asked clients what their mothers thought about adoption. Counseling a married woman in 1962, the case worker urged her to tell

her mother about her adoption plan before the baby was born. Mrs. P,
mother of a toddler, was separating from an abusive husband and concerned that she could not support two children on her own. But when
the baby was born, she changed her mind. Her worker believed she had
been unduly pressured by her mother: "It seemed as though Mrs. P was
no match for her mother who did not approve of adoption . . . I can
only hope that Mrs. P's decision to keep her baby was her own." In 1961,
a twenty-one-year old African American college student came to the
bureau late in her pregnancy, struggling with family members who opposed adoption. Her social worker lamented that she had been refused
at FCH (since she was so near term): "I felt more than ever it was regret-
table that maternity home care was not available because she certainly
could use the support and protection in order to carry through her plan
of adoption." When the baby was born, her father called to report, "almost triumphantly," in the social worker's estimation, that she had decided to keep the baby.

As another case suggests, communal opposition to relinquishment
was sometimes directly at odds with women's aspirations for upward
mobility. One African American woman wanted to place her child for
adoption in order to pursue her dream of becoming a nurse. Twenty-
one years old, Lorna knew the sting of racism; she told her social worker
she had been rejected from one hospital school of nursing because of
her color. Instead, she worked as a nurses' aid, where coworkers urged
her to become a licensed practical nurse, the next notch up in the nursing hierarchy. But the spirited young woman resolved to earn her RN:
"She had no interest in becoming a practical nurse when she knew she
had the ability to be a graduate nurse and she was not content to be second best just because her skin was the wrong color."

Her unexpected pregnancy in 1957 threatened these aspirations. Engaged to the birth father, Lorna had seen her marriage prospects disappear abruptly when her fiancé impregnated another woman, eighteen
years old, and then yielded to her family's insistence that he marry her.
Adoption seemed the only way to secure her hoped-for future: "She said
that if she had to be responsible for a baby she would just never be able
to amount to anything and she wanted most of all to continue her education." But in the face of family opposition, she gave up her plan for

adoption and instead moved in with a cousin who cared for the baby while she worked. Smart and ambitious, perhaps Lorna found a way to realize her dream even as she supported her son. Still, her story suggests the ways in which communal claims constricted women's choices, even as they affirmed women as single mothers.

A married woman in Delaware could not relinquish a child without her husband's consent, regardless of whether or not he was the biological father. (By contrast, unmarried fathers had no legal rights to children until the 1970s.) Sometimes, women who were separated but still legally married sought adoption to hide their pregnancies from estranged husbands, fearing that the men would use their sexual misdeeds against them in child custody battles. Bureau workers then had the unhappy task of explaining that husbands held parental rights to any child born in the marriage, and thus their consent was required to execute a relinquishment. Very often, women in this situation then promptly disappeared from the bureau's records.

Husbands sometimes withheld consent to adoption to control or punish wives who were trying to leave them. In 1954 one woman was planning to separate from her husband only to find herself surprised by another pregnancy. She wanted to place this expected child for adoption, for she and her husband had two daughters already. In and out of jail, he supported them only erratically, and she was already struggling to provide for herself and the two girls. But he refused his consent: "He said all she wanted to do was have a big time. That's the only reason he won't sign." Later in the pregnancy he agreed to the adoption plan, but then changed his mind when the baby was born. Without her husband's consent, Mrs. Z had no recourse but to keep the child.

Another young woman had left her abusive husband to escape his beatings and was living with her parents as she awaited the birth of her second child in 1972. She applied to the bureau to plan adoption for the expected baby, concerned that she could not support two children as a single mother. Mrs. D feared that her husband would refuse to sign relinquishment papers: "He wants to get back at her for leaving him and going home." In this case, the bureau resolved to go to court on behalf of Mrs. D: the agency was prepared to seek involuntary termination of this husband's parental rights if he tried to oppose his wife's adoption plans. Most often, though, wives could rely only on persuasion and good will when they sought husbands' consent for adoption.

The most sobering examples of women's constrained choices lie in the largely forgotten underside of the history of African American adoption. African American communities have often been outspoken in disapproval of relinquishment. Some contemporary evidence suggests that, compared to other groups, African Americans remain somewhat reserved in their endorsement of formal "stranger" adoption. In a 1997 survey, for example, more than twice as many black as white respondents believed that "adoptive parents get less satisfaction out of raising an adopted child," and just half, compared to 70 percent of whites, agreed that "it is very likely adopted children will love their adoptive parents as much as they would have loved the parents who gave birth to them."[47] Still, other studies have found that African Americans adopt children in the same proportions as do whites (once data are controlled for class).[48] And many observers have noted the widespread practice of informal adoption in black communities, evidence of another form of child-sharing and communal provision for child welfare. At times, such practices and attitudes have been celebrated as cultural resistance to the individualism of the best solution. Historian Rickie Solinger, for example, writes that "the black community organized itself to accommodate mother and child while the white community was totally unwilling and unable to do so."[49] But these communal bonds were repressive as well as sustaining. Moreover, black women did not simply eschew adoption. Instead, most had no choice but to seek alternatives, since they were virtually excluded from agency adoption.

CBD records show that black women turned to adoption for the same reasons as did many white women: because they wanted educational opportunity and hoped to secure better prospects for their children than they could provide. But black women ended up relinquishing far less often that white women. However, that comparison is in itself profoundly misleading. Adoption was far more insecure and unpromising for black women and children—so much so that we cannot say that black and white women even operated within the same system. The low rate of relinquishment among African Americans reflected not only different cultural attitudes but also the stark constraints on black women's access to adoption. Indeed, postwar adoption can be seen as a striking instance of de facto segregation, evident even in the records of the CBD, an agency that served both black and white clients for its entire history.

Racial matching and racially based class disadvantage combined to raise formidable barriers to African American participation in formal adoption. The supply-and-demand situation that dominated white adoption was reversed for African Americans. That is, for years, African American children needing adoption heavily outnumbered black adopters and foster parents. Other studies have shown that black couples adopt in the same proportions as other groups, but not in numbers large enough to accommodate the greater numbers of black children needing homes. The imbalance, then, bespeaks the economic disadvantages of African American communities: hard-pressed families were seldom in a position to extend their meager resources to strangers, and black couples who did apply for adoption were likely to find that they did not meet agency requirements. Meanwhile, the mandate of racial matching was so strong that very few agencies were willing to consider white adopters, in abundant supply, as prospective parents for African American children. The adoption services available to black women and their children were, in practice, separate and unequal.

The adoption prospects of a black child had long been uncertain, and this knowledge undoubtedly influenced some women's decisions about relinquishment. As a white woman contemplated relinquishment, she too faced the fear of consigning her child to an unknown fate; but her confidence in the promises of the best solution was well founded. Agencies could select from a large pool of eager applicants hoping to adopt, weeding out prospective liabilities and enhancing the prospects of a good "match." White women had good reason, then, to believe that their children would fare well in adoptive families. Black women could have no such confidence. They knew, or learned, that black children without their parents often grew up in foster care—sometimes in long-term and loving homes but without the assurance of permanency. Moreover, as social workers were uneasily aware, adoption itself did not always clearly enhance the life chances of black children. The shortage of black adopters meant that the agency had to apply more lenient standards to African American applicants, and at the same time, the constrictions of racism flattened the economic profile of the African American community: adopters, like birth parents, confronted limited educational opportunity, narrow job prospects, housing and social discrimination. Indeed, in a bitter irony, the black women most likely to relinquish—women with real prospects of mobility themselves—were also probably the least likely to improve their child's life chances through adoption. A white college student who relinquished could be almost certain that her child would be placed with adopters who could and would send a child to college; a child of a black college student, by contrast, was much less likely to be placed with adopters who could support such aspirations.

The most immediate deterrent to adoption, though, was the threat of outright rejection from the agency. After 1951, as the CBD specialized in adoption, it accepted children into care only under the presumption of relinquishment—and, tacitly, with the bureau's expectation that it would be able to place the child for adoption. Most white women who sought to relinquish their children never even realized that there was some chance that the agency would turn them away. After 1940, only a half-dozen records document refusals of white clients. By contrast, black women routinely faced the prospect that their child would be rejected. Social workers warned their African American clients that the agency could not guarantee placement, owing to an acute shortage of foster homes and a chronic dearth of black adopters. This caveat undermined and complicated the agency's own prescribed course, in which a woman's studied deliberation led to a firm decision. The scarcity of foster and adoptive homes for black children introduced a nearly insupportable burden of uncertainty about the timing and execution of relinquishment. A white woman who made the decision could sign as soon as she was ready. A black woman had to wait until a home was ready—and, in the meantime, she had to assume responsibility for her child's care.

Bureau workers were well aware that this condition tipped the balance for many black women who were considering adoption. Miss D supported three children already, with her mother's help, some assistance from the father of two of her children, and her wages as a worker in a food processing plant. In 1963, when she discovered she was pregnant again, she tried to abort at home, with help from the birth father. When their efforts failed, he denied paternity, and Miss D then turned to adoption. But as her pregnancy advanced, Miss D found her resolve tested by friends and family, who vigorously argued that she would regret relinquishing her child. In the end, she withdrew her application.

Was Miss D enabled to keep her child, with the support of her community, or was she coerced by the friends and relatives who discouraged her adoption plan? Her social worker advanced another explanation. She believed that Miss D had turned away from adoption, in part, because she realized how little the bureau could offer her, as she mused in her summary: "It may be that her decision . . . is partly influenced by her knowledge of our dire foster home situation and the fact that there more than likely would have been a great delay in our taking her baby."

For Miss S, the bureau's provisional commitment likely rendered a difficult decision all but impossible. Nineteen years old, she was already caring for a toddler, with some help from the child's father. Pregnant again in 1960, she applied to the bureau for adoption services after her expected child's father denied paternity. She soon felt the pressure of the concerted opposition of her mother and siblings; as her social worker noted, "It's been a little hard for Miss S to keep to her course of adoption which to her seems right." As her social worker recognized, the bureau's routine caveat came as a staggering blow. "When I had to tell her about the uncertainty even doubtfulness that we would have a home for her baby when it was needed, this was really quite distressing for her and despite her effort to hold back tears they did pour forth and I think she was really quite hurt. In one sense I suppose it's doubly hard because she has taken a stand against her family in favor of adoption only to told now by me that it might be hard if not impossible anyway." The case worker tried to help Miss S figure out an interim plan, in case a home was not available, but her client, she reported, was very upset and seemed "stymied." When her baby was born, she turned to other resources, resolving to sue the father for child support and perhaps to apply for ADC.

When she became pregnant in 1965, sixteen-year-old Brenda felt adoption was the best decision for her expected child. Her parents agreed; they had already told her they could not take the baby into their home. Nonetheless, Brenda ended up keeping her child. Her case worker felt certain that the bureau's limited service was the reason. "If I could have given Brenda any kind of assurance that her baby would be placed directly for adoption or shortly thereafter, I feel certain she would have followed through with a minimal amount of conflict and upset." Instead, learning that it was "most unlikely" that the bureau could place her child, Brenda prevailed upon her parents, who "begrudgingly accepted the fact that [she] needed to bring her baby home." The worker summarized, "Brenda could not bear this kind of uncertainty. She had too much fear and guilt that the baby might never be adopted and might fare worse than if she had kept him." Such outcomes strained social workers' own equanimity, for they recognized that the bureau was failing black clients who shared their own assessment of adoption as the best solution. "I had tremendous feeling about the CB's inability to meet the needs of Brenda and her baby," she lamented at the end of this record.

When Brenda became pregnant again in 1967, she tried determinedly to abort. First, she traveled to New York in hopes of getting an abortion there. Unsuccessful, she returned home to make two separate attempts to abort, once taking quinine and another time using turpentine and sugar. Still pregnant, she turned to the CBD. The bureau failed her again. As her case worker summed up in an unusually blunt note, when the baby was born, Brenda "was forced to keep him because of CB's inability to provide placement . . . she had a difficult time accepting the fact and I was very concerned for her and her baby . . . She was extremely depressed."

In a few cases, African American women did follow through with adoption plans even though the bureau was not able to help immediately. Miss R, mother of one child, was living with her parents and an older sister, also a single mother. When she learned she was pregnant again in 1958, she was certain that she could not take responsibility for a second. The bureau did not have a home for the child when it was born, though. Miss R took the baby home and cared for her for two months, during which, her social worker believed, she "never wavered" in her decision for adoption. When the bureau did find a placement for the little girl, a "very composed" Miss R brought her to the agency and "reaffirmed her decision of adoption." It was not surprising, though, that few women could summon such resolve.

By the mid-1950s, the National Urban League had identified the dearth of adoption services as an instance of discrimination. In speeches, committee reports, and internal memoranda, NUL affiliates refuted arguments that African American communities did not need adoption services because they took care of their own through informal arrangements. "The Negro family has often been forced to meet its needs as best it could with whatever resources it had. The fact that Negro families 'take in' another child is no excuse for the lack of adequate and needed services for potentially adoptable children."[50] Commenting on black women's lower rates of relinquishment, another observer challenged the view that such women were choosing to raise their children, enabled by the tolerance of their communities. Instead, the writer concluded, "It is a fact that many agencies will not encourage Negro unmarried mothers to surrender their babies and, in fact, actively discourage such surrenders because of the dearth of adoptive families. Thus, in essence, many of these young women are not confronted with a free choice as how to proceed."[51] As another NUL member understood, adoption was a vehicle for upward mobility denied to most black mothers and their children: "In the adoption picture which offers ten families for every white child available for adoption, the guarantee of the American ideal is not out of reach. On the other hand, when only one family is available for every seven Negro children, the American dream for them fades unless *we* are willing to see that they have at least an equal chance of a life with parents of their own."[52] The experience of African American women and children marks the boundaries of the expansive postwar consensus: adoption was a strategy of upward mobility that, in practice, benefited whites almost exclusively.

For all women, discussion of relinquishment has frequently focused too narrowly on the drama of an individual at a moment of consequential decision. A larger understanding of relinquishment requires us to bring into view the prospects that women faced as single mothers—what social workers termed "realities." For many women, the primary motivation for adoption was their pressing awareness of the limits of their resources—social, emotional, and financial. In bureau case narratives, those women who were already single mothers knew these necessities from experience. One after another, they told social workers that they were turning to adoption because they were "unable to care for another child." CBD records document the formidable array of daunting circumstances that led women to this conclusion.

Most single mothers faced severe financial constraints. The bureau encouraged single mothers to consider paternity suits to compel reluctant fathers to help support their children. Not infrequently, men disappeared upon receiving the news of their impending paternity, placing themselves beyond the reach of any claims that might result. Many women themselves were loath to undergo the public scrutiny of Family Court, and even successful paternity suits were no guarantor of regular child support payments. A nineteen-year-old single mother, expecting her third child in 1965, rejected the suggestion that she seek child support: "Miss S knew from experience that if she did take him to Court, she would not get very much money anyhow and then there was the matter of having to always keep after them and going back to Court when the father does not make his payments, etc." As some recognized, or learned, a court order was a futile measure against a man who himself had no secure access to a living wage. The mother of a young drugstore clerk urged her daughter to take the father of her expected child to court in 1947. But she was reluctant to face the censure of Family Court, and besides, she recognized, since the man was unemployed she was unlikely to get financial help from him even if she obtained a court order. In a 1950 case, Family Court had sent Mrs. M's husband to the Workhouse when he repeatedly failed to pay mandated child support, "but she felt that was not the answer since what she needed was the money." Pregnant by another man, she doubted that he would be any more responsive to a court order, since he was in a common-law relationship with another woman and not likely to have any money to spare. Some independent-minded women preferred to rely on their own resources. One such woman was annoyed to learn that her mother had gone to her boyfriend's mother, hoping to enlist her support in getting her son to pay the girl's hospital bill, at least. She didn't want his money, she told her social worker in 1956, because then he would "think he owned me and the baby too."

Social workers also advised their clients to apply for public support. But Aid to Dependent Children required that single mothers attempt paternity suits before they could qualify for benefits, a step that many were unwilling to take. ADC benefits were often grossly inadequate, as illustrated in case records. When a single mother appealed to the bureau for help in 1956, the social worker found that "her ADC budget is only $75 a month and she pays $50 of that for rent." In another case, Mrs. B was seeking temporary placement for her children in 1957. Her husband was in jail, and she was struggling desperately to care for her five children. Impoverished and indebted, she still hoped to become a licensed practical nurse and then, perhaps, a registered nurse. The Department of Public Welfare, which referred her to the bureau, blamed the miserly administration of ADC for her situation: "According to our agency budget Mrs. B had a total monthly need of $214, [but] legislative maximum limited our grant to $121." Some bureau clients avoided ADC because of the widespread stigma of dependence on "the welfare." In the 1950s, single mothers and their children were excluded by policy from another source of public support: as noted in a number of CBD case records, housing projects would not accept families "unless there is a man and a bread winner."

The low wages of "women's work" kept single mothers and their children on the margins of economic survival. Few of the occupations represented in CBD records would have enabled a woman to sustain herself and her children. The bureau's single mothers were household workers, waitresses, hospital workers, retail clerks, beauticians, bank tellers, and clerical workers; others labored in Delaware's poultry processing plants (aptly known as "chicken factories"), or in the few light industries in the state, such as leather-processing and glove-making shops. Sex work was more remunerative; a few of the CBD's clients told their social workers that they earned their livings as "exotic dancers" in local clubs, or as prostitutes.

Finding child care during working hours posed formidable difficulties for single mothers. St. Michael's Home for Children was the only public child care mentioned in pre-World War II CBD records, and it accepted only children over three years old. During the war, the Works Progress Administration operated a day nursery in Wilmington.

Seeking foster care for her three-year-old so she could accept shift work in 1942, one woman learned from the bureau that the nursery was planning to extend its hours into the evening. "Her face lighted up" with relief, the social worker noted.

With little public child care, Delaware's single mothers relied on a patchwork of informal and public assistance. Many lived with their own parents or other relatives, contributing their wages to the household in exchange for child care. A few pooled resources by sharing households with other single mothers and their children. Some had landladies or neighbors who cared for their children during the day, though paid child care pared down a meager paycheck to even less. All of these arrangements were subject to sudden renegotiation as caregivers became ill, moved away, or took other jobs themselves. In the midst of such transitions, single mothers often lost their jobs because they had missed work or been late too many times. CBD records are full of women who turned to the bureau for foster care because they desperately needed to earn a wage and had exhausted the available options for child care. Overwhelmed and discouraged, some sought to place older children for adoption rather than continue to raise them in penury. In a 1950s case, for example, a single mother of three children applied to place all of them for adoption. The record summarized a dilemma common to many single mothers: "If she works she does not earn enough money to pay a baby sitter and keep the household going otherwise and when she lives on ADC as she is doing now she gets only $99 a month which hardly keeps them decently."

What does it mean to speak of choice in such circumstances? Certainly, a liberal model of choice—as a broad menu of options from which individuals can freely select—has limited relevance to these women's lives. Their options were narrow, and they were rarely in a position to make choices as unconstrained individuals. Instead, they made decisions as members of families and communities, decisions both enabled and constrained by the people around them. In many ways, they lived in dependency, confined by women's inequality and by class and racial oppression. As mothers, they confronted the formidable responsibility conferred by children's dependence.

CBD workers knew that single mothers could manage; they worked with them daily. They also knew that motherhood severely constrained the prospects of such women and limited their children's futures. Against communal resistance to adoption, CBD workers held out the possibility of individual mobility. The tension between CBD's endorsement of the best solution and local communities' resistance to adoption was a replay of classic American conflicts about upward mobility. Social workers wanted to extend the possibilities of social mobility to women. Communitarian values, by contrast, offered a modicum of security at the cost of immobility.

The "best solution" commanded broad support between World War II and 1970. The flourishing adoption practice of those years both confirms and complicates the critique of adoption that emerged by the end of the twentieth century. In many ways, adoption did serve as an instrument of repressive sexual and domestic ideologies. In their prescriptions for adoptive mothers and single women pregnant out of wedlock, social workers firmly endorsed postwar conformity. They sought adopters who conformed to the ideal of motherhood approved by psychology and celebrated in popular culture. Counseling single women, they used a therapeutic narrative that encouraged clients to renounce their sexual transgressions and to return to the path of respectable marriage and motherhood. Social workers willingly served a system that confined women within the gender ideologies of domesticity and sexual respectability. At the same time, though, they recognized the acute inequalities that bore down upon women, and they resisted the most punitive policing of gender boundaries by refusing to consign gender transgressors to the margins of postwar society. Compassionate observers of the harsh realities of single mothers' lives, social workers expressed no larger vision of the kind of social change that might enable single women and their children to live in security and dignity. But neither were they complacent about the victims of social inequality. Social workers reached out to society's most vulnerable members—women and dependent children—seeking to make a place for them at the table of postwar prosperity.

4

Redrawing the Boundaries:
Transracial and International Adoption

In ringing testimony to the pervasive environmentalism of the era of the "best solution," some adopters reached beyond the "as if begotten" family to claim children of other nations and races as their own. For some, international adoption was an extension of the United States' global mission in the twentieth century, a way to sweep the world's needy children into the peace and prosperity of the much-touted "American century." For others, it was reparation for that century's history of bloody wars. American adopters reached out to children orphaned, displaced, or rejected in Korea, and later in Vietnam. In countries around the world—China, India, Russia, Romania, Ecuador, Peru, El Salvador, Mexico, and others—Americans sought sons and daughters among children who were casualties of political oppression, civil war, poverty, and hunger. At home, longstanding racial barriers were breached as, for the first time, white adopters embraced African American and American Indian children as their own. Though biracial children had long been accepted by African American adopters, adoption across racial boundaries became more visible culturally and was renamed "transracial adoption," as white adopters, too, extended themselves to children born of interracial unions.

Adoptions like these had a newly public face, and not only because members of such adoptive families were often visually identifiable as biological strangers. For some adopters, their interracial families were visible signs of their personal commitment to postwar ideals of racial integration. "The personal is political," the New Left would declare in the early 1960s; for some adopters, that translated into the resolve to break down racial barriers in the family as well as at the voting booth, the lunch counter, and the work place. Some white adopters saw in their interracial families a hopeful harbinger of an imagined future—beyond tolerance and civil rights to color-blind mutuality, the vision Martin Luther King, Jr., had named the blessed community. Similarly, for some adopters of children from other countries, their "rainbow" families expressed a Judeo-Christian ethos of humanitarian outreach that affirmed human community over ethnic and racial difference. In the case of white adoption of American Indian children, the social engineering of the best solution reached its apogee in a mass transfer of children from impoverished reservations to middle-class communities. Between 1958 and 1967, about seven hundred American Indian children were placed with white adopters through the Indian Adoption Project, a collaborative effort of the Bureau of Indian Affairs and the Child Welfare League of America.[1] Initiated as postwar culture proclaimed American assimilation and tolerance against Nazi racism and Communist dictatorship, adoptions across racial and international borders seemed a seamless extension of a national ethos. But as the political climate shifted, some critics at home and abroad saw them as galling examples of white arrogance and American global domination.

Adoptions such as these pose a provocative test of the limits and character of American pluralism. They were and are exceptional, never accounting for more than a small percentage of placements. Adoptions of African American children by white parents, unknown before the 1950s, never became common; they represented no more than two or three percent of all adoptions even at their peak in 1971.[2] Crossing the most enduring and significant racial boundary in American history, such adoptions have been marked as controversial and named as "other" most consistently: "transracial" adoption, in most contexts, means adoption of African American children by white adopters.

Adoption of American Indian children by white parents is now virtually outlawed, rendering these particular adoptive families a historical artifact of a now-repudiated social experiment. In parts of the country without large American Indian populations, such adoptive families were probably not clearly marked as transracial. Some "passed" as matching families, and others were likely recognized as "different" in a way that was not necessarily categorized as racial difference.

Widely publicized stories of international adoption have produced the perception that such families now constitute the typical adoptive family; but they, too, remain in the minority. International adoption represented only 15–20 percent of the adoptions finalized in 1993.[3] Many of such adoptions were also "transracial" according to one common postwar categorization (black, yellow, white, red, and brown), but by the late twentieth century, people native to Asia and Latin America were not consistently accounted as racial "others" in the United States. Still, such families were recognized as "non-matching" even when observers could not specify what made them different. By contrast, Russian and Romanian children—even those who might be regarded as ethnic "others" in their own country, such as the highly stigmatized gypsies of Romania—were a match because they were considered white in the cultural lexicon of race in the United States at the end of the millennium.

Transracial and transnational families violate the boundaries of adoption in two directions. The relationship of family members to one another, in most cases, is visibly and irrefutably not "as if begotten." These families face together the pain of ethnic and racial discriminations directed against some of their members. Internally, they deal with perceptions of difference among family members that are shaped, in part, by larger histories of power and inequality and by cultural categories of race, ethnicity, and national origin. Such placements also create adoptive families that are themselves subject to boundary violations. Because most are visually identifiable as adoptive families, they lose the privacy available to the "matching" adoptive family. Unlike most adopters and adopted persons, who can decide when and to whom to disclose adoption, unmatched families are subject to routine invasions of privacy as others observe and comment upon their difference. For families themselves and for the communities in which they find themselves— whether their extended families, their neighborhoods, their cities, their nation, or the world—adoption across these boundaries raises, with new intensity, overarching questions about what makes a family, who belongs, and how family members and others negotiate difference.

As adoption reached its peak numbers of 1970, few would have predicted the broad critique that would ultimately challenge every tenet of the best solution. The conflict over transracial adoption was the first consequential expression of that critique, a signal of the social changes that would reconfigure the practice and cultural meanings of adoption. The American civil rights movement reached a historic divide by the late 1960s, as some African Americans, disillusioned with the gradualist and conciliatory politics of integration, asserted a nationalist agenda. This shift fundamentally reshaped adoption after 1972, when the National Association of Black Social Workers declared its opposition to the placement of African American children with white foster or adoptive parents. These adoptions, never numerous, dropped down to under a thousand per year by 1975. Soon after, some American Indians likewise took up the politics of nationalism, pressing historic claims to tribal autonomy. As part of that movement, activists forcefully protested the adoption of American Indian children outside of their tribal communities. For them, the American Indian project became a potent symbol of the damage inflicted by paternalistic outsiders, and in response they demanded and won tribal control of child placement in the 1978 Indian Child Welfare Act. At the end of the twentieth century, transracial adoption remained controversial.

The critique of transracial adoption challenged but did not overturn postwar universalism among adopters. Though nationalist claims fundamentally reshaped domestic adoption, some adopters continued to cross racial lines as they searched the world for children. Though many children from other countries were recognizable as ethnic "others," they often eluded assignment to available American racial categories. Such children did not escape entirely the racism and xenophobia directed toward stigmatized outsiders, but unlike black or biracial children of white adopters, they did not experience the stress that comes from transgressing racial boundaries established by long histories of power and oppression. As the century ended, the conflict over domestic transracial adoption continued to smolder while international adoption expanded—an indication of the ambiguous and contradictory status of adoption in the era that dismantled the best solution.

By the early 1970s, transracial and international placements were arranged in an environment of scarcity. The perennial imbalance in adoption, in which white adopters outnumbered available children of their own race, eventually undid the entire system of social-work adoption practice represented by agencies like the CBD. "Healthy white baby" was a request deemed "unrealistic" by social workers in the 1970s. At the CBD as elsewhere, social workers would warn adopters that restricting their options by race, age, and state of health would drastically reduce their chances of becoming parents at all. In response, some turned away from traditional agencies to pursue their quests for healthy white babies through independent adoption. Others would embrace a new vision of adoptive parenthood. They would reach out to older children, or those challenged by illness, disability, or psychological problems. Still others would relinquish the "as if begotten" family by extending their searches across racial and national boundaries.

Adoptions across national and racial lines have claimed a public visibility disproportionate to their actual numbers, a measure of the ways in which such families remain provocative—evoking utopian possibility, for some; and for others, providing a galling instance of white privilege at home and abroad. The charged debates emerge in newspaper and magazine coverage and find expression in fiction and film. Such adoptions are also documented in a spate of contemporary memoirs by adoptive parents. These sources offer maps of the cultural landscape of transracial and international adoption, supplementing the evidence of case records and professional literature.

At the CBD and elsewhere, racial and ethnic matching gave way well before the changing demographics of adoption in the 1970s. By the mid-1950s, social workers at the CBD and elsewhere no longer assumed racial matching as a given. Instead, they routinely asked white adopters if they would consider "Oriental," American Indian, "Negro," or mixed-race children as family members. The bureau itself did not handle international adoptions, but CBD social workers could refer interested prospective adopters to Welcome House, a branch of the organization established by Pearl S. Buck in 1949 for adoption of Amerasian children born of Korean women and American servicemen. The CBD was a participant in the national American Indian adoption project, and thus its records afford a glimpse inside this short-lived and, ultimately, much maligned effort. Along with some other social work agencies, the CBD began to place a few African American children with white adopters, in a new response to the old problem of too few black adopters. Adoption across racial and national lines had become sufficiently common—or well publicized—by the late 1950s that some clients came to the bureau already aware of this possibility, or because they knew the agency placed American Indian children.

The first CBD records of transracial adoption are remarkable for their silence on the question of how racial difference might shape the lives of adoptive families. Instead, these home studies focused almost exclusively on a new kind of matching. Social workers explored adopters' feelings about racial difference through discussions of perceived appearance and qualities of children who would not "match" families visually. "Fitness" of white adopters for transracial placements was largely defined as parental acceptance of children's differences. These records were marked primarily by an expanded vocabulary of race. As adopters indicated their openness to a wider variety of children, the tacit consensus underlying racial matching was breached; clients and workers alike needed a new language for exploring the shifting boundaries of adoptive kinship. Case narratives of white adopters came to include the same nuanced lexicon of color, appearance, and racial assignment that had characterized African American home studies, and for the same reason. Notably, though, such records contain no discussion about parenting children of another race.

By comparison, both social workers and clients appeared to attach more significance to the child's sex. Home studies frequently revealed the widespread assumption that boys and girls presented distinctive pleasures and challenges. Moreover, parental preference alone did not settle the question of parental fitness to raise boys or girls: social workers sometimes decided that prospective adopters would not be good parents of one sex or the other, regardless of what these clients said about their preferences. In startling contrast, neither prospective adopters nor case workers seemed to consider that parenting a child of a different race might pose any distinctive challenges or require any special attributes of parents. At times, home studies did acknowledge the social pressures of race in discussions of whether or not white adopters' families and communities were likely to welcome children of color. But in effect, case workers accepted white adopters' self-assignments. If prospective adopters indicated their willingness to consider children of other races, and if they believed their immediate social environment would be supportive, social workers tended to take such declarations as adequate evidence of their fitness to raise these children.

Social workers applied their customary protocols in making transracial placements. They used interviews to probe adopters for more detail, to prompt disclosure, and to assess the sincerity and depth of stated preferences. For example, in placing American Indian children, social workers showed prospective adopters pictures of a number of such children as a way of clarifying and verifying their openness to observably "different" family members. When Mr. and Mrs. M came to the bureau in 1964 hoping to adopt an American Indian child, their case worker presented photographs and recorded their reaction: "They responded with sincere delight over the appearance of many of the Indian children in the pictures and seemed equally related to the child with the darker coloring, not seeming to pick out just the light color Indian." At the same time, the worker was mindful of the limitation that these adopters had expressed: they had considered the possibility of applying for a biracial (white and African American) child, but decided that this was not something they could undertake. She concluded, "I felt that the medium complexioned copper toned Indian complexion would be quite acceptable to the Ms while the very dark, black skinned Indian could present more of the problem they felt would be involved in the more Negro child."

Posing the same test to Mr. and Mrs. W in 1966, another CBD social worker "felt they would be ready for any degree of Indian and any complexion. In fact some of their most positive remarks seemed to be about some of the darker children." Another couple, parents of one child by birth, adopted an American Indian child and then returned in 1971 indicating they would consider a biracial (white and African American) girl. The record dealt with this unmatching family with the same protocols applied to other home studies, assessing the strength of racial preference compared to other preferences. For this couple, sex loomed larger than color, their social worker concluded: "They would both prefer the full Negro dark skinned child who was a girl far above the interracial child who was a boy."

The optimism of the early civil rights movement inspired some white adopters to claim African American children as their own. As Douglas Bates recalled in his memoir of their interracial family, "When Gloria and I adopted the girls [in 1970], race relations in the United States seemed to be brimming with hope and promise."[4] Consequently, he remembered, they gave little thought to the challenges they might face as an interracial family: "Compared with our adoption decision," he recalled wryly, "Gloria and I would expend far more time and energy a decade later researching the purchase of our first VCR."[5] Like the CBD, the agency where they applied—Oregon Children's Service Division— placed little emphasis on racial difference in the home study. It was enough for the prospective adopters to indicate that they had no preference about race. Four months later, the Bates became parents of an African American girl.

Relatively unmarked as "difference," these early transracial placements were testimony to the confidence in assimilation that expanded the boundaries of adoption in the 1950s and 1960s. They also tacitly embody another tenet of the postwar consensus: that the fact of adoption has little significance once the family is certified by law. Adoptive parents needed to disclose adoption sensitively to their children, but beyond that, home studies, manuals for adoptive parents, and social work literature assumed that the tasks of adoptive parents were no different than those of biological parents; thus, there was no advice literature on raising adopted children until the 1970s. At the same time, the records do register an underlying caution about the special challenges of interracial or international placements—families whose difference would be visible. CBD social workers framed a new and more capacious view of adoptive families when they asked white adopters if they wanted to consider Asian, American Indian, or African American children; the very question breached the old tacit consensus that had governed matching. But aware that clients might perceive even the question as pressure, social workers deliberately avoided doing anything more to encourage adopters to broaden their horizons. And, as ever, they approved adopters who minimized ethnic and racial difference. Of one white couple who had adopted a Cherokee daughter, the CBD social worker noted approvingly in 1964, "The Ys have been open and comfortable in acknowledging Suzy as an Indian child without seeming to be too inclined to overadvertise the fact unnecessarily." Her implied standard was faithful to postwar ideals of tolerance and social conformity.

Set apart by their visible difference, families of transracial and international adoption pressed the limits of the postwar conception of adoption as "substitute family" modeled on blood kinship. Such families proclaimed the possibility of kinship across groups separated by national and ethnic particularism and, sometimes, riven by long histories of discrimination, oppression, and conflict. Such adoptions were audacious assertions of American individualism and self-construction, celebrations of a family formed by private choice and unfettered by public life or history. The pluralistic ideology and ethnic diversity of a "nation of immigrants" rendered American society more open to adoption than any other country. In the 1990s, Americans claimed an estimated seven to ten thousand children a year from countries around the world, accounting for more than half of the world's transnational adoptions.[6]

As transracial adoptions became more common, they also became more clearly marked as different. By the mid-1960s, CBD workers were actively directing some adopters to such children. A new kind of matching emerged, in which "hard to place" children were assigned to adopters who were themselves considered lower priority by agencies. Fertile couples, for example, had long posed something of a dilemma to agencies. Most American agencies considered them less desirable as adopters. Since they were not motivated by the need that compelled infertile couples to broaden their ideas of parenthood, social workers worried that they might be less accepting of their adoptive children, or that adoptive children would feel themselves at a disadvantage in competition with siblings born to their adoptive parents. Many agencies excluded fertile adopters on the basis of a distributive logic: as white prospective adopters clamored to claim scarce children, social workers were reluctant to place children with parents who could have offspring by birth. Few agencies accepted fertile adopters on exactly the same terms as infertile adopters, and by the mid-1960s the CBD was openly advising such clients that they could not be considered for healthy white babies.

Mr. and Mrs. H arrived at the adoption of a biracial Indian-white child by this route. Early in 1966, Mrs. H called the bureau to inquire whether she and her husband could apply for adoption: they were parents of two children born to them and knew of no reason they could not give birth to another. They were told that "at the present time couples who could readily have children of their own could be considered for children not so much sought after by other families." Mr. and Mrs. H apparently had no trouble decoding this message, and seven months later they called to apply for an American Indian child, having read of this program in *Good Housekeeping*.

Fertile adopters reshaped—even subverted—the home study's vocabulary of motive. The postwar consensus promoted adoption as the equivalent of biological kinship—as a social kinship that could substitute for the family that nature had failed to provide. Fertile adopters, though, had no need for substitute kinship. Rather, they came to agencies because they chose to extend their families beyond the usual limits imposed by biology—and, often, for reasons that violated social work conceptions of adoptive parenthood. Social workers had long insisted that there was only one acceptable motive for adoption: the desire to raise a child as one's own. Adopters seeking children of other races or from abroad, though, often cited altruistic or political motives—the desire to help needy children; a commitment to limiting population growth; an affirmation of human solidarity across racial and national lines. Openly skeptical of such motives, social workers had long endorsed a personalistic vision of parenthood, centered on desire and sentiment. Implicitly, they also approved a democratic family balanced by a kind of parity of need, readily perceptible when infertile adopters longing for children were matched with children who needed homes. Within this kind of emotional exchange, social workers felt more confident that adopters would perceive their children as cherished gifts, not as second-best strangers or beholden wards. The demography of adoption among whites itself had long abetted this aim, undermining the notion of adopters as rescuers or benefactors; since available children were far outnumbered by prospective adopters, the calculus of need ran in the opposite direction.

In a significant reversal, social workers accepted altruistic and political motives in cases of transnational and international placements. In the mid-1960s, for example, Mr. and Mrs. S wanted to adopt an American Indian child because they "felt an Indian child probably needed parents more than some other children . . . They said that they had never thought from the beginning of adopting a White child, and this did not seem to be related to the feeling that there might not be a possibility of getting a White child to adopt, because they had a couple of children already"—and so, presumably, did not "need" another.

The bureau placed another American Indian child with white adopters who had one child by birth. Though they assumed they were still fertile, they wanted to expand their family by adopting a child with "special need for a family." A few years later, Mr. and Mrs. R returned to the bureau to adopt a child with African American and white parents. This time, they added a political spin to altruism: "They were not wanting to add to the population when they felt they could offer themselves as parents to children who might not otherwise have parents." Another couple, parents of one child by birth, advanced the same explanation in 1972: "[We] want a larger family but prefer not to bring any more children into the world but to adopt because of the many children in the world needing a family."

In part, this shift in perspective arose from social workers' uneasy awareness of the pressures of scarcity. They wanted to make sure that prospective adopters were not turning to unconventional adoptions out of desperation, a situation that social workers feared might end in unfortunate placements of children that adopters would come to regard as second best. In some of these adoptions, then, social workers seemed to value a focused intention to adopt a racially different child even over the much-vaunted "flexibility" that they had come to prize by the 1950s. Prospective adopters who already had children, they believed, were more likely to accept a child who could not have been born to them. Or perhaps social workers themselves felt more confident that such applicants were truly choosing these children, since they did not "need" adoption to expand their families.

Case records suggest an underlying doubt that visibly different children could join a family as the full equivalents of biological kin. Consider, for example, the revealing home study of a young childless couple, who in 1972 came to the bureau in hopes of adopting an "interracial" child (with one African American and one white parent). Hesitant at the outset, their social worker became even more wary as she considered their potential fertility. Their medical report provided no clear explanation for their inability to conceive, and the social worker suspected that Mr. and Mrs. A still hoped for a pregnancy. Mrs. A "visibly cooled" upon receiving the bureau's standard instructions about practicing contraception during the home study. Social workers were always alert to signs that adopters were not really reconciled to infertility—and therefore possibly were turning to adoption reluctantly. In this case, the worker found their attitude even more worrisome because of their interest in a biracial child. "Our experience thus far has been that Caucasian couples applying for an interracial child have been somewhat older than they, have had whatever children they plan to have by birth so that the make-up of their family has been known and the child with some differences placed in these families has come in as the baby, actually chosen for his difference." Mr. and Mrs. A managed to convince their worker to approve them. They argued that they had talked with their families about their plans (improving the possibility that the child would be welcomed in the extended family). They insisted that they were not trying to "prove" anything, responding to the CBD's suspicion of political motives for adoptions. Finally, they averred that they preferred a biracial child for altruistic reasons—because such a child might have "less of a chance" for adoption otherwise. Reassured, the bureau placed a biracial child with these adopters and approved a second placement when the couple returned a year later.

Biracial children became more consistently identified as a separate category in the 1960s, deemed "interracial" in the vocabulary used in CBD records and elsewhere. Presumably most Americans were aware that the wide variety of skin tones and features among African Americans was the result of a long shared history in the United States that included sexual contact between the races. In fact, many Americans have an interracial heritage, a biological kinship that is often obscured by cultural categories of race that allow nothing in between black and white. But the term was specifically reserved for children who were born of parents identified as members of different races; most often, it referred to children of white and African American parents. Before 1960, the bureau occasionally placed such children with African American adopters—though never with whites—without identifying them as interracial. That silence reflected American racial categories, in which any detectable African American heritage led to the assignment of a person to that group. Interracial children were visually indistinguishable from light-skinned children born to parents both identified as African American. In these adoptions, social workers and adopters had seemed more concerned with color than heritage. This concern with appearance rather than actual heritage, as we have already seen, was also typical of white adopters' attitudes toward ethnic difference in the 1930s and 1940s.

However, by the mid-1960s case records began to mark color and parentage as distinctive categories. In a 1969 record of an African American adoption, for example, the social worker wrote that the prospective parents preferred "a fairly light complexioned children and [were] also quite ready for an inter-racial, Negro-White child." That these categories were understood as discrete is revealed in a misunderstanding that emerged in a 1968 placement of a biracial child. As the prospective African American adopters prepared to legalize their adoption of the little boy that the bureau had placed with them, they were startled to read that he had one white parent. Their social worker, in her turn, was incredulous that the adopters had not realized this all along. "Although I had not specifically mentioned that the mother was white and the father was Negro upon presenting this baby, I was quite surprised that they had not understood that he was an interracial child *since I had described him as such.*" [emphasis added] It is possible that Mr. and Mrs. P simply had not heard the word "interracial" in the swirl of emotion evoked by hearing about a potential child for the first time. Or perhaps "interracial" did not mean the same thing to these adopters as it did to the social worker. The worker also felt sure that the baby "was obviously interracial in his appearance and coloring," an evaluation that is puzzling in its own turn, since there is no unambiguous marker of such parentage.

Interracial sex was freighted with historical significance and competing cultural meanings. For some, it invoked the historical memory of white exploitation, the slave owner's rape of his female chattel. Among some race liberals in the 1940s and 1950s, interracial relationships were a hopeful indication of the lowering of racial barriers. For others, interracial sex carried the charge of transgression, an act of rebellion against the constrictions of bourgeois culture. By the early 1970s, for some African Americans allied with black nationalism, consensual interracial sex came to be seen as a form of false consciousness or race betrayal.

Mr. P admitted he was especially discomfited to learn that his son had been born to a white woman: he "had felt that if the mother . . . had been Negro and the father had been white, it would not have struck him so strongly." Of course, this reversal would have made no difference in the child's racial heritage, and the social worker and Mrs. P both seemed nonplussed by Mr. P's reaction. But his response suggests his identification with the black birth father, and the multiple meanings attached to such unions. Black men's sexual relationships with white women had long been highly charged. Whites had used such relationships, real or imagined, to justify a gruesome history of lynching. In recent memory, the murder of fourteen-year-old Emmett Till in 1955 had served as a galvanizing instance of white terrorism, this time one that lent energy and resolve to the civil rights movement. In any case, Mr. P's qualms were soon dispelled. He and Mrs. P agreed that it made no difference that their child was interracial, though they had been startled to learn it belatedly, and he and Mrs. P proceeded to finalize the adoption.

The brief experiment in transracial placement took place, in part, as social workers confronted a chronic scarcity of foster or adoptive homes open to black children, and sometimes were forced to refuse service to black women who turned to the bureau. The National Urban League took action to address the needs of these children in 1953, announcing plans to launch a national adoption program. From the outset, the project focused on recruiting more black adopters. A survey of African American prospective adopters exposed many agency practices that discouraged or offended such couples.[7] Income requirements, geared to the higher wages and living standards available to whites, set minimums that few black families could meet. Requirements for women's withdrawal from paid work exacerbated the problem, since many African American households relied on women's contributions to the family income. Age restrictions, often implemented primarily to cut down the numbers of white adopters, eliminated black adopters who were otherwise promising parents. The sensitive issue of color often made black clients uneasy, and many felt put off by the responses of their social workers, most of whom were white. In interviews or home studies, some African American clients complained that social workers were insensitive to issues of matching. "The agency wanted us to take a child we did not want," one former applicant reported. "They wanted us to take a light-skinned child, but we didn't accept it. We are brown-skinned."

Others found social workers overconcerned and offensively blunt about appearance. One NUL respondent recounted that the couple's case worker had asked, "'Do you consider yourself colored? You don't look like an American Negro.' What does she expect a Negro to look like? That's the trouble with whites, they are always trying to divide us.'" Discussions of the shortage of black adoptive homes had often tacitly assumed that African Americans were reluctant adopters. The NUL survey countered this view head on, demonstrating that agencies often alienated promising adopters.

NUL correspondence, speeches, and memoranda set out a sharp critique of the racial exclusion of postwar adoption practice, but largely affirmed the tenets of the best solution and the ideal of the "as if begotten" adoptive family. The project that developed, dubbed Adopt-a-Child, thus focused on ways to recruit more black adopters. One writer protested, "A child is not neglected merely because he is illegitimate . . . only a very small number of the illegitimate babies born to Negro mothers are in need of adoptive homes." Instead, she argued, the NUL should advocate for increased ADC grants to support single mothers and their children.[8] In a 1954 letter to the NUL, a Minnesota public welfare worker suggested extending the program to white adopters: "You might be interested to know that we have been, to a degree, successful in the placement of the obviously white-appearing child of mixed Negro or Indian, etc., in families of the Caucasian race."[9] These divergent responses foreshadowed the fracturing of the adoption consensus that would occur in the 1970s. Many would come to advocate renewed caution about relinquishment and adoption, even as some others would press to expand the boundaries of adoption.

The NUL itself never officially advocated transracial adoption, but a few of the member agencies of Adopt-a-Child reported that they had begun to place children across racial lines. The most obvious reason was pragmatic. After the three-year project (1955–1958), an intensive effort to establish national registries for hard-to-place children (including but not limited to African American children) and to recruit more black adopters, Adopt-a-Child could report only very limited results. In state after state, even agencies that returned optimistic reports revealed that they had done very few placements. In Milwaukee, for example, the County Department of Welfare placed only three to eleven black children per year during 1954 to 1956. In another Wisconsin county, an NUL member agency sent out 1,000 newsletters to recruit black adopters: "Result—one adoptive home secured."[10] Members of Adopt-a-Child also complained of the indifference of most agencies in their communities. As one discouraged member confided in 1954, "We have been laboring [in Cincinnati] on this matter of adoptions for Negro children for the last couple of years without too great success." Local agencies turned a deaf ear to the league's advice about recruiting black adopters, this correspondent reported, and he concluded in disgust, "It became quite obvious . . . that if possible, Children's Home would shove off the responsibility onto someone else."[11] Swamped by relinquishments of white babies and adopters eager to claim them, most did little to assist those black women who sought their aid, let alone to make special efforts to reach out to black women and their children.

Under these conditions, some agencies began to turn to white adopters. Catholic Charities in Ohio, for example, quietly placed a child "of mixed racial background" with a white family.[12] Committed to religious matching, Catholic agencies faced even more difficulties in recruiting black adopters, few of whom were Catholics; likely, this agency chose to cross racial boundaries rather than to breach religious ones. "Should we encourage placement of Negro babies in other than Negro families? Are we realistic?" pondered members of the Urban League chapter in New Brunswick, New Jersey. Minnesota League members answered in the affirmative. In one sample year, between July 1956 and July 1957, the state supervised 179 Negro children and 306 Indian children in foster care, all waiting for adoption: 5 black children and 37 Indian children were placed. All of the Indian children and one "part Negro" child were placed with white adopters. The league chapter designed an interagency project to "include encouragement and education toward assimilation of non-white children in white homes," while also advocating efforts to recruit more black adopters.[13]

If transracial adoption was often a default response when efforts to recruit minority adopters fell short, it was also the logical extension of the postwar adoption consensus. In 1948 the Child Welfare League of America's new standards had overturned two decades of social work assessment of adoptive "fitness" by declaring, "Any child is adoptable who needs a family and can develop in a family setting and for whom a family can be found that can accept him as he is."[14] For at least some postwar liberals, race was no longer an absolute barrier to such acceptance. Liberal discourses of race minimized the differences between black and white Americans. In a 1959 conference on minority adoption, held in San Diego, participants invoked Gunnar Myrdal's monumental study of race to assert, "Negro culture is basically American." The summary session considered whether or not agencies should recruit minority staff to work with clients of their own group. The group apparently agreed that agencies should hire "Mexican-American" social workers for those clients, but need not do so for "Negro" clients, because "there is not very much cultural difference between negro people and Anglos." One participant cited recent sociological theories about the changing role of American families to argue that "the matching of children to families becomes more and more irrelevant because the family really is just a place to grow up in, and not a place in which one develops a sense of identity."[15]

In 1968 transracial adoptions were reported at 733—accounting for only about one percent of all stranger adoptions, but a notable figure considering the long history of an intensely defended color line. By 1971 the figure had increased three fold to reach its historic peak of 2,574.[16] This number still represented a very small percentage of all adoptions, and hardly a number large enough to reconfigure the racial demography of American families. Nonetheless, such families loomed large in the symbolic landscape of the late 1960s and early 1970s. As African Americans confronted entrenched white racism, some grew disillusioned with the integrationist goals of the civil rights movement. Those inspired by the new politics of black nationalism rejected the claims of postwar colorblind universalism. For them, transracial adoption was simply another galling instance of white intrusion into black communities, and they made their protest public.

In April 1972 the National Association of Black Social Workers issued a strongly worded statement opposing the placement of black children with white foster parents or adopters.[17] These professionals declared, "Black children should be placed only with black families whether in foster care or for adoption." African American children could develop healthy self-concepts and a positive sense of racial identity only within racially matched families, they argued. They concluded by resolving to find alternatives to transracial placements that they deemed "a form of genocide." Arising from the politics of black nationalism, the NABSW position embodied that movement's disillusion with integration and its agenda of sustaining and strengthening black communities to defend African Americans against the corrosive effects of white racism.

American Indian activists took up their own nationalist claims. In July 1972, just months after the NABSW statement, the Sisseton-Wahpeton Sioux passed a resolution vowing "to make every stand possible to keep these children on the reservation" in Indian foster and adoptive homes.[18] Other tribes followed suit in resolutions that echoed the language and intent of the NABSW statement; the Oglala Sioux, for example, supported in-race adoption of Indian children so that they might "associate themselves with their own race and learn their own culture."[19] The 1978 Indian Child Welfare Act gave tribes exclusive jurisdiction of children living on reservations or who were wards of the tribe. In other placements of Indian children, Congress established the principle of preferential matching: that is, in placements of Indian children, members of the extended family were to have first priority, followed by members of the tribe and then by other Indian adopters. At the end of the twentieth century, congressional debates that contested racial matching still made exceptions for American Indian children.[20]

Expressed in the language of an emerging nationalism, such challenges reprised conflicts that had long defined American culture—and that had profoundly shaped American adoption. The conflict over transracial adoption cut to the core of the postwar consensus, exposing the class and racial privilege underlying its affirmations of upward mobility and assimilation. Like earlier demands for religious matching, pressure for racial matching came, in part, from within embattled communities that saw adoption as theft of their most precious resource— the children who constituted their legacy and their future. For some white adopters, colorblind universalism inspired a newly expansive definition of family. But for some African Americans and American Indians, these capacious families represented yet another assault on communities struggling to survive in white America. They responded by emphatically reclaiming these children as their own.

The NABSW statement was followed by a precipitant decline in transracial adoptions of black children. By 1973 the numbers had fallen to 1,091, less than half that of the peak year, 1971; in 1975, there were only 831 transracial adoptions.[21] During this four-year period, adoptions overall were also declining sharply, but transracial placements fell at more than twice the rate of all adoptions. Most sources attribute the decline to the NABSW position, and indeed it has been frequently cited in both court cases and the professional literature of adoption. Black nationalism did win a sympathetic audience among some white liberals and leftists, who responded to black Americans' frustration with the slow pace of the civil rights movement. Still, it seems unlikely that NABSW, a 5,000 member professional organization, had the clout to turn around adoption policy single-handedly—and just as unlikely that its chilling effect on transracial adoption meant that most Americans endorsed black nationalism. Elizabeth Bartholet has suggested, instead, that NABSW's position supplied a rationale for social workers who were already reluctant to support placement across racial lines, and had done so only under pressure from white adopters.[22]

The NABSW position provided a new language for affirming practices of racial matching that had been in effect for decades, only briefly challenged by a flurry of transracial placements in the 1960s. Though no state has achieved the absolute standard set by the NABSW—all black children in foster and adoptive placements with black families—social workers and other adoption experts have widely accepted (or, more accurately, reaffirmed) the principle of racial matching, now renamed "in-race placement." The commitment to racial matching persisted in the face of energetic challenges from critics who condemn racial matching as the repugnant remnant of a segregationist society, and as a practice that has left thousands of black children without the security and stability of permanent families.[23] And, tellingly, it persists even though twenty years of empirical studies have concluded that outcomes of transracial adoptions do not differ from those of adoption in general—that is, by the various standards used to measure outcome, black children raised by white parents fare as well as children adopted into "matching" families. On the question of racial identity, outcome studies also find that black children raised by white parents have a strong and positive sense of themselves as African Americans, and that most feel a sense of belonging within both white and African American communities. Nonetheless, most adoption experts continue to advocate same-race placement.[24]

Cases of contested adoption demonstrate the influence of nationalist defense of racial and cultural boundaries. In a 1999 case, for example, an Illinois juvenile court judge returned a three-year-old African American boy to his mother, who had lost custody of her son because of drug use. The court ruled that the state family services department had "placed too little emphasis on black culture" when it recommended that the little boy stay with the white foster parents who had raised him since he was eight days old.[25] The 1978 Indian Child Welfare Act and its affirmation of tribal sovereignty have lent powerful support to tribal claims to Indian children placed with white adopters. In one landmark case, decided by the Supreme Court in 1989, Choctaw Indians invoked the act to contest the adoption of Choctaw twins by white adopters.[26]

The twins' parents had moved off the reservation in order to avoid tribal jurisdiction, and they voluntarily relinquished the twins for adoption without racial restrictions. The twins were three years old by the time the Supreme Court ruled. Nonetheless, the Court affirmed the tribe's claim to jurisdiction in the case. Ruling that the birth mother was still an official resident of the reservation, the Court reasoned that her children were residents also (though they had never been on the reservation) and thus under the jurisdiction of the tribe.

As in earlier conflicts over religious matching, debates about in-race placement turned on different understandings of family. Critics of transracial placements challenged "best interest" as a standard that was too narrowly conceived, grounded in psychological views of individual parent-child relationships. In fact, custody and adoption cases are often adjudicated by consideration of the "psychological parent," adapted from the influential argument posed by Joseph Goldstein, Anna Freud, and Albert J. Solnit in 1973.[27] The concept affirmed that parenting is not a matter solely of biology or of contractual rights but rather a status forged and validated by a social relationship of nurture.

However, arguments about the psychological parent also rest on underlying assumptions of the family as it has been constructed within a twentieth-century middle-class culture: as essentially autonomous from social groups such as religious communities, extended kin networks, and ethnic or cultural communities. Implicitly, adoption posits identity as self-construction. By contrast, nationalist arguments pressed communal claims and argued for social considerations in placement. They emphasize that children are members of larger social groups that confer on them a social identity shaped by assignment, not simply voluntary affiliation. In the Choctaw decision, the Supreme Court directly addressed the conflicting models of best interest that fueled this legal battle, and affirmed the collective claims of the tribe. "It is not ours to say whether the trauma that might result from removing these children from their adoptive family should outweigh the interests of the Tribe— and perhaps the children themselves—in having them raised as part of the Choctaw community." And yet, attesting to the powerful sway of arguments about the child's attachment to psychological parents, the tribal court itself ultimately ruled that the children could stay with their adoptive parents.[28]

In the 1980s and 1990s, mainstream media coverage of transracial adoptions was commonly rendered in a frame that affirmed psychological parenting over communal claims. Stories about transracial adoption presented interracial families favorably, as shown in a 1993 article from the *New York Times* entitled "Revisiting Old Debate: Race and Adoptions."[29] Accompanying photographs portray white adopters with African American or biracial children in scenes of comfortable domesticity. In one, the adoptive father looks fondly at his biracial son, who lies on the couch and looks inquisitively toward the camera. The adoptive mother sits behind him, regarding the photographer unsmilingly. Below, an interracial adoptive family gathers in the kitchen to celebrate the birthday of twenty-five-year-old Andrew, who is African American and the son of white adopters. He avers, "I don't have any regrets."

The story frame of news reports commonly presents racial contests over adoption as battles mounted by cold-hearted ideologues against loving parents and innocent children. Accompanying photographs serve as testimony of domestic harmony, set against headlines announcing the intrusion of conflict. "Bitter Racial Dispute Rages Over Adoption/White Couple Seeks Custody of 2 Blacks," a 1995 headline declares.[30] Right under the headline, a transracial family presents a picture of loving devotion. A white mother embraces a black boy as he kisses her cheek; her white husband drapes one arm affectionately around her, as he looks fondly at a smiling African American boy nestled in his lap. The family sits close on an outdoor bench, implying a scene of shared leisure. In the body of the story, we learn that the foster mother is actually American Indian, and that their family already includes an eleven-year-old biological daughter, an eight-year-old adoptive daughter born to one white and one African American parent, and two black foster children. The story interviews experts who both support and oppose transracial placement and provides background on the larger conflict. Still, the frame and the most prominent elements—headline and photograph—telegraph the drama of love disrupted by legalism. Coverage of contested adoptions often subtly denigrates birth parents, who seem selfish and unstable by comparison to settled middle-class foster parents or adopters. In the coverage of the Illinois case cited above, for example, journalistic objectivity is belied by the initial identification of the birth mother as "a former cocaine addict."[31]

The promise of upward mobility often associated with adoption is directly invoked in an op-ed piece in the *Wall Street Journal* about Sara, "one child who was given a chance at a better life" when her African American parents relinquished her at eight months with the intention of freeing her for adoption by a white couple, Mr. and Mrs. G.[32] In this frame, white adopters are seen as heroic rescuers of a discarded infant "who was found to be HIV positive, was born cocaine-addicted, weighed less than five pounds, and was in intensive care when Mr. and Mrs. G agreed to take her into their homes." The story made the news when the Maryland Department of Social Services balked, concerned about placing Sara across racial lines. The viewpoint of the agency is depicted only through the perspective of the frustrated adopters, who charged officials with delay and obstruction of their adoption on grounds of race. Stories like these appeal to readers' empathy for children, their identification with parents threatened with losing their children, the common American disposition to resent professional expertise exercised through faceless bureaucracies, and a favorable view of colorblindness in race relations. Still, it is worth noting the underlying assumptions of this characteristic frame: it implies that adoption is a private negotiation, best left to the adults most directly involved. Ultimately, this position endorses a kind of privatism that reinforces older formulations of parental rights as property rights. Moreover, it assumes that children's welfare is best served by private families protected from public intrusion and the scrutiny of the state. At its extreme, though, this principle has sometimes served to screen neglect and violence from public view, against the best interests of women and children.

Coverage of contested adoptions involving American Indians often presents communal claims more favorably, in telling contrast to the media frame on transracial adoption of black children. "A Cultural Gap May Swallow A Child," reads a 1993 *New York Times* headline of a story covering the Sioux's legal challenge of the Swensons, white adoptive parents of a child with a white mother and Oglala Sioux father.[33] The photograph shows a smiling toddler sandwiched between her parents, whose expressions are relaxed and happy. The three are posed in a cornfield. Readers might assume that the child pictured is the subject of the headline, but the caption makes clear that this is not the adoptive family. Instead, the photograph shows the Indian father whose tribe is trying to reclaim his son from white adopters; the woman and child in the photograph are his wife and the daughter born to them. The dominant media frame is not quite in place. The headline follows the conventional frame by portraying children in contested adoptions as the hapless victims of adult struggles. And yet the "cultural gap" causing the problem seems benign by comparison to the "bitter racial dispute" of the headline on transracial adoption of black children. Moreover, this story is told from the viewpoint of the Indian birth parent.

Transracial adoptions of African Americans and Americans Indians occupied the same historical niche, and both groups challenged the practice with similar nationalist arguments. Their subsequent trajectories were markedly divergent, however. Though cultural nationalism has strongly influenced adoption practice for biracial or African American children, it relies on a web of policy and judicial decisions rather than on any legislative mandate. Moreover, the postwar endorsement of colorblind universalism has proved durable: in the 1980s and 1990s, racial preference in adoption was repeatedly assaulted, both on constitutional grounds and with best-interest arguments. American Indians, by contrast, achieved legal autonomy in child welfare decisions. In effect, the 1978 Indian Child Welfare Act accorded the force of law to the cultural claims of the American Indian movement.

This difference arises from American Indians' distinctive historical relationship to the United States government. In land transfers and treaties, the U.S. government had long recognized some form of tribal sovereignty. It also signals the complicated politics of American Indian identity. Those on reservations occupy enclaves more closed than any comparable social space occupied by African Americans—a parallel citizenship marked with formal borders, legal sovereignty, and official enrollment. For those off the reservation, though, identity is blurred by different tribal definitions of who belongs, by assimilation (marked and accelerated by a 60 percent rate of intermarriage), and by the absence of uniform assignment by others.[34]

In the case of transracial placements of African American children, the reigning question is: where do black children belong? In contests of transracial placements involving American Indians, the Indian Child Welfare act heavily weights the answer to the tribe; a court must find "good cause" to override its intent, and few have done so.[35] Commitments to tribal sovereignty have, at least thus far, shielded tribes from constitutional challenges to racial preference. Thus, in racial contests over Indian adoption, the question is not "Where do American Indians belong?" but rather "Who is an Indian?"

For African American children, racial matching remains the common practice, yet it has been repeatedly criticized. The protracted debate over the 1994 Multiethnic Placement Act illustrates the complicated politics surrounding race and adoption. Sponsored by Senators Howard Metzenbaum of Ohio and Carol Moseley-Braun of Illinois, both liberal Democrats, the legislation sought to curtail racial matching in adoption by withholding federal funds from agencies that delayed or denied placements solely on the basis of race, color, or national origin. Supporters of the bill invoked traditional best-interest arguments, portraying black children as the helpless victims of adult ideologues. Metzenbaum declared, for example, "It outrages me that poor little kids suffer because of the views of some social workers."[36] Such formulations were empathetic responses to the real pain and loss of children who lived without the security of permanent families. At the same time, though, they were also staunchly individualist interpretations of best interest that denied the claims and the resources of ethnic communities.

The bill's appeal to colorblind individualism won support that crossed political lines usually dividing liberals and conservatives. Writing in the *Wall Street Journal*, Alfred R. Hunt praised the bill and cited the NABSW position as yet another pernicious example of political correctness. But liberals were themselves divided over the legislation. Congressman Mfume of Maryland, head of the Congressional Black Caucus, endorsed the bill, acknowledging, "I've caught some grief because of this. But I've seen a lot of kids who have been denied the opportunity to be adopted, and that breaks your heart." Prominent liberal Democrats, though, found the initial bill troubling: Secretary of Health and Human Services Donna Shalala and Marian Wright Edelman, head of the Children's Defense Fund, successfully lobbied for amendments that softened the original legislation's assault on racial matching. The bill's final language captures the contemporary liberal discourse of race; its acknowledgment of cultural identity indicates the influence of 1970s black nationalism, even as it rejects the NABSW argument for in-race placement only. Agencies could not make race the sole reason for placement, but they could "consider the cultural, ethnic, or racial identity needs of the child and the capacity of the prospective . . . parents to meet those needs." Disappointed supporters of the original bill feared that MEPA might actually strengthen the racial matching policies it had been designed to remove. Even as it sought to encourage transracial placement, the legislation also lent the endorsement of law to considerations of race; it could be interpreted or used, then, as a partial mandate for the kind of racial preference already dominating placement practices.[37] The law was amended in 1996 to clarify its intent and strengthen enforcement.

Strikingly, the ICWA has so far survived legal challenges, even though it openly uses the racial preference that MEPA sought to overturn. Moreover, ICWA allows the accounting of tribal membership by blood portion, an abhorrent survival of nineteenth-century scientific racism. (Some tribes, such as the Cherokees, place little importance on blood lineage in determining who is a Cherokee; for others, though it is the defining criterion of who belongs.) Efforts to amend the ICWA have raised this issue, and one California judicial opinion ruled that tribal membership cannot be decided on the basis of blood alone.[38]

These debates found expression in fictional representations of transracial adoption. Three widely circulated examples offer further evidence of the cultural politics of adoption in the 1990s. Two focused on contested adoption. *Losing Isaiah* (a 1993 novel by Seth Margolis, made into a film released in 1995) tells the story of an African American boy adopted by whites, who becomes the subject of a legal battle when his mother returns to reclaim him. Barbara Kingsolver's 1993 *Pigs in Heaven* weighs the claims of a white single mother against tribal law and the Cherokee community, as an Indian lawyer challenges her adoption of a Cherokee child. Sherman Alexie's 1996 novel *Indian Killer* uses transracial adoption as a provocative plot device in an ironic and politically self-conscious representation of race and identity. All three stories use fiction to propose new vantage points on the polarized debate of colorblind universalism versus racial particularism.[39]

Losing Isaiah sets up a schematic treatment of contested adoption. The Lewins are upper west side New Yorkers, parents of a 12-year-old girl; both employed in professional jobs, they struggle nonetheless to keep up with the high costs of Manhattan rent and private school tuition. Isaiah enters their life when Margaret Lewin encounters him as a newborn in her volunteer work at an urban hospital, where Isaiah has abandoned by his mother, Selma, a drug addict. Margaret finds Selma, who agrees to relinquish him for adoption. But in the opening pages of the novel, Selma reappears to reclaim her son, now almost three years old. She has turned her own life around and is intent on becoming a mother to the son she has lost.

This scenario establishes the grounds for two alternative plots, drawing on the competing narratives of transracial adoption in public debate. In the dominant media frame, adopters are heroic rescuers beset by selfish birth parents and held hostage to political ideologues. In the counter-narrative most clearly articulated by the NABSW, adopters use their class and racial privilege to steal the children who rightfully belong to their birth parents and their racial communities. *Losing Isaiah* invokes these polarized positions in order to undermine and complicate them. In the book and film, the dramatic fulcrum is the conflict between two mothers and the ways that both fall short of the exalted expectations attached to motherhood.

The court case comes down to an agonizing Solomon's choice. And as in the biblical story, the law alone cannot supply justice. The judge, an authoritative older white woman, defers to the claims of racial affiliation and biological kinship, ordering the Lewins to return Isaiah to Selma. But the women themselves both recognize that the law cannot decide who is a mother. The novel makes the point through parallel vignettes of the protagonists as the trial ends, as each waits for the decision to be announced the next day. Margaret (soon to be declared the loser) feels at peace as she watches Isaiah sleeping, for she knows—whatever the court says—that she is his mother. Selma (who will win the court case) spends a troubled night, blank and numb, for she realizes with dismay that a legal proceeding cannot make her his mother. As Selma cares for a little boy devastated by his removal from the only parents he has known, she decides to return him to the Lewins. On their doorstep, though, she changes her mind, resolving to raise him herself. Black children belong with black mothers, she affirms in the last line of the novel, observing, "Trouble with this city is all the kids is with all the wrong people."

Losing Isaiah was released as a film in 1995. The screenplay, by Naomi Foner, rendered the birth mother more sympathetically; played by Halle Berry, she is a survivor who is justifiably wary of the class and race politics of her child's white adopters. Yet she herself decides that Isaiah needs to return to the people he knows as parents. In the end, she proposes a compromise in which Isaiah will return to his adoptive parents on her terms. "You'll have to deal with me," she warns Margaret (Jessica Lange), who agrees as they embrace tearfully. The two women's selfless maternity enables the just solution that the law could not provide.

The film closes on a black frame with a printed quotation from Isaiah 11:6: ". . . and a little child shall lead them." Pointing to the prophetic naming of this child, the filmmakers gesture to the larger significance of this interracial family and its refusal of exclusive kinship, either of blood or adoption. Instead, "Isaiah" suggests the utopian possibilities of the new world imagined in the prophetic vision of Hebrew scripture, the "holy mountain" where all are reconciled. This ending is credible, though, only because of the erosion of the postwar consensus supporting adoption. Despite its affirmation that blood alone does not make one a mother, *Losing Isaiah* ultimately rests on the tacit assumption that adoption is *not* the equivalent of biological kinship but is rather a form of substitute care that is potentially always open to challenge on the grounds of best interest. As this story inadvertently demonstrates, this version of best interest vacates any notion of "good enough" mothering. Both adoptive mother and birth mother are flawed, characterizations that could undercut the pressures for impossible perfection that surround motherhood. Instead, both pay dearly for their imperfections with devastating loss, and they reclaim their maternity only after saintly transcendence of their own selfish desire for maternal pleasure.

Both conclusions defer to a pessimistic view of American race relations. At a time when more and more Americans are claiming multiple racial identities, the practice of racial matching insists that we are one or the other, and immutably "other" to one another. In the novel, even selfless maternity cannot rise above the divisions of race. The film imagines racial reconciliation by way of a sentimental version of womanly empathy and self-sacrifice. And finally, both versions oddly undercut their own politics, dramatizing mother love as a bond between woman and child that transcends law, community, and social life.

Barbara Kingsolver's *Pigs in Heaven* features a contested transracial adoption that takes up the same issues as *Losing Isaiah* but in an exposition that more fully imagines the role of community, thus lending more credence to the politics of identity and affiliation. The novel itself is in part an explicit response to critics who objected to the ending of *The Bean Trees* (1988), in which Taylor Greer decides to adopt the American Indian child whom she finds abandoned in her car.[40] Kingsolver recounted her second thoughts to an interviewer: "I realized with embarrassment that I had completely neglected a whole moral area when I wrote about this Native American kid being swept off the reservation and raised by a very loving white mother. It was something I hadn't thought about, and I felt I needed to make it right in another book."[41] Though *The Bean Trees* dodges the charged politics of adoption by making Taylor an accidental mother, it could be taken as reinforcing racial and class stereotypes by casting Taylor as benign white rescuer of a tribeless Indian child.

Where does Turtle belong? As in *Losing Isaiah,* in *Pigs in Heaven* the question is explored through a conflict between two women. Annawake Fourkiller is a Cherokee lawyer deeply committed to the politics of tribal autonomy. She learns of the little girl when Turtle and Taylor appear on Oprah Winfrey to tell of Turtle's role in the rescue of a young man who fell into the reservoir at Hoover Dam. Annawake recognizes the girl as Cherokee and, outraged, she resolves to reclaim her for the tribe. Family history fuels her political commitment, for Annawake's own twin brother Gabe was "stolen from the family," removed during the era when many American Indian children were taken from the reservation and placed with white adoptive families. Kingsolver provides a nuanced depiction of different positions among Cherokees themselves as they struggle with tribal politics and community identity. Franklin, another "born again Indian," shares Annawake's self-conscious defense of tribal identity, but he is skeptical of her crusade to reclaim Turtle: "No matter what her story is, a lot of hearts are involved," he cautions her (67).

Soon, Taylor and Annawake confront one another in a scene that closely parallels the mothers' exchange in *Losing Isaiah*. "Your people let her fall through the crack and she was in bad trouble," Taylor accuses Annawake. "How can you possibly think this is in Turtle's best interest?" In reply, Annawake first reframes best interest as a community matter: "How can you think it's good for a tribe to lose its children?" But she also responds to the individualist version of best interest, arguing that Turtle herself needs the tribe: "Turtle is Cherokee. She needs to know that" (76).

Race matters, but so does maternal nurture. Even as Taylor responds to Annawake's claims, so Annawake is moved by Taylor's mothering. In an unconvincing fairy-tale ending, Annawake determines to resolve the conflict by extending tribal kinship to embrace the adoptive family. She contrives to pair up Alice—Taylor's mother and Turtle's grandmother by adoption—with Cash, Turtle's grandfather. Meanwhile, Alice proposes another version of this resolution. When she meets with Annawake, she asks the lawyer if she and Taylor could enroll in the tribe, since they do claim some Cherokee descent. Conveniently for Kingsolver, Cherokee definitions of Indianness are more capacious than those prevailing in some tribes, and they do not depend on a rigorously demonstrated blood portion—a definition of racial identity that sits uneasily with many Americans (and particularly American leftists, part of the audience Kingsolver addresses).[42] Annawake replies, "Yes, if you enrolled you would be Cherokee. We're not into racial purity'" (278). In the end, the connection is doubly secured. Alice and Cash conveniently fall in love, so kinship is established both by marriage and shared tribal identity.

Still, this personal connection does not dislodge Annawake's tribal claim. "Our children are our future," she proclaims. Taylor agrees to an arrangement which declares Cash guardian of Turtle, to share joint custody with Taylor. The novel does acknowledge the loss that this resolution involves for Taylor, but these notes register as minor reservations that carry little weight as Kingsolver shamelessly resorts to the classic ending of comedy: a marriage, and a double marriage at that.[43] As Cash and Alice plan their wedding, Taylor tells her mother that she is ready to affirm a long-term commitment to her lover, Jax, counting him as family. In this novel, then, the web of kinship is woven by biological relationship, social identity, legal contract, and freely chosen mutuality.

In *Indian Killer*, Sherman Alexie uses transracial adoption as an instance and metaphor of white violation and Indian deracination. Alexie cleverly deploys the conventions of popular fiction—the thriller, mystery novel, and police procedural—in a novel that is also a recasting of Richard Wright's 1940 *Native Son*. The author uses and then subverts readers' expectations of genre in what becomes a complex, ironic commentary on American Indian racial identity. The text on the back of the paperback edition frames the novel as a recognizable contemporary version of the search for self-knowledge: "Born Indian, raised white, Smith desperately yearns for his lost heritage and seeks his elusive true identity." Alexie anticipates and undercuts the liberal defense of transracial adoption. John's parents, model adopters, raise him in a tolerant liberal community. Conscientiously following the liberal script on cultural difference, they affirm John's Indian identity and strive to understand and embrace Indian culture. But Alexie mocks such efforts as superficial and ineffectual. Deprived of any knowledge of his actual tribal origins, John grows up with a painful sense of racial difference and inferiority. Under intolerable pressure, he seeks the catharsis of violence: "John needed to kill a white man" (25).

This statement initially appears to be a straight-faced exposition of motive. Soon, though, with the introduction of Marie, *Indian Killer* breaks from the conventions of the thriller. An activist and fellow student of John at the University of Washington, Marie is an Indian who energetically presses the claims of tribal identity even as she recognizes that her own affiliations are more complicated than prevailing political categories allow. In one scene, Marie critically observes the thoughtless and uninformed assumptions of non-Indian students as they discuss life on the reservation—but even as she resists their views, she recognizes that she herself is alienated from reservation Indians. Often excluded by pervasive racism at the predominantly white university, she is also uncomfortable and out of place on the reservation, rendered an outsider by her own upward mobility. Through Marie, Alexie comments ironically on the internal divisions wrought by identity politics. She muses, "Indians were always placing one another on an identity spectrum, with the more traditional to the left and the less traditional Indians to the right. Marie knew she belonged somewhere in the middle of that spectrum and that her happiness depended on placing more Indians to her right" (39). John's unknown heritage torments him, but in the dense political context supplied by Marie's activism, his uncertain identity is less an exceptional effect of adoption than a dramatic instance of a dislocation experienced by many Indians.

The novel never discloses the real identity of the killer. Rather, Alexie makes his characters' assumptions and theories a kind of Rorschach of racial attitudes. Like Bigger Thomas, the brutal tormented murderer of Wright's *Native Son*, the Indian Killer is rendered ultimately as a kind of racialized projection—the white man's Indian. Moreover, the killer might not even be an Indian. As the novel unfolds the reader becomes aware of the significance of the title's semantic puzzle: the Indian Killer could be a killer who is an Indian, or it could refer to a killer of Indians.

Through most of the novel, Alexie uses transracial adoption to represent white exploitation and racism. Alexie characterizes John Smith as a young man in anguish, and finally despair, over his fractured identity. In a provocative naming, "John Smith" is both a cipher and sign of deracination—a common name attached to many Americans, and a name that refers ironically to the John Smith of Jamestown, Virginia, a white man saved from "hostile Indians" by the Indian princess Pocahontas. In recurring fantasies, John imagines his life as it might have been with the birth mother who relinquished him. He longs for the imagined warmth of his loving, stable family and the security of a known and shared racial identity. Through this upbeat depiction, Alexie counters the stark portrayals of deprivation and pathology that appear in many journalistic accounts of reservation life.

Alexie is clearly challenging the narrative of the best solution, for neither the material well being nor the loving concern of John's well-meaning white parents is enough to offset the losses of adoption. In one scene, Daniel, his adoptive father, muses, "Oh, there were lots of times when John was simply their son, with no need for any qualifiers, but the stark difference in their physical appearances was a nagging reminder of the truth. If Olivia and Daniel could not forget that John was adopted, then John must have carried that knowledge even closer to his skin" (114). John himself feels unhappily different. As a child, he observes his parents' pale skin next to his own, and feels excluded from their intimacy: "He wanted to look like his parents" (306). His wish is phrased with Alexie's characteristic ambiguity. Olivia and Daniel's whiteness is described almost squeamishly; John does not necessarily want to be white. Maybe he simply wants parents who look like him; or maybe he does look like his parents—his birth parents, that is.

At the novel's end, Alexie throws the reader another curve by suggesting an ironic distance on his own metaphor of transracial adoption as deracination. John's problem may not be adoption after all but rather a deluded fixation on stable identity. In understated gallows humor, Alexie has John get a job as a high steel worker, attracted to this hazardous construction work because he wants to identify with the Indians famed for their balance and fearlessness at dizzying heights—even though he's not sure which Indians have this skill, much less whether he is a member of that tribe. Marie, the novel's most sympathetic character, manages a sophisticated double-think in which her political clarity coexists with her ironic view of identity as unstable and shifting. Indians themselves cannot agree on what it means to be an Indian or who counts as Indian, she recognizes. Still, she embraces a strategic essentialism, for she understands very well how she is assigned as an Indian by others. Regardless of how she might see herself, she cannot escape the meanings that others attach to Indianness and the histories of domination that produce those meanings.

These three stories all refuse the prevailing media frame that poses transracial adoption as a struggle between colorblind individualism and a communally minded nationalism. All acknowledge that colorblind universalism is also a politics, and one that has too often served the interests of those already in power. All three implicitly argue that race does matter. *Losing Isaiah* and *Pigs in Heaven* both imagine solutions in which participants come to understand and respect one another's positions and that propose alternatives to Solomon's choice, with its assumption that only one woman can be mother to a given child. *Indian Killer* avoids any such closure, but the novel's deliberate indeterminacy also makes the point that the existing either-or framework is not satisfactory. All three, then, try to move the discussion to new terms.

Public policy has yet to enact the kinds of creative compromise proposed in these fictions. Inconsistent and shifting, it instead reflects a telling indecision. American Indians have asserted more sweeping claims to children as tribal members, but they have won these demands as part of a larger struggle for tribal autonomy, rather than because of public assent to the specific claims of racial or tribal identity as considered in adoption. African-American nationalism has had a more limited and indirect influence. The Multi-Ethnic Placement Act and its amendments specifically repudiated the main tenets of the NABSW argument. And yet social work policy still upholds same-race placement as the ideal solution when possible, and social workers continue to struggle over how to reconcile racial matching with the mandate of "permanency planning"—avoiding the protracted uncertainty and upheaval of children growing up with no secure place. In a study published in 1999, investigators found that social workers remained more cautious and skeptical about transracial adoption than prospective adopters. Their outcome study, like most others, found that black children raised by white adopters had positive racial identities and fared as well as other adopted children. The social workers they surveyed, however, believed otherwise. Seventy-one percent thought that such children were "likely to have problems developing a sense of identity," and under half assented to the statement that "when black children are in need of homes, white applicants should be encouraged to consider adopting a black child." The investigators also found that agencies applied more rigorous screening to prospective white adopters of black or biracial children, a deterrent to adopters who might consider transracial adoption.[44]

Meanwhile, as many urban black communities were devastated by cocaine and HIV infection in the 1980s and 1990s, tens of thousands of children entered a foster care system totally inadequate to meet their basic needs for shelter and security.[45] Adoption—whether same-race or transracial—could help some children find secure havens, but it could not solve the deeper problems accounting for these shattered lives. That would take a new social contract that claimed public stewardship of children through a generous welfare state.

International adoption, involving far more children than domestic transracial adoption, came of age at the same moment of postwar prosperity and Cold War politics. Pearl S. Buck's Welcome House, established in 1949, initiated a global migration that would involve thousands of children by the end of the century. A celebrated humanitarian and novelist, Buck wrote widely about her own life experience as an American raised in China, an advocate of children's welfare, and the adoptive parent of seven children. Welcome House eventually placed about five thousand Amerasian children with American adopters. Buck's efforts on behalf of Amerasian children appealed to the consciences of Americans, whom she called to account for these young victims of war. Korean adoption expanded in the mid-1950s after Henry Holt, who adopted a child himself in 1956, established Holt International, which became a prominent organization facilitating intercountry adoption in Korea and many other nations. Korean children remain one of the most common subjects of intercountry adoption, and Korean-born adoptees are by far the most numerous single group of persons adopted from abroad.

Intercountry adoption got under way when the best solution dominated adoption practice, and it came to represent a much larger proportion of adoptions after 1970, when domestic adoption became more difficult. As more adopters began to extend their searches beyond the borders of the United States, some indicated that they were motivated, in part, by local pressures on adoption. As fewer children were relinquished, prospective adopters faced either longer waits for agency adoptions or the uncertainties of independent adoption (in which adopters and birth parents worked out placements without agency involvement). Some prospective adopters, dismayed by news of contested adoptions, turned to transnational adoption to find children whose birthparents would be far away and unlikely to reclaim their children.[46] For others, transnational adoption appealed because it held out hope for applicants who were disqualified or disadvantaged by American adoption practices: those over forty years of age; single parents; adopters who had been rejected for medical reasons. In a 1991 survey conducted by the U.S. Senate Committee on Intercountry Adoption, many adopters explained that they were seeking children abroad because they thought they would not meet requirements for domestic adoption.[47]

Adoption from Korea remained the most common kind of intercountry adoption until 1991, when over 2,500 Romanian children left that nation with American adopters. In the wake of the collapse of the Soviet Union, Russia became another major "sending" nation. In 1995, for unknown reasons, China began to allow intercountry adoption, and thousands of Chinese daughters abandoned in response to the one-child policy for population control were claimed by American adopters.

Americans' enthusiastic participation in intercountry adoption sometimes touched raw nerves abroad. In the 1970s North Korea had repeatedly criticized the South Korean government for allowing so many children to emigrate, and in 1988, during the Olympics in Seoul, NBC broadcaster Bryant Gumbel reported that such adoptions were "embarrassing, perhaps even a national shame," for some Koreans. In response, the Korean government resolved to phase out intercountry adoption by 1996. By 2001 the government was still allowing some adoption, but the numbers had been sharply reduced.[48] Exposés of neglect in Romanian orphanages, chaotic adoption procedures, and a flourishing black market likely influenced the abrupt policy shifts of the Romanian government: in 1991, Romania led the world as a "sending" nation, only to shut down adoption almost completely the next year, when it released only 121 children.[49] In Latin America, rumors periodically circulated about children taken by Americans, ostensibly for adoption, and used as involuntary donors in an international ring of black market organ selling. The grisly stories had no basis in fact, but their persistent resurfacing served as testimony to the suspicion that attended intercountry adoption in some quarters.

At home, depictions of international adoption often relied on self-congratulatory images of adoption as rescue. "Operation Babylift," the name given to one program sponsoring the immigration of Vietnamese children of American servicemen, captured this sentiment. A memoir written by the adoptive mother of a Romanian child presents women like herself as heroes: "these adoption pilgrims, these unstoppable American moms who literally took on the world for the sake of a child they had never met."[50] Such accounts dramatize the encounter of once impoverished children with American bounty: speaking of their two daughters adopted from Romania, adoptive parents reported that "the girls' biggest thrill was going to the supermarket for the first time. They had never eaten a banana before. And now they each have a doll, another thing they had never had."[51]

Memoirs and media stories rely on themes of upward mobility and assimilation, long identified with American historical narratives of progress and abundance. Pygmalion stories emphasize the transformation of abandoned waifs into prosperous American babies, with market metaphors abounding. On its April 11, 1993, cover, for example, the New York Times Magazine featured a portrait of a Chinese baby wearing a red velvet dress with ecru lace at collar and wrists. Underneath, the copy read "China's Market in Orphan Girls: How Li Sha, Abandoned in Wuhan, Became Hanna Porter, Embraced in Greenwich Village." The photograph presented the baby as a precious object, set against a black background and dramatically lit—the same visual convention used in many of the magazine's glossy advertisements, its consumer metaphor underscored by the title's use of "market." Inside, the table of contents develops both the Pygmalion theme and the market metaphor. The baby's prospects before her adoption are implied in a black-and-white photograph that shows her dressed in Chinese clothing, gripping the sides of a scarred wooden trunk. "Unwanted and abandoned, baby girls have become the newest Chinese export," the copy announces.

Viewing such stark disparities from a political perspective, some critics of international adoption have seen it as a form of imperialism—a transfer of children from poor to rich nations that is a repugnant extension of the transfer of natural and human resources that structures global capitalism. For such critics, as Elizabeth Bartholet observes, "international adoption . . . can be understood as the ultimate form of the exploitation that some see at the heart of all adoption—the taking by the rich and powerful of the children born to the poor and powerless."[52] In defense of transnational adoption, Bartholet and others counter that adoption provides a means of helping some children in ways that their own communities cannot, even though adoption is not a comprehensive or adequate response to the needs of displaced children around the world.

Transnational adoption is charged with political meaning. Its history maps the global suffering wrought by war, hatred, hunger, and political oppression. Americans who adopt children from other countries come into intimate contact with deprivation and suffering on a scale most have never known. For some, the result is an unreflective celebration of American prosperity and disdainful recoil from the "other." In a revealing self-published memoir, Barbara and Patrick Canale turn to Romanian adoption after they are defeated by the rigors of domestic private adoption, portrayed as a kind of ritual humiliation.[53] Anxiously performing ideal domesticity, Barbara prepares blueberry muffins for the social worker's visit. Passing the test of the home study, the couple works to craft a self-presentation that will appeal to a birth mother. With the advice of an expensive lawyer, they put together "a marketable photo album" (23–24). Learning of Romanian adoption from a speaker who addresses their infertility group, they turn to this possibility in part, it seems, because they prefer the role of magnanimous rescuer over their insecure position as adopters competing for scarce American children. "We felt good about adopting from a country where we would actually make a difference in a child's life" (34).

As this adopter encounters the shock of conditions in Romania, though, her tone changes to petulant entitlement. Painfully naïve about the realities of life in a country wracked by political conflict and economic chaos, she complains about dirty accommodations, streets riddled with potholes, and bad coffee. In one passage, she records, "I was perplexed over the shopping methodologies. I couldn't understand how stores could be empty except for a few little things that cost next to nothing and still no one could afford to buy them" (123). Longing for home, she fantasizes about the comforts of American consumer goods: "I wanted my Jacuzzi, and my microwave oven . . . I wanted to reach into my refrigerator and have a diet Coke with ice whenever I wanted one . . . I wanted a big tall glass of whole milk with Oreo cookies before I hopped into my queen-size four poster bed" (134).

Canale had imagined she was going to Romania "because God wanted one less child to suffer in an orphanage there" (31), but once there, she discovers that most children in orphanages were not available for adoption. Soon, the couple is drawn into the underworld of adoption brokers. "Love at first sight" goes awry when Auriel, the child they meet in an orphanage, turns out to have two living parents who do not want to relinquish him. Outraged, the author insists, "It was evident that Auriel would be better off with us" (96). When the birth parents later return to offer adoption in exchange for a cash payment and a radio, the Canales leap at the deal. But they end up arguing over what model of radio, and in the court room negotiations break down. The author unself-consciously describes her own transformation into the classic ugly American: "I pointed my index finger approximately two inches from his crooked and ugly nose and in my meanest voice I told him that we had a deal, and if he didn't honor it, then he could keep his son . . . I asked him one last time if he would accept our original offer, and when he declined, I told him to go to hell, and to take his whole family with him" (112). As the author herself admitted earlier, "We . . . noticed that we started to lose sight of what was actually 'right' and what was actually 'wrong'" (100–101). By the end, their altruism has yielded to American arrogance and cultural supremacy.

Others, though, consider and reject the narrative of rescue. In his independent-minded account of adopting a Russian boy, Robert Klose recalls his encounter with an evangelical Christian, a fellow passenger on his flight to Russia. She enthuses over his anticipated adoption and praises him for rescuing a needy child: "So, you feel that God is working through you to bring this boy out of misery and to America where he'll have a great deal to be grateful for . . . this little boy is waiting for you to save him." Klose muses that he has met some prospective adopters like her, those "who seem to feel that every foreign child yearns for a crack at life in America. But children who don't live in America can be happy, too." Instead, he affirms the ideal of mutuality long endorsed by social workers: "I feel that my own needs simply complement Alyosha's. He needs a father and I need a son."[54] For Klose, international adoption is not a charitable act but rather a pragmatic means to surmount barriers to single male adopters.

In other personal narratives, adopters grapple with the public meanings of transnational adoption. For some, adopting across national boundaries leads them to rethink parenting in the light of global issues of children's welfare. In *Sudden Family,* Debi and Steve Standiford, both ambitious young lawyers, unexpectedly find themselves moved by their church's call to aid Vietnamese children.[55] Serving as teachers in a Thai refugee camp, they decide to adopt two Vietnamese boys who are among the refugees. The preface frames this memoir as a sentimental account of adoption as rescue, promising the reader "a delightful, humorous, heartwarming account of a remarkable family" (7). The narrative itself opens with the image of birds in a storm: "our family has been an oasis for two boys caught in the maelstrom of war" (9). But *Sudden Family* challenges this view of adoption by taking the story past the usual ending of family formation to describe the boys' painful adjustment to an alien culture. In a counterpoint of alternating sections, Hy and Nhi Phan tell their own story. The Standifords believe that they are adopting orphans; in reality, Hy and Nhi are sons of two living parents who urged their boys to say they were orphaned during the war. The boys also lie about their ages—they are fourteen and sixteen years old, not nine and thirteen, as they claim in order to make themselves more appealing to prospective adopters.

The memoir counters the Pygmalion frame with a complex realism about the cost of cultural dislocation and the limits of affluence. The boys eagerly anticipate a bountiful table, as one writes: "in the refugee camp, we learned that Americans eat six times a day, and I was looking forward to always being full. But my first two months in America, I never got enough to eat" (89–90). The boys are hungry in the midst of abundance because, unbeknownst to the Standifords, Vietnamese custom dictates that they eat less than their elders out of respect. Nhi, who is partly paralyzed, dreams of the restored body that he imagines American doctors can provide. Though he benefits from superior American health care and from a more accepting attitude toward disability, Nhi feels isolated by American expectations for independence and autonomy. Once carried everywhere by his brother, Nhi now negotiates the world alone, in a wheelchair, and he fears that he will be abandoned as his brother responds to Americans' more truncated sense of obligation to disabled family members.

The adoptive parents' perspective proves unreliable: the Standifords' sections, recounting the boys' successful adaptation to American life, are abruptly interrupted by Nhi's attempted suicide. Meanwhile, in ironic counterpoint, Hy reads Dale Carnegie as he tries to discern American ways. Both boys are guilt-ridden about their deception; both mourn the loss of their parents left behind in Vietnam. In his epilogue, Hy acknowledges "both gain and loss in coming to America" and muses about the difficulties of naming an identity that is neither American nor Vietnamese. Steve's final reflections affirm adoption as response to God's call, which had led them on a journey from facile assumptions about American benevolence to a more critical and realistic under-standing of international adoption.

Adopters like the Standifords have established a political presence, forming self-help and advocacy organizations for international families. Both memoir and manual, Sheri Register's *"Are Those Kids Yours?"* ad-dresses international adoption in its political and ethical context.[56] As she makes the decision to adopt a child from another country, Register muses, "Taking a child out of her original culture and moving her to a very different setting where she would be in a racial minority seemed a rather drastic measure. I did not want to think of myself as a greedy, im-perialist consumer of imported children. On the other hand, I wanted a baby, and a chronic illness prevented me from bearing one myself; moreover, the baby we were to adopt needed a family" (p. x). But even as Register acknowledges the political critique of international adoption, she affirms its possibilities for individuals and for social change. "Fo-cusing on the particular—a single child's life—can sharpen our vision of the whole, if we stay attentive. Seen in its broader context, interna-tional adoption may increase our sense of urgency about the millions of lives still at risk" (23).

This sensibility is poignantly evident in Laurel Strassberger's account of her adoptions of Latin American children. In Chile to pursue a sec-ond adoption, Strassberger sees the faces of her own children in the young beggars who eat crusts from their restaurant table.[57] Her response is a continued effort to assist Latin American children through sponsorship and charitable donations, and to educate herself and others about the politics and peoples of Latin America.

In Register's title, *"Are Those Kids Yours?"* she quotes a familiar query directed to non-matching adoptive families, and her manual encourages such families to acknowledge and celebrate their differences. Like Strassberger and others, she advises adopters to educate themselves and their children on their countries of origin and to promote positive images of places often denigrated in American culture. Adopted persons themselves have returned a divided verdict on such efforts. In Frances M. Koh's *Adopted from Asia,* a collection of brief accounts by eleven young people adopted from Korea, some recall their annoyance at being sent to Korean "culture camp" to learn about their home countries.[58] But most affirm a dual identity, both Korean and American, and from the perspective of their twenties, some appreciate the efforts they once spurned to acquaint them with their Asian heritage.

Transnational adoption itself has emerged as a new source of affiliation. There are national associations for adoptive families of Korean, Chinese, and Latin American children, and these groups themselves link adopted persons and parents with others like them. The Internet facilitates the formation of such communities; websites offer access to chat rooms and information about heritage tours, culture camps, and international resources for finding biological kin. Parents are encouraged to recognize their children as members of both birth and adoptive families. *Rain Forest Girl,* for example, a children's book written by an adoptive mother of a girl born in Brazil, ends by affirming, "Her first home and first people will always be a part of who she is."[59] This embrace of difference drew support from a wider acceptance of multiculturalism in the 1980s and 1990s.

At the margins, domestic transracial and international adoptions still represent a small number of all American adoptions. But these practices, and the response to them, offer an index of the complexities of American adoption at the close of the twentieth century. At home, the reaction against transracial adoption signaled the limits of American pluralism and the constriction of adoption itself. Yet at the same time, the steady growth of international adoption—often transracial—suggested just the opposite response. Once again, some adopters pressed against a prevailing consensus to expand the boundaries of family. As they did so, some also openly challenged the old tenets of the "as if begotten" family. And yet, even as their families drew curious glances, their difference also made them quintessentially American. Their diversity captured the larger history of this nation of immigrants, even as it offered a proleptic image of an America that would soon be more multicultural than ever before.

5

"Tell It Slant":
Adoption and Disclosure

"Tell all the Truth but tell it slant," Emily Dickinson's poetic counsel, aptly sums up the guarded attitude toward disclosure that has been typical of all parties to adoption for much of its history. An intricate dance of secrecy and disclosure shaped private life, professional protocol, and public policy.

The most discussed kind of disclosure was the adoption story—telling children about adoption. Social workers were more unified and consistent on this issue than any other: from the 1920s on, they counseled parents to tell their children they had been adopted. But beneath this apparent consensus lay a welter of contradictory advice on the management of disclosure. Experts (including social workers, psychologists, and psychiatrists) disagreed about what and when adopters should tell, how they should disclose adoption to children, why telling mattered, and whom to tell outside the immediate family. Adopters themselves, social workers complained, often responded by procrastinating unconscionably, leaving children at risk of learning about their adoption from others. As experts equivocated and adopters dragged their feet, both revealed the persistent uneasiness that attended adoption.

Managing information was a matter of consequence for social workers, relinquishing parents, adopters, and adopted persons alike. Guilt and shame were potent motivators: many birth mothers hoped to conceal their pregnancies and their adoption plans; adopters often felt shamed by infertility. For some, concealment was strategic: birth fathers sometimes denied paternity to avoid child support or social censure; birth mothers might lie to improve their children's chances for adoption; adopters might dissemble to social workers, hiding discrediting information to improve their chances of getting approved for adoption. For social workers, secrecy and disclosure were the fulcrum of professional practice. Their access to confidential information was crucial to their professional authority.[1] Agency adoption offered the inducement of expert matching and the promise of professional discretion, placing tact and knowledge-gathering at a premium. Social workers' commitment to children's welfare demanded careful investigation of their backgrounds and their prospective adoptive parents. Agency adoption also gained ground as birth mothers and prospective adopters turned to social workers as intermediaries, strategically positioned to protect the confidentiality of both parties. Throughout, social workers wrestled with ethical questions about how to manage their knowledge about clients—in particular, what to tell adopters about children and their birth families.

Attitudes toward secrecy and disclosure are a measure of the cultural status of adoption—its acceptance by mid-century, its marginality after 1970, its anomalous position throughout. Confidentiality was both the vehicle and the mark of the wide acceptance of adoption by the late 1940s. Birth mothers and adopters alike had long sought the safety of secrecy. Relinquishing mothers wanted to escape the stigma of pregnancies outside of marriage; adopters feared interference from adopted children's birth relatives, and some hoped to conceal adoption altogether. By the 1940s, as adoption of infants became more common, the "as if begotten" family emerged with the support of agency practices and state laws that concealed the origins of adoptive families. The amended birth certificate and the sealed record were the sign and technology of adoption secrecy, an indication of the social consensus supporting families formed by law.

Adoption case records offer rich testimony of negotiations over disclosure, as social workers and their clients sought to manage information to their own ends. The case record illuminates social workers' pivotal roles as both procurers and stewards of confidential information. Through the home study, they studied prospective adopters in order to decide whether hopeful applicants were fit parents and which children to place in their care. In the 1920s and 1930s, their studies of children aimed to sort out the select few who were "fit" for adoption; throughout the century, they gathered information to guide their efforts to match children and adoptive parents. In the 1950s, direct placement revised these protocols. Placing children directly from hospital to adoptive home, social worker could not rely on information gathered from their extended observation and testing. Instead, they sought to understand children by getting more information about birth families.

Birth mothers and adopters sought discreet and trustworthy assistance as they undertook relinquishment and adoption. Confidentiality was a matter of high importance to both. No state required adopters to use agencies in 1950, and only a few passed such laws even by the end of the twentieth century. Clients came to agencies—or avoided them—of their own volition. Adoptions done outside agencies equaled or outnumbered agency placements throughout the twentieth century, except for a few years at the height of the postwar adoption consensus.[2] Some clients chose agencies because they were convinced by social workers' claims to professional expertise and by the view that agency adoption was "safer" because of expert testing and observation of children placed for adoption. In turn, some birth mothers came to agencies because they, too, believed that expert intervention afforded an advantage—that their children's futures were more securely entrusted to social workers than to other professionals, such as lawyers or doctors, or to their own unassisted judgment. The agency's other key advantage was its social location: its ability to act as an intermediary between relinquishing and adoptive parents, shielding the privacy of both parties. Social workers' professional authority turned on their reputations as trusted intermediaries—as professionals who could be relied upon to use what they knew effectively, humanely, and discreetly. Clients voluntarily submitted to social work scrutiny in order to gain the perceived advantages of social work expertise—in large part, social workers' scrutiny of the *other* parties to adoption. At the same time, they also sought to minimize the intrusion of the expert gaze when it was directed toward their own lives.

Stigmatized as sexual transgressors and bad mothers, women relinquishing children for adoption had reason to try to shield themselves from public disclosure. Confidentiality was the primary advantage of agency adoption, but it came at the cost of submission to social work investigation. Social workers tried to persuade relinquishing mothers that disclosure was therapeutic for the women themselves, and salutary for their children because it would enable better placements. Some birth mothers apparently acquiesced to this logic, providing extensive medical information and participating in the therapeutic narrative of case work. Others engaged in selective disclosure. Some refused to divulge the names of birth fathers—to protect married lovers, to conceal incest, to avoid contact with men they feared, or to prevent former lovers from learning of their pregnancies. Others dissembled about the circumstances of their pregnancies. One woman, embarrassed that she was not sure of her baby's father, claimed that it was her fiancé even though she suspected she had gotten pregnant in a casual encounter with another lover. (The calendar betrayed her, for her social worker quickly calculated that her fiancé, assigned elsewhere on military duty, could not have been the father.) Some claimed that they had gotten pregnant the first time they had sex, or even in the absence of full penetration—both scenarios possible but unlikely. In any case, social workers noticed that their clients seemed unusually prone to such mishaps. Some credulous experts, in thrall to psychological explanation, solemnly interpreted such data as evidence that unwed mothers were more fertile than married women.[3] A more commonsense interpretation suggests that some of these women, at least, were simply trying to downplay their sexual experience. Unmasked by their pregnancies, they nonetheless did not have to confess to more than the minimum of one "offense."

Social workers trod a fine line as they pressed clients to disclose discrediting information. They risked losing women's trust when they probed to verify stories of men slipping drugs into their drinks, rape by strangers, or sex forced by an intimidating and insistent date. As they were well aware, sexual intercourse did not in itself imply consent;

women were vulnerable to coercion that ranged from psychological manipulation to outright physical force. They also recognized that women caught in the disgrace of a transgressive pregnancy had reason to conceal their consent to sex.

There is some evidence, too, that women tried to suppress other kinds of stigmatizing social histories, such as prison terms or sex work. Lesbian desire was also intensely denied. Social workers in the Children's Bureau of Delaware regarded a "homosexual problem" as a serious psychiatric disorder, far more troubling than the "mistake" of an out-of-wedlock pregnancy. Women who found themselves suddenly alone in dealing with an unwanted pregnancy were often bitter about their male lovers; even as social workers acknowledged this understandable response, they were vigilant about identifying "man-haters"—in their definition, women who went so far in their reaction against their partners that they were at risk for repudiating heterosexuality itself. The few women who ventured to admit sexual attraction to other women retreated promptly into denial—and for good reason. Suspected homosexuality could in itself be grounds for labeling a girl delinquent, with the cascade of consequences that might follow for a minor, including involuntary commitment to Woods Haven, the state's facility for juvenile correction. Medical histories were potentially another ground for dissemblance. Pregnant women knew from their social workers that sick or disabled babies would not be accepted for adoption. Some, then, may have feared to disclose family histories of hereditary disease or admit to drug use or abortion attempts.

By the 1950s, as more young women resorted to maternity homes for their confidential service, social workers themselves became active agents and collaborators in a system of sanctioned and institutionalized deception. For some women, hiding a shameful pregnancy was itself the primary motive for relinquishment. The sequestered space of the maternity home marked the boundaries of acceptable concealment. At the margins, unsanctioned concealment and untoward candor both threatened the rehabilitative agenda of the "best solution." Young women who concealed their pregnancies from everyone eluded both chastisement and rehabilitation and, at the extreme, risked the health and lives of themselves and their children. Abandonment of an unwanted child—

the ultimate secrecy—was rare. Some young women confided to their social workers that they hoped to use a social fiction to achieve the same effect: they planned to conceal their relinquishments by saying that the baby had died. Social workers rejected this idea as frankly unrealistic and warned young women against it. On the other margin, those who endorsed the best solution also disapproved of full disclosure—going public with out-of-wedlock pregnancy and motherhood. Women who carried to term in their communities and then raised their children as single mothers flouted ideals of postwar femininity that held marriage as essential to sexual fulfillment and motherhood. By refusing the secrecy proffered by the maternity home, they also refused its sentence of shame and ritual of penance.

Maternity homes served as a space of limited disclosure, where social workers and matrons abetted women's efforts to conceal their pregnancies from all but a few intimates. They did encourage women to tell their babies' fathers, so that social workers could investigate family background. Parents of young women were necessarily parties to the secret, for they had to participate in relinquishment when executed by mothers under twenty-one years old, and few young single women could afford maternity home care without help from parents. In some cases, though, no one else knew: friends, neighbors, schoolmates, even siblings were kept in the dark.

By the late 1950s, as direct placement became more common, social workers grew more exigent in their efforts to identify birth fathers. Earlier, family history held less weight in evaluation of children for adoption, since social workers could rely on extensive testing and observation of children in their care. History and observation of birth parents loomed larger as testing protocols became more truncated and early placement became the goal. "Unknown history" on the father's side made a baby too much of a risk for direct placement, social workers thought, so they redoubled their efforts to interview birth fathers. As they became more confident about placing newborns, they sometimes did so without paternal histories. But in the 1970s, their efforts to find birth fathers gained new impetus as several influential Supreme Court decisions accorded legal rights to unmarried fathers.[4] Many states still do not require the consent of unmarried fathers on relinquishments, but judicial defense of fathers' claims in contested adoptions sent a clear message: placing children for adoption without the father's consent was risky.

Hoping to avoid foster care for their babies, many relinquishing mothers strongly preferred direct placement themselves, and this proved an effective lever in getting birth mothers to disclose the identities of birth fathers. CBD workers pursued birth fathers tactfully, since they recognized that men had ample reason to avoid disclosing paternity—fear of paternity suits, marital disruption, and community censure. Nonetheless, they were persistent and resourceful in their efforts. A man who refused to meet with a social worker who contacted him on the matter might find her waiting for him as he left work, hoping to get a word with him. When men refused direct encounters, social workers sometimes approached other family members, most often the men's mothers, to get information about family history. If a man resolutely denied paternity, social workers might still try to catch a glimpse of him to use his appearance as testimony: case records included the case worker's visual impressions of birth fathers, along with assessments of whether the baby resembled him or other family members.

Prospective adopters were also subject to the scrutiny of social workers, and like birth parents they often squirmed uneasily under the professional gaze. Though a few arrived with the image of themselves as benevolent rescuers of a needy child, such clients were speedily disabused of their illusions. At the CBD, they had to present themselves in a preliminary interview in order to get an application and then had to wait until a worker was assigned to their home study. Recognizing their position on the unfavorable side of the supply-and-demand equation, adopters generally entered the home study with considerable apprehension. As one adoptive mother recalled wryly in a memoir, "[receiving] an adopted babe depends on one's worthiness to have him. It's the profoundest difference there is between natural and adoptive parents."[5]

Confronted with the technology of social work investigation, prospective adopters would have been dim indeed not to understand that they were under surveillance. It was not surprising, then, that adopters sought to manage social workers' impressions and, at times, practiced outright deception. Some attempted to conceal unfavorable medical or psychiatric histories—for good reason, as these were the most common reasons for the agency's occasional rejections of prospective adopters. A few lied to cover up criminal records. Others dissembled over their marital histories by not disclosing failed unions or by backdating their weddings in order to conform to agency requirements about duration of marriage. Still others convinced social workers that they were happily married, only to separate acrimoniously soon after placement as the added stress of new parenthood exacerbated longstanding conflicts.

Social workers sought to ferret out any signs that a couple was divided on the desire to adopt. Marital consensus on this crucial subject was a prime requisite of approval of a home study. Husbands and wives were interviewed separately at least once, to enable a reluctant spouse to disclose his or her reservations. A few times, couples successfully concealed their disagreements. In one such case in the 1970s, as the bureau decided to remove the child from a conflict-ridden home, the prospective adoptive mother admitted that her husband had harbored doubts about adoption all along.

Attempting to establish relationships of trust with clients, social workers encouraged voluntary disclosure by touting the therapeutic value of the home study for adopters and its importance as a safeguard for vulnerable children. At the same time, the protocol of the home study included many strategies for corroborating such information— some disclosed to adopters, and others that social workers used discreetly behind the scenes. Asked to request confidential medical reports and to supply names of references, for example, adopters knew that social workers were consulting outsiders about their qualifications. Still, it seems likely that few recognized the range of resources that social workers brought to bear or the sweep of their investigative gaze. Public and professional record-keeping widened the scope of the adoption home investigation. Some clients obviously failed to anticipate the agency's protocols for confirming information that they disclosed voluntarily or its resources for uncovering what they had tried to conceal. Couples who had dissembled about the duration of their marriages soon found themselves awkwardly backtracking, confronted with the agency's request for a copy of the marriage certificate. (The court required verification of marriage as part of the legalization process.) Clients who appeared for an initial interview knew they were on stage, but in all like-lihood most did not realize that the agency recorded every contact with clients and that even their initial telephone inquiry had been entered as part of the data of the home study. Even such a slight datum might be interpreted as meaningful. Prospective adopters who called to inquire about adoption and then let a year lapse before following up, or who made an appointment and then cancelled it, or who failed to heed the deadline for returning their applications, would find themselves having to explain away delays that their social worker interpreted as ambiva-lence.

With the formidable resource of the agency's voluminous case files, CBD workers could identify a client as a family member of another cli-ent or as a person who himself or herself had had prior contact with the agency. In Delaware as in many other states, agency workers could draw on the pooled knowledge of many local agencies: through the Social Service Index, professionals shared confidential information about cli-ents.[6] Public records, such as marriage records, provided other sources of confirmation. The CBD could also use criminal record checks, as one chagrined client discovered when her social worker confronted her about a shoplifting conviction that she had tried to conceal. Clients caught in lies found themselves at a double disadvantage: they had to explain away their deceptions as well as defend themselves against the discrediting information that had come to light.

Social workers and clients negotiated the boundaries of privacy in dealing with sensitive issues of infertility and sexuality. Even before they arrived at the agency, most clients had already suffered invasions of pri-vacy regarding their infertility, as physicians probed their bodies and bodily functions and intruded into the intimate domain of their sexual-ity. Infertility was easier to conceal than an out-of-wedlock pregnancy, but it carried its own social stigma. Adoption required couples to dis-close infertility more widely, first to the agency (the CBD, like many others, required medical documentation of infertility) and then, im-plicitly, to others who were likely to assume that infertility was the moti-vation for adoption.

One man admitted to a CBD worker that he was reluctant to adopt at first because adoption would publicize their infertility, and he feared the derision of male co-workers for a man who could not impregnate his wife. Even social workers sometimes lapsed from the objectivity of social science as they recorded who was "responsible" or "at fault" for a couple's inability to conceive, a language of agency—and blame—ill suited to the involuntary nature of infertility. No wonder, then, that many clients were reluctant to revisit painful histories of infertility in the course of the home study.

For some, the diagnosis of infertility was deemed so traumatic that doctors or partners tried to conceal it even from the principals themselves. In 1963, when one man found that his low sperm count was probably the cause of the couple's inability to conceive, he was devastated. After unsuccessful efforts to treat the problem, their physician advised his wife not to let him know just how "weak" he was. Another couple, Mr. and Mrs. W, came to the agency in the late 1960s after they had undergone unsuccessful treatment for infertility. After her second surgery, Mrs. W's doctor was convinced she would never get pregnant, but he advised her husband not to tell her so. He kept the secret for a while, believing it "the kindest thing for his wife," but finally did tell her the truth. In another 1960s case, the prospective adopters had separated briefly when an outraged husband discovered that his wife had not told him that she was the cause of their inability to conceive. She defended herself by explaining that she had had reason to fear his response to the truth. When she had asked him what he thought about a woman who couldn't have children, Mr. J (not recognizing that he was in the middle of a high-stakes marital test) had replied "that such a woman was finished and washed up."

Social workers viewed attitudes toward infertility as a telling marker of marital stability and fitness for adoptive parenthood. As clients narrated the trials of infertility, social workers scrutinized them for signs of discord or blame, or for positive indications of mutual support. "Acceptance" of infertility was itself a crucial indicator of readiness for adoption, they believed: they wanted assurance that adopters had relinquished their hopes for biological children. In home studies, they watched closely for signs of preoccupation with infertility, either excessive emotion on the subject or a telltale admission that one or both prospective adopters still hoped for a conception.

CBD workers also probed for undisclosed ambivalence about adoption through the bureau's policy on "safeguarding"—use of contraception. Prospective adopters were required to agree to practice contraception during the home study and for at least a year after adoptive placement. Clients were exempt only if a pregnancy was absolutely impossible—if the woman had undergone a hysterectomy, for example. In practice, few adopters met that test. Even a man with practically no viable sperm occasionally ended up as a biological father; couples who had endured years of infertility might still be surprised by a conception. Some Catholic adopters objected that their church forbade mechanical contraception; the bureau respected this religious prohibition but required such couples to promise that they would use the rhythm method conscientiously. When clients openly demurred, as a few did, their home studies were deferred until they declared themselves ready to comply.

The requirement served to protect children and to prepare clients for adoptive parenthood. Social workers explained to prospective adopters that they needed to avoid pregnancy so that an adopted child would not end up competing for parents' time and affection with a birth child close to the same age. For the CBD, "safeguarding" also served as a warrant that clients meant what they said about accepting their infertility: by taking active measures to prevent pregnancy, clients demonstrated that they were ready to commit themselves unreservedly to adoptive parenthood. It discouraged prospective adopters from using the home study as treatment for infertility, in case any were tempted to test the enduring folklore which holds that adoption often leads to conception.[7] Perhaps the practice of contraception served as a symbolic marker for adopters, too. It replicated, in reverse, the intentionality of planned parenthood. Many clients had likely begun their quest for parenthood by deliberately deciding not to use contraception. As they complied with the bureau's directive, they marked the beginning of a new quest for parenthood—this time through adoption—by taking up contraception again.

Of course, social workers had no way of enforcing compliance on this intimate matter. Some prospective adopters became pregnant during the home study or probationary period; in shame-faced discussions with their social workers, they admitted that they had feigned agreement to this policy while privately flouting it. It seems reasonable to suppose that others, though not exposed by a pregnancy, may also have dissembled on the matter. Practicing contraception after longstanding infertility might well have seemed irrational to some couples, a pointless exercise in reproductive control that might serve as a galling reminder of their involuntary infertility. Why give up the unsought boon of infertility—liberation from contraceptive regimens? Others surely felt loath to foreclose the possibility, however remote, of a long-desired pregnancy. The CBD feared that this attitude meant that such clients saw adoption as inferior, the default solution when biology failed. Alternatively, though, perhaps some clients simply wanted to maximize their chances of becoming parents by any means.

The CBD, like most other agencies, required its clients to confine their efforts to adopt to a single agency. Given the state's small size and tight-knit networks, clients who tried to pursue multiple applications close to home were likely to be found out. But adopters themselves could take advantage of the state's geography by applying to agencies in nearby states, a tactic less likely to be discovered. Independent placements were much more difficult to police, and CBD records contain many mentions of adopters who found children without agency supervision. After 1951, when Delaware outlawed non-agency adoption, the bureau was in a better position than most agencies to enforce the dictum of applying in only one place. Likely many people who might have sought private adoptions were deterred by the statutory prohibition.

Nonetheless, CBD records also show that private adoption continued and that courts typically did not enforce the law with any rigor. No doubt judges were reluctant to remove children from homes that seemed satisfactory, even if they had arrived there illegally. Indeed, one 1959 record contains revealing evidence that at least one Delaware judge had little sympathy for the spirit of the law—its effort to enforce social work standards. A board member of the agency and former judge on Delaware's superior and orphan court, the man intervened energetically when the CBD tried to discourage one couple from adopting a child from a well-known independent agency in another state—an adoption mill, by CBD standards. Though this was not technically a private adoption, since an agency was involved, the bureau made it clear that this agency did not meet the standards that the law was intended to uphold. Nonetheless, this judge could not understand why the bureau would not abet the efforts of these adopters (who were his friends). Confronted with this dissension in its own ranks—and from a former judge—the bureau had no choice but to back off.

Adopters found ready allies among other professionals when they flouted agency policy—even law—in their quest for parenthood. A mid-1950s case placed the CBD at loggerheads with a local minister who had helped his parishioners to find a child. These adopters were also clients of the CBD. Though the law prohibiting non-agency placement had been in effect for four years, these people were either unaware or unafraid of it: they reacted indignantly to the bureau's stern warning that the placement was illegal. Another couple, Mr. and Mrs. M, came to the CBD after a long history of disappointment: three pregnancies had ended in stillbirth. Mrs. M. got pregnant again during the home study, a fact they managed to conceal from the agency with the collusion of their doctor, who omitted mention of the pregnancy in his medical report. Their caution proved warranted, since this pregnancy, too, ended in fetal death when Mrs. M. was close to term. Unaware of these events, the CBD approved their application. Not content simply to wait for a CBD placement, Mr. and Mrs. M leaped at the chance to adopt a baby born to a woman in another state. The CBD learned of this plan and warned the couple that they would not be able to adopt the child legally in Delaware. Undeterred, Mr. and Mrs. M legalized the adoption in a third state.

If clients sometimes bent the truth to advance their own aims, social workers themselves practiced sophisticated and self-conscious deceptions in their casework. "Tell it slant" amounted to a professional protocol, one intended both to serve therapeutic goals and to express an ethos of compassion.[8] At times, they used indirection to deliver a tactful version of a painful truth. Rejection letters to prospective adopters, for example, rarely contained a full and frank disclosure of the reasons the agency deemed a couple unfit as adoptive parents. Instead, social workers relied on a few stock phrases. In the form letter used in the 1950s, the CBD avoided naming specific reasons for rejection in a message that instead emphasized the general situation of adoption scarcity. "We are extremely sorry to write you that we are unable to go further with your request at this time," the letter opened. "We do receive a great many more applications to adopt than we ever have children available. This means, unfortunately, that we are unable to fill many of the requests and must disappoint many fine families." The revised form used in the 1960s was slightly more forthcoming: "We are unable to help all of the couples coming to us and do need to consider first the couples who would be in the best physical and emotional health." Still, clients receiving such letters were left to infer for themselves exactly what had led the agency to conclude that they were not among those couples "in the best physical and emotional health." Upon occasion, a hurt, puzzled, or angry client would request further clarification, and social workers would explain more by phone or in a meeting. Most often, such letters ended the agency's contact with these clients.

Case records reveal workers' concern about the pain that such rejections might inflict, or their potential to stir marital disharmony when one partner's perceived liabilities were the cause for rejection. Maybe that was the reason the bureau "told it slant" in a 1960s rejection letter that cited medical reasons. One of the prospective adopters had a potentially worrisome history of cancer, the record showed. But in fact, on the evidence of other cases, this history by itself would probably not have been cause for rejection. The case record revealed the agency's major concern—that the healthy spouse was ambivalent about adoption.

Outright rejections were relatively uncommon. More often, the CBD delivered a tacit rejection by gently discouraging unsuitable clients, or by pursuing a strategy of stalling and evasion. In a 1955 example, the case worker recorded her vague but persistent misgivings about one couple, including her observation that the prospective mother talked too much and that the couple "seemed uncomfortable" dealing with the agency. Relatively trivial, these factors did not amount to a clear contraindication of adoption. Still, the worker was not prepared to proceed with this couple, either. The result was that the agency decided simply to let the contact lapse. Such multiple factors—none conclusive on its own, but in the aggregate damning—also led to a silent rejection of Mr. and Mrs. Q. In their deliberations, the agency staff members pondered several negatives: the prospective father's age (over forty); the couple's extended infertility treatment (possibly a sign of negative views of adoption); and Mrs. Q's "rather intense" personality. Rather than reject the couple outright, the agency decided to "offer little encouragement."

We do not know what most of these couples concluded from the agency's silence or discouraging responses. Probably some realized they were getting the brush-off. Others might have been too disheartened to persist in the face of discouragement, or too diffident to challenge the agency's apparently dilatory behavior. In a few cases, clients considered "unpromising" by the agency did persist—and sometimes their persistence paid off. When social workers were concerned that their clients were lukewarm about adoption, backing off was a deliberate ploy, a test of motivation. When clients did nothing about the agency's retreat into silence, social workers took this as confirmation of their suspicions. Conversely, when clients actively pursued their applications in the face of discouragement, social workers were ready to revise their estimations of such couples' motivation.

Intricate management of disclosure shaped the rituals of presentation. In a carefully staged drama of successive disclosure, social workers introduced a child first through verbal description and a photograph; prospective adopters then could choose to meet the child in person. Disclosure of background information was a marker of the boundary between foster care and adoption. Foster parents were typically told little about the child's family; by contrast, prospective adopters were the privileged audiences of social workers' carefully guarded knowledge. In keeping with the tenets of the "as if begotten" family, in which the adoptive family completely displaced the birth family, information flowed only one way: birth mothers were refused any knowledge of adopters.

Claiming their own place as mediators of adoption, social workers were deliberate and highly selective in their practices of disclosure. Later, as adoption activists denounced the entire system of confidential adoption, they castigated social workers as custodians and brokers of lies. Social workers, though, understood themselves as professionals entrusted with clients' secrets and as stewards of knowledge that had the power to hurt. CBD practices conformed to the professional consensus on disclosure established in the early 1920s, as illustrated in records of the U.S. Children's Bureau. In a revealing exchange forwarded to the USCB in the early 1920s, a reviewer from the Ohio Board of Charities criticized a children's home in the state for its policy of telling adoptive parents little or nothing about birth parents. The superintendent countered, "We do not think that it is advisable to tell the unfortunate history of the children who are to be adopted. If there is any good reason for telling any part of it, we do so but the more that is told, the worse the result as a rule."[9] By the late 1930s, the USCB was advocating "that relatively complete information should be given to [adoptive] parents about the background of the child that they are taking into their home, but that this should be given without identifying information."[10] By "relatively complete," other letters reveal, the USCB meant disclosure of physical and "mental" history, but not "adverse social history" such as criminal convictions.[11] The recommendation—and its ambiguities—suggest the underlying view of knowledge as power, to be exercised and dispensed with discretion. Professional management of disclosure had two objects: to equip adopters as parents and to enable parental disclosure of adoption to children.

In service of the first aim, social workers dispensed information on a need-to-know basis, guided by contemporary understandings of genetics. They told prospective adopters about conditions that might be heritable, but sometimes did not disclose other medical information. This practice was complicated by changing understandings of genetic inheritance. By the 1930s, social workers had rejected eugenicist views of the heritability of criminal behavior, for example, and a virtual consensus prevailed on not disclosing such information about the birth parents. Mental illness proved a more difficult case, for its causes were uncertain. Medical and psychiatric opinion was often divided, and the tenuous consensus of one era might be overturned in the next. In the late 1930s, the federal Children's Bureau advocated disclosure of mental illness. But the CBD often deemed it irrelevant, likely responding to newer ideas of psychiatric illness that emphasized social causation—poor parenting or traumatic experience. By 1960, this view was widespread. A few critics declared that mental illness was a fiction; psychiatric diagnoses were forms of social control used to enforce conformity. But by the end of the twentieth century, psychiatric illness was increasingly described as a physiological disorder, caused by chemical imbalances in the brain—and more likely to be seen, again, as inheritable.[12] Throughout, social workers weighed the potential value of such information against the risks of stigma and undue anxiety that might accompany it.

Through testing, observation, interviews, and medical examinations, social workers worked diligently to know the children in their care, but they controlled that information carefully. Full disclosure was unusual, so much so that social workers remarked upon it in the case record. "The situation was very uncomplicated," commented one CBD worker in 1966. "I did not purposefully omit anything except [a sometimes heritable condition in a collateral relative]." In phrasing that implicitly marked another presentation as unusually thorough, another worker noted in 1959, "The family background was presented in some detail because of the many positive factors present."

In this process, case records themselves served as a crucial technology of collusion. Social workers used these records to keep their stories straight, a complicated task given their highly selective disclosure of information in their possession. Virtually every account of a presentation included careful notes about what was *not* revealed, as shown in these examples from 1960s records. Most often these were lies of omission, in which the bureau shielded adopters from the knowledge of stigmatizing social histories. "I do not name that the mother and several other relatives repeated grades" or that members of the birth father's family had relinquished children to the CBD. Another noted, "I did not mention that [the birth mother] had had other illegitimate children . . . I did not mention that . . . the alleged father was now incarcerated." One summary recorded, "I stressed the positive elements regarding the natural mother and her family and did not indicate that she had had other illegitimate children nor did I indicate that she had been promiscuous nor her general present pattern of living"—a euphemism clarified elsewhere in the file, where the worker described this client as "more or less a prostitute." Sometimes social workers did not disclose that a child had been removed from a prior placement, especially one of short duration. At times, social workers offered coded versions of the truth, as in this case: "I purposely omitted that this mother herself apparently was born illegitimately—I put in that her parents were separated when she was an infant." On occasion, the CBD concealed ethnic or racial identities that were widely stigmatized. One worker "" "let them know that some of [the birth father's] ancestors are of Spanish extraction and I purposely avoid naming that he is a Puerto Rican." In several cases, social workers did not tell African American adopters that their prospective child had one white parent.

Social workers appeared to regard such exchanges as tacit negotiations of disclosure, and there is some evidence that adopters, on their part, understood them as such. Workers assumed that adopters would notice the clues proffered in presentations and would ask for more detail if they wanted it. When clients did ask more questions, social workers usually responded with successive disclosure: they would provide more information but not the full story. If clients continued to press, social workers met their queries with increasing candor.

At times, such clues were so indirect that it is difficult to imagine that clients would have recognized them as signals of hidden truths. A worker wrote in one 1960s record, "I omit . . . the fact that the agency has known and actually placed several children related to this alleged father on his maternal side. My way of giving this to the [adopters] is that we know that several children on his side of the family have shown good ability." Though the social worker tacitly disclosed the agency's contact with other family members, in fact it seems highly unlikely that prospective adopters would have recognized this as a clue about their social history of relinquishment; social workers might easily have discovered such information about relatives' academic achievements in their routine interviews of relinquishing parents. In some cases, social workers' presentations combined lies of omission with misleading half-truths: "I did not mention to them that the alleged father was married," one worker recorded, "but did mention that the couple did not feel that it was advisable for them to marry [because one was white and one African American]."

In other cases, it seems more likely that adopters would have recognized—or guessed—that social workers were choosing their words to soften painful truths. Rape, prostitution, or very casual sex were often rendered through vague euphemisms that described the birth father as "someone she did not know" or "someone she did not know well," respectively. Suspected or known incest was rarely disclosed directly, instead indicated through descriptions such as "someone close to the family." In a rare case of an infant girl left on the bureau's steps, the CBD worker noted that the adopters "knew from me that we did not have specific information on the health, etc. of [the] natural parents," but she recorded, underlining the sentence so that it would not be overlooked, "*I never used the word abandonment in describing the way in which L was released for adoption.*" These studied euphemisms could scarcely have escaped any but the most unwary adopters, but significantly, none pressed for clarification. It seems likely that in such cases, adopters and social workers collaborated silently to obscure origins that might bring stigma or pain to adopted children. Social workers engineered such collaborations by their selection of adopters: they offered children with unknown or "unspeakable" family histories to adopters who had already indicated, in home studies, that they were unconcerned or incurious about a child's origins.

Social workers and prospective adopters sometimes engaged in open negotiations of disclosure. In presenting a child to Mr. and Mrs. Y, the CBD worker told them that the child had been placed for adoption before and then removed, but that she was sparing them the sordid details: "I was not going to tell them about these things because they were unpleasant and they really hadn't affected the child and that was all that counted for them. They agreed this was true and that they'd rather not hear that part of it." In fact, the removal resulted from neighbors' complaints that the prospective adopters were heavy drinkers and gamblers, and unmarried in the bargain. The CBD had had some inkling of these liabilities: during the home study, the case worker had observed that Mr. O had liquor on his breath, and when the bureau tried to confirm their marriage, no record of it could be found. The agency went ahead anyway, swallowing its misgivings in the absence of any other prospects for this African American child. Selective disclosure in this case, then, spared not only the adopters' feelings but the agency's reputation: this was a risky placement, and the bureau knew it. In a 1974 record, a prospective adoptive father worried aloud that "too much knowledge" would color his attitude toward an adoptive child: he might expect too much of a child of highly educated birth parents, or anticipate behavior problems if he knew a child came from a "bad" background. His worker complied with his desire to be left in ignorance, offering only a few general comments on the child's background.

In some cases, the bureau and adopters were subtly at odds on the issue of disclosure. When foster parents went on to adopt the little girl in their care in a 1940s case, they tried to fend off their social worker's narrative of her past. "It might seem silly," the adoptive mother explained apologetically, "but . . . Judy seemed so much their child that she would almost rather not know much about the background. She said that they loved Judy as she was with all her little faults she was gradually overcoming, but if they knew that her father or mother had had certain characteristics maybe if similar characteristics appeared in Judy they would think 'unfairly,' she said, that it was because of her background." Placing "unfairly" in quotation marks, the recording social worker implied that adopters might profit from information about characteristics that *could* be heritable. This worker encouraged her clients to ask her more by telling them, "We were willing to share what we knew." But even when the adopters demurred, she pressed them to listen to the background information so they could tell their daughter if she were to ask. One couple adopting in the 1960s resisted their social worker's attempts to fill them in on their child's background: "They felt the less they knew the better they would feel about it." She agreed "this was true up to a certain point" but encouraged them to listen to the information "because you certainly want to be able to give your child some kind of explanation in the future." In a 1950s case, the bureau worker clearly disapproved when another couple described their first adoption, from a local Catholic agency: "They know nothing of [his] background, and they are glad for this, feeling that their only interest and concern is in the child." She explained that the bureau would provide "general" information about background because this was important for their parenting of an adopted child.

The unusually direct discussion of disclosure as policy in a 1960s case reveals the CBD's endorsement of a middle ground of limited disclosure. These clients had previously adopted a child from an agency in another state. They had received a very detailed history and anticipated the same from the CBD. Their social worker observed that these parents apparently derived considerable satisfaction from the knowledge of their child's "desirable" background. But she prepared them for a less abundant disclosure from the bureau, explaining that "a more generalized presentation is sometimes equally or more helpful." In another 1960s home study, a social worker approvingly quoted a prospective father who affirmed the wisdom of the bureau's ideal of limited disclosure: "Mr. S said that he can see how having information about the biological parents would really not help to raise the child." Still, throughout the CBD's history, telling something of the child's background was deemed an important professional practice.

Disclosure assumed new dimensions after 1970. Like other traditional child welfare agencies, the CBD was placing fewer and fewer white infants. The caseload was dominated by "special needs" adoption—finding families for children who were "hard to place" because of their age, race, medical needs, or psychiatric histories. Placement of such children was often no longer a local matter. Instead, agencies turned to regional and national networks to share information about children waiting for adoption and to match them with suitable parents. Photographs (later, videos) and written descriptions assumed new importance in presentation. The brief biographical sketches seek to convey the individual appeal and strengths of each child, even as they also allude to troubled histories and alert prospective parents to the child's ongoing medical and psychiatric needs.

An example from the 1990s illustrates the formula that emerged, a mixture of cheery optimism and professional candor. The National Adoption Center, an organization dedicated to finding homes for hard-to-place children, circulated this description as an introduction of two siblings available for adoption: "K is a bright, handsome youngster who likes to ride his bike, swim, and roller skate. K's behavior has been disruptive in the past, but he's been doing better in a home where limits, boundaries are given. He's in a SED [special education] class and doing well. F is a bubbly, happy little girl with a great sense of humor. She's in a group home and has post traumatic stress disorder and attention deficit hyperactivity. She takes Ritalin and Tofrin. Both children are in counseling to help them work through previous traumas." Hand-written notes in the margins of this document tell a grimmer story. Likely, they were notes taken by a CBD social worker who called to inquire about the children and who received, in return, the more candid response offered to a professional colleague. The children had both been abused sexually by their adoptive father and were currently in separate placements because they were sexually active with one another. The "previous traumas" of the description also included "Satanic worship and cult issues." The girl's "group home" served residents who were mentally ill.

By telling it slant, social workers served as children's advocates by presenting them positively as they searched for parents who would have the resilience and resources to meet their needs. In the successive disclosure of the home study, adopters would learn more about the histories revealed in the handwritten notes. But how much, and what, did adopters need to know? Such cases raised the ante on disclosure. In a 1997 memoir, one adoptive mother charged that agency euphemisms had profoundly misled her and her husband, to the detriment of their adoptive daughters and their biological children. Ann Kimble Loux's *The Limits of Hope* unfolds a wrenching story of nearly unrelieved bleakness.[13] Adopted at ages three and four, the two girls had suffered abuse and neglect. Beyond adoption was no happy ending, but a nightmarish account of intractable behavioral and learning problems, delinquency, drug abuse, and prostitution. Her daughters, Loux believes, were irreversibly damaged by the devastating effects of early deprivation and abuse. In part, her narrative is an impassioned critique of social work disclosure: she believes that the agency that placed the children did too little to prepare them for the girls' severe problems and the possibility that they would never recover. "Wrongful adoption" became a new category of litigation after a 1986 case brought by an adoptive couple found an Ohio agency guilty of misinforming them about their child's background.[14] Notably, though, the decision in that case explicitly affirmed the agency's professional prerogative to manage disclosure—including withholding some information about the child.

"Tell it slant" was also the consistent counsel about disclosing adoption to children. From the 1920s, social workers declared that children should know the "truth" about adoption. Rarely, though, did anyone advocate for the standard of disclosure that guided legal testimony: the truth, the whole truth, and nothing but the truth. Social workers could control parental disclosure to a point, by withholding some information—manifestly, parents could not tell their children things that they themselves did not know. Beyond that, how much should they tell their children, how, when, and why? Outside the boundaries of the immediate family, who else should know, and what should they know, about adoption?

In the 1920s and 1930s when most adoptions were of older children, disclosure was not an issue because concealment was not a possibility: children themselves might remember their birth families, and others in the community knew them.[15] As adoption among strangers became more common, and as children were adopted at younger ages, concealment became more feasible—presenting opportunities that some agencies and adopters seized upon with alacrity. Social workers again endorsed a middle ground, advocating disclosure to children but not to others.

Many correspondents to the federal Children's Bureau expressed concerns about the confidentiality of adoption. Most often, they wanted the assurance that birth families would not "interfere," threatening the security and permanence of the adoptive family. In the 1930s and 1940s, more and more states passed laws that affirmed adoption as the equivalent of blood kinship. Formal transfer of parental rights and the amended birth certificate, used in Delaware as early as the mid-1930s, marked this acceptance. In this document, the names of birth parents were replaced with the names of adoptive parents, so that the child's birth certificate concealed the fact of adoption. Initially, Delaware adopters still had access to the names of birth parents, which were recorded on legalization papers. Soon after, Delaware began to use amended birth certificates in concert with sealed records. The link between birth and adoptive parents was documented for the court and then sequestered from public view in a closed record. By 1948 this practice was used in most states.[16]

Social workers supported the sealed record, but they opposed the notion that some considered a corollary to confidential adoption: that adoption erased a child's prior identity. Some advocates of adoption proposed more radical measures to protect adoption secrets. In 1939 an alarmed social worker wrote the USCB to appeal for support. The judges responsible for adoption in her state wanted all records destroyed once the adoption was completed, in order to assure confidentiality for the adoptive family. The bureau replied promptly to affirm the social worker's commitment to preserving the record: "Probably most records of adoption will never be called for after the legal aspects of the case have been completed. Yet it would be unfortunate if a single record that may be needed for an important purpose . . . had been destroyed. Since one never knows which *one* will be needed, we must keep them *all*."[17] In a 1946 paper presented at the National Conference of Social Work, Grace Louise Hubbard declared, "The identity of a child is his sacred right."[18] Identity, according to Hubbard, was neither determined by environment nor set in stone by nature; rather, it was a conscious process of self-invention that used the materials of both background and experience. "It includes both what we know about ourselves, our origin and pedigree, and also what we have been able to take at any given time out of our life experience . . . Lineage and ancestry are a part of this sense of self, but these things do not create one's identity."[19] In *Adopting a Child*, published in 1947, Frances Lockridge voiced the expert consensus of social workers as she emphasized the professional duty of good record-keeping. "Good adoption agencies keep careful records of children placed . . . Believing that an agency has no right to take, irrevocably, from a child the information about his own identity, such information is kept. He may never want it, but it is there if he does want it."[20] The role of social workers as stewards of such information was key to their definition of expert practice and their claim to professional authority.

Though CBD social workers did not tell all that they knew, they regarded the gathering and preservation of information as crucial. Like Lockridge, they believed that such data offered a resource that might be needed in the future, and perhaps for reasons that could not be fully anticipated in the present. Maintaining information, then, was part of an agency's continuing responsibility to the adopted person as a client with a history that preceded the transfer to an adoptive family and a future that might require some access to that past. Agencies like The Cradle, a commercial maternity home, operated from a radically different view of identity. In its practice, adoption was not a transfer of custody but more fundamentally a transformation of identity itself. Agencies approved by the social work consensus functioned as mediators between past and present; agencies like The Cradle sought, instead, to erase the past to make way for the substitute family of adoption. When criticized for "meager" record keeping, the director of The Cradle countered that the home deliberately maintained very sparse records, so that if adoptive parents or children asked, "the agency could honestly say that nothing was available."[21] Adamant in their view that the adoptive family entirely replaced biological kinship, agencies like The Cradle sought to make the child into a blank slate.

Some prospective adopters sought a privacy that far exceeded the legal and social work mandate for a barrier between birth and adoptive families. A few sought to conceal the fact of adoption altogether. When they wrote the USCB, some requested replies in plain envelopes and asked for assurances that their inquiries would be kept confidential. Some correspondents asked for referrals to agencies far from their homes; as one such writer explained, "We want no one not even our own relations to know that it does not really belong to us."[22] In a few highly unusual examples, female adopters sought to conceal adoptions even from their husbands. A prospective adoptive mother wrote Franklin D. Roosevelt to request his assistance in such a ploy. Her husband was "very desirous of having a child" but opposed to an adoption that might expose his infertility. She hoped to adopt an infant while her husband was away on military duty and to represent the baby to him and others as their biological child.[23] Though the practical difficulties of such a plan seem all but insurmountable, *The New York Times* reported the exceptional case of a woman who apparently did sustain such a deception for many years. According to the 1921 story, an adoptive mother of eleven children had successfully represented herself as their biological mother to everyone, including her husband (a man who must have been frequently absent from home, not to mention singularly—perhaps willfully—unobservant).[24]

More commonly, prospective adopters resolved that they would keep the adoption secret from their children. One women, who hoped to adopt a boy and a girl, had thought about the matter in some detail and recognized the difficulty of concealment in her letter to the USCB: "We would not want them to know of their adoption, so feel it would be necessary to keep it from everyone, if that could be done."[25] Social workers persistently discouraged such plans for concealment. The head of the USCB remonstrated gently with this woman, "Children cannot be adopted without a court record . . . and it is not possible to keep the matter the entire secret that you would perhaps like."[26]

Social workers spent much time and energy advising adopters about disclosure. Throughout the twentieth-century history of adoption, the most frequently advanced argument for truth-telling has been one of simple pragmatism: parents should tell because children will find out anyway. As social workers recognized, secrecy is a relative matter at best, for absolute control of information is seldom a realistic possibility. Case records and memoirs include many instances of inadvertent disclosure of adoption. Children might learn of adoption from neighbors, relatives, school mates. Some suspected the truth and confirmed it in confrontations with parents. Others found legalization papers, incriminating correspondence, or original birth certificates among family papers. And in still other cases, parents themselves blurted out the secret, often in the midst of bitter family battles. In virtually all such instances of unplanned disclosure, the truth came as a shock: adopted persons felt stigmatized by the recognition that they had been relinquished by birth parents and profoundly betrayed by adoptive parents who had withheld the truth. Aware of the damage wrought by unexpected disclosure, social workers sought to convince adopters of their duty to tell children about their adoption, at the right time, in the right way, and under the right circumstances.

Social workers regarded willingness to tell as a measure of adoptive parents' fitness. They assumed that most adopters would feel some reluctance about telling. But when clients expressed strong and persistent reservations about disclosure, social workers suspected that they might be harboring doubts about adoption itself. One worker confronted her clients outright during a 1955 home study: "I asked Mr. B if people minded telling about things they were proud of . . . I asked if the Bs felt that adopting a child was anything to be ashamed of or to hide." As early as 1941, CBD social workers considered reluctance to tell as a reason to question adopters' fitness. When foster parents of a little girl pressed the bureau to consider them for adoption, their social worker hesitated: "I do not feel that the agency could responsibly offer Ellen to them for adoption until they have worked out more clearly the fact that she is not their own child and they are able to allow Ellen the knowledge that she isn't their own." This strong reservation seems odd, given that the little girl was already happily settled with a family she saw as her own. However, it suggests the weight that social workers attached to "telling" as an indication of a healthy attitude toward adoptive parenting.

A psychological rationale emerged in some sources. In her 1936 manual for adoptive parents, Eleanor Garrigue Gallagher warned about the destructive potential of family secrets: "The parents' fear of telling a child that he is adopted is frequently based on their own feeling of insecurity in the relationship, and sooner or later this feeling will be communicated to the child."[27] Yet parents who mentioned adoption at every possible opportunity were also suspect. One record from the 1960s succinctly expressed the ideal that was pervasively endorsed in CBD case narratives: "The "Ls feel that they are Betsy's 'real parents' but do not ignore the fact of adoption."

Before 1935, when the agency supervised adoptive families for a two-year probationary period after placement, home visits provided ample opportunity to counsel adopters about disclosure, and case records show that workers returned to the subject until they were satisfied that parents would tell. In a 1935 record, the adoptive parents resolved at first to move out of the neighborhood to "some place where no one knew about the child" to mitigate the risk that he might learn about his adoption from others. The CBD worker used supervisory visits to try to persuade Mr. and Mrs. A of the folly of this position. On one visit, she asked Mrs. A to review the details the agency had provided about the child's background. When the adoptive mother proved herself a poor historian on the subject, the worker went over the information again and prodded her on the issue of telling. "Although Mrs. A superficially agreed, she said she supposed someday she would tell her, [I] had doubts on the subject. She seems more in favor of felling her than she did a year ago, however. She said she thought more about the community aspect and knows that neighbors will undoubtedly tell Nancy as she grows older." Recognizing that they had no control once an adoption was finalized, social workers tried to make the most of the teaching opportunities of the home study and the supervisory period.

Though social workers consistently hewed to the position that children should be told that they were adopted, they were seldom stern advocates of the whole truth. Adoptive parents frequently confided that they planned to fabricate some story about the circumstances of the adoption—typically, telling the child that birth parents were dead. In earlier records, CBD workers did not always oppose even this complete fiction. During a home study conducted in 1936, the prospective adoptive mother told her social worker that she would not tell her son that he had been born out of wedlock; instead, she mused that "they would probably say his parents are dead. However, as he becomes a man and insists upon having more details they may give more information about his parents." The worker reported this conversation without comment, and she did not try to talk her out of the lie. Perhaps this client's ability to imagine disclosure as a continuing process, and to consider telling the truth eventually, seemed a promising enough sign to workers who feared that many parents would avoid telling altogether.

On some occasions bureau workers entered enthusiastically into their clients' planned fabrications. In one unusually detailed record of a 1935 case, worker and adoptive mother discussed disclosure over a number of home visits. A college graduate, this adoptive mother set out to school herself in the professional literature: "She has read a good many books and articles about adoption, and is very well informed on child psychology." Sometimes, clients such as these used their research as a way to challenge workers' professional authority; in this case, though, the adoptive mother embraced the expert consensus that the bureau represented. Mrs. T had already absorbed the contemporary expert opinion on telling: "She believes it very bad to bring up a child not knowing it is adopted. She plans to begin to tell her as soon as she can understand words, even before she can really comprehend it." In the same breath, though, she indicated that she planned to tell this truth slant: "They are going to tell Helen that they picked her from a great many children to adopt." The bureau worker raised no objection to this idea. On the contrary, she reported approvingly that Mrs. T "was quite aware of the necessity for having Helen think that her mother loved her and that it was not carelessness or neglect" that motivated the relinquishment. As they went on to discuss possible narratives, the worker suggested explaining that the mother was too immature to undertake care of a child. By contrast, "The economic motive of relinquishment for adoption seemed to both adoptive mother and worker needlessly cruel, since it would always seem to the child that if someone had just helped the mother at that time that she might have kept the child."

In this extended exchange, adoptive mother and worker collaborated to construct a good story, one that might have only a contingent relationship to the truth. The worker told her client, "In some cases she has known adoptive mothers to tell a young child first asking about his mother that mother is dead, which is, of course, emotionally true since the mother no longer plays any part in the child's life." Later, this narrative could be reframed: "When the child is much older she could tell her the difference between emotional death and physical death." Tacitly acknowledging the taint of bad faith that colored this scenario, the worker assured her client, "This need not seem a lie to her unless the adoptive mother had actually felt guilt in telling it."

This elastic notion of truth attests to the social worker's concern for telling as a therapeutic narrative—a story of the child's origins that would support healthy self-esteem and bond the adoptive family. In 1940, when one adoptive mother wondered aloud about what to tell her child, her worker encouraged her to come up with a story that she could deliver with ease and conviction: "The thing that would be easiest for her to say would be the thing that would be best for them." Notably, this mother was considering the use of a common deception—that the child's birth parents were dead. As a 1930s record makes clear, social workers regarded telling the story as therapeutic for adopters as well. The CBD worker wrote down her counsel to an adoptive mother: "I said that I thought the exact way that a person went about discussing adoption with a child had to be their own—the main thing seemed to me to be for the [adoptive] parents to feel free about it and to be able to accept the fact that even though an adoption was different from having an own child, it was a thing which they should face and accept."

When social workers discouraged direct lies, it was on pragmatic rather than ethical grounds. In a 1936 case, the CBD worker demurred when an adoptive mother was planning to say that the birth parents were dead and they knew nothing of them. In the tactful phrase that appeared in many records, this social worker counseled, "It might be best to make the story entirely factual." But the purely pragmatic motivation for this advice was clear as social workers raised no objection to the less risky deception of lying by omission. Many clients resolved outright that they were not going to tell adopted children that they had been born out of wedlock, and social workers readily countenanced this deception. In counseling adoptive parents, workers emphasized that "illegitimacy" did not necessarily mean that a child was tainted by poor "background." A 1937 case narrative recorded the dismay of prospective adopters when their worker told them that most available children were born out of wedlock. In response, "I tried to bring out that often illegitimate children might have a better background than legitimate ones. Legitimate parents who are living who give up children are perhaps pretty irresponsible." But in the next breath, she advised that telling a child of illegitimacy "almost always would be unnecessary." In acquiescing to parents' concerns about the stigma of illegitimacy, social workers acknowledged the strength of public opinion on the subject. One adoptive mother vowed in 1939 that "she would absolutely never tell a child that his parents weren't married." She claimed that she herself "did not care at all about the fact that the parents were unmarried, but she would care tremendously about having her baby know that . . . I said she had perhaps 90% of the population to back her up in that feeling." Discretion on this matter would shield the child from the unfortunate prejudice of others.

The emphasis on a therapeutic narrative remained constant even as social workers shifted their recommendations about what constituted a good story. The rise and fall of the "chosen child" story is illuminating. The story first appeared in 1916, in newsletters of the Illinois Children's Home and Aid Society. The didactic children's story celebrates the intentionality of adoption: unlike birth parents, who must take what comes along, adoptive parents select a particular child to make their own. By the late 1920s, the USCB recommended this story to adopters asking for advice about disclosure.[28]

This story was codified and widely circulated in a children's book that quickly became an adoption classic, Valentina P. Wasson's *The Chosen Baby*.[29] Published in 1939, the book was the first children's book on adoption. Revised in 1950 and again in 1977, the book's subsequent editions registered changes in adoption practices and shifting prescriptions about disclosure. *The Chosen Baby* is ostensibly directed to children, but it is meant to be "overheard" by the adults who read it to and with children. In the story, adoption brings joy to infertile adults who find children with the help of social workers. The title underscores the message of adoption's positive difference, even its superiority: adoptive children are chosen with an intentionality denied to families formed the old-fashioned way. The story achieved remarkable currency and influence, as attested in memoirs of adoption and case records that recount children's understandings of adoption. Obviously all three versions of the story favored disclosure tacitly, since the book itself was likely read primarily by adoptive families as part of family narratives of adoption. By 1977 disclosure itself was directly represented in the story as one of the shared pleasures of the adoptive family. "Peter and Mary like to hear the story of how they were adopted. James and Martha and Peter and Mary Brown are a very happy family."

The three editions all emphasize the difficulty of adoption, a realistic representation that supports the theme of the chosen child as prized and desirable. In the 1939 edition, the hopeful man and wife are warned at their initial interview that they will have a long wait, and subsequent pages illustrate the eager adopters begging for a baby. When they complete their first adoption and return for a little girl, the worker warns again, "You may have to wait a long time. More and more people wish to adopt babies." This time the man and wife wait for nearly a year before they get their daughter. In the 1950 and 1977 edition, adopters get the same warning and, like the man and wife, wait a few months for their son and almost a year for their second adoption.

The 1939 edition portrays adopters who choose a specific child, a theme removed in subsequent revisions. Summoned to the "Home," they survey three babies before selecting one. In the 1950s edition, the revision reflects instead the approved protocols of presentation: social workers choose a baby for the Browns. The 1977 edition elaborates on the experience of "meeting." James and Martha (updated from the Man and Wife) go to the agency where they first see the baby sleeping in his crib. He wakes up and smiles; they hold him and exchange glances with one another and the baby. They decide to adopt the baby and return the next day to bring him home. This more detailed portrayal of presentation emphasizes both the chemistry of meeting and the deliberative process of adoption.

Before the mid-1950s, CBD workers often recommended the book to adopters casting about for a way to present adoption to their children. Along with other experts, though, bureau workers came to regard this narrative with disapproval—but not because it was untrue.[30] Rather, the chosen child story was rejected because of its disquieting acknowledgment of adoption's intentionality. The idea of chosenness, social workers feared, was shadowed by the reality of relinquishment. As a child became old enough to understand more, the positive story of adopters' choice would gain a disturbing undertow: adoptive children were available to be chosen only because they had first been relinquished by the parents to whom they were born. Chosenness also introduced an idea of merit that fundamentally violated the ideal of unconditionality that was associated with blood relationships. Parental love is supposed to be unconditional, and so choosing has no place in it. Children who were told they were "chosen" might feel pressured to earn and deserve the love that biological children were accorded by birthright.

Before the 1970s social workers virtually never urged full and unmediated disclosure, fearful that the bald truth might hurt both adopters and children. Instead, they counseled that adopters tell a story that would not be readily contradicted by facts that might come to light; that portrayed birth parents positively; and that explained relinquishment gently, protecting the child from feeling rejected or unworthy. If the truth advanced these goals, so much the better; if not, selective omissions were in order.

Later advice was much sterner in advocating full disclosure, if still attentive to softening its impact on a vulnerable child. A 1989 manual offered unflinching advice about how to tell a child he had been abandoned in a gas station rest room.[31] The very young child might be told, "We don't know much about your birth mother. We think she was probably very young . . . She probably decided she didn't know enough about taking care of babies to take care of one." As the child matured, this story could be "expanded" to include direct disclosure of the abandonment. "She went to a gas station and tried to hide you in the restroom. But, of course, you cried, and someone in the gas station heard you and found you right away." The author provides sample dialogues that anticipate the child's questions and reactions and then suggest possible responses. The manual explains how to deal with "difficult situations" in talking about adoption with adolescents—situations such as a birth mother who was a prostitute impregnated by a client or a birth father who was a rapist. "It may be . . . difficult to provide final details," the author concedes. "With a little planning, however, it is possible to explain what happened in a way that does not condone their actions, but allows the teenager to view the situation in a way that will leave him feeling all right about being related to that person."[32] Published in 2000, *Telling the Truth to Your Adopted or Foster Child* offered the same counsel of candor, with pages of advice on "sharing the hard stuff," including "law-breaking behavior," rape, incest, abuse, abandonment, prostitution, and drug abuse.[33] Rehearsing with a tape recorder, the authors advised, would help parents convey such information matter-of-factly. Disclosure had changed radically since the days when social workers agreed with clients that it might be best to conceal a child's birth out of wedlock.

Concerned adoptive parents were buffeted by ambiguous and shifting prescriptions on another key issue: at what age children should learn of adoption. A virtual truism of social workers—that a child should know of adoption as soon as he or she could understand— begged the question and probably offered some parents a rationale for putting off disclosure. Meanwhile, social workers admonished parents to make sure they told early enough so that the child would not learn of adoption from others. This was difficult to anticipate, though common sense would suggest that the risk of such inadvertent disclosure would rise sharply as children became more verbal and came into contact with more people outside the immediate family. By the 1950s, social workers assumed that disclosure was not a one-time event but a process of talking about adoption. Some experts even advised talking to infants about adoption. "When you feel like it occasionally say something like 'We're so glad we adopted you.' He just needs to hear the word 'adopted' said in a happy tone."[34] Another manual coached, "practice using the word *adoption*," and offered a script for adopters to rehearse: "You can say 'We're so happy we adopted you' while you are hugging and holding your baby. 'We're so lucky to have adopted you into our family' is an alternative." In a final stage direction, the author cautioned, "use the word *adoption* spontaneously."[35] Such "telling" probably did not convey much to young children, experts admitted, but it was therapeutic for parents—good practice for later telling, when children would ask hard questions and scrutinize parents' body language and emotional responses as well as their answers.[36] Though not all experts advocated talking to infants about adoption, most did seem to agree that children should learn of adoption between the ages of three and five and that parents should tell "early and often."

In the late 1950s and early 1960s, psychiatrists challenged this conventional wisdom, warning that early and repeated disclosure of adoption damaged children's self-esteem and sense of identity.[37] Those oriented to Freudian accounts of development feared that the disquieting facts of adoption would complicate children's resolution of the Oedipal conflict. The "family romance"—the common childhood fantasy that one is adopted—might prove deeply traumatic for children who really were adopted. Such experts recommended that parents should not disclose adoption until children were ten to thirteen years old, even given the considerable risk that they would learn of their adoption from others. Social workers and other adoption experts never embraced this recommendation, but it did resurface occasionally. One 1993 manual acknowledged the psychoanalytic counsel in favor of later disclosure, but the authors themselves made the case for telling early.[38] "Some psychologists," they noted, recommended waiting until children were five years old before telling them about adoption, though they advocated for earlier disclosure. In her 1992 manual *The Adoption Lifecycle*, Elinor B. Rosenberg, a social worker and adoptive parent, cautioned adopters about the dangers of early disclosure. Children younger than six or seven years old, she wrote, "lack the capacity to understand the concepts of adoptive and biological parenthood . . . News of the adoption at this stage, then, paves the way for confusion." She acknowledged the risk that children would learn of adoption from others if parents did not tell early. Her advice left adopters with a knotty dilemma, as she conceded: "Disclosure at this age is a trade-off of trust over comprehension."[39]

Throughout the century, advice about disclosure to others remained much more consistent. Even in the 1980s and 1990s, when experts counseled very frank disclosure to children, they continued to advocate discretion when it came to dealing with others. Social workers advised that it was unnecessary (and impractical) to try to conceal the fact of adoption from others—but also that it was unnecessary (and imprudent) to disclose any particulars to those outside the family. CBD workers raised no objection when clients revealed that they welcomed a job transfer because it would allow them to keep adoption secret from those outside the family. In fact, this version of confidentiality won social workers' imprimatur, as a 1935 case record reveals. Of clients who were about to move to a distant city, the social worker noted, "They seemed very glad to take Patsy with them as they wished to make her so completely their own that no one would know that she had been adopted— they do not hide the fact of her adoption [from the child herself] but wish to be removed from the place where she was known to a number of people." The case also suggests how the possibilities of disclosure might shift with changing circumstances. In Delaware, Patsy, adopted as a five-year-old, would have encountered people who knew her birth relatives, and her adoptive parents had no choice about disclosing the fact of her adoption. In a new place, though, they could tell their own story—or not—about their family.

Social workers looked askance at adopters who disclosed the family's circumstances indiscriminately. In a 1955 record, the case worker found her clients, already adoptive parents of one child, "perhaps too ready to introduce the fact of [their son's] adoption to people whom they meet casually." A record from the late 1960s approved the discretion of the prospective adopters: "They don't anticipate needing to give details about the child they adopt to even their families," a comment followed by a cautionary tale of some adopters who had been too free with details of a child's background. In some cases, social workers explicitly advised adopters to conceal some information. Explaining their child's mixed-race parentage to his African American adopters in 1946, the bureau worker counseled, "In view of this situation they very well could see how important it was for them never to breathe anything to anyone about the parentage of this child." Even after 1980, the same experts who urged parents to tell their children the whole truth also coached adopters on how to deflect curious questions from anyone else.[40]

Prescriptive literature purveyed the same message. *If You Adopt a Child*, a 1957 manual, advised, "Experience has shown that the less others know about your child before he came into your home, the quicker they are able to accept him as *your* child."[41] The authors counseled adopters to resist the temptation to set the record straight when others assumed a biological relationship. If someone were to comment on the resemblance between adoptive parent and child, they coached, the adopter might simply say "thank you" or agree. Disclosure to others was advocated only on a need-to-know basis, and most agreed that few outside the family needed to know anything beyond the fact of adoption. Discretion served to protect children from outsiders who might make them feel uncomfortably different. Moreover, privacy maintained family boundaries; it was an entitlement of family life by law and custom and a potent mechanism of family solidarity.

Before 1970 social workers agreed that parents had a duty to disclose adoption to their children, but they assumed that in loving and secure adoptive families, the issue would not loom large. Social workers sought to assure themselves that adoptive parents would tell, and they offered guidance on what, when, and how to tell. Their advice could be summarized succinctly: tell, but don't dwell on it. Adoptive parents, on their part, had won social and legal support for the privacy of the adoptive family: legal procedures of relinquishment made parental rights transferable, and the sealed record and amended birth certificate served as a firewall between birth and adoptive families.

But as the postwar adoption consensus eroded, even those who supported adoption began to see disclosure in a different light. The new conventional wisdom of the 1980s held that "adoption is a life-long process." The language of risk returned to adoption. Now, though, it was not the adoptive family that was threatened by the "bad seed"—the possibility that an adopted child would carry unknown defects. Instead,

adopted children were themselves at risk, in the eyes of a new generation of experts who argued that separation from blood kin rendered
adopted children vulnerable to a formidable list of disorders. To negotiate the hazards of growing up without birth kin, adopted children required expert guidance. This attitude indirectly influenced disclosure,
mostly by revising the counsel of reticence. Since experts had come to
consider adoption a persistent liability as children negotiated the developmental tasks of growing up, then more people outside the family
needed to know they were adopted. A 1989 manual, for example, advised parents to tell their children's teachers: "Because children in the
middle childhood years are working through a lot of issues concerning
how they joined their families, it is important for teachers to be aware of
the child's adoption and the issues the child might have as a result."[42]
Previously advised not to overemphasize adoption, parents were now
admonished to be aware that it would likely shape every stage of their
children's development.

The biggest change in adoption disclosure was wrought by adopted
persons themselves. As the large cohort of children adopted in the 1950s
came of age, they challenged the law and practice of adoption secrecy
and disclosure. As these voices reached a national audience, social work
practice changed in response. By the 1990s, social workers at the CBD
were endorsing a radically different version of the "good" adoptive parents' attitude toward disclosure. A 1994 case record revealed the new
ideal: "They have totally accepted Edward and yet recognize that as an
adopted person he has the right to grow up with the knowledge that he
was not born into his family. They are not threatened by the fact that he
has biological family members and may want to locate them at some
point. [The adopters] are comfortable with this and will give help and
support should he decide to search." Prospective adopters had once
turned to agencies so they might receive assurances that birth parents
would not "interfere." Now, those same agencies counseled adoptive
parents that accepting "the fact of adoption" meant that they should be
"comfortable with" the possibility that their child would one day reclaim biological kin. A seismic upheaval was transforming the contours
of adoption. At the epicenter was the drama of search and reunion.

6

Adoption Challenged:
Beyond the Best Solution

*The Adoption Tri-
angle,* published in 1978, registered a new wave of caution about the
risks of adoption. It was the most influential and widely circulated
statement of a wider retreat from the postwar "best solution."[1] The title,
suggesting illicit sex and betrayal, sets the tone; and throughout the
book, adoption is rendered in the language of illness and disability. The
first page warns that adoption is a "lifelong process . . . an all too real
and complex phenomenon that can be the cause of many potential
problems" (13). In wrenching letters, birth mothers write of their sorrow and unrelieved grief over relinquishment, a loss that the authors
name "psychological amputation." "Adoptees," the authors warn, inevitably suffer the "handicap" of being "severed" from biological kin. Their
disease is "genealogical bewilderment."[2] Their "true identity" has been
stolen; only lifting the veil of secrecy can make the adopted person
whole.

Written mostly from the perspective of adopted persons and relinquishing mothers, *The Adoption Triangle* also held a cautionary tale for
adoptive parents. Without the "bond" of birth, the authors write, adop-

tive mothers have an "inherently unstable primary identification" with their children, even those adopted in infancy. Adopted children are more "vulnerable" than others to stress, and are over-represented on psychiatric wards and in counseling practices. Their "special needs" are often overlooked by adoptive parents, whose own sense of inadequacy blinds them to their children's pain. With adolescence, the "trauma" of adoption intensifies. As adults, adopted persons often "suffer from low esteem" and "feel embarrassed at their adoptive status." In the face of this pervasive malaise, the authors offer the panacea of expert guidance: "Mental health practitioners today recognize the unique problems of triangle members and are better able to help them" (16).

By 1970, the broad consensus that had supported adoption began to crumble. Further liberalization of sexual attitudes, new birth control technology, and legal abortion broadened the choices available to women, and led to a stigmatizing of relinquishment. Women could terminate unwelcome pregnancies or, alternatively, raise children born out of wedlock without automatically forfeiting middle-class respectability. In this cultural context, relinquishment rapidly lost the respect accorded to it under the tenets of the best solution and came to be regarded with suspicion and condemnation. At home and abroad, the shifting politics of race qualified the enthusiasm once accorded to the rainbow families of color-blind universalism. Sociobiology—a strange bedfellow of sexual revolution, Black Power, and anti-imperialism—contributed to the dissolution of the adoption consensus in the 1980s. In both scientific and popular discourses, environmentalism gradually yielded to a pervasive biological determinism that renewed old fears of the risks of adoption.

The narrative of the best solution was directly challenged by adopted persons themselves, in a recognizable subgenre of memoirs that emerged in this period. Such memoirs were themselves an indicator of the sharp shift in views of adoption: according to the postwar consensus, there was no adoption story once the adoptive family had formed. In autobiographical accounts of their pervasive sense of difference and loss, these authors rejected that view. The improved life chances promised by adoption, they argued, did not compensate for the rupture of separating from biological family. In the growing search movement, adopted persons fought cultural and legal prohibitions against disclosure to establish ties with biological kin.[3]

At the same time, women who had relinquished children for adoption began to speak out, no longer constrained by the fading stigma of unwed motherhood. Rejecting the shield of silence provided by confidential adoption, they challenged the postwar consensus. In an autobiographical act of renaming and self-construction, they claimed the new identity of "birth mother."[4] Against the tenets of the best solution, the term asserts a lifelong relationship: relinquishment can transfer parental rights, but not the inalienable bond of biology.

Search narratives as a distinctive category had their origins in adoptee organizations which began to spring up in the 1970s; the life stories shared in oral accounts and newsletters were one important element of the movement's shared culture.[5] During the 1980s and 1990s, stories of search and reunion reached beyond these groups to claim new audiences and attention. Adoption reunion became a subject for advice columnists like Ann Landers and a staple of radio and television talk shows. These narratives recruited new participants to the movement. Many published memoirs reveal that the authors decided to search after hearing the stories of other adoptees on radio or television, and then received inspiration and assistance from organized search groups or their publications.[6] Adoptees' stories of their search for hidden pasts and their reunions with blood relatives drew sympathetic audiences. Soon, they were followed by memoirs from birth mothers themselves, who cast aside confidentiality in order to tell their stories. They, too, sought to heal the wounds of the past by finding the children they had relinquished for adoption.

Four influential books served as foundations of the adoption rights movement and as prototypes for the search narrative. Jean Paton, adopted as a child, interviewed adult adoptees in the early 1950s in a project she named Orphan Voyage. After numerous rejections of the resulting book, *The Adopted Break Silence*, Paton published it herself in 1954. *Orphan Voyage* followed in 1968. In this book, also privately published, Paton interspersed the story of her own search for biological relatives with interviews of other adopted adults and advocacy for reform of adoption practice, including allowing for the possibility of contact between parents and children after relinquishment.[7] Again, Paton's work drew little public notice. *Book Review Digest,* which indexes a wide range of newspapers and periodicals, lists no reviews.

Florence Fisher's *The Search for Anna Fisher,* published in 1973, was reviewed in both *Library Journal* and *The New York Times Book Review.*[8] Detailing her long effort to discover the identity of the woman who gave birth to her and relinquished her for adoption, Fisher ended her narrative with a call to action. The book publicized Fisher's ALMA (Adoptees' Liberty Movement Association), founded in 1971 to advise adoptees and birth parents on how to carry out a search and to press for access to sealed adoption records. Soon after, Betty Jean Lifton, a well-known playwright and author and the wife of the nationally known psychiatrist Robert Jay Lifton, published *Twice Born* (1975).[9] Her memoir and subsequent advocacy for adoption reform brought wider visibility to the claims of Paton and Fisher.

Written by Arthur D. Sorosky, a child psychiatrist, and Annette Baran and Reuben Pannor, both social workers, *The Adoption Triangle* brought the cachet of expert credentials to a gathering movement that was challenging traditional adoption. The sealed record, the instrument of confidential adoption, became the target of the movement for "adoption rights" or "adoption reform." *The Adoption Triangle,* subtitled *Sealed or Opened Records: How They Affect Adoptees, Birth Parents, and Adoptive Parents,* exemplified and advanced this argument. In challenging the sealed record, critics of confidential adoption used the language of exposé: they were ferreting out hidden secrets in a moral quest, shining the light of truth on adoption. Accolades for *The Adoption Triangle* illustrate this pervasive metaphor. Florence Fisher praised its "searing condemnation of secrecy," its "rare and penetrating insight," the "truth" revealed in its "voyage through the looking glass." The *Los Angeles Times* characterized the book as "a bright glimpse of a previously dark subject . . . true and open."[10]

Such rhetoric reflects the language and traditional ideals of American political culture. Secrecy has long been associated with conspiracy, from the anti-Masonic movement of the nineteenth century to the anti-Communist crusades of the 1940s and 1950s. In the 1970s, the sensational revelations of the Watergate scandal provided concrete demonstration of what many Americans were already prepared to believe: secrecy was suspect, a veil thrown over clandestine and illicit activity.[11] The challenge to secrecy supplied a potent political language for adoption activists, and it also served to define a unifying goal—the demand to open sealed records.

For many, the critique of sealed records was a response to galling personal experience. As persons adopted in the 1940s and 1950s began to search for birth relatives in the rights-oriented decades of the 1970s and after, they encountered the wall of the sealed record. Some surmounted that wall with relative ease. Search narratives reveal that adoption secrecy is uneven and sometimes highly permeable, often an open secret rather than a closely guarded one. Others, though, spent years in futile quests for the identity of birth relatives. As adopted persons turned to courts, public records, and social work agencies, they confronted bureaucratic obstacles at every turn: layers of officialdom stood between them and even the most ordinary facts of their origins. Most courts refused access to those records except in cases of extreme medical exigency. Social work agencies like the Children's Bureau of Delaware that upheld professional standards of record-keeping maintained the wall as well. Some agencies required adult adoptees to get permission from their adoptive parents before they would release even nonidentifying background information. Angered and humiliated by such treatment, adoptees used the language of rights to assault the law and practice of confidential adoption.

Some moved beyond the demand for open records to a comprehensive critique of confidential adoption, a shift illustrated in the growing militance of successive editions of *The Adoption Triangle*. In the 1978 edition, the authors endorsed the release of confidential information to adopted persons who had attained legal majority. In the revised edition of 1984, they called for an expanded agenda. "Opening the sealed records is merely the tip of the iceberg, under which lies a vast mosaic of contradictions that questions the entire institution of adoption as it has been practiced" (217). In garbled syntax and obfuscating passive voice, the authors hedged on what that might mean, as in their final recommendation calling for "consideration on the part of the authorities of new adoption alternatives to provide stable homes and families for children who would not be relinquished otherwise" (224). But the authors tipped their hands in the previous chapter's review of "contemporary adoption issues," where they issued caveats about every conceivable alternative to the biological family. Their brief commentaries combined dire warnings about children's vulnerability with covert scare tactics about the risks of adoptive parenting. "Abandonment depression" was the fate of the "older child" placed for adoption. Children with "special needs" "pose a variety of problems." Transracial and international adoptions have been the subject of "controversy," and though some see them as successful, the experts—"adoption social workers"—"have become concerned about the potential identity crises created in transracial homes." Single parents must be screened to exclude "recluses" or persons not "comfortable" with their gender roles. Artificial insemination lets parents deny and hide their infertility, and tragically cuts off children from their birth fathers (the sperm donors). The black market lurks in the background, with unscrupulous persons ready to exploit "desperate" adopters. In the end, the only "alternatives" that appear in a positive light are open adoption and "alternative ways of parenting." The chapter closes by advising "desperate" couples to "exercise caution and develop a perspective." Perhaps medical technology will yield a miracle baby. Otherwise, would-be parents are encouraged to get over their attachment to the "nuclear family concept" and "develop meaningful relationships with children on different levels."[12] The message was clear: the best solution was best avoided.

Ironically, this assault on adoption developed in the wake of its precipitant decline. After 1970 the number of adoptions dropped dramatically, even as births out of wedlock increased. "Stranger" adoptions dropped steadily as relinquishment became uncommon and stigmatized. In 1970 there were 89,000 adoptions; by 1975, there were 48,000. The federal government has not collected national statistics on adoption since 1975, but subsequent estimates suggest that this number has remained relatively constant.[13] Of course, the dropping number of adoptions was not inherently a cause for concern. In the best of all possible worlds, children would be born into families sustained by intact communities and humane public support, including adequate health care, quality day care, and secure employment for their parents. Under such conditions, very few would end up dependent on the kindness of strangers. But as the twentieth century waned, children's welfare was declining in one of the richest nations in the world.[14] Children born out of wedlock were often raised by hard-pressed mothers on the edge of economic survival. After a decade of Republican assaults on public funding for women and children, Democrats, too, took up the agenda of "ending welfare as we know it." Tens of thousands of children grew up in foster care, even as critics challenged adoption as inhumane and unnatural.

By the 1980s, adoption occupied a smaller and smaller part of the case load in public child welfare agencies, church social service agencies, and voluntary agencies like the CBD. In the 1970s, the bureau reversed its historic decision of 1951, when in response to pressing demand it had become an agency solely devoted to adoption. Now, the agency resumed its older role as a community agency offering a range of social services—family counseling, supervision of foster care, child welfare and protection services. Its adoption practice, increasingly, was restricted only to "special needs" adoption—placing children who once would have been considered "unadoptable." As some of the children the bureau had placed for adoption began to return to the agency seeking clues to their pasts, the CBD also began to define a role for itself in "post-adoption services," including agency assistance in search and reunion.

Testimony to the adoption reform movement, the search narrative became a popular genre, often organized around a recognizable stock plot. Initially addressed to an esoteric and informal audience of "triad" members—in actuality, mostly adopted persons and birth mothers—it soon reached wider audiences through published memoirs, advice columns, and radio and TV journalism. The search narrative's distinctive story of identity lost and found appealed for its novelty, but at the same time it borrowed conventions from other, established literary genres. In the tradition of detective novels, it embodied the compelling search for a hidden truth. The search narrative resembled the quest novel in its account of obstacles confronted and overcome in the search for reunion with blood relatives. Search narratives also echoed the themes of coming-of-age stories: for adopted persons, self-knowledge is hard won and the hardships of the search serve as a distinctive initiation into full self-hood. This subgenre was influenced by the formal conventions of auto-biography but also by popular confessional forms such as "real TV," radio and television talk shows, and Internet list serves and chat rooms.[15]

In a common narrative trajectory, search stories define the problem (a lost or incomplete self) and then recount the search for wholeness. While some adopted persons find birth parents easily, for most the search is an intricate story of clues gathered and pursued, dead ends and discouragement, obstacles encountered and overcome. The recounting of such quests serves both to dramatize the search and to offer practical instruction and encouragement to other persons engaged in search. Most end with the drama of reunion, followed by a brief coda about the aftermath. These exceptional stories of relatives separated at birth are preoccupied with a pervasive theme of contemporary culture: the quest for individual identity.[16]

Search narratives, and adoption memoirs more generally, are women's stories. In part this reflects the actual predominance of women in the search movement. As many observers have noted, women are much more likely than men to undertake searches.[17] And overwhelm-ingly, searchers (both male and female) are looking for their mothers, not for their fathers. Organizations of birth "parents" are gender neutral in name only; actual membership is almost exclusively female.[18] To date, not a single birth father has published a full-length memoir, and few men claim the name "birth father" publicly.[19] Women also predominate as authors of memoirs about adoptive parenting. Despite the emphasis on genetics as justification for undertaking a search, adoption stories are almost always stories about motherhood, not about heredity; and conflicts over adoption are struggles over who can claim the name of mother.

Typically, writers begin by explaining their motivation for searching. Writing against the postwar consensus, with its assumption that the adoptive family completely replaces birth kinship, the authors describe separation from blood kin as deprivation and, often, as stigma. In *Mother, Can You Hear Me?* Elizabeth Cooper Allen writes, "I was never without a feeling of loss and a sense of being different from others.

There was some essential void in my connection with the natural order of origin—or birth. I was a foundling, a changeling."[20] Katrina Maxtone-Graham describes adoption as "amputation from history" in her autobiography, *An Adopted Woman*.[21] This language echoes the view of genealogical bewilderment advanced by some adoption rights activists, a sense of rupture from biological and historical origins. For some, the search is an effort to redeem a hurtful childhood. Doris McMillon hopes that finding her birth mother will relieve the "deadly emptiness" of a spirit scarred by her abusive, mentally ill adoptive mother.[22]

Most narratives assert that the motivation to search is natural and intrinsic, and they specifically refute the notion that search is a symptom of unhappy adoptive families. Search organizations have tirelessly made the same argument, challenging the earlier assumption that secure and happy adopted people would have little curiosity about their origins. Some memoirs exhibit a telling "over-correction" on this matter. Even in narratives that portray markedly painful relationships with adopted parents, the authors insist that their desire to search has nothing to do with their unhappy childhoods, but instead is a natural—even universal—response to adoption. Allen, for example, describes her adoptive mother as "strong, controlling, and unbending . . . harsh." She waits until both parents are dead before she begins a search for birth parents and, after her reunion with her birth mother, proclaims that the experience has yielded "a new appreciation for the many very positive things my parents were able to give me."[23] Amy Dean's adoptive mother drank heavily, and when Dean was two and a half she was placed in foster care. Two years later, her adoptive parents divorced and her adoptive father got custody of her. Nonetheless, she reassures her father that her search is not motivated by a longing for another mother: "It's not so much the *person* I want to find as the *answers* to my questions. I want to find my roots."[24] Maxtone-Graham avers, "I was learning more and more . . . how little my search had to do . . . with my adoptive parents. My unhappiness as a child had not been their doing, I was beginning to realize, but the simple fact of adoption."[25]

In some accounts, adopted persons experience themselves not only as incomplete but as defective. Ironically, the rights-oriented adoption movement has been oblivious to the critique of another contemporary rights-based movement, that of disabled persons, which has challenged the use of disability as a metaphor of inadequacy or brokenness. In *Mixed Blessing*, McMillon describes an adoptive mother who might have come from central casting's wicked stepmother roster. Angry and mentally unstable, she constantly warns her daughter of the taint of her "bad blood" and admonishes her to be grateful that her adoptive parents rescued her from her "whore" of a mother.[26] Frances Lear fears her unknown heredity; when she gives birth to healthy daughters, she is tremendously relieved. "The miracle was their existence, that I would actually give birth to a child, that I was capable of normal everything—conception, pregnancy, delivery—that the unknown genetic tracks that preceded me and that I had traveled would not, suddenly, in the body of my issue, lead to unimaginable diseases and traits and congenital poisons."[27] For Jean Paton, writing in 1968, adoption is inevitably second best. "No adoption can attain the potentiality of family life. I do not like this; it makes an illegitimate birth like a clubfoot or a harelip. But it is true."[28] In this disturbing image of physical deformity, adoption is not simply rupture; it is marked by indelible stigma.

Other accounts attest to lasting pain associated with relinquishment. Jean Downie remembers feeling "second best" when she learns of her adoption at age fourteen, inferior to children born to the parents who are raising them and uncomfortably obligated to adoptive parents.[29] Her account might simply serve as a cautionary tale about the importance of early disclosure; some others, though, share her feelings even though they learned of their adoptions as young children. Tim Green describes the anxious striving of his childhood and adult life as an effect of adoption, derived from his sense of rejection by his birth mother and his fear that adoptive parents, too, will find him unacceptable unless he can earn their love.[30] Robert Andersen, a psychiatrist, depicts his crushing sense of inferiority as a result of his adoption in a bitter memoir titled *Second Choice: Growing Up Adopted.*[31]

Search narratives characteristically proceed to recount the process of finding birth relatives. Like protagonists in detective stories, searchers try to solve the mystery of their hidden pasts, and the narratives build suspense through plot lines that include red herrings, unreliable witnesses, and obstructions to the investigation. Adopted persons begin their search by appealing to agencies and judges and pursuing leads through newspapers, telephone books, and public records. If those methods fail, they hire private investigators, consult mediums and psychics, and use insider contacts, subterfuge, or direct action to gain access to sequestered records. Adoptees often find themselves pitted against established authority in their quest for justice. These authors are united in their critique of sealed adoption records, a position that again reflects the politics of the search movement. One prominent national figure in that movement, Sandra Kay Musser, served a jail term for her illegal use of Social Security Administration records to assist searches.[32] For some in the adoption rights movement, Musser is a martyr whose principled civil disobedience was punished by a repressive legal system.

The reunion scene provides the climax to most search narratives. In all but one account (Robert Andersen's), the search leads the author to a birth relative.[33] Invariably, the moment of physical encounter between birth mother and adoptee is dramatized. In a restaging of the mother's intense scrutiny of her newborn infant, the reunited mother and child exchange searching gazes, looking eagerly for a physical resemblance that represents and confirms their biological kinship. Downie finds a birth aunt who shows her photographs and exclaims over her resemblance to a grandmother and half-sister.[34] Green encounters "the mirror image of myself"; at the reunion, his birth mother is even wearing a leather trench coat like his. Green portrays the moment as a reversal of the disembodiment that many adoptees describe; it is "to see oneself incarnate."[35]

Allen is disappointed at her first sight of Almeda, her birth mother: "I looked at the small body in the heavy winter clothes and could feel no connection." Her birth mother doesn't resemble her at all, she feels—instead, she is disconcerted to see that Almeda looks a lot like her adoptive mother. Scrutinizing old photographs of Almeda, she later discerns a faint physical resemblance between herself and her mother; she notes with satisfaction, "It was then that I knew that I truly was Almeda's daughter."[36] Dean looks in vain for some physical sign of her kinship with her birth mother. Writing in epistolary form, she addresses her birth mother: "I look now at the pictures of you and me together. I glance back and forth, from me to you and you to me, but I can't discern any resemblance. This disappoints me. I think I had expectations, prior to seeing you, that we would look just like each other, or at least share some visible similarities."[37] Physical resemblance, these memoirs reveal, serves as a powerful sign of genetic connection. When it is absent, the reunion seems incomplete. Some search memoirs include photographs, allowing readers to participate in the process of searching the faces of participants to discern physical similarities.

In the characteristic denouement, the narrator describes the relationship that develops after the initial reunion. For some, the search yields an ideal affinity with a welcoming mother. Maxtone-Graham, for example, feels an immediate rapport with her birth mother that she attributes to their genetic relationship. "If I made an allusion, or cracked a joke, or uttered an abbreviated opinion, I never had to wonder, 'Will she get it?' As with people one has known all one's life, there was no need to make explanations."[38] Dean portrays a more confusing and ambivalent relationship with her birth mother, "one that has a built-in closeness because of our mother-daughter connection and our blood bond, but also has a limited emotional 'comfort zone' to handle such closeness because we've never connected as mother and daughter. In reality, we're strangers."[39] McMillon finds her birth mother and birth father, but not the love and intimacy she had sought. "The problem was, I now had two new parents—strangers."[40]

Most of these narratives affirm the credo of the search movement: reunion heals the losses of the past. For some adopted persons, the search establishes a broader network of kinship as newly identified relatives name themselves as family. In some narratives, shared rituals affirm the expanded boundaries of family, as in weddings attended by birth and adoptive relatives. In virtually every account, photographs are a vital medium of reunion. Typically searchers take photographs and have others take photographs of themselves with birth relatives. Reunited persons tell their stories by reviewing family photographs. Through visual images, participants share vicariously the years they have spent apart; in photographic documentation of reunions, they lay claim to a shared future.

Some memoirs seem to strain for a happy ending even when reunion proves disappointing. Some assert that the process of discovery is itself healing, even when reunions do not result in sustained connections. As Maxtone-Graham reflects at the conclusion of her long search, "I . . . had been at last an instrument of my own fate . . . I had had the power of action. And thus it was that I had become a real human being" (267). For Allen, reunion is symbolic rebirth: "I was giving birth to Almeda [her birth mother] within myself, and I was giving birth to myself as a more complete Elizabeth" (73). McMillon redefines her quest as she decides that she was searching not for her mother but for a psychic wholeness to heal the wounds of her childhood. "Louise [her adoptive mother] was the vital factor in my life . . . Josefine? Josefine was a total stranger, conjured up for comfort like an imaginary playmate, and I felt fear and anticipation at the meeting in Germany but no sense of homecoming, of family. Only the knowledge of finally finishing old business" (225). With reunion, McMillon relinquishes the fantasy of "the perfect mother-image . . . It was asking for an intimacy that few people ever reach, and the fact of the blood tie meant nothing at all." For her, healing comes not with reunion but as she becomes a mother herself. She recognizes a new tie with her stepdaughters—"My *real* daughters. *I* was their real mother, now, the mother who would raise them from this point on." And the last line celebrates her impending maternity of a child by birth: "I was pregnant. The real test of my growing up was just ahead" (247). Still, even though McMillan's search for a mother is not satisfied by reunion, the experience of the search helped her claim an adult identity as a mother herself.

Search memoirs rarely document unsuccessful searches or end in disillusionment. The few exceptions help illuminate the tacit rules of the genre—and its role in promoting the search movement. In one such exception, Andersen's *Second Choice,* privately published, the author's unsuccessful search serves only to deepen his torment about the past. He uncovers evidence that he was sold in a black-market adoption and comes to suspect that his mother was a prostitute. The unrelieved bitterness of this memoir is at odds with the tone of most search narratives, and it challenges a fundamental claim of the search movement—that the process of search is itself healing and empowering. This is also the only published memoir of a search that comes to a dead end. Its lack of closure violates popular conventions for a tidy ending. It also under-

cuts the conventional trajectory of memoir, with its movement from in-
nocence to experience to wisdom. The scraps of information that
Andersen acquires do not liberate him from the past; rather, they only
confirm his feelings of rejection and betrayal.

James Stingley's *Mother, Mother* breaks from the genre in a bitter
story of his betrayal at the hands of a birth mother who finds *him*.[41] His
first encounter with her is jarringly at odds with others: rather than
searching his mother's features for resemblances, Stingley regards her
with the assessing sexual gaze of a man looking at a woman: "She
seemed in her mid-forties, but even by Los Angeles standards, she was
stunning. Her cheekbones were high and wide, her chin dimpled. Her
eyes were electric blue. Her lips were supple and sensuous. Her hair was
fiery red, styled dramatically . . . Her body, what I could see of it, was no
less spectacular"(8). This reunion leads to a tempestuous sexual relationship between mother and son. The conventions of the quest novel
yield to film noir in this story of female betrayal, which ends with
Stingley's bitter repudiation of both of his mothers: "If I believed anything now, it was that I had been a pawn between two women, each
seeking her own satisfaction, each finally seeing me only as a disturbing
reminder neither could wash her hands of" (192). For him, reconciliation comes not in reunion but when he fathers a son: "It is because of
him that I have come closer and closer to being the whole man that I
have needed so desperately to become" (219).

Perhaps it is significant that these two stories of bad reunions are
both authored by men, though three other reunion accounts by male
authors follow the conventions of the genre: Frank Law's and Michael
Watson's stories, both privately published, and Tim Green's *A Man and
His Mother*.[42] In any case, Andersen and Stingley both write at the margins of the search movement and outside its dominant narrative.
Andersen's perspective is more immediately shaped by his psychiatric
training, and his search is undertaken in isolation; he makes no reference to support groups or the inspiration of media accounts of searches.
Stingley does not initiate the search himself, and his story is not written
in dialogue with the search movement. Though his story might be taken
as a caveat about the unanticipated consequences of reunion, he himself
does not present it as such: instead, it is simply a sensational story of

manhood attained by escape from the past—for him, both biological and adoptive mothers.

Sarah Saffian writes with a consciousness of the search movement and its literature, and her memoir self-consciously inverts the genre in a story of unexpected reversal.[43] She herself had been contemplating a search for birth family when her birth parents contact her. This unexpected turn of events leaves her confused, self-protective, and wary. It is three years later when she finally feels ready to meet her birth family in person. Saffian's apparently contrary response undercuts a core claim of the search movement, the assertion that all adoptees long for reunion. But her experience confirms a corollary tenet of reunion literature, which emphasizes the importance of the adopted person's initiative in search. Infantalized by the sealed record with its lock on the past, the argument goes, adopted persons are consigned to permanent childhood. To grow up, they must take their fates into their own hands by conducting the search themselves.[44] And like most authors of search narratives, Saffian does not write beyond the ending of reunion.

Why do most search narratives drop the curtain soon after reunion? One likely reason is that such endings sustain a fantasy of ideal kinship that is seldom realized in actual reunion aftermaths (or, for that matter, in family life more generally). In research that has been done on adoption reunion, observers have found that most reunited kin do not establish close or sustained relationships.[45] After the initial excitement of rediscovery, strain sometimes develops as newly found family members struggle to define their relationships with one another. Only rarely do reunions result in radically reconstituted families. Birth families seldom displace adoptive kin, and faced with the daunting prospect of assuming all the mutual obligations associated with two sets of kin, many adopted persons back off. In most cases, the initial intensity of reunion yields to a more casual and limited relationship. Such endings would diminish the dramatic momentum of search and reunion memoir. Exploring the aftermath of reunion also subtly undercuts the political agenda of adoption rights activists, since the occasional bad reunion and the more common anticlimactic aftermath might seem to diminish the value of the search. Activists argue that the outcome of the search is less important than the process—a view affirmed in accounts that do not explore the outcome in detail. Whatever the result, they assert, adopted persons have an unconditional right to information about their past and access to birth families. Reunion endings, then, indirectly suggest the extent to which these memoirs are shaped by the concerns of the adoption rights movement. They also suggest the renegotiated boundaries of talk about adoption. For even as search and reunion memoirs break the silence around confidential adoption, they also themselves mark out a new terrain of the unsaid and unspeakable: few explore what happens after the initial meeting, much less venture onto the territory of bad reunions.

Birth mother memoirs offer another challenge to the tenets of the postwar adoption consensus by telling stories once veiled in silence. Most of them re-enact the shaming of pregnancy out of wedlock to explain their adoption decisions. For them, even more than for adopted persons, stigma is written on the body as the young women's pregnancies mark them as illicitly sexual. Recounting her stay in a maternity home, Carol Schaefer recalls the residents' preoccupation with stretch marks. "We were all concerned whenever a little line would appear. To hide the fact that we were damaged goods, we could lie that we had broken our hymens riding a bike when we were nine years old, but we were terrified that stretch marks would brand us forever as unwed mothers."[46] Margaret Moorman remembers her dismay when her doctor tells her the stretch marks on her breasts will remain after she gives birth: "I hadn't realized there would be visible scars. I had been told, again and again, that I would give my baby up and *put all this behind me.* How could that happen if I, like Hester Prynne with her scarlet A, bore the sign of my disgrace forever?"[47] In these memoirs, the authors refuse the shame of silence by volunteering the stories that they had once feared would be told on their bodies.

All of these narratives directly contest the spoiled identity of unwed motherhood as they portray it for contemporary readers. And significantly, most of them also contest the postwar narrative of adoption as the best solution for the woman confronted with an unexpected and unwanted pregnancy. Refuting the received wisdom of that era, one such birth mother asserts flatly, "Leaving one's child in the care of total strangers whom one has never met and will presumably never meet is crazy behavior. It is not a true 'choice' but a choice born of low self-esteem, a lack of options, and a sense of hopelessness."[48] By telling their stories, they refuse the secrecy that was supposed to protect them. Most refute the sanguine narrative of "second chance" that was part of the best solution: instead, they argue that relinquishment inflicted lasting wounds, unresolved grief, and intense longing for the child who was surrendered. Many say they were told they would forget these children; their memoirs are testaments to their remembering.[49]

Rebecca Harsin, for example, writes, "A birth-mother gives the most precious of gifts—her child—and society expects her to forget and go on with her life as though nothing had happened. That's just not the way it works."[50] A contemporary bumper sticker declares, "Birth-mothers Don't Forget." In her title, *Waiting to Forget: A Mother Opens the Door to Her Secret Past,* Moorman simultaneously dramatizes the impossibility of forgetting, underscores the decision to leave secrecy behind, and claims the identity of "mother." These authors seek to explain and justify their decisions to relinquish children by showing readers the intense pressure generated by restrictive sexual codes. At the same time, they contest that stigma by refusing the shield of secrecy that was part of the postwar bargain.

As they repudiate one spoiled identity, however, they confront another that is potentially as damaging. As Schaefer writes, "We [she and her child's father] could not speak the unspeakable even to one another, that we had given our own baby to total strangers and abandoned him to an unknown destiny."[51] Relinquishment as well as pregnancy is experienced as a stigma expressed on and through the body, as amputation and psychic dissociation. Schaefer writes that she was left with "half of myself," and in response, "I disconnected my feelings and was left with half a soul."[52] After her marriage, Harsin tries to conceive for a year without becoming pregnant, though no medical problem is apparent. She interprets her infertility as divine judgment: "I wasn't fit to be a mother. God didn't want me to have any more babies."[53] Schaefer worries that her son might somehow bear the stigmata of her pregnancy and relinquishment: "I still had doubts about my fitness to be a mother. Would my 'sin' hurt my second child somehow?'"[54]

Louise Jurgens believes that the emotional wound of relinquishment expresses itself on the birth mother's body. Narrating her own gynecological disease and hysterectomy, she opines that medical problems have their sources "in the emotional paths of our lives." She believes that birth mothers suffer more disability than others, and she attributes this to self-punishing emotions: "Fifty percent of the women who came to the meetings [of Concerned United Birthparents] had created disease in their bodies."[55] Lynn Franklin acknowledges that psychogenic theories of illness lack firm scientific grounding, but she too is inclined to believe that "my unresolved feelings [about relinquishment] caused a lack of harmony in my body" and that her gynecological problems were an expression of her "poor self-image as a woman."[56] Another writer, a birth mother herself, recounts the story of a birth mother raped by a stranger three months after she had relinquished a child. Citing other such cases, she concluded that relinquishment had left a "hole" which made the woman vulnerable.: "Until that place is filled, during the time the woman is psychologically unprotected, it marks the birth mother as a potential victim for any psychopath who is looking for one, for any accident waiting to happen."[57] Even as these women shed the stigma of unwed motherhood, they assume the shame and guilt of relinquishment.

This reversal, in which unwed motherhood is accepted and relinquishment shameful, marks the demise of the postwar consensus. The authors express guilt and intense regret over this decision, again refuting the postwar narrative of relinquishment as a recuperable loss rather than a wound that never heals. As these women are painfully aware, their decisions were intelligible—even laudable—within a context that no longer exists. Now, they are barely legible to audiences located within radically different sexual mores. In the 1950s and 1960s, 80 percent of white children born out of wedlock were relinquished for adoption; by 1980, fewer than 4 percent of unwed mothers made that decision.[58] These writers are women caught between two stories, neither of which is adequate to explain their experience. They violated the postwar narrative by their continuing regret and longing for relinquished children. Meanwhile, their stories of the shaming of illicit pregnancy have been rendered anachronistic; and in a social milieu far more skeptical of adoption, they are stigmatized as women who gave away their children.

In these autobiographies, the authors forcefully reclaim the identity of "mother." Lorraine Dusky's *Birthmark* captures the cultural anomaly of the mother without her child: "I read in a book by Margaret Drabble that the world is divided into two groups: those who have children and those who don't . . . Me? Well, I can flit back and forth into either group. I fit in both, I fit in neither."[59] Schaefer repudiates the use of "birth mother," now widespread in expert and popular literature. "I hated the term . . . right away. It sounded like we were brood mares and implied that the relationship to our children ended at birth."[60] Jurgens describes the wrenching experience of seeing another woman's name on her son's amended birth certificate: "Her relationship as his parent was one I could never have. I would never dare to pretend to be his parent. That was a privilege I could not have and a loss I would always mourn. But I had given birth to him. I had never stopped loving him. I was his mother, too."[61] In this revealing distinction, Jurgens considers "parent," unmarked by gender, as a transferable social role; by contrast, "mother" is an irrevocable identity conferred by biology ("I had given birth to him") and demonstrated in maternal feeling ("I had never stopped loving him").

But to claim this identity, as these accounts do in active autobiographical acts of assertion, is often to *dis*claim their own agency in relinquishment. Most portray themselves as powerless victims of circumstance, pressured by parents and social workers, brainwashed by the rhetoric of the best solution. *Torn from the Heart,* Jurgens's title, graphically depicts adoption as coercion. Some birth mothers describe their relinquished children as "lost" to adoption, as if they had unaccountably wandered off—a choice of words that obscures the actual scene of relinquishment, in which birth mothers themselves sign papers to execute their voluntary termination of parental rights.[62] This revealing language testifies to the potent stigma of relinquishment. The postwar adoption consensus portrayed relinquishment as an act of love, the mark of the "good" and selfless mother. With the faltering of that consensus, relinquishing mothers have no defense against the full cultural judgment brought to bear on the "bad," selfish mother who rejects and abandons her child.

To explain the remarkable agency that they do exercise—in writing these accounts; in pursuing exhaustive searches for their children; and, in some cases, in speaking, writing, and organizing for the adoption rights movement—the authors invoke nature and maternal instinct. Dusky explains that she relinquished her child because she felt forced to choose between career and children. In retrospect, she regrets her decision and portrays her desire for a career as a misguided effort to deny her female nature: "I thought I could outsmart my gender."[63] Explaining the overwhelmingly female constituency of birth parents' organizations, Jurgens attributes it to biology: "The birthmother's physical bond is so much stronger." When she finds her daughter, she presses the reluctant young woman to contact her birth father, motivated, she says, by her "maternal urge" to reunite father and daughter.[64] Sandra Musser's "found" daughter cuts her off a month after their reunion, but Musser insists nonetheless that "Blood is thicker than water." In fact, she takes her daughter's rejection as a test that proves the tenacity of mother love. She writes her estranged daughter, "You were a part of me for nine months and share my flesh and blood—that makes you important to me . . . a mother's love is always stronger for her child than vice versa . . . You can reject me, ignore me, or hate me—I will still continue to love you as one of my own."[65] Concerned United Birthparents, founded in Massachusetts in 1976, uses the acronym of CUB and the logo of a mother bear to claim motherhood as an inalienable natural bond. Having given up the social role of motherhood, these authors insistently press the claims of biology. But these are treacherous waters, for the more they proclaim the power of nature, the more vulnerable they become to the censure of others ready to regard them as "unnatural" mothers for relinquishing their children.

Two birth mother memoirs suggest an alternative critique of the best solution, one that does not rely on an idealized natural motherhood. Margaret Moorman's *Waiting to Forget* reaches beyond personal narrative in a form that brings historical sources into dialogue with her remembered experience. In contrast to other birth mother memoirs, presented as testimony to the adoption rights movement, Moorman resists drawing a clear conclusion. Instead, she reflects on the shifting self-construction of autobiography, the way we tell and revise our stories, how they shape our lives. In her account, autobiography is not a single coherent story but something more like collage. Embodying the layers of memory in its own form, this memoir includes a document of earlier self-construction: the seven-page autobiography she wrote for the adoption agency as she prepared to relinquish her son. As she considers this experience from the perspective of the present, she reflects on current debates about adoption as they appear in birth mother narratives, news stories, and media representation. Moorman affirms, with other birth mothers, that the best solution was deeply mistaken in its facile assumption about loss: she is still "waiting to forget." But unlike others, she is not convinced relinquishment was a tragic mistake. Ultimately her narrative refuses closure: she can neither wholly condemn nor wholly embrace her own decision. Moorman searches for her birth son, and that narrative too remains unresolved. By the end of the book, she has established contact by letter, but her son does not want to meet her.

Like Moorman's memoir, Jan L. Waldron's *Giving Away Simone* stakes out a critique of the postwar consensus without fully endorsing the tenets of the adoption rights movement. Like other birth mother narratives, Waldron's challenges the narrative of the best solution, with its "willful romanticizing and reactionary rhetoric." Like Moorman, she uses memoir as cultural criticism as well as self-construction: "There are stakes, beyond the personal, in the telling of this story."[66] Waldron's story extends the genre of the search memoir by writing beyond the conventional ending. Half the book is devoted to exploring the dimensions of a reunion which is often difficult and fraught with tension.

Waldron tells her story as both representative and exceptional. Her forays into the sexual revolution include a relationship with an older black man (Waldron is white). When she gets pregnant in 1968, Waldron considers adoption on the crest of a turning tide; she finds mentors who counsel "keeping" as well as those who promote adoption. In the middle of her pregnancy, her high school art teacher mentions that he and his wife want to adopt a child, and Waldron tentatively agrees. When her daughter is born, she decides not to relinquish her, but after a few months changes her mind and places Simone with the couple. Though Waldron herself does not have direct contact with the adoptive family, her brother visits annually and Simone (renamed Rebecca) knows that he is her birth mother's brother.

In most other accounts, the protagonist is an outsider, stigmatized by her break from middle-class respectability. Waldron's account is unusual in portraying relinquishment as part of a family legacy of ambivalent motherhood; she sees herself as one of many female relatives separated from their children by adoption, abandonment, divorce, or emotional disengagement. Confronted with five generations of such losses, Waldron sets out to reverse her family's history and reunite her "kept" and relinquished children. Again exceptionally, Waldron arranges to meet her daughter in 1980, when she is just eleven years old. With the support of the adoptive parents, she seeks to forge a continuing relationship with her relinquished daughter.

The moment of reunion signals the difficulties that are to follow. Like other searchers, Waldron scrutinizes her daughter for shared characteristics. Instead, she finds a child who is emphatically other. "I saw no signs of me in her. She did not have my nose, or eyes. Her skin was buttery brown. I was white. She seemed shier than I imagined a girl of mine to be. More withdrawn. Is a mother's daughter meant to seem so unrelated?" (115). Waldron recounts the awkward and painful task of developing a relationship on this terra incognita of kinship, for Rebecca is "a daughter, but not a daughter" (131). They proceed in fits and starts, with Waldron at first uncomfortable with Rebecca's demands for gifts and her transgressions of Waldron's domestic turf when she is staying in her mother's house. Driven by guilt and obligation, Waldron tries to respond generously but finds herself awkward and lacking in mother-love. Ten years later, they are estranged, separated by mutual recriminations and accusations.

As the memoir ends, they have established an uneasy truce. Waldron's memoir ultimately rejects the claims of most birth mother memoirs, for she finds that biological kinship alone means little. Instead, she recalls the strain of their connection, "the unnaturalness of having a child who is not mine and, for her, having a mother who belongs to someone else." She claims Rebecca as daughter through a relationship established by blood, but realized only through language and intention: "For more than half her life, the force and persistence of our communication have both liberated and bound Rebecca and me. And that, finally, is why we are family" (210–211).

Saffian, Moorman, and Waldron all participate in the contemporary critique of the best solution even as they refuse the uncritical celebration of biological kinship as "natural"—with its corollary that adoptive kinship is unnatural. At one extreme, though, critics of the best solution argue precisely that. The adoption rights movement is a rather limited, even esoteric, constituency. But it has had considerable impact on wider public discussions of adoption. In contrast to the confident endorsement of adoption in the 1950s and 1960s, contemporary representation of adoption kinship reveals a pervasive ambivalence.

One highly exceptional memoir offers a provocative instance. Michele Launders titles her story *I Wish You Didn't Know My Name,* for she is the birth mother of Lisa Steinberg, a child who suffered fatal abuse at the hands of her adoptive father, who also beat her younger brother and her mother.[67] Lisa's story graphically embodies the deepest fear of a parent who relinquishes a child to an unknown fate. Launders's narrative opens with an anguished confession: "This poor tortured child. I, her mother, had delivered her into the hands of her killers. I hoped that God had watched over her, because I certainly hadn't." Lisa's life and death might seem to offer the ultimate cautionary tale about adoption, and the most adamant critics of adoption have used it as a telling instance of the consequences of severing kinship ties. Significantly, though, this memoir is framed in a way that subtly deflects that reading. Co-authored by Penina Spiegel, the book opens with a brief note on their collaboration which reveals that Spiegel is an adoptive mother, who dedicates the memoir "to birth mothers everywhere."[68] This dedication prepares us for the framing of the story as a birth mother narrative, a recognizable genre by the 1990s. Yet the identification of Spiegel as an adoptive mother, at the same time, prepares the reader to expect that the book is unlikely to repudiate adoption altogether.

Launders's story borrows many of the elements of the conventional narrative of birth mothers who relinquished their children in the 1950s and 1960s. Betrayed by her unfeeling boyfriend, Launders portrays herself as "naïve . . . alone and desperate" (42). Under the circumstances, adoption was the best solution: "I did it for Lisa. I had wanted her to have a good life, better than I could give her. I wanted her to have two parents, parents who were married" (7). But in Launders's story, the narrative of the postwar consensus is anachronistic. In fact, Launders relinquished Lisa in a shady transaction in the early 1980s. By this time, many women raised children born out of wedlock; those who chose adoption could exercise a range of options, including selecting the adoptive parents themselves. For reasons that are not explained, Launders instead turns to an unscrupulous physician and a lawyer who demanded $500 in cash.

The birth mother's worst fears are realized in this story: her trust is violated and her child suffers at the hands of strangers. The lawyer promised to place her daughter with married, Catholic adopters, and instead gave Lisa to Steinberg and Nussbaum, unmarried and Jewish. What went wrong? Media coverage invariably identified Steinberg as Lisa's "adoptive father." Advocates of adoption repeatedly protested this identification, which seemed to suggest that adoption somehow figured in the abuse. Steinberg, often called a "monster," was not a "natural" father. Such critics pointed out that Lisa and her brother had never been legally adopted, in another effort to avoid the stigma attached to adoption in the coverage.

In the conventional happy ending of the search memoir, reunion provides the relief of knowing that sons and daughters have fared well in their adoptive families. Launders's story is a Gothic inversion: she learns of her daughter's violent death in a swirl of publicity. For some birth mothers, reunion initiates complicated negotiations over mutual obligations and claims with newfound relatives. For Launders, this negotiation takes place on the public stage of the courtroom, where she reclaims Lisa's body, as her rightful mother. Yet even this highly unusual story includes the conventional ending's acknowledgment of both blood and adoptive kinship. Launders acknowledges Lisa's two identities as she arranges her daughter's funeral rites, which include both a Catholic priest and a rabbi. The gravestone reclaims Lisa as child of "Michele Launders" and "Kevin," but Lisa herself is identified by the name she used all her life: Lisa Steinberg.

Launders's place in the events and her memoir itself both attest to the wide reach and success of birth mothers' critiques. Within the postwar consensus, it is difficult to imagine that the media would have sought out birth relatives in such a case. Touted as the rightful restoration of Lisa to her real mother, this act drew no public criticism. Even a decade earlier, it might have been seen as deeply inhumane, inflicting unthinkable suffering on a woman who had already made hard choices about her child's future. Equally striking is the judicial support for reinstating kinship between the Steinberg children and their birth relatives, first by recognizing Michelle as the rightful mother in the gesture of releasing Lisa's body to her; and then by returning Lisa's brother to his birth mother. This is an exceptional, even singular, case, and yet its complicated negotiations reveal much about prevailing discourses of adoption.

For some, the Steinberg case stands as a grim instance of the risks of adoption. Marsha Riben dedicates her book to Lisa and "to all others for whom adoption has been a tragedy." Her title signals the book's rhetoric of exposé: *Shedding Light on the Dark Side of Adoption.*[69] Riben, an activist for adoption reform, opens her book with the story of a Holocaust survivor who recalled his despair in the death camp. Assigned to the horrifying job of removing bodies from the gas chambers, he nearly lost hope. Another inmate urged him to struggle to survive, so that he might bear witness. "I, too, am a survivor of tragedy. I am one of the thousands who survived the loss our children to adoption."[70] Though she acknowledges that relinquishment was "far less tragic than mass murder," the comparison sets the tone for what follows. Noting the higher rate of child abuse in stepfamilies, Riben extrapolates this finding to adoptive families. Indeed, "I would not be at all surprised to find that it is higher among adoptive parents. Firstly, because of absence of kinship and secondly because of expectations" (13). The difficulty of finding a child to adopt, Riben speculates, fuels adoptive parents' fantasies of a "perfect child," and when their expectations are disappointed, abuse results. The frustration and stress of adoption, she believes, lead tragically to outcomes like the Steinberg case. Conceding that this is "an extreme example," Riben goes on to bolster it by offering anecdotes of several cases like it.

This pathologizing of adoption revives older stereotypes of the adoptee as a "bad seed," modernized through the frame of psychology. One chapter explores cases of adoptees who murder their parents; an-

other features serial killers who were adopted. These apparently exceptional cases, Riben believes, are symptomatic of a pervasive condition.
She quotes the expert testimony of Arthur D. Sorosky (co-author of *The
Adoption Triangle*) in the 1986 case of a fourteen-year-old boy who
killed both his adoptive parents by setting fire to their bedroom. The
defense argued for his acquittal on the basis of a newly invented psychiatric disorder: "adopted child syndrome," marked by "conflict with authority; preoccupation with excessive fantasy; setting fires; pathological
lying, stealing, running away from home; learning difficulties and lack
of impulse control" (62). This list indiscriminately lumped ordinary adolescent rebellion ("conflict with authority") and attention disorder
("learning difficulties and lack of impulse control") with serious anti-
social behavior (setting fires, lying, and stealing), with no coherent argument of how any of them was related to adoption. Challenged in
cross examination, the expert witnesses themselves conceded that such
behaviors were not limited to adoptees or found in all of them. Nonetheless, they stoutly averred that "most adoptees exhibit some of these
traits as a result of their confusion about heritage" because of "feelings
of rejection and abandonment" (62).

Riben's "suggestions for future research" presuppose a causal relationship between adoption and family pathology, as seen in the questions she considers most urgent: "Does the stress of adopting add to the
divorce rate? The incest taboo and its effect on sexual abuse in adoptive
families; Absence of kinship and its effect on abuse in adoptive homes"
(168). Riben's own exposé has produced not a shred of credible evidence on any of these questions, but no matter: she is convinced that
further research will bring the "dark side" to light.

The book jacket describes Riben as an advocate of "adoption reform," but the book itself implies the more radical agenda of abolishing
adoption altogether. Riben advocates search and reunion according to
the agenda of CUB and the American Adoption Congress (she is a
member of both) and dismisses the fear of adoptive parents that birth
parents will "steal" their children. In fact, this is a highly unlikely outcome of reunion, by all accounts. Most searchers are adults, and reunions rarely end by displacing adoptive parents—often, adopted persons affirm that the search deepened and clarified their relationships

with adoptive parents. However, Riben herself approvingly recounts two searches in which the birth mother rescues her child from "bad" adoptive parents. Rife with unexamined assumptions—that adoption causes attention deficit; that substitute care is neglect—Riben's analysis, at the least, fails to consider plausible alternative explanations. But for her, these accounts provide unassailable evidence that adoption is tragic for mother and child. The rhetoric of the best solution is completely reversed in this fervent denunciation, rendered by a birth mother who Riben quotes approvingly: "[Adoption] is an institutionalized form of symbolic infanticide, with all the horrors, revulsion and guilt intact . . . We feel like murderers because we ARE murderers—but we killed with a pen, not a gun . . . Adoption does not kill the body, but it surely kills a large part of the soul, both of the mother and of the child."[71] If this is so, then only the most dire circumstances would justify adoption.

Riben's view of the "dark side" of adoption remains on the margins. Her book is circulated primarily within the adoption rights movement—and even there, few are as critical of adoption as she. Still, the book is a startling indication of the reservations that have developed around an institution once heralded as optimal for unwed mothers and their children.

Doubts about adoption reach well beyond the adoption rights movement. The confident environmentalism of earlier years has wavered, yielding to a renewed sense of adoption as "risky." One indication of this shift can be seen in memoirs by adoptive parents themselves, published since the 1930s and thus predating the search-and-reunion stories that began to proliferate in the 1970s. Stories of adoptive parents are negotiations of identity that proclaim the equivalence of biological and adoptive kinship. They are also quest narratives, tales of obstacles overcome on their unconventional roads to parenthood. Some, especially those written in the last ten years, combine memoir with advice about finding a child to adopt and critique of contemporary adoption practice.

These adoption stories typically endorse the tenets of the best solution, and they are themselves assertions of the equivalence of adoptive and biological kinship. In the stock plot of these narratives, the protagonists (heterosexual and married) decide to have a child, only to find themselves thwarted. They wait with growing concern for a pregnancy that does not materialize; pursue medical treatment for infertility; and then turn to adoption. Then, they encounter more obstacles. Adoption narratives invariably express the protagonists' sense of bitter irony: biological reproduction, seemingly effortless for most, is impossible for them; and adoption, though ultimately a solution, demands resourcefulness, fortitude, and endurance. Prospective adopters must prove themselves under the scrutiny of social workers, endure long waits and protracted uncertainty, and negotiate the maze of adoption law. They also face limits and choices outside the experience of biological parents, such as becoming parents of older children or children from racial or ethnic groups different from their own. The narrative typically ends with finding and adopting a child, an ending that implicitly endorses the logic of the "as if begotten" family. Once the adoption takes place, the adoptive family assumes its place among happy families who "are all alike."[72]

In the 1980s and 1990s, several narratives broke from this formula to write beyond the usual ending. For these authors, the difference of adoption was far-reaching and consequential, a story that only began with family formation. Michael Dorris's *The Broken Cord* (1989) is a daunting story of the author's oldest son; Dorris, a single man, adopted Adam when he was three years old.[73] Born to an impoverished American Indian woman, Adam suffered severe physical, emotional, and intellectual impairments that were eventually attributed to fetal alcohol syndrome. Charged with anguish over his son's difficult life and intractable limitations, Dorris's memoir is a polemic against alcohol abuse, controversial for its harsh advocacy of controlling maternal drinking by any means necessary. Dorris never suggested that he had any regrets about adopting Adam, and he went on to adopt another boy and a girl as a single parent. In 1981 he married Louise Erdrich, a celebrated poet and novelist, and had two daughters by birth. Erdrich adopted Dorris's three children.

Still, readers might readily interpret *The Broken Cord* as a formidable caveat about adoption itself. Dorris's story of fetal alcohol syndrome lent itself to fears of the unknown birth mother. With heightened awareness of fetal development, medical protocols and popular prescriptions for prenatal care became ever more elaborate. Surrounded by pregnant women who would not drink a sip of coffee, much less quaff a beer or smoke a cigarette, many prospective adopters worried about the practices of women surprised by an unwanted pregnancy. Young women pregnant out of wedlock might not even consult a physician until they encountered one in the delivery room, let alone commit themselves to a rigorous regimen of healthy diet, adequate rest, prenatal vitamins, and abstinence from drugs, alcohol, and tobacco. Although most babies are born healthy—the species is designed for survival, after all—middle-class anxieties about health and fantasies of control fueled adopters' fears about the unknowns of adoption. In a secondary theme, the book implied that social workers had not been candid enough about Adam's prospects, though Dorris acknowledged that the risks of fetal alcohol exposure were not yet widely recognized when Adam was a baby. Some readers, taking a different tack, took Dorris's story as confirmation of their objections to removing Indian children from their tribes.[74]

The memoir repudiates the confident environmentalism that under-girded the postwar adoption mandate. At three, Adam could barely speak, and he had spent most of his life in foster care or institutions. When his social worker tried to warn Dorris that Adam's handicaps might be permanent, Dorris insisted, "I believe in the positive impact of environment, and with me he'll catch up."[75] In retrospect, he regards this optimism as naïve and ill-informed. The memoir ends with his la-ment for Adam, as Dorris grieves the insuperable limitations of congen-ital damage.

Dorris's book, published by a major commercial house, was widely circulated and discussed. The marketing frame for the book underlined its challenge to the most venerable tenet of the best solution. "He knew that his new three-year-old son, Adam, was badly developmentally dis-abled; but he believed in the power of nurture and love," the blurb be-gan. "This is the heartrending story, full of compassion and rage, of how his son grew up mentally retarded, a victim of Fetal Alcohol Syndrome whom no amount of love could make whole." Love was *not* enough.

Ann Kimble Loux implied as much in the title of her memoir, *The Limits of Hope*. Adopted at ages three and four, her girls never formed meaningful bonds with their adoptive parents and siblings (born to the adopters). They suffered learning disabilities, school failure, and discipline problems; as they grew older, the list lengthened to include severe emotional disorders, drug abuse, and prostitution. Loux and her husband struggled to maintain their family life for years under pressure of these formidable difficulties; eventually they divorced. The memoir ends on a note that is positive only by contrast to the pain of what comes before. One young woman has achieved a kind of tenuous stability in an early marriage motivated by her pregnancy; the other is supporting herself and her drug habit, albeit as a prostitute. In this grim account, Loux assails the truism that love conquers all. With painful honesty she considers the possibility that she and her husband have failed these girls. But she also asks probing questions about adoption. Resisting the contemporary social work view that "every child is adoptable," Loux proposes that some children are too damaged for family life; she believes that her daughters might have fared better in institutional care. The foreword lent the authority of professional credentials to Loux's sobering conclusion. Dr. Hugh M. Leichtman wrote approvingly that the memoir "will help shatter the myth that adoptive children, regardless of their histories, invariably thrive in genuinely loving families."[76]

International adoption generated wider awareness of the risks of early child abuse and neglect, as illustrated in "The Orphan Ranger," a *New Yorker* article published in summer 2000.[77] With the expansion of adoption to countries such as Romania and the former Soviet Union, American adopters became parents to older children raised in orphanages, where they endured extreme overcrowding and neglect. As adopters struggled with the special needs of such children, their experiences and advocacy led to the emergence of a new species of expert: medical consultants on adoption. Developmental pediatricians such as Dr. Jane Aronson, the focus of the *New Yorker* piece, offered advice to prospective adopters by assessing videos and medical records of available children. In specialized clinics, they also examined and treated children who had been adopted from other countries. Such services are emerging as a new medical specialty, offered in "about a dozen" practices around the country, and physicians undertaking this work have sought to establish "adoption consultation" as an official section of the American Academy of Pediatrics.[78] The article notes that most babies are healthy and that delayed children often make rapid and complete recoveries from early neglect. Dr. Aronson herself provides compelling witness to this confidence, for the story includes an account of her own decision to adopt a child from Vietnam. Still, the article's stark depictions of listless, unresponsive children lend weight to a general perception of adoption as risky, and even its success stories might well give pause to prospective adopters. The Russian boy featured in the story ends up a happy four-year-old, but his recovery has involved two years of intensive rehabilitation in a special-needs nursery school. The article implies that successful adopters have to be willing to undertake exceptional risks and overcome formidable obstacles—they are "orphan rangers," the intrepid cowboys of contemporary adoptive parenthood.

In a book that combined adoption memoir with expert advice, Nancy Newton Verrier argued that even children adopted as infants were at risk of serious psychiatric disorders. An adoptive mother and psychotherapist, Verrier opened her book by recanting the gospel of environmentalism. "My belief was that love would conquer all. What I discovered, however, was that it was easier for us to give love than it was for her to accept it."[79] When her daughter Gisele, adopted at three days old, began "acting out" and showing signs of depression and anxiety, a therapist suggested the symptoms revealed "the pain Gisele was suffering as a result of her adoption experience" (xvi).

Verrier also has a biological child, and throughout, her conclusions about adoption rely on comparison between the "problem" child (Gisele) and the apparently untroubled sibling. She does not consider other possible explanations for their differences. One alternative hypothesis might be that these parents, rather than Gisele herself, experience adoption as a wound: perhaps they are too ready to make invidious comparisons between adoptive and birth child, or prone to identify with their biological child and to see Gisele as alien. Or perhaps Gisele's problems have nothing to do with adoption: "acting out," after all, is hardly restricted to adopted children.

Regardless, this personal experience convinces Verrier that all adopted persons suffer the devastating effects of "the primal wound, a wound . . . caused by the separation of the child from his biological mother, the connection to whom seems mystical, mysterious, spiritual and everlasting" (xvi). Verrier waxes lyrical on the irreplaceable intimacy of the birth bond. She feels bonded to her adoptive daughter, "but it is a bond forged in the fire of sacrifice and pain, not the easy, fluid, continuity of bonding she might have had with her birthmother" (xvii). She exhorts adoptive parents to recognize their children's sadness or anger as signs of the primal wound. When adopted babies and toddlers cry, for example, it means they are mourning their birth mothers. Adoptive mothers should respond by murmuring consolingly, "I know you must miss her." Adoptees, she argues, are like victims of post-traumatic stress disorder, burdened by guilt and shame, feelings of defectiveness or incompleteness, mistrust, fear of abandonment, and avoidance of intimacy.

Verrier does not explain her sampling procedure or indicate how many informants contributed to her study; she does not describe her protocols for interviews and observations. Instead, she candidly admits that the idea of the "primal wound" is not subject to empirical verification: "at the current state of our understanding, such inferences can neither be proved nor disproved, only believed or disbelieved." Casting aside rational examination, she appeals instead to the authority of motherhood: "As a biological mother, I can know it through my own intuition and experience" (2). But Verrier grants authority to other people's personal experience only when it conforms to her own conclusions. Adopted persons who claim to have little interest in their adoptions are dismissed summarily: "This is a defense" (121). Birth mothers who refuse reunions with their relinquished children are in denial. "Often the birthmother negates the importance of the birth bond and convinces herself that her child had a good upbringing and doesn't need her. This is rationalization. She doesn't want to face her pain and has found an excuse not to do so" (177). In this tautological argument, even apparently contradictory evidence is marshaled as proof of Verrier's a priori conclusions.

Not surprisingly, Verrier's work has gone unremarked in social science professional literature, and *The Primal Wound* was not widely reviewed in publications addressed to general readers, either. Nonetheless,

Verrier has become a poster child for the adoptive rights movement. She is often a featured speaker at adoption conferences, and her blurbs appear as a kind of imprimatur on search memoirs. Unflinchingly, this adoptive mother proclaims the primacy of the birth bond. Unlike most advocates of open records, and against the testimony of most reunion stories, Verrier believes that reunion inevitably exposes adoptive kinship as inferior. "One thing every adoptive mother knows in her heart is that her child's reuniting with her birth mother will change forever their relationship to one another" (160). The good adoptive mother must be prepared to step aside magnanimously: "While she has every right to her feelings about this, she does not have the right to interfere with the reunion between the biological mother and child. Their fundamental right to be together transcends any feelings she may have about it" (162). Verrier's stern advocacy of maternal altruism has an oddly familiar ring. It is the same kind of advice and judgment meted out earlier to birth mothers in the era of the best solution, who were supposed to relinquish their babies selflessly and never look back.

The adoption rights movement has contributed to a pronounced shift in media coverage and popular culture, which now widely echoes activists' challenge to the tenets of the best solution. In one measure of the impact of the critique, journalists began to assume many of their arguments as truisms. Coverage of adoption reunions borrowed wholesale the frame of search narratives. "She Just Wanted to Know Who She Was," ran the headline on a typical story, published in *Health* magazine in July 2000. Adopted as an infant, Mary Anne Duffy had long felt like an outsider: "I wasn't part of the family."[80] She needed to "feel the tug of the genes and test the pull of the heart," the narrative explains. In a covert critique of the economic disparities between birth and adoptive families, the reporter portrays Duffy as a poor little rich girl. Raised in an affluent upper-middle-class community, repeatedly told the "chosen child" story, Duffy still lacked the essence of family love. "With her parents often away and a sister seven years older, she was lonely." "A poor student in a family of intellectuals," and worse, overweight in "a family of thin people," Mary Anne grew up with a feeling of painful difference. "Lacking answers, lacking roots, Mary Anne detected that in the place where a full sense of her self could be nourished there grew instead . . . a void." True to formula, Mary Anne is the victim of a "string of unhappy relationships with uncaring men," until she is rescued by the love of a good man. When she is more than fifty, she finally fills the void of her missing self when she finds her birth family. Fulfilled through this re-union, Mary Anne achieves a goal as elusive as true love: weight loss. The pounds fall away as "she realized—how trite but true!—that the emptiness she'd tried vainly to stuff with food had disappeared" (172).

There is another adoption story within the framing story, one that subtly undercuts its formula. Duffy's birth mother, it turns out, had her-self adopted two baby girls and then given birth to three more daugh-ters. Her adopted daughters "also sometimes felt that their family was not wholly their own. They were the two who acted out as teens, the ones who wound up living far from [their adoptive parents] as adults." But in a discordant note, reunion doesn't solve their problems. One daughter does find her birth mother, but "while the reunion was sweet, it was also uncomfortable, and the two are only rarely in touch" (170). This experience might seem to undermine the theme of reunion as the necessary vehicle of wholeness and healing, but the reporter leaves the apparent contradiction unremarked.

The story concludes with a revealing twist on the chosen-child theme. "We usually think of family, at least parents and siblings, as peo-ple we have no choice about. But sometimes, if we're lucky, they might also be people whom we choose to know and love." In this reversal, the intentional family is the chosen family of reunion, not of adoption. Re-union affords adopted persons an agency that is otherwise not theirs: "After more than fifty years, the chosen child finally got to make that choice." For Duffy, reunion offers an alternative to the unchosen family of adoption. She "will always feel tenderness for Mary [her adoptive mother], but it's Joanne she now refers to when she says 'Mom.'" And though Duffy is never reunited with her birth father, reunion still sup-plies a replacement for the father who raised her. "In place of the father she never knew, or the one she knew but who couldn't give her what she needed, she has the father she always wanted: Joe," her birth mother's husband (172).

This fairy tale reunion embodies the fantasy of the family romance—Duffy actually finds her ideal parents. Though adoption activists portray adoptees as uniquely powerless, since they did not make the adoption decision, in this regard adopted persons share a universal human condition. None of us choose our families, whether we arrive in them by way of birth or adoption. In ideal reunions, adopted persons gain an exceptional agency: they get to choose their relatives.

To suggest that this story is clichéd and formulaic is not to challenge the authenticity of Duffy's lived experience. For her, as for many of the authors of search narratives, the story of adoption loss and reunion supplied meaning and direction. We all live by stories. Touched by postmodern sensibilities, some would even argue that identity itself is a story, an autobiographical self-construction, subject to ongoing revision. What stands out here, though, is the reporter's uncritical acceptance of the search narrative and its assumptions about adoption. Her commitment to the frame overrides countervailing evidence in the story itself and keeps her from exploring alternative explanations. It seems reasonable to assume that adopted persons would struggle with the gaps and silences surrounding their origins, especially in a culture that is currently more inclined to seek biological explanations for the classic questions of modern identity: who am I, and where do I belong? Certainly, adopted persons stand in a different relationship to the "family romance," for they really do have another family. But is it self-evident then that all suffer fundamental identity problems, an emptiness at the core?

We have the testimony of many adopted people that this is their experience. Others, though, see their adoption as relatively insignificant; and still others experience its unknowns as a wellspring of imaginative possibility and creativity. In the new orthodoxy of adoption, such views are either dismissed as denial or actively suppressed. In Internet discussions, for example, adopted persons who do not share the truisms of the search movement often find themselves marginalized. One such person hoped to find a birth sister but did not want to encounter his birth mother along the way.[81] He turned to an Internet discussion for advice, only to withdraw in frustration when other participants repeatedly insisted that he must really want to find his mother.

Gatherings of adoption activists often have the same dynamic of self-confirming conclusions sealed off from alternative views. When I went to meet the author of a recent book on birth mothers at a local book-store, the small group assembled began to talk about search and re-union. As usual at such gatherings, the speaker invited us to introduce ourselves and to indicate if we were "triad members." I explained that I was an adoptive mother. My son, I elaborated in response to questions, was then fourteen years old. As a young child, he had been very curious about adoption, and we often discussed it; on the cusp of adolescence, he had become more reticent and impatiently dismissed my periodic ef-forts to discuss adoption or to elicit his response to news coverage on search and reunion, open records legislation, and the like. "He's just afraid of hurting your feelings," one participant promptly opined. Si-lently, I considered her response. She could be right, I allowed. Yet she had never met my son, and she had known me for just five minutes. At the least, her conclusion seemed premature—unless, that is, one was al-ready convinced a priori that all adopted persons longed for reunion.

A young woman spoke next. She knew she had been relinquished in large part because her white mother felt unable to raise a biracial child as a single mother. She recognized that adoption reunion might pose particular difficulties for her birth mother, who might be living in a family that thought of itself as exclusively white. Moreover, she was an-gry at the knowledge that she was relinquished because of her race. "I've thought about it a lot," she ventured, "and I've decided I don't want to search." Across from her, another participant replied, "I felt that way too. I'm so glad I finally had the courage to search." Exchanges like these are common at meetings of "triad" members (usually mostly adopted persons and birth mothers). Facilitators and participants use the ges-tures of therapeutic empathy to silence any dissenting views, diagnosing any objection as denial.

Once subject to a veritable media blackout, adoption activists have won a large public audience. To a considerable extent, they have also moved the expert consensus in their direction. By the late 1970s, social work and child welfare journals included favorable coverage of activists' efforts to open sealed records, and advice manuals intoned the new mantra: "Adoption is a life-long process."[82] Social workers and thera-pists offered expert guidance in a newly minted specialty—post-adoption services that included family counseling and acting as intermediaries and counselors for searchers. In yet another measure of the influence of the critique, supporters of traditional confidential adoption were now on the defensive. Organizations like the Adoptive Parents Committee and the Association for the Protection of the Adoptive Triangle formed in the 1970s to advocate the confidentiality that had been the foundation of postwar adoption. In 1980 those organizations merged in the National Committee for Adoption, which remains the primary organizational advocate for confidential adoption.[83]

In just a few years, adoption rights activists reshaped the terms of the debate and unsettled many of the truisms of the postwar consensus. Yet their critique has thus far had a limited impact on law and public policy.[84] Attitudes about disclosure occupy a spectrum that indicates the scope and the limits of a changing consensus on adoption. On one end, we see widening public sympathy for adoptees in search. Mutual consent registries abound. The most cautious version of revised disclosure, these registries provide a matching service for adopted adults and birth parents who hope to contact one another. In a few states, recent laws facilitate searches by opening access to sealed records under some conditions. In Delaware, adopted persons who are at least twenty-one years old may get their original birth certificates unless birth parents have filed an affidavit requesting confidentiality. In effect, some legislatures and courts have ruled that there is no public interest in maintaining the sealed record if adopted person and birth parent agree to waive its protections of privacy.

At the same time, though, adoption activists have had little success in advancing a broader argument based on rights. Some have used the language of natural rights to oppose arguments based on privacy rights: "There is no right of privacy between the child and its mother as to the fact of birth, for every human is born of a woman and no sealing of records, no cloak of secrecy, no act in the name of privacy can wash away that fact."[85] Bastard Nation, an adoption rights organization that appears to appeal to a younger constituency, takes another tack, arguing for open records on the grounds of citizenship: adopted persons have a right to information about their origins, apart from their interest in search and reunion. However, constitutional challenges to sealed records have repeatedly failed.[86]

The campaign for open records has won some important victories. In the summer of 2000, Oregon became the first state to pass a voters' referendum favoring unrestricted access of adopted persons to once-sealed records. The Oregon legislation was a litmus test of the "rights" position, for it openly rejected the objection usually mounted about the privacy rights of birth mothers. Some Oregon birth mothers made this argument themselves during public debate over the referendum and filed a class action suit challenging its constitutionality. In the referendum, adoption activists had won a unilateral right to information about their birth families. Alabama soon followed, opening sealed records to adoptees who were at least nineteen years old. There, birth parents could file legally unbinding "preference forms" to indicate whether or not they wished to be contacted by their relinquished children. The law also made provisions for birth parents to file updated medical information, presumably so that adopted persons could have access to this material without directly contacting birth families. Landmark victories for the adoption rights movement, these laws nonetheless fell short of endorsing its larger claims about the inviolability of blood kinship. Allowing unilateral access to sealed records, the laws affirmed the adopted person's right to find his or her origins but accorded no complementary right to birth relatives seeking relinquished kin. Moreover, the privacy shield remains in place for adoptive families with minor children. Birth mothers who are trying to find relinquished minor children have gained some support within the adoption rights movement, but little sympathy outside it. In fact, in widely publicized contested adoptions like the Baby Jessica or Baby Richard cases, public sentiment runs high against birth parents who claim children who have settled into adoptive families.

In the adoption rights movement, the demand for open records led some to demand an end to confidential adoption. *The Adoption Triangle* ended with a moderate advocacy of open adoption, which the authors defined as one in which "the birth parent meets the adoptive parents, relinquishes all legal, moral, and nurturing rights to the child, but retains the right to continuing contact and knowledge of the child's whereabouts and welfare." They advised "serious consideration" of this kind of adoption, though noted, "Such an arrangement could never be expected to replace the traditional adoption."[87] But six years later, two of the three co-authors were advocating just that. In a 1984 article in *Child Welfare*, Baran and Pannor issued a manifesto calling for the end of confidential adoption. "All adoptions, including the placement of newborn infants, should now be open, in the best interests of the child, birth parents, and adoptive parents."[88] Likewise, Sandra Musser explicitly called for a sweeping revision of a historical mistake, symbolized and facilitated by sealed records: "Adoption as we know it today was a legal invention of the 1940s—it was a misguided attempt to both imitate nature on the one hand and help those who had gone 'astray' on the other. We now know that it created many more problems than it ever hoped to solve. Therefore, open adoption must become the order of the day."[89] Baran and Pannor soon extended their critique of secrecy to artificial insemination in a 1989 book titled *Lethal Secrets*.[90] By 1991 Pannor and Baran had lost confidence in adoption altogether, traditional or otherwise. They now advocated an increased emphasis on family preservation—providing all possible support to enable single mothers to raise their children. For children who still needed substitute parents, the authors proposed a kind of guardianship in which birth parents remained legal parents, while guardians assumed custodial and financial responsibility.[91]

Some psychoanalytically oriented experts responded with skepticism, even as their essays indicated that many agencies had begun to encourage, or even require, some degree of openness. In a 1984 article in *Child Welfare*, one author deplored agencies' precipitant shift from the rigidity of secrecy to an equally rigid orthodoxy of openness. She referred to new rituals of adoption, such as requiring adoptive parents to write notes of appreciation to birth parents and to provide photographs of the relinquished child; agencies also encouraged birth parents to leave gifts and pictures for the child. Such exchanges, she argued, obscured the realities of relinquishment and impaired attachment among adoptive family members. "Biological parents must fade into the background and, acknowledged but not emphasized, must give the adoptive parents the sole role of caretakers and thus, in actuality, parents to the child."[92] In a three-part series that appeared in 1985 in the newly established *Child and Adolescent Social Work Journal*, five co-authors pondered "Some Theoretical Considerations of Confidential Adoptions" and raised doubts that open adoption offered benefits for any of the triad members. For birth mothers, openness could interfere with the process of grieving. Adolescent birth mothers, they believed, often got pregnant because of "underlying conflict or deficit," with the risk that "the pathology can be played out with the adoptive parents and the adoptive child to the detriment of all involved." With confidentiality, and, of course, professional counseling, birth mothers could confront their pathologies more constructively.[93] Adoptive parents, they feared, were not in a position to resist open adoption if agencies promoted or required it, but they had little to gain from it. Open adoption might make them defensive and anxious, interfering with their attachment to adopted children.[94] The adopted child faced the confusion of dealing with two sets of parents; these psychoanalytically-minded experts were concerned about the effects as children encountered the conflicts of the Oedipal stage and later of adolescence. Flatly refuting the advocates of open adoption, they concluded, "There is no inherent benefit in such knowledge. To the contrary, there may be definite risks for the child at each stage of development."[95]

Advocates of open adoption swept aside such objections. This skeptical view of open adoption, based on extrapolation from psychoanalytic theory, had no case histories to support it, they charged. The same was true for the more optimistic scenarios advanced by those who favored open adoption. Nonetheless, open adoption soon claimed a new place in adoption practice. Just as confidential adoption had been installed, in large part, in response to birth mothers' desire for secrecy, the shift to open adoption in the 1980s was driven by birth mothers themselves.[96] By meeting and choosing their child's parents, relinquishing mothers assuaged their fears of consigning their children to an unknown fate. Their control over placement also overturned old relationships of dependence and expertise, in which social workers or other mediators called the shots. "Openness" encompassed a range of practices, from initial meetings between birth and adoptive parents (identified only by their first names) to arrangements for lifelong contact between birth and adoptive families. In some open adoptions, agencies mediated between birth and adoptive parents, doing home studies and advising birth mothers on prospective adopters. Others were arranged by adoption attorneys who advised couples about how to find women who were considering adoption.

Open adoption could be implemented with ease because no state required confidential adoption (this would have been a practical impossibility, in any case), and "independent adoption" (done outside approved agencies) was legal in all but six states. Even in states that prohibited use of unlicensed intermediaries in adoption, birth mothers themselves were usually exempted: on the basis of traditional parental rights, they could place their children directly, without agency involvement. Reprising a common theme in adoption history, social workers followed rather than led this change in practice. But rather quickly, agencies began to endorse some version of open adoption. Even the venerable Spence-Chapin agency in New York City, a bastion of traditional adoption, began to do "semi-open" adoptions in the 1980s and to encourage contact between birth and adoptive parents.[97] In the largest study of open adoption to date, researchers charted the rapid shift in agency practices. By 1993, of 35 agencies studied, 32 discouraged confidential adoption, with 13 of these advocating full disclosure; only two agencies encouraged confidential adoption.[98]

Open adoption, in many ways, represents a reframing of the postwar adoption consensus. In contrast to critics like Riben and Verrier who saw adoption as inherently destructive, advocates of open adoption affirmed the possibilities of adoption reform. Freed of the denial, shame, and secrecy of the "as if begotten" family, they believed, adoption might yet achieve its promise of healing for all three members of the triad. Symbolically, it overthrew the stigma associated with adoption by rejecting the veil of confidentiality. Women who relinquished their children for adoption could claim a social role to go with the identity of birth mother. They themselves could help to shape their children's futures by selecting adoptive parents, rather than leaving this consequential decision to others. Advocates of open adoption affirm the current legal system of transfer of parental rights; Pannor and Baran's more extreme position of replacing adoption with guardianship has won few adherents. But in open adoption, relinquishment did not necessarily entail lifelong separation of birth mother and child. (In principle, open adoptions might also involve birth fathers; in practice, very few did.) In open adoptions, proponents argued, children would be freed from the uncertainty and emptiness of unknown origins. Adoptive parents would benefit, too, as their children would have the information that adoptees in confidential adoption were denied, and, sometimes, access to real birth mothers that would forestall their romantic fantasies of the perfect mother. Open adoption proponents also revived the theme of chosenness, long anathematized in advice about disclosure. Now, however, it was adoptive parents who were chosen. Being selected by birth mothers, advocates argued, would help heal the losses of infertility and bolster adopters' confidence in themselves as parents. *Adoption without Fear,* echoing the title of Grantley Dick-Read's classic *Childbirth without Fear,* proclaimed open adoption as the equivalent of natural childbirth.[99] A new genre of prescriptive literature sprang up to offer advice on open adoption. Agency protocols, too, changed to reflect the accent on disclosure.

Advice manuals and intermediaries advised adopters on how to present themselves to birth mothers. Soon, standard practice included "Dear Birthmother" letters, in which prospective adopters introduced themselves and explained their motives for adopting. The epistolary form, with its personal address, was somewhat misleading: in fact, these letters were written according to formulas suggested by agencies or in advice literature.[100] Strive for "an open, appealing manner," one author advised. "The autobiography should make a person want to reach out and touch you."[101] Another coached, "You are trying just a bit to tug at the birth mother's heartstrings. You want to consider her emotional side and convince her that as a pregnant woman she would be doing a service for the world or for you by giving her child to you. Don't be maudlin, but don't be too aloof. People open their hearts to other real, down-to-earth people in our society."[102] In the letters, couples hoping to adopt presented themselves in the image of good parents as defined by social work literature. To a person, on the evidence of these letters, prospective adopters were stably employed, happily wed, and living in comfortable but not luxurious surroundings. In one memoir, adoptive mother Jana Wolff commented ironically on the artifice of the form by publishing two versions of her own "Dear Birthmother" letter. The first opened,

"Dear Birth Mother: Screw you. Do you think I want to beg a complete stranger for a kid whose own mother doesn't want him? You messed up and now you get to sit in judgment of the perfect parents for your baby." The letter they actually sent deployed the calculated warmth and pre-scribed clichés of the form. It began, "This must be a very difficult time for you. It takes courage to think about what would be best for your child and choose adoptive parents for him or her."[103] True to formula, the letter continued by citing the prospective adopters' qualifications for parenthood.

Photographs accompanied the letters, and these visual images com-plemented and amplified the text. Most were outdoor shots, with the couple posed in casual clothes and in scenes that suggested their shared leisure, companionability, and good health. Such scenes tacitly coun-tered concerns about "desperate" adopters by presenting happy couples with balanced lives. By showing prospective adopters engaged in ener-getic outdoor pursuits, the photos also minimized the typical age gap between birth and adoptive parents. Perhaps, too, the outdoor setting served as a kind of class equalizer. Shown outside their homes, adopters were in a neutral setting that did not disclose economic status, deflect-ing birth mothers' possible class resentments; almost by definition, sin-gle mothers were disadvantaged economically compared with married couples. Visual images also provided a convenient way of conveying what etiquette generally leaves unsaid: photographs disclosed adopters' physical appearance, including signifiers of race.

In new rituals of placement and relinquishment, birth mother and prospective adopters met one another face to face. Memoirs of open adoption described the nervous anticipation that adopters brought to such meetings. The elation of being "chosen" becomes a turning point in the stock plot of these memoirs. Some adoptive parents soon discov-ered the downside long identified with the chosen-child story: adopters who had been chosen could also be unchosen. Most open adoptions are arranged before a child is legally relinquished, usually even before he or she is born; most birth mothers want to avoid placing infants in foster care, and most adopters hope for newborns. Laws governing relinquish-ment vary widely from state to state; in some, it is effective immediately upon the birth mother's signature; in others, such as California, relinquishment cannot be finalized until six months after the birth mother first signs her intention to relinquish. Open adoptions, then, are often legal-risk placements—since babies go home with adopters before they are legally free for adoption. "Buy the crib, but hang on to the receipt" was the counsel shared by prospective adopters preparing for expected babies whose mothers might yet decide to raise them.[104] New adoptive parents in legal-risk situations endured anxious waits for final relinquishments and struggled to maintain some distance from babies that might yet be taken from them. As the birth mother wavered, one prospective father recalled his hesitation about entering into one of the rituals of new parenthood: "Part of me was afraid to take pictures, everything was still so uncertain."[105]

Almost certainly, open adoption has contributed to public perceptions of adoption as risky. In a widely aired episode of L.A. Law, shown in April 1990, a lawyer couple joyfully welcomed a new baby, only to lose the child after three months when the birth mother returned to reclaim her. Lincoln Caplan's An Open Adoption, first published as a three-part series in the New Yorker in 1990, gave wide publicity to such arrangements.[106] Caplan's reportage centered on the complicated relationship of Dan and Lee Stone, prospective adopters, and Peggy Bass, a young single woman who was pregnant and planning to relinquish her baby for adoption. From that focal point, Caplan covered the contemporary social science and public debate about adoption in a measured and wide-ranging discussion. The core story ended happily, with all parties affirming the adoption, and some read Caplan's account as a measure of the public acceptance accorded to open adoption.[107]

At a minimum, though, Caplan's story was open to other readings. Caplan was himself an adoptive father of a child placed in a traditional confidential adoption. He recorded the optimistic expectations of Bass and the Stones, and then effectively juxtaposed an unfolding story of risk, vulnerability, and pain. Several months after the birth and placement, the Stones were dismayed to learn that Peggy had concealed her ambivalence about relinquishment from them; when Peggy's parents learned of it, the Stones feared they might disrupt the placement. Caplan came down squarely in the middle on the question of open adoption. Reasoning that no solid evidence existed to favor one practice over the other, he argued that both confidential and open adoption should be available. Still, readers might well have been unsettled by his depiction of the uncertainty and anxiety that attended open adoption.

In a classically American repudiation of bureaucratic authority, open adoption reclaimed placement as a private decision that affirmed personal autonomy. Kathleen Silber and Phylis Speedlin's *Dear Birthmother* and Suzanne Arms's *Adoption: A Handful of Hope* celebrated open adoption through stories of women who chose adoption with deliberation and dignity.[108] Advocates of open adoption endorsed a revised version of the best solution. With other critics of postwar adoption practices, they rejected the pressure and shame of earlier years. But in contrast to critics like Riben, Verrier, or Baran and Pannor, they continued to affirm that adoption might be the best solution. Arms argued that the contemporary stigma attached to relinquishment was itself a new form of coercion: "The overwhelming majority of young women simply do not see adoption as a positive choice; they see it as a sign of weakness and a lack of caring. Because they rule adoption out without even considering it, how can we say that they have real choice in their decision to keep their baby?"[109] Others took up this theme of responsible choice, proclaimed on a bumper sticker that read "Adoption Is an Option." *Open Adoption: A Caring Option* tacitly countered negative stereotypes of relinquishment as abandonment.

"Option" appealed to the American ideal of choice, and it also provocatively echoed language that had long been used to advocate and defend legal abortion. Some, including extreme anti-abortion groups like Operation Rescue, advocated adoption as a political strategy in opposition to abortion. For them, adoption was a way to shore up traditional families and prevent abortion.[110] Others defended both abortion and adoption as legitimate responses to unwanted pregnancy; Suzanne Arms, for example, advocated adoption within a new-age feminist cultural politics. For those like her, open adoption represented a utopian kind of family, unconstrained by the boundaries of tradition.

The best outcome study of open adoption to date confounded both the worst fears of traditionalists and the most optimistic claims of advocates. Published in 1998, Harold D. Grotevant and Ruth G. McRoy's

Openness in Adoption reported survey and interview data from 35 private agencies and over 700 persons involved in open adoption.[111] Opponents of open adoption had argued that this arrangement would render adopters more anxious about birth parents and therefore insecure as parents themselves. The study found that, on the contrary, adopters in fully disclosed adoptions were *less* likely than others to harbor fears about birth parents reclaiming their children, and that measures of "sense of permanency" and "sense of entitlement" to parenthood did not differ according to degrees of openness (122, 127–128). Those skeptical about open adoption also cited fears of birth parents' "interference" with adoptive families. But the study found that most adopters were themselves satisfied with the degree of contact; moreover, with only two exceptions, those who were dissatisfied wanted more rather than less contact with birth parents (121). Surprisingly, it was birth mothers themselves who were most negative about the prospect of future meetings in open adoptions. "These observations are consistent with the notion that over time, birth mothers may begin to pull away from contact and the relationship with the [adoptive] family" (193).

Advocates of open adoption claimed that birth mothers who chose their child's adopters were better able to overcome the losses of relinquishment. The study supported this argument in part: only 12 percent of birth mothers regretted their decisions in fully disclosed adoptions, compared with 22–24 percent in other arrangements (140). Against the prediction of advocates of openness, though, birth mothers in confidential adoptions were no more likely to regret their decision than those in either mediated or time-limited mediated adoptions—that is, adoptions that included some contact of birth and adoptive parents through an intermediary, or those that involved some contact for a limited time after placement. Contradicting the claims of advocates, the study found no significant differences between birth mothers in confidential adoptions and those in fully disclosed adoptions when it came to adjustment after relinquishment. Birth mothers in time-limited mediated adoptions actually suffered more difficulties, a finding that confirms the predictions of critics who argued that openness made it more difficult to resolve the losses of adoption. Perhaps, the authors speculated, such birth mothers had harder adjustments because they were struggling both with maintaining contact (in the short term) and anticipating separation at the same time. Other studies returned contradictory findings on the question; some found that openness eased resolution of birth mothers' grief, while others documented more intense grief among birth mothers in open adoptions (154–155). Regardless of the type of adoption, Grotevant and McRoy found, follow-up studies showed that birth mothers were coping well four to twelve years after relinquishment (171).

Overall, *Openness in Adoption* offered qualified support for fuller disclosure in adoption. Its depiction of adoption outcome countered fears of prospective adopters. For birth mothers, the picture was less clear: the study failed to confirm some of the more optimistic claims of advocates of openness. Grotevant and McRoy themselves concluded that adoption "can be fraught with risks and lifelong concerns for birthparents," echoing concerns repeatedly raised by groups like CUB. At the same time, they also quoted findings that there were no significant differences in "negative psychological outcome" between teenagers who relinquished children and those who kept them (153–154).

Struggling with the silences and gaps of confidential adoption, many adopted persons in the postwar generation have taken up openness as an unqualified good. But if openness solves the problems of secrecy, it also may bring new challenges. In particular, the finding that birth mothers tend to want less contact over time is potentially troubling. We know from their own accounts that many adopted persons experience relinquishment as rejection, even if adoptive parents have portrayed birth parents positively and offered empathetic explanations for relinquishment. We know, too, that many adopted persons experience separation from birth families as painful. But in confidential adoption, relinquishment is a decision made once and, usually, on behalf of an infant with whom the birth mother has only a brief relationship. In contrast, children in open adoptions are vulnerable to the withdrawal of a birth mother who could see them but who chooses not to do so. Surely such adopted persons are more, not less, likely to experience separation from the birth mother as a personal rejection, even something for which they are to blame. And yet it also seems unreasonable to imagine imposing some contractual obligation upon birth parents who have already made the difficult decision to relinquish their children.

The demand for openness in adoption is a telling barometer of the ambivalence surrounding contemporary adoption. Its repudiation of secrecy is, in one way, an extension of the affirmation of adoption that characterized the postwar mandate: it calls for a vision of adoption that is wider than the "as if begotten" family. Its new rituals of placement and relinquishment express a fuller and richer vision of adoption, one that both acknowledges loss and celebrates new possibility. At its limit, though, the demand for full disclosure in adoption is also an indicator of the renewed stigma attached to contemporary adoption. The assault on secrecy strikes a familiar and resonant chord in American political rhetoric, and therefore it can seem self-evident that secrecy is bad and openness desirable. On closer examination, though, this rhetoric is susceptible to challenge.

Even as Americans have assaulted secrecy as conspiracy—a threat to democratic institutions—we have also long defended privacy as fundamental to maintaining those institutions. Without privacy, there is no freedom: relentless scrutiny is the hallmark of totalitarian states. In public and private life alike, we maintain zones of confidentiality in a host of formal institutions and customary practices. Attorney-client privilege, our legal system insists, is crucial to the right to a fair trial promised by the Bill of Rights. The state honors religious freedom by accepting the secrecy of the confessional, which in turn sequesters sinners from secular judgment so they might be free to seek forgiveness and absolution. The trust of the doctor-patient relationship rests on the assurance of medical discretion, affirmed in physicians' traditional Hippocratic oath. Secrets define the boundaries of intimacy. In recognition of the significance of marital privacy, the law asserts that husbands and wives cannot be compelled to testify against one another. By sharing secrets and keeping confidences, friends enact their mutual trust and loyalty. As adoption rights activists argued, secrecy does have the power to destroy; what they did not acknowledge is that secrecy is indispensable to social life.

When we subject the adoptive family to more public scrutiny than other families, we are marking it as marginal and inferior, outside the boundaries of privacy accorded to "real" families. Probing questions posed to biological parents are widely recognized as rude and intrusive; few ask, "Was it a mistake, or did you plan this pregnancy?" "This baby doesn't look like your husband; are you sure he's the father?" "What did your obstetrician charge?" "Did you want a girl (or boy)?" "Maybe you'll have a boy (or girl) next time." Adoptive families, by contrast, are routinely subject to intrusive questions. "Are those kids yours?" is a frequent query posed to adopters in "non-matching" families. Adoptive parents are often asked, sometimes in earshot of their children, "Why was he put up for adoption?" "Who are his real parents?" "What did it cost?" Congratulations to new adopters are often offered along with the comment, "Maybe you'll still have a child of your own."

"Wanted: a child to raise as our own." That had long been the plaint of adults seeking children to adopt. The twentieth century had seen the rapid expansion of formal adoption, followed by an enthusiastic public endorsement of families formed by law. By the end of the twentieth century, though, it had become harder and harder to find such children. Adoption had become highly exceptional, and the public confidence of the 1950s and 1960s had been sharply tempered. And yet adoption continued to have a place in child welfare—and to expand in ways that its most committed postwar advocates would never have imagined.

Epilogue

"Adoptive kinship is not and cannot be the equivalent of blood relationship," declared the sociologist H. David Kirk in 1981.[1] Kirk himself argued eloquently for the utopian potential of this difference, which for him offered a vision of families joined by choice, not bound by blood. In the 1980s and 1990s, adoption has been pervasively depicted as difference, and—in contrast to Kirk's view—often as defect. Popular search narratives portray adoption as rupture. Even the professional literature of adoption emphasizes risk and vulnerability. The numbers of adoptions have declined for many reasons, but surely one is that fewer people are inclined to imagine that adoption is a good solution—let alone the "best"—when they are confronted with infertility or an unwanted pregnancy.

And yet, adoption had also expanded in ways that few would have predicted in the 1950s. Children once considered unadoptable—older children; those with severe physical disabilities or delayed development; those wounded by histories of abuse and neglect—are now the primary clients of agencies like the CBD, who rallied to their assistance. Social workers repudiated their old insistence on "fitness" with a new commitment to finding homes, proclaiming that "No child is unadoptable." The old laws of supply and demand seemed suspended, too. In the 1950s and 1960s, adopters that social workers considered marginal had little chance, as they were assessed against the claims of those who looked more promising. But in the 1980s and 1990s, even as print and television reports described "desperate" prospective adopters scouring the country and the world for children, many customary restrictions were lifted. Single women, accepted as adopters before 1940, had been pushed aside as postwar ideals touted the heterosexual nuclear family. By the 1980s, agencies were again placing children with single women. For the first time, lesbians and gay men found some agencies willing to help them find children, as well as courts that would approve their adoption petitions. Single men remained rare among adopters, but they too now found ways to become adoptive fathers. Age limits became more flexible; some persons in their fifties were adopting infants and young children. And though the numbers of adoptions had dropped, it seemed that adoptive families were everywhere, their diversity rendering them highly visible. American parents came home with Chinese-born daughters—more than five thousand of them in 2000—the latest addition to fifty years of children who had emigrated from Europe, Asia, and Latin America to join American families.

By the end of the century, adoption had undergone another consequential change, largely unremarked. Since 1970, agency adoption has again declined sharply, in what amounts to a massive de facto deregulation of child placement. Social workers, who had finally gained a certain negotiated authority in adoption, now again found themselves responding to changes forged outside the expert consensus. Adoption practice had essentially divided into two tiers. Traditional agencies like the CBD were now specialized almost exclusively in special needs adoptions, while their old constituency—predominantly white adopters and white birth mothers—had turned to independent adoption. Birth mothers increasingly chose to avoid agencies, making their own arrangements with adopters. Prospective adopters deserted agencies in droves, deterred by long waits and discouraging prospects. By the end of the century, most healthy babies were being placed through independent adoptions or in the new private agencies which had sprung up as intermediaries; some adopters sought children from abroad. Open adoption has been touted as an innovation, but in many ways it represents a return to the kind of child exchange that has prevailed for most of American history. Before 1940 and after 1970, most placements have been made as private agreements executed between consenting adults, with minimal involvement from the state.

Does it matter? By most accounts, adoption has been a success. Outcome studies have repeatedly found that children flourish in adoptive families, whether they are facilitated by agencies or formed by independent adoption, and that adopters are deeply satisfied with the children that they claim by law and love, not by blood.[2] Advocates of open adoption argue that the birth mother's choice of birth parents restores dignity and autonomy to relinquishment. This argument appeals to the American ideal of individual choice and to the feminist ideal of women's autonomy. But these arrangements tacitly embody and reinforce another troubling assumption: that children are property, belonging to their parents by right of ownership. It is reassuring that most adoptions turn out well, testament to the resilience of children and to the fundamental human capacity for altruism, nurturing, and love. Still, it is bad social policy and poor ethical practice to rely on a laissez-faire system of adoption that, in practice, becomes modeled on the market place.

What happens to the principle of a child's best interest in a situation where market models prevail? Social work protocols for placement have not been perfect; they reflect the commitments and blind spots of their own historical moments. But can we assume that children are better served by placements made according to the unassisted judgment of a young woman—usually a teenager—facing an unplanned and unwanted pregnancy?[3] Sometimes, adoption practice has been paternalistic, even coercive, in its attitudes toward both adopters and birth mothers. But can we assume that the different interests of each will be fairly served when they are on their own, negotiating from their vulnerabilities and with a child's future at stake?

It seems evident, too, that the market model of adoption has increased the economic disparities between adoptive families and others. Some observers believe that birth mothers in domestic adoptions have tended to favor more affluent couples as they select their child's parents from the many adults eager to adopt.[4] The structure of independent adoption favors adults with the kinds of skills and resources that are more likely to accompany middle-class standing. Finding a birth mother relies on being able to understand how the system works and deploy it to one's own advantage with energetic use of personal networks, access to professional networks, persuasive self-presentation in written narratives and on the telephone. In both domestic and international adoptions, adopters usually have to travel to find their child, often at short notice and for indeterminant times; this kind of flexibility is a prerogative of professional employment, seldom available to those in other jobs. Reliance on the market has also driven up the costs of adoption, excluding persons of modest income. The prominence of market considerations, I believe, also contributes to the stigmatizing of adoption. High costs for adoption violate deeply held beliefs about family by interjecting money into the domain of love.

Even as the vision of the best solution was repudiated in the 1980s and 1990s, there were many indications that Americans remain confident about the value of adoption. In the 1980s and 1990s, adoption was publicly endorsed by both George Bush, whose praise for the Adoption Option was in part an expression of his anti-abortion sentiments, and by William Jefferson Clinton, a pro-choice president who approved Adoption 2000 in 1996, legislation intended to assist special needs adoptions, and the Adoption and Safe Families Act in 1997, to speed permanency planning for children in foster care. In 2000, Congress passed the Intercountry Adoption Act, ratifying the 1993 Hague Convention proposal to establish uniform standards to regulate international adoption. The federal government has also given public support to adoptive families by passing the adoption tax credit. Some of these initiatives are motivated by efforts to punish and stigmatize single mothers, a giant step backward. Others, though, bespeak a resilient confidence in the kinship of strangers and a compassionate outreach to children who need homes.

As the twenty-first century opens, there are signs of an emerging new consensus, one that moves beyond the best solution to a vision of adoption grounded in realism and hope. The "as if begotten" family has been rejected as inauthentic; yet most Americans have refused the corollary of some adoption activists that blood will tell. Instead, there is a new affirmation of the family of adoption that recognizes both blood kinship and adoptive kinship. It seems likely that more and more states will open adoption records, facilitating connections between adopted persons and birth families. At the same time, the adoptive family's powerful legal sanction remains unshaken: the law recognizes only one set of parents, according adoptive parents the same rights and obligations as biological parents. Adoptive families might now be seen to represent not the families we never were—the "archaic and nostalgic" ideal of postwar domesticity—but instead the families that we are becoming—diverse, flexible, multicultural.[5]

As we consider the enduring questions of human identity—who am I, and where do I belong?—we bereft postmodernists often conclude that the answer is "nowhere." Perhaps this is one reason for the popularity of search and reunion stories. Apparently exceptional, they are in some ways paradigmatic of family life writ large. Their stories of fractured kinship resonate with readers touched by other experiences of family loss: of families divided by alienation, desertion, betrayal, divorce. Many people experience contemporary life as fragmented and atomistic; as families, too, falter and fail, we seem to have no secure place. Adoption confronts us with the realities of loss and limitation that attend every human life. Some have responded by insisting that only blood relationship can constitute enduring solidarity. Adoption challenges us, instead, to add a much older question to our reflections on identity: Who is my neighbor? By that question we are called to hope and trust anew in the only authentic kinship we know: bonds forged in love and sustained by will and commitment.

Notes

INTRODUCTION

1. This description of the women's reform network draws on Robyn Muncy, *Creating a Female Dominion in American Reform, 1890–1935* (New York: Oxford University Press, 1991), pp. 42–46.

2. Several excellent books document the history of the USCB; see Muncy, *Creating a Female Dominion;* Molly Ladd-Taylor, *Mother-Work: Women, Child Welfare, and the State, 1890–1930* (Urbana: University of Illinois Press, 1994); and Kriste Lindenmeyer, *"A Right to Childhood": The U.S. Children's Bureau and Child Welfare, 1912–1946* (Urbana: University of Illinois Press, 1997).

3. See Christine A. Bachrach, "Adoption Plans, Adopted Children, and Adoptive Mothers," *Journal of Marriage and the Family 48* (May 1986): 243–253, esp. p. 245; and Bachrach, K. London, and P. Maza, "On the Path to Adoption: Adoption Seeking in the U.S.," *Journal of Marriage and the Family 53* (August 1991): 705–718.

CHAPTER ONE: WANTED—A CHILD TO RAISE AS OUR OWN

1. Mayor of Bogalusa, LA, W. H. Sullivan to Children's Aid Society of New York, April 27, 1918. Central File 1914–1918, National Archives and Records Administration, Record Group 102, Box 211 [Records from the U.S. Children's Bureau at the National Archives hereafter cited as RG 102.]

2. Sent to the USCB and filed in Central File 1914–1918, RG 102, Box 211.

3. Viviana Zelizer, *Pricing the Priceless Child: The Changing Value of Children* (New York: Basic, 1986), esp. pp. 169–207.

4. Marilyn Irvin Holt, *The Orphan Trains: Placing Out in America* (Lincoln: University of Nebraska Press, 1992), and Stephen O'Connor, *Orphan Trains:*

The Story of Charles Loring Brace and the Children He Saved and Failed (Boston: Houghton Mifflin, 2001).

5. Holt, *Orphan Trains,* pp. 178–179.

6. Mary Kathleen Benet, *The Politics of Adoption* (New York: Free Press, 1976), p. 77.

7. Elazar Barkan, *The Retreat of Scientific Racism: Changing Concepts of Race in Britain and the United States between the World Wars* (Cambridge, UK: Cambridge University Press, 1992), and Carl N. Degler, *In Search of Human Nature: The Decline and Revival of Darwinism in American Thought* (New York: Oxford, 1991).

8. Christina Simmons, "Modern Sexuality and the Myth of Victorian Repression," in *Passion and Power: Sexuality in History,* ed. Kathy Peiss and Christina Simmons (Philadelphia: Temple University Press, 1989), pp. 157–177, and Nancy F. Cott, *Public Vows: A History of Marriage and the Nation* (Cambridge: Harvard University Press, 2000), p. 50.

9. David Rothman, *The Discovery of the Asylum: Social Order and Disorder in the New Republic* (Boston: Little, Brown, 1971).

10. On the network of women reformers and the 1909 White House Conference, see Robyn Muncy, *Creating a Female Dominion in American Reform, 1890–1935* (New York: Oxford, 1991), pp. 42–46, and Kriste Lindenmeyer, *"A Right to Childhood": The U.S. Children's Bureau and Child Welfare, 1912–1946* (Urbana: University of Illinois Press, 1997), pp. 19–20.

11. Some important contributions to this historiography include Leroy Ashby, *Endangered Children: Dependency, Neglect, and Abuse in American History* (New York: Twayne, 1997; Dorothy M. Brown and Elizabeth McKeown, *The Poor Belong to Us: Catholic Charities and American Welfare* (Cambridge: Harvard University Press, 1997); Joan Gittens, *Poor Relations: The Children of the State in Illinois, 1818–1990* (Urbana: University of Illinois Press, 1994); Michael Katz, *In the Shadow of the Poorhouse: A Social History of Welfare in America* (New York: Basic, 1986); and Susan Tiffin, *In Whose Best Interest? Child Welfare in the Progressive Era* (Westport, CT: Greenwood, 1982).

12. Quoted in George Walker, *The Traffic in Babies: An Analysis of the Conditions Discovered during an Investigation Conducted in the Year 1914* (Baltimore: Norman, Remington Co., 1918), p. 141.

13. Regina G. Kunzel, *Fallen Women, Problem Girls: Unmarried Mothers and the Professionalizaion of Social Work, 1890–1945* (New Haven: Yale University Press, 1993), and Katherine G. Aiken, *Harnessing the Power of Motherhood: The*

National Florence Crittenton Mission, 1883–1925 (Knoxville: University of Tennessee Press, 1998).

14. Zelizer, *Pricing the Priceless Child*, p. 174.

15. Walker, *Traffic in Babies*, pp. 1, 30–31, 38.

16. Ibid., pp. 102, 7.

17. Ibid., p. 4.

18. Ibid., p. 94.

19. Linda Gordon, *Pitied But Not Entitled: Single Mothers and the History of Welfare* (Cambridge: Harvard University Press, 1994), pp. 28–29, and Lindenmeyer, *"The Right to Childhood,"* pp. 158–160.

20. Zelizer, *Pricing the Priceless Child*, pp. 195–198.

21. *Journal of the House of Representatives of the 48th General Assembly of the State of Illinois*, 1913, p. 1235. Thanks to Leslie Reagan for sending me a copy of this report.

22. USCB to Charles Edward Pell, June 23, 1920. Central File 1914–1920, RG 102, Box 67.

23. The USCB expressed sympathy for the agency's dilemma but, predictably, declined to get involved in a controversy with a state court. Mrs. W. C. Ross to USCB, September 30, 1939; reply October 4, 1939. Central File 1937–1940, RG 102, Box 822.

24. Testimony to such methods of child placement is abundant in USCB records; see, for example, Helen Schuster, Director, Oklahoma Children's Service to Agnes K. Hanna, USCB, April 9, 1934, on commercial maternity homes, Adoptions 1934–1935, RG 102, Box 548; Hanna to Elizabeth H. Webster, Council of Social Agencies of Chicago, IL, October 5, 1940, on The Cradle, a large commercial maternity home, Adoptions 1937–1940, RG 102, Box 821. Correspondence concerning "The Doorway to Happiness," a radio show proposed by Walter White, which aimed to "entertain a listening radio audience" and "to find responsible homes . . . for Fatherless and Motherless children" filed in Adoption 1937–1940, RG 102, Box 821; Elizabeth M. Owens to Grace Abbott, November 4, 1921, reporting child placement on the radio in California, Adoptions 1929–32, RG 102, Box 406.

25. Minutes for December 10, 1918, Minute book, Children's Bureau of Delaware.

26. Summary of state laws on adoption in Hanna to Mr. K. L. Messenger, Commissioner of Child Welfare, Hartford, CT, April 1, 1929. Central File 1929–1932, RG 102, Box 406.

27. Grace Abbott (head of USCB) to Margaret Hughes, State Department of Public Institutions, St. Paul, MN, March 3, 1933. Parental Responsibility, RG 102, Box 550.

28. Henry Winfred Thurston, *The Dependent Child* (New York: Columbia University Press, 1930; rpt. Arno, 1974).

29. Ibid., p. 157.

30. Ibid. p. 261.

31. Ibid., p. 159.

32. Ibid., p. 230.

33. Jim LePradd, Chicago, IL, to Franklin D. Roosevelt, November 7, 1936, referred to Children's Bureau for reply. Adoption 36 (2), RG 102, Box 549.

34. Mrs. W. R. Lambert, Thomasville, GA, to USCB January 4, 1939. Central File 1937–1940, RG 102, Box 822.

35. Mrs. George Tuscan, Wollaston, MA, December 24, 1938. Central File 1937–1940, RG 102, Box 822.

36. This example is Hanna to Mrs. Will Solomon, Temple, TX, December 16, 1932. Central File 1929–1932, RG 102, Box 406.

37. Mrs. Charles M. J. Norton, La Porte City, IA, to Eleanor Roosevelt, June 16, 1939. Central File 1937–1940, RG 102, Box 822.

38. Zelizer, *Pricing the Priceless Child*, pp. 198–199.

39. Eleanor Garrigue Gallagher, *The Adopted Child* (New York: Reynald and Hitchcock, 1936), pp. 33–34.

40. Kunzel, *Fallen Women, Problem Girls*, pp. 52–54.

41. Philip R. Reilly, *The Surgical Solution: A History of Involuntary Sterilization in the United States* (Baltimore: Johns Hopkins University Press, 1991), p. 84.

42. On the origins of intelligence testing during World War I, see JoAnne Brown, *The Definition of a Profession: The Authority of Metaphor in the History of Intelligence Testing, 1890–1930* (Princeton: Princeton University Press, 1992), pp. 109–125, and Leila Zenderland, *Measuring Minds: Henry Herbert Goddard and the Origins of American Intelligence Testing* (Cambridge, UK: Cambridge University Press, 1998), pp. 281–294.

CHAPTER TWO: FAMILIES BY DESIGN

1. Eleanor Garrigue Gallagher, *The Adopted Child* (New York: Reynald and Hitchcock, 1936), pp. 32, 34.

2. Judith S. Modell, *Kinship with Strangers: Adoption and Interpretations of Kinship in American Culture* (Berkeley: University of California Press, 1994), p. 226.

3. A comprehensive review of studies on sex preference in the United States may be found in Nancy E. Williamson, *Sons or Daughters? A Cross-Cultural Survey of Parental Preferences* (Berkeley Hills: Sage, 1976). Williamson's study confirms the persistence of preference for boys among biological parents as revealed in numerous studies conducted from 1930 to the mid-1970s. There is no comparable study on American sex preference since *Sons or Daughters?* Subsequent work on sex preference focuses mostly on population policy in underdeveloped nations. Sex preference in the United States is a topic of investigation in relation to reproductive technologies that enable sex selection; there is no broader study of attitudes about sex and family composition. Williamson also reviewed six studies on sex preference in adoption, five of which confirm a preference for girls.

4. Albert R. Bell, Frederic, WI, to Eleanor Roosevelt, November 20, 1935 (sent to USCB for reply). Adoption 1936, RG 102, Box 549.

5. "Baby Market," *Pathfinder*, vol. 54, no. 7, p. 40. Clipping in Adoption 1941–1944, RG 102, Box 170.

6. Lloyd G. Clift to Eleanor Roosevelt, February 5, 1940 (forwarded to USCB for reply). Central File 1937–1940, RG 102, Box 821.

7. Clara C. Clayton, Director, State Child Welfare Bureau (Nebraska), to Hanna, USCB, February 26, 1935. Adoption 1934–1935, RG 102, Box 548.

8. I reviewed all correspondence sent to the USCB from prospective adopters between 1912 and 1948. (After 1948, I was not confident I was capturing a complete sample, because of erratic filing methods and the huge volume of correspondence). Of these, 56 percent expressed no preference or indicated "either boy or girl"; 32 percent indicated they were seeking daughters, and 12 percent stated they wanted to adopt sons.

9. These figures are based on my review of 314 home studies of clients adopting for the first time at the CBD between 1930 and 1970. (After 1970, sex preference was essentially mooted: the bureau placed so few children that clients who held to a preference for one sex only were dismissed as "unrealistic.") I selected first-time CBD adopters to diminish the effect of sex preference shaped by children already in the home. My sample does capture some clients who were already parents, though; some had children by birth or had adopted a child previously from another source. African American and Jewish adopters are both over-represented in my sample, because I sought to capture all adop-

tions involving these groups, while sampling white Christian adopters. To adjust for this sampling bias, I sometimes cite figures for "white Christians" rather than composite figures of all CBD adopters.

10. Williamson, *Sons or Daughters?* pp. 29–33.

11. I cite the data from white Christians adopters separately here to correct for the bias introduced by over-representation of African-American and Jewish adopters in the sample.

12. Ibid., p. 33.

13. This disposition is documented in "parity progression ratios," that is, measures of how likely a couple is to continue having children. Studies of this behavior reveal that U.S. parents with two girls are more likely to have a third child than parents with two boys; or, to state it another way, parents tend to stop having children once they have one of each, or at least one boy. However, the difference between parents of sons and parents of daughters is relatively small—smaller than one might predict from surveys of couples' stated sex preferences. For an excellent summary and comparison of these studies, see Williamson, *Sons or Daughters?* pp. 43–46. See also Jeanne E. Clare and Clyde V. Kiser, "Social and Psychological Factors Affecting Fertility: XIV. Preference for Children of Given Sex in Relation to Fertility," *The Milbank Memorial Fund Quarterly* 29 (1951): 440–492.

14. Except where otherwise indicated, all cases in this paragraph are from the 1930s.

15. For another version of this argument, see Julie Berebitsky, *Like Our Very Own: Adoption and the Changing Culture of Motherhood, 1851–1950* (Lawrence: University Press of Kansas, 2000), pp. 140–142. Berebitsky argues that "social workers attempted to form adoptive families in such a way as to replicate the prevailing social class structure." This is true only to the extent that IQ does predict class, and CBD social workers recognized the barriers to upward mobility that rendered such predictions faulty. It also suggests more conscious intention than my evidence would support.

16. For a detailed history and critique of attachment theory, see Diane Eyer, *Mother-Infant Bonding: A Scientific Fiction* (New Haven: Yale University Pres, 1992), and Eyer, *Motherguilt: How Our Culture Blames Mothers for What's Wrong with Society* (New York: Times, 1996). On re-evaluation of placement practices in the 1950s, see J. Richard Wittenborn, *The Placement of Adoptive Children* (Springfield, IL: Charles C. Thomas, 1957). On influence of Bowlby on social work, see Eyer, *Mother-Infant Bonding,* p. 61, and Wittenborn, *Placement of Adoptive Children,* p. 4. Quotation from Wittenborn, p. 170.

17. *Revised Code of Delaware*, 1935. 3551 Sec. 4, p. 764.

18. See Romans 8:23; Galatians 4:5.

19. Reena Sigman Friedman, *These Are Our Children: Jewish Orphanages in the United States, 1880–1925* (Hanover, NH: Brandeis University Press, 1994), pp. 2–5; see also Dorothy M. Brown and Elizabeth McKeown, *The Poor Belong to Us: Catholic Charities and American Welfare* (Cambridge: Harvard University Press, 1997).

20. Nina Bernstein, *The Lost Children of* Wilder: *The Epic Struggle to Change Foster Care* (New York: Pantheon, 2001), pp. 57–58.

21. *Delaware Laws* 48 (1951), chap. 134, 3551E Sec. 4E, pp. 283–284.

22. *Delaware Laws* 56 (1967), chap. 323, p. 1102.

23. *Delaware Code Annotated*, 911, p. 128.

24. Ellen S. George and Stephen M. Snyder, "A Reconsideration of the Religious Element in Adoption," *Cornell Law Review* 56 (May 1971): 782–789.

25. The term comes from the celebrated study of American religion, Will Herberg, *Protestant, Catholic, Jew* (1955; Garden City, NY: Doubleday/Anchor, 1960).

26. Lawrence List, "A Child and a Wall: A Study of Religious Protection Laws," *Buffalo Law Review* 13 (1963): 17.

27. *In re Adoption of "E"* was a landmark case decided by the New Jersey Supreme Court in 1971; it reversed the lower court's denial of adoption to petitioners who were atheists. A useful brief summary may be found in Douglas J. Patterson, "Constitutional and Statutory Aspects of Religion as a Factor in Adoption Proceedings," *University of Missouri-Kansas City Law Review* 40 (1971–1972): 211–227. Another argument about the constitutionality of religious protection statutes is Linda A. Beerbower, "Religious Matching in Adoption: New York's Approach and the First Amendment," *University of Pittsburgh Law Review* 33 (1972): 601–610.

28. A discussion of *Petitions of Goldman* may be found in Harold B. Kivlan, "A Study of Religious Requirements for Adoption," *Dickinson Law Review* 76 (Spring 1972): 531–532.

29. See George and Synder, "Reconsideration of the Religious Element," pp. 786–787.

30. Shelley Kapnek Rosenberg, *Adoption and the Jewish Family: Contemporary Perspectives* (Philadelphia: Jewish Publication Society, 1998), pp. 2–20.

31. Florence D. Walrath to CB, April 8, 1941. Central File 1941–1942, RG 102, Box 170.

32. Ruth F. Brenner to Colby, July 23, 1942. Central File 1941–1944, RG 102, Box 169.

33. Colby to W. Hopkirk, CWLA, November 5, 1943. Central File 1941–1944, RG 102, Box 169.

34. C. A. Weslager, *Delaware's Forgotten Folk: The Story of the Moors and Nanticokes* (Philadelphia: University of Pennsylvania Press, 1943), p. 13. Thanks to Rebecca Knight, reference librarian at the University of Delaware, who tracked down this and other sources on Delaware Moors.

35. Mrs. Henry Ransdell, Portland, ME, to USCB. Central File 1929–1932, RG 102, box 406.

36. Mrs. Guy Hedgpeth, Newman, CA, to USCB, August 31, 1926. Adoption 1925–1928, RG 102, Box 294.

37. NUL Conference Report, "A Suggested Community Organization Program in Child Welfare," September 8, 1953, p. 6; National Urban League records, Group I, Series II, 1953–61, Box 19, file 1. In Library of Congress manuscript collection. [Hereafter cited LC-NUL.]

38. Nelson C. Jackson, Director, Community Services, to Lester B. Granger, Executive Director, re Child Welfare conferences, March 8, 1954. LC-NUL, ibid.

39. Working copy of the Report for the Study Committee on Adoptions of the Urban League of Kansas City, January 1954, p. 14. LC-NUL, Box 20

40. Confidential report to Study Committee, March 26, 1956, p. 8. LC-NUL, ibid.

41. Ibid., pp. 11–12.

42. NUL Conference Report, "A Suggested Community Organization Program in Child Welfare," September 8, 1953, pp. 6–7. LC-NUL, Box 19.

43. Mrs. Stella Thomson, NYC, to Eleanor Roosevelt, June 30, 1951. Central File 1941–1944, RG 102, Box 170.

44. Mary Ruth Colby, "Protection of Children in Adoption," paper presented at National Conference of Social Work, June 28, 1938, p. 7. Manuscript in Central File 1937–1940, RG 102, Box 821.

45. Hanna to Walter Pattey, January 13, 1931. Central File 1929–1932, RG 102, Box 406.

CHAPTER THREE: THE "BEST SOLUTION"

1. Mary Ruth Colby, "Protection of Children in Adoption," paper presented at National Conference of Social Work, June 28, 1938, in Central File 1937–1940, RG 102, Box 821; USCB estimate for 1945 cited in E. Wayne Carp, *Family Matters: Secrecy and Disclosure in the History of Adoption* (Cambridge: Harvard

University Press, 1998), p. 29; 1957–1970 statistics from National Center for Health Statistics data, tabulated and analyzed in Gordon Scott Bonham, "Who Adopts: The Relationship of Adoption and Social-Demographic Characteristics of Women," *Journal of Marriage and the Family* 39 (May 1977): 295–306.

2. This chapter extends the history of out of wedlock pregnancy set out in Regina G. Kunzel's *Fallen Women, Problem Girls: Unmarried Mothers and the Professionalization of Social Work, 1890–1945* (New Haven: Yale University Press, 1993).

3. An influential historical work that illustrates and argues this perspective is Rickie Solinger's *Wake Up Little Susie: Single Pregnancy and Race before Roe v. Wade* (New York: Routledge, 1992). On 1950s gender roles and sexual containment, see Elaine Tyler May, *Homeward Bound: American Families in the Cold War Era* (New York: Basic, 1988).

4. U.S. Children's Bureau report, "Protecting Children in Adoptions," delivered at Washington, D.C., conference, June 1955, p. 14. In National Urban League papers, Group I, Series II, 1953–1961, Box 19, file 3, "Adoption Programs: Reports and statements, 1953–55." Library of Congress manuscript collections (hereafter cited as LC-NUL); National Urban League conference report, "A Suggested Community Organization Program in Child Welfare," September 8, 1953, p. 4, LC-NUL, Box 19, file 6, "Adoption Program, reports and statements 1957–61."

5. Viviana A. Zelizer, *Pricing the Priceless Child: The Changing Social Value of Children* (New York: Basic Books, 1985), p. 263n119; 1951 figure from a survey of 17 states conducted by the U.S. Children's Bureau, reported in *Social Work Yearbook,* Social Security Administration, 1954; William Meezan, Sanford Katz, and Eva Manoff Russo, *Adoptions without Agencies: A Study of Independent Adoptions* (New York: Child Welfare League of America, 1978), p. 10.

6. CBD records contain frequent references to private (nonagency) adoptions occurring even after 1951; judges were probably loath to disrupt successful placements of some duration because of procedural defects. But given that Delaware was the first state to make agency adoption mandatory, it is reasonable to assume that its rate of agency-mediated adoption would be higher than the national average.

7. For the history of confidential adoption, see Carp, *Family Matters.*

8. Linda Gordon, *Pitied But Not Entitled: Single Mothers and the History of Welfare* (Cambridge: Harvard University Press, 1994), pp. 28–29, and Kriste Lindenmeyer, *"A Right to Children: The U.S. Children's Bureau and Child Welfare, 1912–1946* (Urbana: University of Illinois Press, 1997), pp. 158–160.

9. Leontine R. Young, *Out of Wedlock: A Study of the Problem of the Unmarried Mother and Her Child* (New York: McGraw-Hill, 1954), p. 22.

10. Ibid., pp. 32–33.

11. Ibid., p. 37.

12. Helen L. Witmer et al., *Independent Adoption: A Follow-Up Study* (New York: Russell Sage, 1963), p. 96.

13. J. Richard Wittenborn, *The Placement of Adoptive Children* (Springfield, IL: Charles C. Thomas, 1957), pp. 164–165.

14. Quoted ibid., p. 165.

15. Carl Doss and Helen Doss, *If You Adopt A Child* (New York: Henry Holt and Co., 1957), pp. 26, 45. For historical analyses of the prevalence of psychological interpretations for female infertility in the 1950s, see Margaret Marsh and Wanda Ronner, *The Empty Cradle: Infertility in America from Colonial Times to the Present* (Baltimore: Johns Hopkins University Press, 1996), p. 196, and Elaine Tyler May, *Barren in the Promised Land: Childless Americans and the Pursuit of Happiness* (New York: Basic, 1995), pp. 143, 153–155, 170–173.

16. May, *Barren in the Promised Land*, pp. 158–159; Marsh and Ronner, *Empty Cradle*, p. 16.

17. On masculine ideals in the 1950s, see Robert L. Griswold, *Fatherhood in America* (New York: Basic, 1993), pp. 185–210.

18. Lynn Y. Weiner, *From Working Girl to Working Mother: The Female Labor Force in the United States, 1820–1980* (Chapel Hill: University of North Carolina Press, 1985), pp. 93–94.

19. Confidential Report to the Study Committee, March 26, 1956, on Adopt-a-Child program, pp. 9–10. LC-NUL, Box 19, file 2, "Adoption Correspondence and Memoranda (General), 1956–1959."

20. "There Are Children To Be Adopted," newsletter from Lake County, Milwaukee, agency, in LC-NUL, Box 20, file 5, "Lake County-Milwaukee."

21. Clark Vincent, *Unmarried Mothers* (Glencoe, NY: Free Press, 1961).

22. Gordon, *Pitied But Not Entitled*.

23. Rickie Solinger, *The Abortionist: A Woman against the Law* (New York: Free Press, 1994), and Leslie Reagan, *When Abortion Was a Crime: Women, Medicine, and Law in the United States, 1867–1973* (Berkeley: University of California Press, 1997).

24. Jane E. Faber, untitled paper for SOC 320, summarizing her work with the bureau during July and August of 1963, n.p. Held at Children & Families First (CFF), Wilmington, DE.

25. Patricia Gottlieb, "Learning to Use Myself Spontaneously in the Imme-

diate Moment to Help an Unmarried Mother Face Emotionally the Realities of Her Pregnancy," Masters of Social Work Practice Project, University of Pennsylvania, 1968. Held at CFF, Wilmington, DE.

26. For an analysis of adolescent sexuality and prescriptions for conduct in the 1950s, see Wini Breines, *Young, White, and Miserable: Growing Up Female in the Fifties* (Boston: Beacon, 1992), pp. 84–126.

27. Shere Hite, *The Hite Report: A Nationwide Study of Female Sexuality* (New York: Dell, 1976), pp. 139–143.

28. May, *Barren in the Promised Land,* pp. 113–116.

29. Philip R. Reilly, *The Surgical Solution: A History of Involuntary Sterilization in the United States* (Baltimore: Johns Hopkins University Press, 1991).

30. Bonnie Shullenberger, *A Time To Be Born* (Cambridge, MA: Cowley Publications, 1996), p. 41.

31. Rebecca Harsin, *Wanted: First Child. A Birth Mother's Story* (Santa Barbara: Fithian Press, 1991), p. 35.

32. See, for example, Merry Bloch Jones, ed., *Birthmothers: Women Who Have Relinquished Children for Adoption Tell Their Stories* (Chicago: Chicago Review Press, 1993), pp. 21–22.

33. In Rita Townsend and Ann Perkins, eds., *Bitter Fruit: Women's Experiences of Unplanned Pregnancy, Abortion, and Adoption* (Alameda, CA: Hunter House, 1991), p. 181.

34. See, for example, Townsend and Perkins, eds., *Bitter Fruit,* p. 199.

35. The classic account of the sociology of "total institutions" is Erving Goffman, *Asylums* (Chicago: Aldine, 1961).

36. Shullenberger, *A Time To Be Born,* p. 30.

37. Jean Thompson [pseud.], *The House of Tomorrow* (New York: Harper and Row, 1966), p. 45.

38. "Molly," interviewed in Kate Inglis, *Living Mistakes: Mothers Who Consented to Adoption* (London: Allen & Unwin, 1984), p. 58.

39. Thompson, *House of Tomorrow,* pp. 165, 178.

40. Ibid., p. 179.

41. Townsend and Perkins, *Bitter Fruit,* pp. 187–188.

42. "Paula," in Townsend and Perkins, *Bitter Fruit,*" p. 232.

43. Jones, ed., *Birthmothers,* p. 12.

44. Prudence Mors Rains, *Becoming an Unwed Mother: A Sociological Account* (Chicago: Aldine, 1971); Rains cites a rate of relinquishment of 70 percent for white unwed mothers, based on a 1963 report, p. 175. In 1970 the year that adoptions reached their highest number in U.S. history, 80 percent of chil-

dren born out of wedlock were relinquished; see Anne D. Brodzinsky, "Surrendering an Infant for Adoption: The Birthmother Experience," in *The Psychology of Adoption,* ed. David M. Brodzinsky and Marshall D. Schechter (New York: Oxford University Press, 1990), p. 297. Brodinsky notes that this rate fell rapidly; in 1983 it was 4 percent. The current estimate is that less than 2 percent of unmarried women place children for adoption; cited in Laura Mansnerus, "Market Puts Price Tags on the Priceless," *New York Times,* October 26, 1998.

45. Young, *Out of Wedlock,* pp. 214, 217.

46. Leslie Margolin makes this argument in a Foucauldian analysis of late twentieth-century social work; see *Under the Cover of Kindness: The Invention of Social Work* (Charlottesville: University of Virginia Press, 1997).

47. Survey conducted by Evan B. Donaldson Adoption Institute, reported in the *New York Times,* November 9, 1997, p. A-16.

48. Joyce Ladner, *Mixed Families: Adopting across Racial Boundaries* (Garden City, NY: Anchor/Doubleday, 1977), p. 68.

49. Solinger, *Wake Up Little Susie,* p. 7.

50. Working copy, "Report for the Study Committee on Adoptions of the Urban League of Kansas City," January 1954, LC-NUL, Box 20, file 3, "Adoption Program, Affiliates Flint-Jacksonville."

51. Draft of research proposal, "Increasing the Life Chances of Negro Children through Improved Child Welfare Services," LC-NUL, Box 19, file 8, "Adoption Program, Pamphlet drafts (Bert Burns)."

52. William S. Jackson, "Our Evolving Task in Adoption," p. 12; paper presented at the Minnesota State Welfare Conference, March 26, 1958. LC-NUL, Box 19, file 2, "Adoption Correspondence and Memoranda (General), 1956–59."

CHAPTER FOUR: REDRAWING THE BOUNDARIES

1. David Fanshel, *Far from the Reservation: The Transracial Adoption of American Indian Children* (Metuchen, NJ: Scarecrow, 1972).

2. Elizabeth Bartholet, "Where Do Black Children Belong? The Politics of Race Matching in Adoption," in *Family Matters: Readings on Family Lives and the Law,* ed. Martha Minow (New York: New Press, 1993), p. 72.

3. A 1993 report estimated the number of international adoptions by American parents at 7,000 to 10,000 a year; see U.S. Senate, Report to the Honorable Arlen Specter, "Intercountry Adoption" (Washington, DC: General Accounting Office, 1993), p. 2. The largest estimate given for stranger adoptions per year in

the 1990s is 50,000. Thus, it appears that international adoption constitutes about 15–20 percent of American adoptions per year.

4. J. Douglas Bates, *Gift Children: A Story of Race, Family, and Adoption in a Divided America* (New York: Ticknor and Fields, 1993), pp. 10–11.

5. Ibid., p. 29.

6. U.S. Senate, "Intercountry Adoption," General Accounting Office, 1993, pp. 2, 10.

7. "Hard-to-Place Children. Part 1: Negro Children, Kansas City, MO, Publication 94, Community Studies, Inc., May 1955." Library of Congress, National Urban League records, Group I, Series II, 1953–1961 [hereafter LC-NUL], Box 19, folder 4, "Adoption Program, Reports and Statements 1955."

8. "Hard-to-Place Children. Part 2: Illegitimate Negro Children, Kansas City, MO, Publication 99, Community Studies, Inc., March 1956," pp. 49, 51. LC-NUL, Box 19, folder 5, "Adoption Program, Reports and Statements 1956."

9. Asley U. Gaskins, Unit Supervisor, Children's Service Division, Hennepin County Welfare Board, to Nelson C. Jackson, Director, Community Services [National Urban League], May 21, 1954. LC-NUL, Box 19, folder 1, "Adoption Program Correspondence and Memoranda (General) 1953–55."

10. William V. Kelley, Executive Secretary of Milwaukee Urban League, to Nelson D. Jackson, March 8, 1956; Perry A. Taylor, Executive Secretary, Urban League of Greater Little Rock [Wisconsin], to Jackson, November 29, 1955. LC-NUL, Box 20, folder 5.

11. Joseph A. Hall, Executive Secretary of Urban League of Greater Cincinnati, to Nelson C. Jackson, June 8, 1954. LC-NUL, Box 20, file 2, "Affiliates Cincinnati-Essex County."

12. 1957 report from Columbus, Ohio. LC-NUL, Box 20, file 2, "Affiliates Cincinnati-Essex County."

13. Memo to Family and Child Welfare Division, Community Welfare Council, from Minnesota Urban League, re "Problem of Adoption for Minority Race Children," April 11, 1958. LC-NUL, Box 20, file 6, "Minneapolis-Pittsburgh."

14. "Some Principles of Adoption Governing the Practices of Member Agencies," Child Welfare League of America, 1948, rpt. in *Child Welfare*, April 1950, p. 11.

15. "Proceedings: Workshop on Cultural Factors, a program for social caseworkers. San Diego Area Recruitment Committee for Minority Adoptive Homes, 1959," pp. 2, 77, 81. LC-NUL papers, Box 19, file 9, "Adoption Program, Miscellany."

16. Bartholet, "Where Do Black Children Belong?" p. 72.

17. National Association of Black Social Workers, position paper, April 1972, in Rita J. Simon and Howard Altstein, *Transracial Adoption* (New York: Wiley, 1977), pp. 50–52.

18. Steven Unger, ed., *The Destruction of American Indian Families* (New York: Association on American Indian Affairs, 1977), p. 87.

19. Ibid., p. 88.

20. Martha Minow, *Not Only for Myself: Identity, Politics, and the Law* (New York: New Press, 1997), pp. 75, 78.

21. Bartholet, "Where Do Black Children Belong?" pp. 72–73.

22. Elizabeth Bartholet, *Nobody's Children: Abuse and Neglect, Foster Drift, and the Adoption Alternative* (Boston: Beacon, 1999), p. 124.

23. Bartholet, "Where Do Black Children Belong?" and Randall Kennedy, "Orphans of Separatism: The Painful Politics of Transracial Adoption," *American Prospect* 17 (spring 1994): 38–45.

24. For examples of outcome studies of transracial adoption, see Joyce Ladner, *Mixed Families: Adopting across Racial Boundaries* (Garden City: Doubleday, 1977); Lucille J. Grow and Deborah Shapiro, *Black Children— White Parents: A Study of Transracial Adoption* (New York: Child Welfare League of America, 1974); Lucille J. Grow and Deborah Shapiro, *Transracial Adoption Today: Views of Adoptive Parents and Social Workers* (New York: Child Welfare League of America, 1975); Rita J. Simon, Howard Altstein, and Marygold S. Melli, *The Case for Transracial Adoption* (Washington, DC: American University Press, 1994). A useful summary of outcome studies is Arnold R. Silverman and William Feigelman, "Adjustment in Interracial Adoptees: An Overview," in *The Psychology of Adoption,* ed. David M. Brodzinsky and Marshall D. Schechter (New York: Oxford University Press, 1990), pp. 187–200. Twila L. Perry notes that outcome studies have virtually all confirmed the success of transracial adoption but that they have not dislodged the widespread commitment to same-race placement (which she herself continues to endorse); see Perry, "The Transracial Adoption Controversy: An Analysis of Discourse and Subordination," *Review of Law and Social Change* 21, no. 1 (1993/1994): 37.

25. "Mother Regains Child in Racial Custody Case," *New York Times,* March 9, 1999, p. A-18.

26. Minow, *Not Only for Myself,* p. 19.

27. Joseph Goldstein, Anna Freud, and Albert J. Solnit, *Beyond the Best Interests of the Child* (New York: Free Press, 1973).

28. Minow, *Not Only for Myself,* pp. 76–77.

29. "Revising Old Debate: Race and Adoptions," *New York Times,* October 24, 1993.

30. Steven A. Holmes, "Bitter Racial Dispute Rages over Adoption: White Couple Seeks Custody of Two Blacks," *New York Times,* April 13, 1995.

31. "Mother Regains Child," *New York Times,* March 9, 1999, p. A-18.

32. Rita Kramer, "Adoption in Black and White," *Wall Street Journal,* October 24, 1994.

33. Timothy Egan, "A Cultural Gap May Swallow a Child," New York Times, October 12, 1993.

34. Minow, *Not Only for Myself,* data from 1990 census cited in pp. 231–232n710.

35. Timothy Egan, "A Cultural Gap May Swallow a Child," *New York Times,* October 12, 1993, p. A-16.

36. Quoted in Albert R. Hunt, "Metzenbaum Breaches the Adoption Color Barrier," *Wall Street Journal,* July 14, 1994.

37. Metzenbaum and Mfume quoted ibid.; Rita Kramer, "Adoption in Black and White," *Wall Street Journal,* October 24, 1994.

38. On the history of blood portion in accounting tribal membership, see Melissa L. Meyer, "American Indian Blood Quantum Requirements: Blood Is Thicker than Family," in *Over the Edge: Remapping the American West,* ed. Valerie J. Matsumoto and Blake Allmendinger (Berkeley: University of California Press, 1999), pp. 223–249. On the issue of the constitutionality of the ICWA's use of race matching, see Bartholet, *Nobody's Children,* 129.

39. Seth J. Margolis, *Losing Isaiah* (New York: Jove, 1993; *Losing Isaiah* (film), 1995, produced by Howard Koch, Jr., and Naomi Foner (screenplay by Naomi Foner); Barbara Kingsolver, *Pigs in Heaven* (New York: HarperCollins, 1993); Sherman Alexie, *The Indian Killer* (New York: Atlantic Monthly Press, 1996).

40. Barbara Kingsolver, *The Bean Trees* (New York: Harper Perennial, 1988).

41. Interview with Kingsolver in Donna Perry, *Backtalk: Women Writers Speak Out* (New Brunswick: Rutgers University Press, 1993), p. 165.

42. See Meyer, "American Indian Blood Quantum Requirements," p. 234.

43. Most readers found this ending unconvincing; Christopher Lehmann-Haupt, for one, called it "treacly" in his review, "Community vs. Family and Writer vs. Subject," *New York Times,* July 12, 1993, p. C-16.

44. Grow and Shapiro, *Transracial Adoption Today,* pp. 75, 53, 50–52, 89.

45. On foster care and the plight of black children in particular, see

Bartholet, *Nobody's Children,* and Nina Bernstein, *The Lost Children of* Wilder: *The Epic Struggle to Change Foster Care* (New York: Pantheon, 2001).

46. See, for example, Maggie Francis Conroy, *A World of Love* (New York: Kensington Books, 1997), p. 8; Susan T. Viguers, *With Child: One Couple's Journey to Their Adopted Children* (New York: Harcourt Brace Jovanovich, 1986), p. 85.

47. This reason was cited more often than any others; see U.S. Senate, "Intercountry Adoption," p. 59.

48. Reported in Adam Perlman, *Adoption Nation: How the Adoption Revolution Is Transforming America* (New York: Basic/Perseus, 2000), p. 266.

49. Statistics from Immigration and Naturalization Services of the U.S. government may be found on the website for Holt International, which lists INS figures for immigration of children for adoption, 1985–2001. www.holtintl.org.

50. Mary Albanese, *To Romania, with Love: Saving the World, One Child at a Time* (Lima, OH: Fairway Press, 1992), p. 9.

51. Ibid., p. 87.

52. Elizabeth Bartholet, *Family Bonds: Adoption and the Politics of Parenting* (Boston: Houghton-Mifflin, 1993), p. 142.

53. Barbara and Patrick Canale, *Our Labor of Love: A Romanian Adoption Chronicle* (Utica, NY: North Country Books/Pine Tree Press, 1994).

54. Robert Klose, *Adopting Alyosha: A Single Man Finds a Son in Russia* (Jackson: University of Mississippi Press, 1999), pp. 99, 100.

55. Debi Standiford and Steve Standiford, with Nhi and Hy Phan, *Sudden Family* (Waco, TX: Word Books, 1986).

56. Sheri Register, *"Are Those Kids Yours?" American Families with Children Adopted from Other Countries* (New York: Free Press, 1991).

57. Laurel Strassberger, *Our Children from Latin America: Making Adoption Part of Your Life* (New York: Tiresias Press, 1992), p. 32–33.

58. Frances M. Koh, *Adopted from Asia: How It Feels To Grow Up in America* (Minneapolis: East West Press, 1993), pp. 59, 70, 76.

59. Chalise Miner, *Rain Forest Girl: More than an Adoption Story* (Childs, MD: Mitchell Lane Publishers, 1998), p. 46.

CHAPTER FIVE: "TELL IT SLANT"

1. This view of professional authority draws on the classic account of Eliot Freidson, *Profession of Medicine* (New York: Harper and Row, 1970).

2. William Meezan, Sanford Katz, and Eva Manoff Russo, *Adoptions without*

Agencies: A Study of Independent Adoptions (New York: Child Welfare League of America, 1978), p. 10.

3. Leontine R. Young, *Out of Wedlock: A Study of the Problems of the Unmarried Mother and Her Child* (New York: McGraw-Hill, 1954), p. 32; Young also cites "medical reports" documenting lower rates of miscarriage among unwed mothers. Obviously women whose unwelcome pregnancies ended in early miscarriage would not be among the clientele of adoption agencies, an objection that Young anticipates but unaccountably dismisses.

4. Mary L. Shanley, "Fathers' Rights, Mothers' Wrongs? Reflections on Unwed Fathers' Rights and Sex Equality," *Hypatia* 10 (Winter 1995), rpt. in *Reproduction, Sexuality and the Family*, ed. Karen J. Maschke (New York: Garland, 1977).

5. Arnolfi, Io, *We Adopted It* (London: Routledge & Kegan Paul, 1963), pp. 51–52. This is a British account, but the sentiment expressed is a stock feature of memoirs of American adoptive parents also.

6. Karen W. Tice, *Tales of Wayward Girls and Immoral Women: Case Records and the Professionalization of Social Work* (Urbana: University of Illinois Press, 1998), p. 31. Tice notes here the importance of centralized registration bureaus and confidential exchanges in extending the reach of case recording. Her book argues that "Record-keeping . . . played a key role in the legitimation of social casework," p. 7.

7. On the persistence of this idea, and for discussion of studies of infertile couples refuting this truism of folk knowledge, see Margaret Marsh and Wanda Ronner, *The Empty Cradle: Infertility in America from Colonial Times to the Present* (Baltimore: Johns Hopkins University Press, 1996), pp. 205–206.

8. A perceptive discussion of professional management of truth-telling and confidentiality may be found in Sissela Bok, *Lying: Moral Choice in Public and Private Life* (1978; New York: Vintage, 1989), pp. 146–164.

9. M. Y. Crouse to Mary Irene Atkinson of Ohio State Board of Charities, Central File 1921–1924, "Placing Out," RG 102, Box 21. Atkinson sent the letter to the Children's Bureau, presumably as an example of the sorts of irregular practices that social work professionals were seeking to reform.

10. Mary Ruth Colby to Norma Rankin, Director of Child Welfare Services, State Board of Control, Austin, TX, July 26, 1939. Central File 1937–1940, RG 102, Box 822.

11. Colby to Dr. Harry S. Mackler, December 4, 1942. Central File 1941–1944, RG 102, Box 170.

12. A 1990s "wrongful adoption" case turned on just this issue: adopters

charged that the agency had failed to disclose relevant background information about birth relatives' severe mental illness; their son suffered from schizophrenia. The agency countered that when the child was placed, schizophrenia was not generally considered heritable. Lisa Belkin, "What the Jumans Didn't Know about Michael," *New York Times Magazine,* March 14, 1999, pp. 40–49.

13. Ann Kimble Loux, *The Limits of Hope: An Adoptive Mother's Story* (Charlottesville: University Press of Virginia, 1997).

14. E. Wayne Carp, *Family Matters: Secrecy and Disclosure in the History of Adoption* (Cambridge: Harvard University Press, 1998), pp. 192–193.

15. Ibid., p. 85.

16. Ibid., p. 55.

17. Colby to Ann M. Bracken, Director of Children's Welfare Department, State Department of Social Services, Phoenix, AZ, December 12, 1939, in reply to Bracken's letter of December 7. Central File 1937–1940, RG 102, Box 832.

18. Quoted in Carp, *Family Matters,* p. 70.

19. Subsequent quotations from Hubbard's speech are contained in Frances Lockridge, *Adopting a Child* (New York: Greenberg, 1947), p. 81.

20. Ibid., p. 80

21. Reported disapprovingly by Miss Shepperson of the Children's Bureau to Dr. Eliot in memo re: "'The Cradle' Society of Evanston, Illinois," February 24, 1944. Central File 1941–1944, RG 102, Box 169. The memo was in reply to a staff member of Eleanor Roosevelt who requested information about The Cradle.

22. Mrs. E. L. Armstrong, Richmond, VA, to CB, February 28, 1928. Central File 1925–1928, RG 102, Box 294.

23. Elsa Castendyck, Director, Social Services Division, to Mrs. George R. Jones, October 6, 1942. A note on the bottom of this correspondence summarizes the situation as described in Mrs. Jones's letter to FDR, not filed with this reply. Castendyck explained at some length why the proposed plan was not to be countenanced and concluded by advising Mrs. Jones to seek marriage counseling. Central File 1941–1944, RG 102, Box 170.

24. Cited in Viviana A. Zelizer, *Pricing the Priceless Child: The Changing Social Value of Children* (New York: Basic, 1985), p. 189.

25. Mrs. G. Unwin, Scotia, NY, to CB, August 29, 1931. Central File 1929–32, RG 102, Box 406.

26. Grace Abbott to Unwin, September 3, 1931. Central File 1929–32, RG 102, Box 406.

27. Eleanor Garrigue Gallagher, *The Adopted Child* (New York: Reynald and Hitckcock, 1936), p. 114.

28. Carp, *Family Matters,* pp. 90–91.

29. Valentina P. Wasson (illustrated by Hildegard Woodward), *The Chosen Baby* (New York: Carrick and Evans, 1939); Wasson, *Chosen Baby,* rev. ed. (Philadelphia: Lippincott, 1950); Wasson (illustrated by Glo Coalson), *Chosen Baby,* rev. ed. (Philadelphia: Lippincott, 1977).

30. Carp dates the expert critique of the chosen child story to a 1955 paper by Irene M. Josselyn, a psychiatrist at the Institute for Psychoanalysis in Chicago (see *Family Matters,* pp. 128–129). However, CBD social workers were making a similar argument against the theme in 1955 case records. It is possible that they were aware of Josselyn's work; it seems more likely that the critique could have had more than one source. As social workers accumulated experience with adoption, they may have developed their own dissatisfaction with the implications of the chosen child story.

31. Lois Ruskai Melina, *Making Sense of Adoption* (New York: Harper & Row, 1989), pp. 109–10.

32. Ibid., p. 168.

33. Betsy Keefer and Jayne E. Schooler, *Telling the Truth to Your Adopted or Foster Child: Making Sense of the Past* (Westport, CT: Bergin and Garvey, 2000), pp. 97–113.

34. Jacqueline Hornor Plumez, *Successful Adoption* (New York: Harmony, 1982), p. 118.

35. Stephanie E. Siegal, *Parenting Your Adopted Child* (New York: Prentice Hall, 1989), p. 25.

36. Melina, *Making Sense of Adoption,* p. 21.

37. See the detailed discussion and astute analysis of this critique in Carp, *Family Matters,* pp. 128–132.

38. Mary Watkins and Susan Fisher, *Talking with Young Children about Adoption* (New Haven: Yale University Press, 1993), pp. 33–34.

39. Elinor B. Rosenberg, *The Adoption Lifecycle: The Children and Their Families through the Years* (New York: Free Press, 1992), pp. 96–97. In her introduction Rosenberg wrote that her views had been shaped by her experience as a social worker at a residential treatment center where adopted children were disproportionately represented, and by the work of Humberto Nagera, child analyst at the University of Michigan Child Psychiatry department.

40. See, for example, Melina, *Making Sense of Adoption,* pp. 36–39; Plumez,

Successful Adoption, p. 121; Sheri Register, *"Are Those Kids Yours?" American Families with Children Adopted from Other Countries* (New York: Free Press, 1991); Siegal, *Parenting Your Adopted Child*, pp. 26–28, 37–38.

41. Carl Doss and Helen Doss, *If You Adopt A Child* (New York: Henry Holt and Co., 1957), p. 131.

42. Melina, *Making Sense of Adoption*, p. 156.

CHAPTER SIX: ADOPTION CHALLENGED

1. Arthur D. Sorosky, Annette Baran, and Reuben Pannor, *The Adoption Triangle: Sealed or Open Records: How They Affect Adoptees, Birth Parents, and Adoptive Parents* (1978; Garden City: Doubleday/Anchor, 1984).

2. Coined in 1965 by H. J. Sants, the term "genealogical bewilderment" was publicized and popularized by the more widely circulated *Adoption Triangle*. See Sants, "Genealogical Bewilderment in Children with Substitute Parents," *Child Adoption*, 47 (1965): 32–42.

3. My discussion of the origins of the adoption rights movement draws on the only comprehensive historical account of it; see E. Wayne Carp, *Family Matters: Secrecy and Disclosure in the History of Adoption* (Cambridge: Harvard University Press, 1998), pp. 138–166.

4. The origins of this term are not entirely clear, but Carp has argued that it was popularized by Sorosky et al., *The Adoption Triangle* (1978); see Carp, *Family Matters*, p. 149.

5. Carp tells the history of the rise of the adoption rights movement of the 1970s in *Family Matters*, esp. pp. 142–147. For an illuminating ethnographic account of the culture of search groups and the role of personal narrative in them, see Judith S. Modell, *Kinship with Strangers: Adoption and Interpretations of Kinship in American Culture* (Berkeley: University of California Press, 1974), pp. 143–199.

6. Of course many organizations of adoptive parents and families also exist, and their newsletters and meetings are sites for the production and circulation of adopters' narratives. However, these organizations are more varied and specialized than organizations of adoptees in search. Many simply supply forums for the sharing of common experiences and sponsor alternative communities, such as organizations of mixed-race adoptive families. Others, like search groups, have activist orientations; for example, some groups are working to change laws on international adoption, or to sponsor a Uniform Adoption Law to replace the variable state law that currently governs adoption. Still others are

primarily directed to prospective adopters, offering support and advice to people undertaking adoption.

7. Ruthena Hill Kittson [Jean M. Paton], *The Adopted Break Silence* (Philadelphia: Life History Study Centers, 1954); Ruthena Hill Kittson [Jean M. Paton], *Orphan Voyage* (New York: Vantage, 1968).

8. Florence Fisher, *The Search for Anna Fisher* (Boston: Arthur Fields Books, 1973).

9. Betty Jean Lifton, *Twice Born* (New York: McGraw-Hill, 1975).

10. Back cover, paperback edition (already cited) of *The Adoption Triangle*.

11. Carp, *Family Matters*, pp. 146–147.

12. Sorosky et al., *The Adoption Triangle*, pp. 197–218.

13. See Christine A. Bachrach, "Adoption Plans, Adopted Children, and Adoptive Mothers," *Journal of Marriage and the Family* 48 (May 1986): 243–253, esp. 245; and C. A. Bachrach, K. London, and P. Maza, "On the Path to Adoption: Adoption-Seeking in the U.S.," *Journal of Marriage and the Family* 53 (August 1991): 705–718.

14. Robert Haveman and Barbara Wolfe, "Children's Prospects and Children's Policy," *Journal of Economic Perspectives* 7 (Fall 1993): 153–174.

15. For a perceptive analysis of the role of internet exchange in the formation of cultural identities, see Carl Elliott, "A New Way To Be Mad," *Atlantic Monthly* (December 2000), pp. 72–84.

16. This description of the genre, and subsequent generalizations about it, are based on wide reading in this contemporary literature. There is no comprehensive bibliographic aid to adoption memoir, and that genre is constantly expanding. Library of Congress subject headings now include "birth mother" and "birth father," providing access to recent memoirs. I limit my discussion to full-length memoirs or autobiographies. Other life writing about adoption appears in compilations of first-hand accounts, some of which are cited in this chapter and elsewhere in the book. Some advice literature contains autobiographical material. For a more detailed discussion of this material, see Melosh, "Adoption Stories: Autobiographical Narrative and the Politics of Identity," in *Adoption in History: New Interpretive Essays*, ed. E. Wayne Carp (Ann Arbor: University of Michigan, forthcoming 2002).

17. Judith S. Gediman and Linda P. Brown, *Birth Bond: Reunions between Birth Parents and Adoptees—What Happens After* (Far Hills, NJ: New Horizon Press, 1989), p. 55; Katarina Wegar, *Adoption, Identity and Kinship: The Debate over Sealed Birth Records* (New Haven: Yale University Press, 1997), pp. 63–64.

A large study of Canadian adopted persons confirmed this finding, with adopted women three times as likely as men to search: see Karen March, *The Stranger Who Bore Me: Adoptee-Birth Mother Relationships* (Toronto: University of Toronto Press, 1995), p. 33. Others argue that adopted girls express more interest in adoption as children than their male counterparts; see Susan Farber, "Sex Differences in the Expression of Adoption Ideas: Observations of Adoptees from Birth through Latency," *American Journal of Orthopsychiatry* 57, no. 4 (October 1977): 643, 649.

18. Modell, *Kinship with Strangers,* pp. 172–175.

19. There is one anthology that presents brief accounts by birth fathers; see Mary Martin Mason, *"Out of the Shadows": Birthfathers' Stories* (Edina, MN: O. J. Howard Publishing, 1995). However, Mason uses the term "birthfathers" more broadly than the customary use of "birth mother." Some of these men write about their children who were relinquished for adoption; others were separated from their children by abandonment, divorce, or imprisonment.

20. Elizabeth Cooper Allen, *Mother, Can You Hear Me? The Extraordinary True Story of an Adopted Daughter's Reunion with Her Birth Mother after a Separation of Fifty Years* (New York: Dodd, Mead and Co., 1983), p. 13.

21. Katrina Maxtone-Graham, *An Adopted Woman* (New York: Remi, 1983), p. 270.

22. Doris McMillon, *Mixed Blessing* (New York: St. Martin's, 1985), p. 127.

23. Allen, *Mother, Can You Hear Me?* pp. 30, 179.

24. Amy E. Dean, *Letters to My Birthmother: An Adoptee's Diary of Her Search for Her Identity* (New York: Pharos Books/Scripps Howard, 1991), p. 42.

25. Maxtone-Graham, *Adopted Woman,* p. 91.

26. McMillon, *Mixed Blessing,* pp. 12–13.

27. Frances Lear, *The Second Seduction* (New York: Knopf, 1991), p. 110.

28. Paton, *Orphan Voyage,* p. 257.

29. Jean Downie, *By Order of Adoption* (Plantation, FL: Distinctive Publishing Corp., 1992), p. 3.

30. Tim Green, *A Man and His Mother: An Adopted Son's Search* (New York: HarperCollins, 1997).

31. Robert Andersen, *Second Choice: Growing Up Adopted* (Chesterfield, MO: Badger Hill Press, 1993).

32. Carp, *Family Matters,* p. 231.

33. Overall success rates of searches are impossible to estimate, since many are ongoing and in any case there is no way of counting everyone engaged in search. However, it seems safe to conclude that this rate of success surpasses

that experienced by searchers who are not writing memoirs. No doubt this reflects the pressure for closure in popular genres, which may also explain why Andersen's account was published by his own press.

34. Downie, *By Order of Adoption*, p. 49.

35. Green, *A Man and His Mother*, pp. 185–186.

36. Allen, *Mother, Can You Hear Me?* pp. 63–64, 102.

37. Dean, *Letters*, p. 107.

38. Maxtone-Graham, *Adopted Woman*, p. 278.

39. Dean, *Letters*, p. 94.

40. McMillon, *Mixed Blessing*, p. 246.

41. James Stingley, *Mother, Mother* (New York: Congdon & Lattes, 1981).

42. Frank Law, *Through the Eyes of an Adoptee: One Man's Compelling Search for His Beginnings* (Layton, UT: Purr-Fection Printing, 1996); Michael Watson, *In Search of Mom: Journey of an Adoptee* (Costa Mesa, CA: Gallery of Diamonds Publishing, 1998); Green, *A Man and His Mother*.

43. Sarah Saffian, *Ithaka: A Daughter's Memoir of Being Found* (New York: Basic/Perseus Books, 1998).

44. See Betty Jean Lifton, *Journey of the Adopted Self: A Quest for Wholeness* (New York: Basic, 1994), esp. pp. 260–61, 271.

45. A study based on analysis of thirty reunions: Judith S. Gediman and Linda P. Brown, *BirthBond: Reunions between Birthparents and Adoptees— What Happens After* (Far Hills, NJ: New Horizon Press, 1989), pp. 67, 125–126, 158–164; a Canadian study of 60 adoption reunions, Karen March, *The Stranger Who Bore Me: Adoptee-Birth Mother Relationships* (Toronto: University of Toronto Press, 1995), pp. 86–87, 98, 106–108; Katarina Wegar, *Adoption, Identity, and Kinship: The Debate over Sealed Birth Records* (New Haven: Yale University Press, 1997), p. 65 (drawing on data from Paul Sachdev's study of 124 Canadian searchers).

46. Carol Schaefer, *The Other Mother: A Woman's Love for the Child She Gave Up for Adoption* (New York: Soho Press, 1991), p. 38.

47. Margaret Moorman, *Waiting to Forget: A Mother Opens the Door to Her Secret Past* (New York: W. W. Norton, 1996), p. 68.

48. Patricia E. Taylor, *Shadow Train: A Journey Between Relinquishment and Reunion* (Baltimore: Gateway Press, 1995), p. 19.

49. CBD records show that agency social workers definitely did not participate in this much-maligned advice; rather, they told birth mothers specifically that they would *not* forget the children they relinquished, and they viewed remembering as therapeutic, part of the lesson learned from out of wedlock

pregnancy. However, their counsel in itself suggests that this advice was often given to women relinquishing children for adoption; otherwise, it is hard to explain why social workers would find it necessary to warn women that they would not forget such a consequential life experience.

50. Rebecca Harsin, *Wanted: First Child: A Birth Mother's Story* (Santa Barbara: Fithian Press, 1991), p. 106.

51. Schaefer, *The Other Mother*, p. 110.

52. Ibid., pp. 91–92.

53. Harsin, *Wanted—First Child*, p. 83.

54. Schaefer, *Other Mother*, p. 155.

55. Louise Jurgens, *Torn from the Heart: The Amazing True Story of a Birth Mother's Search for Her Lost Daughter* (Lower Lake, CA: Aslan Publishing Co., 1992), pp. 70, 81.

56. Lynn C. Franklin (with Elizabeth Ferber), *May the Circle Be Unbroken: An Intimate Journey into the Heart of Adoption* (New York: Harmony Books, 1998), p. 103.

57. Suzanne Arms, *Adoption: A Handful of Hope* (Berkeley: Celestial Arts, 1990), p. 356.

58. Eva Y. Deykin, Lee Campbell, and Patricia Patti, "The Postadoption Experience of Surrendering Parents," *American Journal of Orthopsychiatry* 54 (April 1984), p. 271.

59. Lorraine Dusky, *Birthmark* (New York: M. Evans and Co., 1979), p. 15.

60. Schaefer, *Other Mother*, p. 181.

61. Jurgens, *Torn from the Heart*, p. 220.

62. See Marsha Riben, *Shedding Light on the Dark Side of Adoption* (Detroit: Harlo, 1988), pp. 9, 13.

63. Dusky, *Birthmark*, pp. 9–10.

64. Jurgens, *Torn from the Heart*, pp. 80, 163,

65. Sandra Kay Musser, *What Kind of Love Is This? A Story of Adoption Reconciliation* (Oaklyn, NJ: Jan Publications, 1982), pp. 37, 13.

66. Jan L. Waldron, *Giving Away Simone: A Memoir* (New York: Times/ Random House, 1995), pp. xvi, xvii.

67. Michele Launders and Penina Spiegel, *I Wish You Didn't Know My Name: The Story of Michele Launders and Her Daughter Lisa* (New York: Warner, 1990), p. 4.

68. My only knowledge of this collaboration is derived from the comments

on it in the text itself; I have not contacted Launders, Spiegel, or the publisher for more information about the circumstances of its writing.

69. Marsha Riben, *Shedding Light on the Dark Side of Adoption* (Detroit: Harlow, 1988).

70. Ibid., p. 13. In another instance of this common usage, Elisa M. Barton proclaims herself a "lost" mother in her collection of e-mail correspondence from relinquishing mothers, *Confessions of a Lost Mother* (Baltimore: Gateway Press, 1996).

71. Mary Anne Cohen, "Death by Adoption: Symbolic Murder," *Origins*, January/February 1984, quoted in Riben, *Shedding Light on the Dark Side of Adoption*, p. 71.

72. "Happy families are all alike; every unhappy family is unhappy in its own way." Leo Tolstoy, *Anna Karinina*, p. 1.

73. Michael Dorris, *The Broken Cord* (New York: Harper and Row, 1989).

74. Elizabeth Cook-Lynn, *Why I Can't Read Wallace Stegner* (Madison: University of Wisconsin Press, 1996), pp. 7–10.

75. Dorris, *Broken Cord*, p. 10.

76. Dr. Hugh M. Leichtman, identified only as the director of Medico Children's Services. In Loux, *The Limits of Hope*, p. ix.

77. Melissa Fay Greene, "The Orphan Ranger: Adopting a Damaged Child," *New Yorker*, July 17, 2000, pp. 38–45.

78. Ibid., p. 39.

79. Nancy Newton Verrier, *The Primal Wound: Understanding the Adopted Child* (Baltimore: Gateway, 1993), p. xiii.

80. Susan Ferine, "She Just Wanted to Know Who She Was," *Health* 14, no. 6 (July/August 2000): 134–140, 166–172. All quotes are in this paragraph, except the last, are from p. 136; ellipses in original.

81. Personal account told to the author in the mid-1990s.

82. On the response of adoption professionals, see Carp, *Family Matters*, pp. 181–183.

83. Carp, *Family Matters*, p. 145.

84. See Carp's assessment of favorable media coverage in the adoption rights movement in *Family Matters*, pp. 167–168.

85. Testimony of Les Waguespack to the Louisiana legislature in hearings about opening sealed records, quoted in Musser, *What Kind of Love Is This?* p. 164.

86. For a more detailed discussion of legal challenges posed in state courts

and for constitutional arguments against sealed records, see Carp, *Family Matters*, pp. 175–180.

87. Quoted from their 1976 article; Sorosky et al., *The Adoption Triangle*, pp. 207–208.

88. Reuben Pannor and Annette Baran, "Open Adoption as Standard Practice," *Child Welfare* 63, no. 3 (May–June 1984): 246.

89. Musser, *What Kind of Love Is This?* p. 168.

90. Annette Baran and Reuben Pannor, *Lethal Secrets: The Shocking Consequences and Unsolved Problems of Artificial Insemination* (New York: Warner/Amistad, 1989). *The Adoption Triangle* had also criticized secrecy in artificial insemination. If genetic inheritance is the issue, obviously the unknown and unreachable father is just as important as the missing birth mother. Notably, though, this issue has failed to capture much public attention, evidence of the primacy of motherhood in debates about adoption and other alternative families.

91. Panel presentation by Pannor and Baran, at 13th International Conference of the American Adoption Congress, Garden Grove, CA, April 11, 1991, described in Elinor B. Rosenberg, *The Adoption Lifecycle: The Children and Their Families through the Years* (New York: Free Press, 1992), p. 181.

92. Rita Dukette, "Value Issues in Present-Day Adoption," *Child Welfare* 63, no. 3 (May–June 1984): 233–243; quotation from p. 242.

93. Adrienne D. Kraft, Joseph Palumbo, Patricia K. Woods, Dorian Mitchell, and Anne W. Schmidt, "Some Theoretical Considerations of Confidential Adoptions, Part I: The Birth Mother," *Child and Adolescent Social Work Journal* 2, no. 1 (spring 1985): 13–21; quotation from p. 20.

94. Kraft el al., "Some Theoretical Considerations of Confidential Adoptions, Part II: The Adoptive Parent," *Child and Adolescent Social Work Journal* 2, no. 2 (Summer 1985): 69–82; material cited on p. 79.

95. Kraft et al., "Some Theoretical Considerations of Confidential Adoptions, Part III: The Adoptive Parents," *Child and Adolescent Social Work Journal* 2, no. 3 (Fall 1985): 139–153; quotation on p. 150.

96. Harold D. Grotevant and Ruth G. McRoy, *Openness in Adoption: Exploring Family Connections* (Thousand Oaks, CA: Sage, 1998), p. 35.

97. Information on Spence-Chapin from Lynn C. Franklin (with Elizabeth Ferber), *May the Circle Be Unbroken: An Intimate Journey into the Heart of Adoption* (New York: Harmony, 1998), p. 116.

98. Grotevant and McRoy, *Openness in Adoption*, pp. 32–33.

99. James L. Gritter, ed., *Adoption without Fear* (San Antonio, TX: Corona, 1989).

100. I noticed the striking similarity in such letters when my father, an obstetrician, began to receive them in the 1980s; prospective adopters sometimes used mailing lists from physicians' professional associations in national searches for children. Accompanied by a cover letter, the letters were addressed directly to women who might be considering adoption. Most included a photograph of the prospective adopters. Their formulaic character suggested a common source. Since then, I have seen advice on writing these letters circulated by adoption attorneys and in manuals such as the ones cited below.

101. Lois Gilman, *The Adoption Resource Book* (New York: Harper and Row, 1987), p. 136.

102. Cynthia D. Martin, *Beating the Adoption Game* (La Jolla: Oak Tree, 1980), p. 139.

103. Jana Wolff, *Secret Thoughts of an Adoptive Mother* (Kansas City: Andrews and McMeel, 1997), pp. 17–18.

104. Ibid., p. 29.

105. Dion Howells (with Karen Wilson Pritchard), *The Story of David: How We Created a Family through Open Adoption* (New York: Delacorte/Doubleday, Dell, 1997), p. 150.

106. Lincoln Caplan, *An Open Adoption* (New York: Farrar, Straus, Giroux, 1990).

107. See, for example, Carp, *Family Matters*, pp. 226–27.

108. Kathleen Silber and Phylis Speedlin, *Dear Birthmother* (San Antonio, TX: Corona, 1983); Suzanne Arms, *Adoption: A Handful of Hope* (Berkeley: Celestial Arts, 1990; rev. ed. of *To Love and Let Go* (1983).

109. Arms, *Adoption: A Handful of Hope,* p. 128.

110. For examples of evangelical Christian advocacy of adoption, see Susan Olasky and Marvin Olasky, *More Than Kindness: A Compassionate Approach to Crisis Childbearing* (Wheaton, IL: Crossway Books, 1990); Ann Kiemel Anderson, *And with the Gift Came Laughter* (Wheaton, IL: Tynale House Publishers, 1987), the account of a well-known evangelical speaker and writer who is also an adoptive mother and informal adoption broker; and Norma McCorvey (with Gary Thomas), *Won by Love* (Nashville: Thomas Nelson, 1997). McCorvey was "Jane Roe" in the landmark case that legalized abortion, *Roe v. Wade*; she has since recanted her support for abortion, and in this memoir describes her embrace of evangelical Christianity. For an example of another reli-

gious community that has embraced adoption as part of its opposition to abortion, see this memoir co-authored by a birth and adoptive mother who are both members of the Church of the Latter Day Saints: Terry Treseder and Terrilyn Ainscouth, *My Child, Your Child: A Childless Couple's Yearning and an Unwed Mother's Decision* (Salt Lake City: Desert Book Co., 1991). Catholic social ministries, of course, also oppose abortion, and Catholic presses have published some recent birth mother memoirs presenting relinquishment favorably; see, for example, Kayla M. Becker with Connie K. Heckert, *To Keera with Love: Abortion, Adoption or Keeping the Baby: The Story of One Teen's Choice* (Kansas City: Sheed and Ward [a service of National Catholic Reporter Publishing Inc.], 1987). For an exceptional example of a liberal anti-abortion argument, see the searching memoir of Bonnie Shullenberger, an Episcopal priest, who recounts her 1967 relinquishment of a child born out of wedlock in her memoir, *A Time to Be Born* (Cambridge: Cowley Publications, 1966).

111. Grotevant and McRoy, *Openness in Adoption.*

EPILOGUE

1. H. David Kirk, *Adoptive Kinship: A Modern Institution in Need of Reform* (Toronto: Buttersworth, 1981), p. 98. In 1964 Kirk anticipated the critique of the best solution in his book *Shared Fate* (rev. ed, Port Angeles, WA: Ben-Simon, 1984).

2. An excellent summary and overview of outcome studies (covering adoption in both the united States and Britain) is David Howe, *Patterns of Adoption* (London: Blackwell Science, 1998); for an outcome study conducted using CBD records, see Janet L. Hoopes, *Prediction in Child Development: A Longitudinal Study of Adoptive and Nonadoptive Families* (New York: Child Welfare League of America, 1982).

3. Two-thirds of birth mothers were teenagers in a 1998 study; see Harold D. Grotevant and Ruth G. McRoy, *Openness in Adoption: Exploring Family Connections* (Thousand Oaks, CA: Sage Publications, 1998), p. 69. The rate of teenage pregnancy has decreased since 1991 but remains one of the highest among industrialized nations.

4. Adam Pertman, *Adoption Nation: How the Adoption Revolution Is Transforming America* (New York: Basic, 2000), p. 200.

5. The phrase "archaic and nostalgic" is from Kirk, *Shared Fate*, p. 161.

Index

abortion, 122, 132, 134, 151, 152, 239, 282
adoptees: and bicultural identity, 199;
   memoirs, 239–240, 244–253, 270–272;
   repudiating adoption secrecy, 241–242.
   See also adoptive children; international adoption; search and reunion;
   transracial adoption
adoption: terminology, 2; as "best solution," 4, 105–108; statistics, 4, 105, 108,
   243; decline of, 4, 239–240, 287; as
   American, 5, 10, 15, 104, 153, 200, 291;
   and inheritance, 16, 66; black market,
   20, 250, 260–262; "shortage," 36, 56; as
   "risky," 38, 39, 40, 42, 45, 236–237,
   242–243, 262–270, 284; as "choice," 46,
   47, 48, 49, 52, 55–56, 231–232, 282;
   and fears of racial mixing, 102–103;
   African Americans excluded from, 108,
   148–153; African American attitudes
   toward, 148–149; as stigma, 245–247;
   outcomes, 289. *See also* international
   adoption; open adoption; transracial
   adoption
Adoption and Safe Families Act, 290
adoption disclosure: to adoptive parents
   in home study, 215–222, 266; advice on
   "telling," 222–223, 226, 232–236, 237;
   as measure of adoptive parents' fitness,
   226–227; as therapeutic narrative, 228–

230. *See also* confidentiality; social
   workers
adoption law: 15, 25–26; 106–107; 290–
   291; in Delaware, 25–26, 76, 77; and
   "best interest," 52–53; and religious
   matching, 77, 81; and sealed records,
   274–275, 278, 280–281
adoption reform (also rights) movement:
   origins of, 240–241; influence of, 260,
   270, 273–274; and open records, 274–
   275
Adoption Triangle, The, 238–239, 241,
   242–243, 263, 275
adoptive children: age at placement, 13,
   30, 55; as participants in placement,
   48–49; religious assignment of, 76–77;
   racial assignment of, 86–87, 94–96; biracial, 93–94, 167, 170–171, 273; social
   workers' gender expectations of, 113–
   114; as "chosen," 230–232; and open
   adoption, 284–285. *See also* adoptive
   parents; child placement; social workers; testing
adoptive parents: qualifications of, 24–25;
   age preferences of, 37, 75; seeking
   agency adoption, 41–42, 73, 108–109;
   sex preferences of, 54–68; intelligence
   preferences of, 72–73; Jewish, 82–83;
   ethnicity preferences of, 89–93; age re-